THE BULLET HILL DIARIES

by Bennett Powers

This is dedicated to Mary Anne and Lorraine...
Two of the strongest women I know.

TABLE OF CONTENTS

Epigraph

Prologue

Hasani

'Welcome to the Islands of Aloha'

'Ding Ding Out There'

As the Crow Flies

Lahaina

The Maui Wowie Potato Chip Factory

The Ship's Wheel

1979

Maui, Take Two

Bullet Hill

'A River Runs Through It'

In Memory Of

Afterword

Acknowledgements

EPIGRAPH

'It is impossible to communicate to you a conception of the trembling sensation, half pleasurable half fearful, with which I'm preparing to depart. I am going to unexplored regions, to "the Lands of Mist and Snow", but I shall kill no albatross; therefore, do not be alarmed for my safety, or if I should come back to you as worn and woeful as the 'Ancient Mariner'. You will smile at my allusion, but I will disclose a secret... There is something at work in my soul which I don't understand... A love for the marvelous, a belief in the marvelous...Which hurries me out of the common pathways ... To the wild sea and unvisited regions I am about to explore.... Shall I meet you again, after having traversed immense seas, and returned?... I dare not expect such success. I love you very tenderly. Remember me with affection, should you never hear from me again.'

Mary Shelley
Frankenstein, 1878

PROLOGUE

'The world grows dark
And bones get caught
And you can look into your heart
And know, that somethings still missing'

'Missing'
Calexico

January, 1994
Guest house on Kaholalele Road,
Wailua Homesteads, Kauai, Hawaii

Leon and I are eating dinner and watching the local news. The Hawaiian anchor woman is saying something about Tucson, Arizona, but she's pronouncing it 'Tuk-son', like when you say 'Tuxedo'. This is really irritating Leon, and he's calling her a 'bonehead', among other things.

I laugh and say, "C'mon man, give her a break... Maybe she's never even been to the mainland."

Leon grunts and says, "That's no excuse.. she's still a bone-head!"

I laugh again...

And I have no way of knowing that in about a year and a half from now I will be working in Tucson. I will come back to my motel room after work and see the little orange light on the top of the room phone blinking, which will mean that I have a message, and it will be from my wife Nancy back home in Scottsdale. She'll be telling me that Leon called from Kauai, and that he said that Andy didn't show up for work, and that

THE BULLET HILL DIARIES

he's missing, and would I please call him as soon as I can...

September, 2009
Wilmington, North Carolina

I'm in the kitchen one evening making salsa, something that I picked up in Arizona, and listening to Calexico. My son Dustin walks in and asks me, "Dad, what does this music remind you of? You listen to this a lot."

I temporarily dodge the bullet and answer his question with a question. "What does it remind you of?"

"It reminds me of that Mexican restaurant in Arizona where we went for breakfast sometimes, and you always got a margarita. You said they were the best!"

This cracks me up. Calexico reminds my son of 'El Encanto', a very cool restaurant in Cave Creek, Arizona, and occasionally on Saturdays we would make the 25 mile road trip up there just for breakfast. And yes, they do have the best margaritas.

"If you really want to know, it reminds me, in a reverse sort of way, of when I first heard that Andy was missing."

"Oh, okay.. that makes sense. I knew it was something."

What I don't say, and what I'm just now remembering, is that Calexico... is from Tucson.

HASANI

January 1st, 1978
Honolulu, Oahu, Hawaii

"You waitin' for the food?"

I'm lying face down on the grass, in a state of complete frustration and utter desperation. With some effort I pick my head up and look to see where this voice is coming from. About eight feet in front of me I see an extremely tall black man laying comfortably on his side. He's wearing a long colorful robe with long flared sleeves. He's got at least a dozen different length necklaces with multi-colored beads around his neck. On his head is a small golden cap. He sort of looks like Richie Havens, minus the beard.

"What's that?" I manage. I'm definitely feeling last night's New Years' Eve celebration.

"I was just wondering if you were here for the free food," he explains. "The Hari Krishna's come here and give hot meals to whoever wants them."

"Um no... but yeah, I am hungry."

The grass I'm lying on is the finely manicured lawn at the front of the Honolulu Zoo. This was my third try at getting on a bus with my oversize Jan Sport backpack. But each time a big Hawaiian hand was thrust in my face..

"No backpacks!"

Someone told me that I could catch the Beach Bus here, and since they allowed surfboards they might allow my backpack. But for the third time I am emphatically denied. I'm starting to wonder if it's just me.. yet another young blonde Haole boy invading the Hawaiian Islands. And now, at wits end, with time to think about it, I really can't blame them.

"Where you headed?" the man asks.

I sit up crossing my legs facing him. "I'm just trying to get to the other side of the island. I have a friend who lives in Kailua, but he won't be here for another week, so I was hoping that I could just camp out somewhere until then."

7

He peruses me for a moment. "That's... probably not a good idea. A young Haole like you is an easy target, if you know what I mean."

I know what he means. But I'm thinking that there's got to be a campground or a Youth Hostile somewhere on this island. While I'm thinking about that, a Volkswagen camper van pulls up to the side of the road next to us and stops. Four Hari Krishna dudes hop out with shaved heads and white robes, and looking for all the world like, well, Hari Krishna's. They slide open the side door and bring out an oriental rug, which they unroll on the grass. Then they bring out many covered bowls of various sizes and place them on the rug, along with paper plates and chopsticks.

And then, seemingly out of nowhere, a bunch of people just materialize. Most of them are dirty looking, with ragged clothing, and I realize that they're homeless. Which is what I am right now.

The man I've been talking to stands up. "This is it," he says.

We fall into the line that's forming. He turns to me and extends his hand. He's even taller than I thought, maybe close to six ten. "I'm Hasani," he says.

I shake his hand, which is enormous. "I'm Bennett, nice to meet you."

"Nice to meet you too."

As we move up in line I notice his attire again, the beads and the long flowing robe. He definitely stands out in this little crowd, and not just because he's twice as tall as everyone else, but it's his general demeanor. And his clothes are clean. He's definitely not homeless.. or if he is, he's the most impeccable homeless guy I've ever seen.

It's our turn to be served, and the Krishna's pile large amounts of yellow rice and other vegetarian dishes on our plates, the steamy aroma's wafting up to my nose and smelling very good. As we sit back down to eat, the Hari Krishna's sit also, but they don't eat. They start softly singing and chanting, ringing little bells from time to time, one of them keeping time on a small drum.

I get a temporary rush of guilt, because the only Hari Krishna's I've had the pleasure to meet were the forceful ones in airport terminals, which weren't very pleasurable at all. But that's not the case here. These guys are feeding me, and keeping their distance, and I'm seeing them in a whole new light.

I know I'm hungry, but this food is delicious. This is my first attempt at using chop sticks, but I'm so famished that I'm making do, just sort of scooping the food to my mouth.

I hear Hasani softly chuckling, probably laughing at my chop stick skills.

Pretty soon he says, "So, when did you first get to Oahu?"

"Just a couple of days ago," I reply.

I tell him how I couldn't get on a bus at the airport because of my backpack. I also tell him how I ended up catching a ride into Waikiki with a limo driver, but I don't tell him the details of that ride, because I'm still sort of thanking my lucky stars...

Two days ago, just after getting off the plane, and all of the buses had left the terminal and I was standing there alone with my backpack, a short black limousine pulled up next to me and stopped. The driver got out, a medium built guy who looked to be in his early thirties, with closely cropped red hair and a neatly trimmed red beard. And he was dressed like a limo driver, vest and all.

"You need a ride?" he asked.

I looked at him and laughed. "I can't afford you."

He put his hands on the top of the car above his door and slightly cocked his head. "How about four bucks?"

There was something about this guy that I instantly liked. I figured that he usually charged five bucks, but knocked off a buck for me at the last minute. Compared to twenty five cents for the bus it still seemed like a lot, but I was going to have to take a cab anyway, and I couldn't imagine that being any cheaper.

He seemed to read my mind and popped the trunk. "You can throw your backpack in here."

I looked at him and smiled, and did as he said. I suddenly felt relieved. Not only did I have a ride now, I had a pretty cool ride.

He opened the shotgun door. "You can sit up front if you want."

As he pulled out of the airport we introduced ourselves, and I told him where I was from. It turned out he was from California also, the San Diego area. In no time at all we're almost talking like old friends.

When he asked me where I was staying and I told him I didn't know, he told me he knew of a smaller hotel in Waikiki, off the beaten path, but still walking distance from the beach. "Cheaper too," he informed me. "Maybe sixty or seventy bucks for the night."

I figured that he probably got some kind of kick back for bringing people there, but whatever, it sounded fine to me. Better than if I just went into town blind. "That sounds great."

A few minutes later he says, "So..." He gives me a sidelong glance and smiles conspiratorially. "You smoke Paka Lolo?"

I hesitate for a moment. Then I say, " Yeah, sometimes."

"Well," he says, "I can get some for you if you want." When I don't say anything he says, "It's right on the way, no trouble at all."

After a pause I say, "What, like a quarter?"

"Sure, I can get you a quarter."

I look out the window at the coconut palms going by. Off to our left is the lush green mountains of the Pali. I'm taking it all in, excited to finally be here. Actually really here, in Hawaii.

"Okay," I say.

"Cool!" he says. "It won't take long."

Pretty soon he turns right, off of the main road. It doesn't take me long to realize that we're headed into the port area. I start to see huge warehouses and container cranes, and a multitude of red, brown and blue containers.

We come to a guard gate, and when he stops to talk to the guard it's pretty obvious that they know each other. They exchange a few words, then the guard laughs and pushes the button that raises the barrier to let us in. We proceed on, turning this way and that, and I catch myself thinking that if I had to find my own way back out of here I would be hopelessly lost. It all looks vaguely familiar to me at the same time though, because I've seen parts of this place many times on episodes of 'Hawaii Five-0'.

We finally pull up to the front of a long camper trailer and park facing the little front door. In seconds the door opens and a skinny Rasta guy steps out onto the landing. He's barefoot, with dirty dreads and wearing faded blue jeans and a wife-beater. Pretty soon he waves his hand, and that's the signal I guess, because only then does my driver open his door.

"I'll be right back," he says with a smile. He goes inside the trailer and Rasta guy shuts the door.

It doesn't take me long to start feeling anxious.

I'm thinking about the two thousand dollars stashed in the 'secret' compartment of my backpack. I'm thinking about just how totally vulnerable I am right now. I'm also thinking that maybe this wasn't such a good fucking idea after all. My driver and Rasta guy are total strangers, and if they wanted to rob me, or kidnap me, or even kill me, there wouldn't be a damn thing I could do about it.

I can see the headlines now.

"Young Stupid Haole Boy Disappears After Leaving Airport."

"Body of Young Haole Boy Found Washed Up On Waikiki Beach."

And oh yeah, Hawaii Five 0. I'm living it right now. That

part where everything takes a turn for the worst, where every-thing goes terribly wrong.

After about fifteen minutes, just as I start cursing myself, the door of the trailer opens and my driver emerges. He hastily makes his way back to the limo and climbs in.

"Sorry that took so long," he says. "That guy really likes to talk story." Then he reaches into his pocket and pulls out a zip-lock bag and throws it on my lap. "Thirty bucks."

I look at it, and it's big beautiful Hawaiian buds. I open the bag to smell them, and the aroma instantly permeates the entire inside of the car. "Wow!" I say. "I've never seen buds quite like this before!" I pull out my wallet and hand him two twenties. "The extra ten is for the ride, and this," I open the bag again and hand him a bud, "is for your trouble."

"Whoa brah," he says, "you're being way too nice!" He gives me six bucks back. "A deal's a deal, but thanks for the bud!"

He starts the car, and as we're heading back out of the port I'm slowly flooded with relief. I'm trying to hide the fact that I'm coming down off of an intense adrenaline rush, a self-inflicted one at that. Me and my imagination, I'm thinking, and try not to laugh. It looks like I'm not about to be killed after all. And now McGarrett and the boys can get back to more important things...

The guy is true to his word, and sets me up at the hotel he was talking about, which is a few streets in from Waikiki Beach. He brings my backpack into the lobby for me, and we say our goodbyes'.

"You take care now man," he says with a wink. "It's gonna get crazy around here, tomorrow night being New Year's Eve and all."

New Year's Eve. I forgot all about it.

"Thanks man, I will." We shake hands, and then he's gone.

I'm figuring that I'll only have to stay here for one night, since my plan is to get to the other side of the island, some-where close to Kailua where my friend Drew lives, and camp out until he shows up a week later. But I never make it out of Honolulu, thanks to my backpack. And so here I sit, eating Hari Krishna food with this man named Hasani.

After we finish eating, and all of the homeless people have vanished, just as rapidly as they first appeared, Hasani asks me, "Is that all of the luggage you have, that backpack?"

"No..." I slowly say. "I have another duffel bag with some clothes in it that I put in a locker at the airport."

He thinks about that for a few minutes. Then he says, "I have an idea... but it's totally up to you." Another few seconds, and then he continues. "I have an apartment back in Waikiki, right behind the International Market Place. It's just a studio apartment with one bed, but since I almost always spend the night with my girlfriend at her place, I hardly ever sleep there." He lets that sink in, and when I don't say anything he says, "You're welcome to spend the week there until your friend shows up, if you want."

I'm not really believing what I'm hearing, and I don't know what to say. I look at this guy again and try to detect any kind of underlying feeling of animosity or ill intent. But the only vibe that I'm picking up from him is pure compassion, and good will.

He seems to read my mind and starts getting up. "C'mon, grab your backpack, and you can think about it on our way back to my place."

Not knowing what else to do, I don my backpack and start following him.

Why is this guy being so nice to me, I wonder? A few scenarios run through my mind. Maybe he's going to get me back to his place and then, what? Knock me over the head and rob me? And then what, drag me off somewhere and dump me? That would be pretty stupid, if I survived I would know where he lives.

As we're walking I take another sidelong glance at him. He's easily six foot nine or ten, probably two hundred and fifty pounds. And even with that loose fitting robe that he's wearing I can tell that he's in good shape. He's built like a pro basketball player, like Wilt Chamberlain or someone. It doesn't escape me that this guy could overtake me in a heartbeat, put me down in two seconds. But that's just not the feeling that I'm getting from him.

We get to his apartment building and, just like he said, it's right behind the International Market Place. It's an older one story stucco structure sandwiched in between new high rise hotels and offices. It strikes me as a building whose days are numbered.

We approach his door and he pulls out a key and unlocks the deadbolt. "C'mon in. You can use the restroom if you need to."

I say I'm okay, so he does. While he's in there I look around. It's really just one big room. The only other door is the bathroom that he's in. There's a big king size bed against one wall, and the only other furniture is a dining room table and a couple of chairs. No torture chamber, or bloody manacles hanging from chains on the walls.

The table is almost completely covered with different containers that have every conceivable size and color of glass beads in them. There's what looks like spools of fishing line, and an assortment of scissors and tweezers and other tools. He's obviously a jewelry maker, and I remember the beads he had around his neck, and the many rings he was wearing.

Lining the walls around the entire room are stacks of magazines and newspapers, and piles of books in semi-neat order, literally thousands of them. I pick up a National Geographic, and as I'm thumbing through it Hasani emerges from the bathroom. I hadn't thought about his age before, but now I'm thinking that he's probably mid thirty's.

Without asking if I've made up my mind yet he says, "I think the first thing we should do, is take the bus out to the airport and pick up that other bag of yours."

We both look at my backpack propped by the front door at the same time.

"You can just leave that here, it'll be safe."

Now I have to make a decision. Do I trust this guy and take him up on his offer? Or do I politely decline, and head back out on my own, not knowing where I'm going, or even how I'm going to get there. And possibly get mugged, or worse.

And then, just like that, my mind is made up. I walk over to my backpack, and then carry it over and prop it against the wall next to the bed. I look back at Hasani, and he gets a big, broad smile.

"Okay then," he says, laughing softly. "Good."

We go back out the door, and when he pulls it shut and I hear that deadbolt 'click', I swallow past something in my throat. My entire life savings, for what it's worth, is locked inside the room of this total stranger that I've just met. Does he have an accomplice? And when we get back will he say, "Oh shit, someone forced my door, and stole your backpack!" It just doesn't seem likely. And anyway, I'm committed now.

"This way," he says, and I follow him down a little walkway that takes us to the back of the International Market Place. Down a passageway and through a door, and we're inside the Market Place itself.

I've never been in here before, and the enormity of it is mind boggling. It's everything Polynesian, from coconut cups and bowls, and palm frond hats, to bright flower print Mu Mu's and Aloha shirts. There's a multitude of sizes of grass skirt hula girls, and ukulele's of all colors. And there's everything else in between that you can think of, and even more that you can't.

We pass through another doorway and I seem to sense something overhead, so I turn around and look up. What I see completely blows me away...

Mounted above the door is the biggest Marlin that I've ever even heard of. It's at least twelve feet long, and the placard underneath the fish says that it weighed just over eighteen hundred pounds when it was landed on rod and reel off the Kona coast, on the big island of Hawaii.

This is forcing me to flash back to a couple of years ago, when I was lucky enough to fly to Cabo San Lucas with my dad and some of his friends in his Cessna. We went marlin fishing, and I narrowly missed my chance to catch one due to the timer bell going off, which meant that everyone rotated to another rod, and the rod that I just had got hit and hooked a marlin. I was kind of crushed at the time, but now, looking at this monster of a fish, I realize that maybe it all happened for a reason, and maybe I wasn't supposed to catch that marlin.

Hasani, who had kept walking, comes back and looks at me questioningly.

I pull my eyes away from this enormous, beautiful dead shell of a creature, and say, "It's nothing. Let's go."

We make our way to the front of the Market Place and out onto Kalakaua boulevard, where we quickly catch a bus, my first one after so many attempts.

I settle into a seat behind Hasani and look out the window. I can't help but notice that Waikiki is not the chaos that it was the previous couple of days. The town was gearing up for New Year's Eve, and there were Chinese fireworks stands on almost every corner. All during the day and into the night people were throwing lit packs of firecrackers off of the high rise hotels. Most of them would make it down to the street where they would continue exploding. Smoke was everywhere, as was the smell of gunpowder, and it looked and smelled like a war zone.

New Year's Eve day was my first morning in Hawaii, and I laugh to myself now at what I decided to do.

The night that my limo driver dropped me off at my hotel, I was given a key but told that my room wouldn't be ready for another half hour or so. I was hungry and wanted to get something to eat, so I asked the kindly Japanese woman if I could leave my backpack with her in the lobby. She was very nice and obliging, and said that would be no problem. She had me put it behind the counter next to her desk.

I thanked her, and as I turned to leave she said, "Office

only open for another hour."

I smiled and told her that was fine, and then stepped out into my first Hawaiian evening.

Finally rid of my backpack, I suddenly felt free, and exhilarated. Moving through throngs of people I made my way towards the beach, and Kalakaua boulevard. When I reached it I turned right, for no particular reason other than it just felt like the right way to go, and started looking for some kind of a restaurant.

People were everywhere, and there was definitely a feeling of anticipation and excitement in the air. I finally came upon a Jolly Roger restaurant, which made me laugh, because Andy and Dean and I would often go to a Jolly Roger in Long Beach when we got paid on Fridays, and have the Buccaneer Burger special. That memory made my mind up for me, so I went in.

I was shown to a booth by the bar, and when the waitress asked what I wanted to drink, I went for it and ordered a beer. When she left to get it I thought, that was too easy. Then I remembered that the legal drinking age in Hawaii is eighteen. I laughed to myself, because I was turning twenty one in a little less than two months, and it didn't even matter anymore.

That first beer, my first legal drink in a public place, went down so good I ordered another. Those two beers and a Buccaneer Burger really hit the spot, and I was luxuriating in my buzz, until I thought of my mom, and got hit with a rash of the guilts.

My parents knew that I was planning to move to Hawaii, but they didn't know when, because I didn't know when. Andy and Dean and I had been planning this for some time, and when our planned departure date got close I quit my job working construction for my uncle, and sold my car. But Andy and Dean weren't ready yet. And I was in a situation where I was more than ready to get the hell out of there. And I didn't tell my parents.

I knew that my mom especially would be very worried, so

I decided right then and there to use the restaurant pay phone and call her.

I had to call collect, and when I got ahold of her I lied a little bit. I told her that I was staying with Drew in Kailua, and that Andy and Dean would be here in a couple of weeks. (That much was true, Andy had promised me that they would meet me "in two weeks, three tops") My mom sounded worried, of course, and I could tell that she was choking back tears. I tried my best to convince her that I was going to be alright, but I think I only half succeeded in my attempt. When I finally said goodbye and hung up the phone, I had tears of my own blurring my vision. I was putting my mom through hell, and she definitely didn't deserve it.

I exited the Jolly Roger and decided to go check out the beach, even though it was nighttime. I cut through the lobby of a posh hotel, walked past the pool with its many lounge chairs, and for the first time walked out onto the sand of Waikiki Beach.

What I saw all looked very Hawaiian, or rather the Hawaii I was familiar with from what I'd seen on TV and in the movies. There were tiki torches everywhere in front of the hotels up and down the beach, and Hawaiian music filtering out of some of the open air bars, along with intoxicated laughter. It was totally dark now, and I could even see a few stars. I could feel the night, my first Hawaiian night, and... then I remembered my backpack!

I got caught up in the moment and totally lost track of time.

"Office only open for another hour.." I knew it was long past that.

I hurried back to the hotel anyway, but sure enough, when I got to the lobby the sliding glass door was locked and the Japanese woman was gone. There was a single light on inside, and I could see my backpack exactly where I left it, behind the counter. What a knucklehead! Me and this backpack! Oh well, at least I had the room key in my pocket, and my backpack was safe.

I went up to my room and took a shower, and then plopped on the bed, where I quickly fell asleep.

When I woke the next morning it took me a few minutes to remember where I was. Oh yeah, I'm in a hotel.. in Waikiki.. in Hawaii!

I got up and walked out to my small lanai. I couldn't see the ocean from here, but it was a bright sunny Hawaiian morning, and I decided that before I tried to catch a bus to the other side of the island I was going to go down to the beach and jump in the water.

I pulled on my blue jeans and my T shirt and went down to the lobby. Instead of the woman from the night before it was a Japanese man, the husband most likely.

When he saw me he smiled and opened the little door at the end of the counter. He obviously knew who I was, and gestured towards my backpack. I walked back and retrieved it, and thanked him kindly, to which he bowed his head and said, "Yes sir, your welcome Mr. Powers sir!"

I don't think anyone had ever called me 'sir' before, and it sounded funny to me. Then again, I have to admit that I kind of liked it. I was being treated like an adult instead of a kid, and that made me feel a little bit more, I don't know, mature? One can only hope.

I went back up to my room and changed into my swimsuit, glad to finally get out of my jeans. I didn't know it yet, but that would be the last time I would be wearing long pants for at least a year.

I checked out of the hotel and proceeded straight to the beach. I walked out through a maze of beach towels and chairs and umbrellas to the water's edge. I instantly recognized Diamond Head Crater off to the left, again thanks to Hawaii Five-O. The light blue water beckoned me, so I propped my backpack in the sand, tore off my shirt and ran in.

To say it felt good is definitely an understatement... It felt magnificent! I swam out maybe fifty yards and turned around, facing the beach and the hotels. And that is when I heard the first firecrackers. What the hell? I thought, and then remembered that it was New Year's Eve tonight.

Slowly starting in that very instant, my immediate plans began to change.

Chalk it up to finally being in the ocean for the first time, but I was having a mini awakening.. I started to realize that New Year's Eve in Waikiki was probably one hell of a spectacle. Why was I in such a big hurry to get to the other side of the island, when the biggest party of the year was about to happen? That thought was answered with more firecrackers, and it wasn't even noon yet.

Whether it was the right decision or not, my mind was made up about what I was going to do for the rest of the day and night.

I swam back to shore, got out of the water and dried myself off as best that I could with my T shirt. I grabbed my backpack and trudged back through the sand and walked into the hotel lobby that I had just come through. In a dripping wet swim suit and no shirt I made my way up to the front desk. The man behind the counter, who looked to be Chinese, eyed me warily. He put down his pen and came over to me.

"Can I help you?" he asked.

"Yes, I would like a room please. Preferably on the beach side, if you have any left."

He looked me up and down, checking me out. "Ah, room expensive. A hundred and fifty dollars."

He plainly didn't think that I could afford it, and the truth is, I couldn't. But I had decided that it was time to celebrate, time to party! If Andy and Dean were here with me right now we'd be doing the exact same thing.

I got my wallet out of my backpack and pulled out two, hundred dollar bills, and started to hand them to him.

But he held up his hand and said, "No have to pay yet." His demeanor instantly changed and he smiled. "One moment please."

He did some checking in his book, then grabbed a key from one of the large boards. He came back over to me and said, "One room left on beach side."

He had me sign my name after making a copy of my driver's license, and handed me my room key. I took it and looked at the number. Room 1978. I couldn't believe my eyes, but took it as a good omen.

I started laughing and pointed at the number. "Room number 1978," I said.

"Yes sir," he said, "nineteenth floor."

"Yeah right," I said. "But it's just that, you know, it's New Year's Eve. It's going to be 1978 at midnight!"

He finally got it. "Ah yes!" He turned to his woman co-worker and said something in Chinese, to which she let out a small grunt. He turned back to me, kind of rolled his eyes, and then smiled.

I started to leave and said "Happy New Year!"

"Happy New Year!" he replied. "Yes Sir!"

There it was, I was being called 'Sir' again. I guess I was going to have to get used to it.

Upon first seeing my room I wasn't ready for how big it was. It had two queen size beds, a sitting area with table and chairs, a large bathroom, a TV and a small electric cooler (with nothing in it , of course. I was going to have to do something about that.) And best of all, a lanai looking out onto the beach, and Diamond Head, and the blue Pacific.

And then I have to admit, I felt kind of stupid. Just me in this big beautiful room. What a waste. That is, unless, I find some someone to share it with me...

Now that I had a room to leave my backpack in, I went back out and looked for someplace to eat lunch. I ended up going to a Jack in the Box thinking that I would save some money. What a financial genius I am! Eating a two dollar lunch in a hundred and fifty dollar room! I picked up some beers as well, a six pack of Primo's, for no other reason than they were Hawaiian.

By mid-afternoon the firecrackers were going hot and heavy. By early evening they blocked off Kalakaua boulevard to car traffic. The streets were starting to swell with people, and it was still six hours until midnight.

After having one of my beers on the lanai, I decided to take the elevator down and walk out onto the beach. The big pre-party was well underway, people walking around with cocktails and open beers. I ended up talking to a guy who was about my age, with longish brown hair and holding a beer in a plastic cup in his hand. After a while he expressed a desire to smoke a joint, but said that he didn't bring anything with him because he was here with his parents, staying in the same hotel that I was. I told him I had some, and that we could go up to my room and smoke one if he wanted to. He brightened at that, liking the fact that I had my own room.

We went up and I fished some papers out of my backpack, and he was happy to roll one. "Wow, where did you get this?" he asked as he broke apart a section of a bud.

I briefly told him about the limo driver and Rasta guy in the port. His eyes widened at that, saying that that must have been pretty hairy. I just laughed and said that yeah, it kind of was. I didn't tell him the part about me being scared shitless.

I got both of us a beer and we went out onto the lanai to smoke the joint. This was the first time that I had smoked any of what I got, and it was very sweet tasting, and, I could slowly tell, very strong. In no time at all we were laughing at anything and everything. He told me his name a few times, but I kept forgetting it.

After a while we went back down to the beach, each carrying a beer in our plastic cups. We mingled with other people, talking and partying, until after a while I realized that he wasn't around anymore. He probably went to eat dinner with his parents. Then I thought, dinner, what a concept! I'd better get something to eat myself. I ended up eating at the restaurant in the hotel, getting the cheapest thing on the menu, which wasn't very cheap. After dinner I went out onto

Kalakaua and joined the throngs of partyers who seemed oblivious to the firecrackers falling all around them.

By the time midnight rolled around, and the night climaxed with skyrockets going off and everyone screaming and shouting, I had had enough. I was in a sea of strangers and feeling pretty lonely. And I hadn't put any effort into trying to get a girl to go back to my room with me. But now I didn't care, I just wanted to get back to that room and crash.

When I got there I walked out onto the lanai one last time, and with the firecrackers and skyrockets finally slowing down I thought, well, it's 1978 now.

What's going to happen in the coming year? I was at a new chapter in my life, and I couldn't wait for Andy and Dean to get here so that I could get on with it. With those thoughts in my head I went back into my room, and fell like a dead man into bed.

It was late the next morning, while I was taking advantage of the complimentary continental breakfast and nursing somewhat of a hangover, that one of the hotel employees told me about the beach bus, and that I could catch it down in front of the Honolulu Zoo.

More and more people are getting on the bus at each stop, so I move up and sit next to Hasani. Eventually we take a turn down Hotel Street. The infamous Hotel Street in Honolulu, with its kitschy nudie bars and red light district. It's quite a sight, and it looks like a movie set. I can easily imagine that I'm back in the forty's, and that I might see Burt Lancaster in his uniform, a little tipsy as he steps out of the New Congress Club. Or Ernest Borgnine walking alone in slacks and an Aloha shirt. And maybe Donna Reed walking arm in arm with Montgomery Clift.

The bus makes a stop and I'm jarred out of my 'From Here to Eternity' fantasy. Three very flamboyant 'working girls' get on. They're all wearing very short, very tight, and very colorful miniskirts. They're also wearing very high, seven or eight inch heels.

It's standing room only on the bus now, and the girls are positioned right next to us. The one closest to me puts her hand on my arm, I guess to steady herself. I look at her long red manicured nails, and absent mindedly notice that she seems to have a lot of forearm hair. I look up at her face and she gives me a big smile and a quick wink. I go to get up to offer her my seat but Hasani shoots out his right arm, blocking me. He then makes a shooing motion with his hand, and the girl lets go of my arm.

Not only are my innocent little eyes seeing their first real live prostitute, but they're also seeing their first trans gender one as well.

After two or three more stops the three hookers get off, along with almost everyone else. Soon we're at the airport, and when we get off of the bus Hasani says he'll wait for me there at the bus stop. I go inside the terminal and make my way to the banks of lockers and find mine without too much trouble. I turn the key and retrieve my small blue 'Aspen' duffel bag. It's really made for carrying ski boots, but I managed to cram quite a few shorts and T shirts in it, along with my mask, snorkel and fins, when I finally get to go snorkeling.

I come back out, and we don't have to wait long for another bus back to Waikiki. I've grown less worried, and less suspicious, and I'm not surprised when Hasani unlocks his door again and my backpack is right where I left it.

Hasani instantly starts pulling the bed apart changing the sheets, and as I sit there feeling a little funny about it, I ask him if I can pay him for his generosity.

He just laughs and says, "No. No need, my friend."

It's late afternoon now, and when he's done making the bed up he grabs a few things to take with him to his girlfriends. Then he pulls a key off of his key ring and lays it on the table.

"Lock up when you go out. And try not to lose this key."

"I won't," I promise.

"I'll be back sometimes during the day to work."

"Okay," I say.

Then he opens the door, tips his golden cap and says, "Aloha."

"Thank you so much for this," I say, and then hastily add "Mahalo."

"You are quite welcome, my friend," he says, and shuts the door.

It's hard to explain the feelings that I have when I'm suddenly alone in this room, the room of a very kind and generous stranger. I'm happy beyond belief, not only because I have a safe place to crash every night, but also because this is going to save me a boatload of money on hotel rooms, if that is what I was going to have to do. I decide right then and there that I'm going to try to pay him somehow, maybe slip a hundred dollar bill under something on his table.

During this week that I have in Waikiki I start falling into a sort of routine. I wake up and go somewhere for breakfast, my favorite place being this little Japanese café that is cheap and I can practice using chop sticks. Then I come back to the apartment and change into my swimsuit and go to the beach.

Some days I'll walk the entire length of the beach, to Ala Wai Yacht Harbor and then back the other way as far as I can go. One day I decide to rent one of those long red surfboards that I've seen many times in the movies. The waves are small, but it's still the most fun I've had since I've been here. I see a couple doing the tandem thing, and they're very good! I also see a guy with his little dog. It's great fun, and the hour goes by too fast.

Other days I just walk around town, meandering about and checking things out. One day I stop to watch the demolition of an old building, probably so they can build yet another high rise hotel. What has me transfixed is this big sledge hammer contraption busting out the concrete slab. It must be diesel powered, because it blows out a big puff of smoke every five seconds or so when the hammer comes down. But what's cool is that sometimes the smoke comes out as a smoke ring, a huge one that goes all the way across the street, getting about twenty feet in diameter before it dissipates. Trippy!

On another day I walk past a theater and notice that 'Close Encounters of the Third Kind' is playing. I've heard about this movie but I haven't seen it yet, and notice that the next showing is about to start. On impulse I buy a ticket and go in, but the only seats that are left are in the front row. Oh well, I go for it anyway. And let me tell you, I feel like I am in the movie, like I'm right next to those spaceships.

Ironically, about three years later I will meet Nancy, who will become my girlfriend, and later my wife, and she will tell me that she was in Waikiki with her family at the exact same time, and that they went and saw the same movie. Did our paths unknowingly cross? We'll never know...

Another thing that I notice more and more as I walk around Waikiki are the 'Pedi-Cabs'. They're three wheeled bicycles with a small bench seat built for two mounted in the rear. They're usually operated by good looking shirtless Hawaiians, or by equally good looking haoles, most times blonde, tan and muscular. Their fares are mostly women, who will always be giggling. Whether they're young twenty somethings, or middle aged women, they will always be giggling.

One of these enterprising cabbies really stands out, and for unique reasons. He has long dark hair, a black eye patch over one eye, and wears a long dark overcoat. He has a very colorful tropical bird on his shoulder, and has a violin case strapped to the side of his bike. He basically looks like a pirate, and I mean the real thing.

One day I see him on a backstreet, leaning against a low wall next to his bike, playing his violin. I'm across the street, and I try to look nonchalant, because I want to hear what he's playing. And what he's playing sounds very cool, melodious, and kind of melancholy.

He finishes, looks up at me, and gives me the slightest nod. I nod back at him, and then he goes into another tune, this one a little more lively. I listen for a little while longer, mar-veling at this guy's life, and then start walking, still hearing his soulful playing as I turn the corner.

I try to keep away from the apartment during the day so as not to bother Hasani while he's working. But every day I come by for a few minutes anyway, usually just to use the rest-room, and there's no sign that Hasani has ever been there. I hope he's not staying away just because of me...

One day towards the end of the week I come back to the apartment in the afternoon and Hasani is there, working at his table.

"I'll just be a minute," I say.

"No, that's alright," he says, setting down his tools. "I need to take a break anyway."

I use the restroom, and when I come back out he is hang-ing the necklace he was working on over a piece of wood on his table.

"I really like your work," I say, truthfully.

"Thank you," he says. "Have a seat, my friend."

I sit down in the other chair. He doesn't say anything for a second, and then he smiles. "You don't happen to have any Paka Lolo do you?"

I laugh. "Yeah, as a matter of fact I do. You wanna smoke some?"

"I'd love to," he says.

I break out my bag and he pulls out a pipe, and we smoke a bowl. I'm curious about his business and ask him where he sells his stuff.

"Usually down at the park, where I met you. I set up a booth down there on the weekends along with a lot of other vendors."

I nod. "Lucky for me you were down there during the week, waiting for the food."

He laughs at that. "So tell me, what are your plans after your friend shows up?"

27

I tell him that I'll be waiting for another couple of weeks with Drew in Kailua until Andy and Dean get here. (I don't know yet that Chris will be coming too.)

"Then we're gonna go straight to Maui, and then to Hana, to the Seven Sacred Pools that my friend Andy has been telling us about. After that our plan is to go to the Big Island, to Kona, and look for jobs."

He thinks about that for a minute. Then he asks, "Are you going to Lahaina while you're on Maui?"

"Oh yeah, we plan on going there too."

After another pause he says, "I think Lahaina is the place for you. You and your friends."

"Yeah, really?" I ask.

"I just visited there a couple of months ago," he says. "Lahaina is an up and coming boom town right now, a lot of haoles your age living and working there." He looks out of the window for a moment, like he's seeing something besides the building next door; perhaps a future that I can't see. He looks back at me. "Yes, I think Lahaina is the town for you."

"Hmmm," I say. "Maybe you're right. I'll definitely talk to Andy and Dean about that when they get here."

After a few moments I ask him, "Why don't you move there? Why do you stay in Waikiki?"

He laughs, loudly this time. "I'm from New York City," he says. "I need the big city around me, the people and the noise. I know this might sound crazy, but it all makes me feel... safe."

I just nod, trying to understand. I've never seen anything like New York City. It's a life I know nothing about.

I decide to let him get back to his work, and go have an early dinner. I thank him for his insights, and walk down to Kalakaua. While I'm eating I think about what he said, about Lahaina being the town for us. And the more I think about it, the more I have a sneaking suspicion that he's right.

Today is the day! It has finally come! Today is the day that

I'm supposed to call Drew, and he will hopefully come and pick me up. I will miss Hasani, but I am more than ready to get the hell out of Waikiki, and see other parts of the island.

At around noon I go to the payphone in the back of the International Market Place. (Hasani doesn't have a phone, or a TV for that matter, and I haven't missed either one.) I pull the slip of paper out of my wallet that Drew's brother Matt gave me just days before I left.

Drew's roommate Mike answers the phone and greets me warmly. He puts Drew on the phone, and it's great to hear a voice that I know. He tells me that he works for a Honolulu radio station, 'KORL', and drives all over the island making deliveries. He'll be able to pick me up in a couple of hours.

"Okay, cool," I say. "I'll be watching for you."

"Just give me the address," he says, "and I can find it with my Thomas Guide."

I tell him the address and he says, "Oh yeah, I think I know where that is. Isn't it right near the International Market Place?"

"Exactly!" I say.

"Okay Cool Ben, I'll see you in a few hours!"

When I hang up I'm so excited that I can barely see straight. Now that it's really going to happen, I almost can't believe it.

I walk through the Market Place, check out the big marlin again, knowing that it might be my last time, and then go out the front door onto Kalakaua. I just walk around aimlessly for a little while, not really caring where I'm going, because I'm finally getting out of this town!

Pretty soon I head back to Hasani's. As I come down the walkway I hear... music. A violin, and someone singing. Next to Hasani's door and off to the side is a Pedi-Cab. The door is open, and I slowly peek in. And there he is, the Pedi-Cab Pirate, playing his violin. And Hasani is singing! At first I'm having trouble connecting it because his voice is a high soprano, and doesn't seem to fit his huge body. But his voice compliments the violin perfectly, and the result is perfect harmony.

I hang by the open door, not wanting to disturb them. Pretty soon they see me anyway, and finish the song. "That was...really cool!" I say, for lack of a better compliment.

They both laugh. Then Hasani introduces me to his friend. "Bennett, this is my good friend McKaw."

We shake hands. "Yeah, I've seen you around."

He smiles and nods. "I've seen you around too."

I look around the room, and then ask him, "Where's that beautiful bird of yours?"

"He's at home," he replies. "He didn't feel like coming out today."

They both laugh, seemingly at an inside joke, so I laugh too. Then I look at Hasani and tell him that I talked to Drew, and that he will be coming by in a bit to pick me up.

To this he raises one eyebrow, and smiles. "So, you'll be leaving soon then."

"Yeah..." I say, suddenly realizing that I never slipped that hundred dollar bill onto his table like I intended to. "You really helped me out, and I want to pay you something."

Hasani cuts me off with a wave of his hand. "There is no need. It has been a pleasure to help you, my friend."

I feel bad, so on impulse I go over to my pack and pull out my bag of buds. I take one out and lay it on his table, to which they both laugh and nod their heads. It's the least I can do.

Then McKaw picks up his violin again and starts playing, and Hasani soon joins in.

I stand half in and half out of the door, listening to them and keeping an eye out for Drew. I can just see the street through the narrow walkway, and it isn't long before I see an old rusty greenish VW bug pull up and stop. Then I see Drew's unmistakable mop of long curly blonde hair as he gets out.

I rush down the walkway to greet him.

"Ben!" he says, with a big smile.

"So good to see you man!" I shake his hand and give him

a quick hug. "C'mon," I say. "There's someone I want you to meet."

We walk the short distance back to Hasani's door, and their song has ended. I bring Drew in and introduce him to both of them, and they greet each other and shake hands. Then Drew looks around and spies my backpack.

"This must be yours, right Ben?"

I nod, and as he picks it up, I grab my Aspen bag. I turn and shake Hasani's hand one last time, thanking him again. I start feeling emotional as I walk out the door, because I know I will probably never see this man again. This man that basically saved my life.

A few Aloha's and, just like that, we're gone.

Drew's bug is a sunroof, but there isn't much of the roof left, so he just drops my backpack through the top and onto the back seat. I do the same with my Aspen bag and then open the door and climb in.

Drew starts the car, and as we pull away I let out a high whoop!

Drew laughs, and high fives me. Then he looks over at me and asks, "Ben, how in the hell did you meet that guy?"

"Well... I'll tell you."

Drew just shakes his head. "Ben," he says, "Somebody up there likes you!"

Amen to that...

'WELCOME TO THE ISLANDS OF ALOHA'

'The traffic lights they turn up blue tomorrow
And shine their emptiness down on my bed
The tiny island sags downstream
'Cause the life that lived is, dead
And the wind, screams, Mary'

'The Wind Cries Mary'
Jimi Hendrix

Drew is whisking me along the 'Kalanianaole Highway'. Yeah, try saying that three times fast. I'm feeling so totally free right now that I can barely contain my excitement.

Drew looks over at me like he's making an announcement and says, "Ben, I'm taking you to a place called Hanauma Bay. I've decided that the best way to introduce you to the islands is to take you snorkeling. I brought along an extra set of snorkeling gear if you don't have any."

"That's cool of you, but I did bring mine. It's one of the main things that I wanted to do when I got here."

"Okay, cool," he says, "Because I can guarantee you brah, you are going to be blown away!"

He's definitely got my attention.

Drew has also packed along a couple of sandwiches; avocado and cheese with sprouts on honey wheatberry bread that he baked himself, and a couple of guava juices as well. As we're driving along he tells me about Hanauma Bay. He explains to me that it is a protected Marine Life Conservation Area and Underwater Park, the only one in the islands. So no one can take any fish, or coral, or anything else out of the bay.

"And what that means, Ben," Drew is saying, "is that it's like snorkeling in a fucken aquarium! A natural aquarium, with more fish and more coral formations than you can imagine!"

"Wow!" I say. "Sounds amazing!"

"Oh it is brah, it is!"

He cracks me up saying 'brah'. Maybe he's lived here longer than I thought, because he has the local talk down. Hawaii definitely agrees with him.

Pretty soon we pull into the parking lot at the bay, and Drew parks in the front row, facing the ocean. Even from here the bay looks incredible. We're both already wearing our swimsuits, so we grab our snorkeling gear and make our way down the trail to the beach. This is my first time on a real Hawaiian white sand beach, (Waikiki's beach is manmade) and the crunchy sand feels amazing on my bare feet.

I follow Drew into the water, pulling on my fins and then my mask. When I finally look underwater, it's the clearest water I've ever been in, and even this close to the beach, there are a multitude of little tropical fish all around me. When I swim out just a little farther the coral formations come into view. Every conceivable size and shape, and color. And I see some bigger fish now, including about a three foot Parrot fish.

I'm freaking out, to say the least! I lose Drew and just start exploring wherever my eyes take me. I occasionally dive down into little niches of sand between the coral and look all around. There's little shell fish, and sea creatures I've never dreamed of, and sometimes I see a Moray Eel stick his head out of a hole in the rock, and I pull back.

Every now and then Drew will call to me on the surface to come look at something. This time when I get to him, it's pretty special indeed. He's hovering over a Brain Coral, about four or five feet in diameter. The sunlight is casting water devils on it, and there are many different fish swimming around it. And I find myself wishing that the super eight movie camera that I have in my backpack was waterproof.

We spend probably close to two hours in this incredible natural aquarium before we crawl up onto the beach. We sit and eat the sandwiches and drink the guava juices that Drew brought while we relax in the sun, which feels really good right now. In fact I'm feeling *so* good that I'm nearly speechless, but I mumble something like, "Just unbelievable..."

Drew laughs, and claps me on the back. "Welcome to the Islands of Aloha brah!"

We're back in the car, making our way around the southwest corner of Oahu. After coming around a bend in the road, Drew points to the right out over the ocean and says, "Maui is straight out there, about a hundred miles. You can sometimes see her on a really clear day."

Maui.

Where we're going...

When they get here...

As we continue around the island he points out 'Makapuu Beach', and not long after that, 'Sandy's', a good body surfing beach he says, known for its fun waves and soft sand.

We're officially on the 'backside' of the island now, and before long we come into Kailua where Drew lives. He pulls down a dirt and gravel drive and we park under a carport next to a white wooden house. It's an older three bedroom, and he lives here with his roommates Mike and Tom. We go inside and I meet both of them, Mike being almost as tall as Drew with a medium build and shortish brown hair. He's pretty tan and looks like he surfs a lot, and I find out later that he does. Tom is a little shorter than me, with glasses and a curly afro. He's soft spoken, and greets me warmly, wearing a kind of tie dye robe and a headband.

Drew is going to make us dinner, but first he is going to bake some bread. He will be making his famous honey wheat-berry bread, the same bread I had the pleasure of enjoying earlier on my sandwich. He explains to me that he makes four loaves, and then has enough dough left over to make two large pizza's.

I watch him through the whole process, and after the loaves are in the oven the kitchen smells like a really good bakery. And he wasn't kidding when he said large pizzas. The two pies he's making out of the extra dough are downright huge, and he loads them up with all kinds of peppers and onions and mushrooms, some tofu chunks, and maybe three or four kinds of cheese. They're veggie pizzas, because Drew's a vegetarian now. He ask's me if I'm cool with that, and I tell him sure, are you kidding? They look and smell amazing.

After we've finished eating Drew's homemade pizzas, Mike and Tom retire to their rooms, and Drew and I kick back in some chairs in the side yard. The sunset is coming on, and I'm loving this right now because it's quiet, and just about the opposite of what I've been used to for the last week.

Drew breaks the silence. "So, when are Andy and Dean supposed to get here?"

"Andy told me two or three weeks," I tell him.

"Okay... and then you guys are going to Maui, right?"

"Yeah, that's the plan. We'll probably go straight to Hana, and the Seven Pools. And then over to Lahaina."

"So you guys are planning to make a go of it on Maui then?" He ask's.

"Well, that was the original plan. But then for some reason we started talking about the Big Island, and Kona." After a pause I say, "But the more I think about it, the more I think that we should probably just stay on Maui."

He thinks about that. "You'd probably have an easier time finding jobs in Lahaina."

"That's funny," I say. "That's exactly what Hasani said."

"Hasani!" Drew exclaims. "He was a trip. Pretty cool guy, huh?"

"You have no idea..."

"And that other guy, the violinist..."

"McKaw," I say. "Didn't know that Hasani and him were friends until I saw them today playing music in the apartment."

After a little while Drew says, "Okay so, this is kind of a personal question, but how much money do you have?"

"Just a little under two thousand," I say.

"Okay, that's perfect. Tomorrow we're gonna get a newspaper and find you a car."

I look at him wide eyed.

He laughs. "Hear me out. Sooner or later you're gonna want a car, you guys are gonna need some transportation." He lets that sink in. "See that beater bug out there, the one that I drove you here in? You can get something just like that for two or three hundred bucks. And you can ship it to Maui for about sixty bucks."

I look at his bug, with the no roof- sun roof, and the doors that fall down about three inches when you open them because the hinges are so rusted.

And now while he's talking, I'm looking at his bug, and thinking how cool it would be to actually own one just like it, to actually drive around on my own, wherever I want to go on this island.

And the other island.

Wait a minute, he said, 'ship it to Maui'.

"You said ship it to Maui? For sixty bucks?"

Drew laughs. "That's right Ben! You guys can drive your new bug to Hana, to the Seven Pools!"

Now he's got me going. 'Your new bug,' like I already own it. He should be a car salesman.

Because I'm sold.

And it's sounding more and more like the smart thing to do…

"Okay man, I think you're probably right about this," I say. "You really think it will be that easy?"

"I'm pretty sure," he says. "I look at the want ads almost every day, and I always see older VW's in there."

He sounds encouraging.

"And the only thing wrong with that bug right there, besides the fact that it's falling apart, was that it had a dead battery. I tried to start the engine, and nothing, so I told the guy that I'd be right back and went straight to Sears and bought a Die Hard. I got back, installed the battery, started it up and drove away!"

"Wow!" I say. "Let's hope that happens again."

Drew sets me up with a single bed in a room off of the living room. I sleep good that night, and when I wake the next morning he's already gone to work. He comes back at around ten am with a newspaper in his hand and a smile on his face.

"Just like I thought," he says. He shows me the ad that he has circled. "A sixty two Bug for three hundred dollars. And I called her already… she says it won't start."

"You're psychic man!"

He laughs. "We'll go check it out first, and then if you want it we'll just go straight to Sears and get a Die Hard. You don't want to get a cheap battery, you want to get a Die Hard and be done with it."

I'll go with that.

"She lives in Hawaii Kai, which is kind of an upscale neighborhood over by Hanauma Bay."

I grab my wallet and we hop in Drew's bug. He has a couple of deliveries to do on the way, so we take a different route than the way he brought me here. We go up and over the Pali. Drew tells me that this is the famous Pali Gap, where some of the Japanese flew through on their way to bomb Pearl Harbor. We briefly stop at the lookout, and walk to the edge of the steep cliff looking back towards Kailua. It's pretty windy, and Drew tells me a story he heard, about a baby falling off of the cliff and the wind blowing the baby back up and into the arms of the mother. Believe it, or not...

When we get to Hawaii Kai it's like Drew said. Nice, bigger homes, but not palaces. Kind of reminding me of Newport Beach, California. When we get to the house we see an old oxidized red bug in the carport. I'm getting curious. Will that car actually be mine?

Drew says, "I have a feeling that she is divorced, living alone. The bug was probably her ex's, and she just wants it gone."

Drew knocks on the door and a very pretty haole woman comes out with long, light brown hair. She's maybe late thirties or early forty's, and looks kind of like Jane Seymour. She's wearing a white sleeveless blouse and blue jean shorts, and Drew and I are both wondering who the knucklehead was that blew it with her.

We go over to the car and aside from the faded paint, I notice that it's really not in bad condition. It has a little rust here and there, but not near as bad as Drew's bug. And the interior

THE BULLET HILL DIARIES

is in surprisingly good shape. Drew has the key, and when he tries to turn it over it just clicks a few times.

Drew looks over at me and smiles. "Do you want it, Ben?"

I think about it for all of two seconds. "Yeah, I want it."

Drew laughs. "Cool! I'll tell her that we'll be right back."

When we get back from Sears, with the new battery and a couple of quarts of oil, just in case, I don't even think of trying to talk her down in price. I just pay her the full three hundred, thinking that this is the best three hundred bucks I've ever spent in my life.

I check the oil, and put a quart in. Then we install the battery, and it starts right up. I'm officially excited.

Following Drew back to Kailua in my new bug, I'm more than excited. I'm ecstatic! Now that I have my own wheels I feel like I really live here. I'm totally free to go anywhere I want. And now we're going to have this car on Maui! I'm really glad that Drew talked me into this, and I can't thank him enough.

Drew has the next day off, and he says that he is taking me to a waterfall with a pool we can jump into. Just a short one mile hike, he says, and the fresh water feels amazing. Sounds great to me.

The trail is easy, and it's my first time seeing the interior of the island up close. Pretty soon we can hear the fall, and when we come over a ledge and I see it, it's like looking at a postcard. I follow Drew to a ledge on the left side of the pool, about twenty five feet above the glistening water. He jumps, and I jump right after him, and the cool clear water feels fantastic. We swim over to the water fall and get right under the falling water itself.

We swim across the pool and crawl out onto the green grass. The sun feels good, and I'm having another Hawaii moment, kind of like Hanauma Bay. But instead of salt water, and fish, and coral, it's a waterfall, and a pool, and green grass.

When we get back to the car Drew says he wants to show

me a little island called Chinaman's Hat, at the north end of Kaneohe Bay. It's real name, he tells me, is Mokolii, which means 'little lizard', but everyone calls it Chinaman's Hat because it resembles the peasant hat worn by the rural men of China. It's only about fifteen hundred feet offshore, with two lonely coconut palms swaying in the breeze. And it looks very solitary in its loneliness, a tiny dab of paradise left to itself.

The following morning Drew tells me that he is taking his roommate Mike to the airport on his way to work. Mike is going to the mainland for a week or so, and that means I'll be spending the day with his other roommate, Tom.

Tom and I have breakfast together, and he asks me about my plans to move to Maui. I briefly tell him about Andy and Dean, and how we started planning this about a year ago.

Tom is kind of shy, but real nice, and we quickly talk easily with each other.

After breakfast he says, "So Ben, I usually go take a swim in the morning down at the beach. Would you like to join me?"

"Sounds great," I say.

It's a pretty short walk down to the beach from their house. When we walk out onto the beach there's a couple of young local kids surfing the two foot shore break on very short boards. We walk down the beach a bit and dive in the water, swimming out past the shore break. Tom starts swimming parallel to the beach, getting some exercise. This is obviously his morning workout routine, so I just follow him and do what he does. It doesn't take me long to tire out though, and I head back in before him.

We towel off on the beach, and then sit for a while soaking up the morning sun. After a while Tom says, "So, are you liking the Hawaiian Islands so far?"

I look out at the blue sea. "I'm loving them!"

I tell him how Drew took me to Hanamua Bay and the waterfall pool. "And I'm loving this beach too... I could really get used to this!"

Tom laughs. "I heard that some guy let you stay with him

in Waikiki last week."

"Yeah, I got lucky. He was really cool."

"Sounds like he was." Tom stretches a little bit, and then says, "Drew also told me that you play drums in a band with his two brothers."

I laugh. "Yeah, sometimes."

"Do you play guitar at all?" he asks.

"Not really," I say. "Well, I know a few chords. Drew's brother Matt teaches me every now and then."

He brightens at this. "Okay, cool. I don't know what your plans are for the rest of the day, but if you want maybe we could jam a little bit."

I look at him and laugh again. "I'm really just a beginner. I don't know if I could hang with you. You've been playing for a while right?"

"Yeah, but that's okay. I have a couple of amps and two electric guitars back at the house. Why don't we just go mess around, see what happens?"

It sounds fun, so I say okay.

When we get back to the house I rinse off at the outdoor shower in their backyard, and then towel off and put on some dry shorts. When I enter the living room Tom greets me and invites me into his room.

The doorway is a curtain of colored beads, and inside the room he has bamboo mats on the floor and a low, Japanese style bed. There's at least three guitars on stands, one of them an acoustic, and a couple of amplifiers in two corners. On the walls are large posters and framed pictures of Jimi Hendrix, and Jimi Hendrix only.

Tom starts tying on a red headband, one of the many different ones that are laying around on his low table and bed. And it all makes sense now...

"You're pretty into Hendrix," I say.

He finishes tying on his headband, then looks at me and smiles.

"Jimi is the King!"

I laugh. "You'll get no argument from me.. I love Jimi!"

Now Tom laughs. "That's good Ben, because that's exactly what we're gonna play."

If someone had told me that today I would be playing parts of Hendrix songs on an electric guitar, and this guy would be playing lead guitar to my rhythms, sounding really close to Jimi himself, I would have laughed in their face. But that's exactly what Tom and I are doing. And he's making it all sound very authentic and psychedelic with the many effects pedals that he has plugged into both of our guitars. He just shows me three or four different chords, along with the rhythm he wants, and when I get that down he just starts taking off.

Tom really has the Hendrix sound nailed, and I'm beside myself with the way we sound. I feel like I've been transported to another world. I've never played guitar like this with anyone else before, or this long for that matter, and after almost two hours we take a break.

I go get us a couple of ice waters, and when I get back to his room Tom is sitting cross legged on the floor rolling a joint. He has put a bootleg Hendrix record on the turntable, where someone recorded him in a hotel room somewhere playing acoustic. It's a Jimi I've never heard.

Tom shows me the rest of his Hendrix record collection, and it looks like virtually everything ever recorded. To Tom Jimi is indeed the King, and although I always loved his music, now I have a new appreciation.

We smoke half of the joint, and then go back to playing. My fingers are sore, but we keep playing. I'm having too much fun, and I want to stay lost in this Hendrix fantasy world all day, which is pretty much what we do.

In the coming few weeks, when Drew has a day off and on the weekends, he will take me to different places on the island. One day we go to the north shore and I see for the first time the home of the world famous surf spots, like Waimea and Pipeline. The waves are small today though, but there's talk of a big swell coming.

We jump in the water at Waimea Beach Park, and then have lunch in the little town of Haleiwa. As we're eating sandwiches and enjoying a cold beer, Drew tells me that Oahu has more accessible beaches than any of the other islands. After what I've seen today I believe him.

On another day we go body surfing at Sandy's, the beach he pointed out to me on my first day driving around the island with him. As soon as we step onto the beach I see where it gets its name. The sand is super soft and stays that way out into the water. The waves are breaking about six to eight foot, which would usually be a little big for me, but these waves look beautiful...

We grab our Churchills and head out into the water. It's so clear that I can see right through the waves, see the people on the other side. It's a Saturday, and there's quite a few of us out. I take off on my first wave and just try not to hit anybody. I've never body surfed waves like these before, waves that are perfectly shaped and crystal clear. Sandy's is a right break, and I'm taking off on eight foot faces, something I would have never done back in California. But they're so easy to judge, and I start having the time of my life.

And now I'm thinking that this is the most fun that I've had since I've been here.

One evening at the house the phone rings, which sounds kind of alarming, because it doesn't ring that often. Drew answers it, first smiling and then laughing, and then looking at me. And I have a feeling I know who it is. Drew talks to him for a little while, and then walks up and hands the phone to me.

"Howzit Brah?" I say, drawing it out, and Andy laughs.

"You're quite the local now, huh Ben?"

"It's pretty fucken cool here man!" I briefly tell him about body surfing, and Hanauma Bay, and the waterfall pool.

"Damn! Sounds like you're having a good time…"

"Oh yeah," I say.

"Hey," he says, and kind of hems and haws for a second. "There's a couple of more guys coming with Dean and I. Chris, and Jeff C.

And this throws me for a loop. It was supposed to be the three of us, Andy and Dean and I. And I don't quite know how I feel about it. "Chris and Jeff huh? Anyone else?"

He must have heard something in my tone. "No, no, that's it. And Jeff isn't coming to Maui with us, he's going to the north shore and staying with his surfing buddies."

"Okay…" I know who Chris is, but I don't know him very well. His sister Mary Jo is my age, and he's a year younger, same as Andy and Dean.

I was going to surprise him about the car, but now I decide to tell him.

"I'll be picking you guys up in my new bug."

"What?" he says. "Are you joking me, Ben?"

I laugh. "Not at all! Drew talked me into buying it, and I'll be shipping it to Maui so we have wheels when we get there."

"That is great Ben!"

"Pretty cool, huh? I have Drew to thank for that. I never would have thought of it on my own."

"That is too cool!" He pauses, then says "I can't believe that we're gonna be there in a couple of days."

He gives me his flight information and I write it down. "That's right," I say. "And in another week or so we'll be on Maui!"

Andy screams like only he can, and I hear it echo in the background. He's obviously working right now, in the garage at Benny Rapp's Chevron.

"It's finally happening Ben!" He is just overwhelmed with excitement.

"Yeah man, it is! And I'll see you in a few days!" Then I say Alo-ha, really dragging out the second syllable.

The last thing I hear is Andy shouting Aloha, the echo loud and clear.

Now that I'm picking up four guys instead of two, I realize that it's definitely going to take two cars. Drew volunteers to drive his bug, and Tom's coming with him. I just hope that we have enough room for their baggage.

This is a pretty big day, the next step in this transition of our lives. As I follow Drew to the airport, up and over the Pali again, I'm pretty excited too. Andy and Dean and I have been planning this for a while, and it's finally coming to fruition.

They have a late morning arrival time, and when we finally meet them they are more than excited; they are stupid happy out of their minds! Andy and Dean practically attack me, and Chris greets me very cheerfully as well. Jeff isn't quite as excited as them, probably because he's just staying for a month.

Since Jeff is being picked up by his friend from the north shore, it isn't as hard as I thought it was going to be fitting the rest of them into our two bugs. Andy rides with Drew and Tom, and Dean and Chris ride with me. Luckily their baggage is duffel bags and daypacks, so they conform more easily into the tight spaces.

Dean rides up front while Chris rides in the back with most of the luggage. They're laughing and shouting, and just plain going off because they're so excited to be here.

At one point Dean says, "Look at fucken Ben, he's gone native on us! He's all tan, and has his own car!" Then he high fives me, and we all laugh.

Chris asks me what I did before Drew got here, and I briefly tell them about Hasani. They both look at me in disbelief. I just tell them that I got real lucky.

When we get to the top of the Pali Drew pulls into the lookout parking lot, and I follow him. I park, and then tell Dean and Chris that they're about to see their first real cool

Hawaiian view.

While we're looking out towards the windward side, the wind itself not as strong as the last time I was here with Drew, Tom tells us that Hendrix wrote a song about this place, aptly called 'The Pali Gap'.

"Jimi loved the islands," Tom says.

Awestruck, Chris says, "I can see why!"

Andy moves over by Chris, and knowing what's ahead he says, "Wait till you see Maui Chris. Wait till you see Hana."

As we start heading back to the cars, Dean, always the explorer, starts climbing up one of the little valleys off of the parking lot. Andy and Chris and I follow him, while Tom and Drew stay behind. Dean keeps going up and up, until he comes out onto a little plateau.

He spies something on the ground up there and walks over to it. "Hey, come look at this."

Andy and Chris and I get to where he is, and we really can't believe what we're seeing. Half in and half out of what seems to be rock is the rusted remains of an engine. But not just any engine, it's a radial engine, like one you'd find in a World War II era plane.

"Is that an engine?" Andy asks.

"Yeah it is," I say. "Out of a really old airplane."

"That's insane!" Dean says. "It must have crashed here. How the fuck else would it get up here?"

We all look at each other.

"You know," Chris says, "The Japanese flew through here when they bombed Pearl Harbor."

Could it really have been from then? I quickly do the math. "That was thirty seven years ago."

It could have been from then.

We look at the rusted relic of an airplane engine a while longer, and then head back down to the cars, mystery unsolved.

After we get back to Drew's house we take Andy, Chris, and Dean down to the beach where Tom and I went swimming. They're loving the water, of course, and we spend some time swimming and sitting around on the beach. While we're kicking back I tell the three of them about my New Year's Eve in Waikiki.

"Why don't we go down there tonight?" Chris suggests.

Dean and Andy are game. And all three of them are a little excited about being of legal drinking age.

"It's right behind here," I say, referring to Hasani's apartment as we drive by the International Market Place on Kalakaua boulevard. I finally find a place to park on a back street, and we walk back to Kalakaua in all of its nighttime partying glory.

As we continue walking down Kalakaua, Dean and Chris taking it all in like kids on Christmas morning, I say, "You guys pick the place."

Andy wastes no time leading us into one of the big Hotels on the beach. We amble up to the bar and order drinks, the first time for Dean and Chris. We drink our drinks, and try to act like we're adults, and don't do a very good job, and laugh and have a good time.

Andy starts chatting it up with our bartender, a Haole guy in his early thirties. I hear him telling the guy about our little hike up at the Gap, and the engine we found, and the guy seems genuinely amazed.

After a little bit the bartender says, "If you guys like to hike, you should check out Manoa Valley, and Manoa Falls."

The four of us are intrigued, and Dean goes and grabs an island tourist map from the lobby. The bartender shows us where Manoa Valley is on the map, and it turns out that it's not all that far from Honolulu, just south a bit.

We decide to go for it in the morning, and we're all excited that we have a mission now. We finish our drinks, thank the bartender and make our way back out onto the street.

We were going to go to another bar, but since we want to get up early for our hike tomorrow we decide to call it a night, and start heading back to my bug. As we're walking along Kalakaua a local kid, maybe sixteen years old, confronts Chris and I.

"Buds?" he says. When we don't say anything he says, "Paka Lolo?"

Chris starts laughing. "Where?"

The kid motions for us to follow him. We both hesitate, and then just for the hell of it, we do. He walks down the crowded sidewalk maybe twenty feet and stops.

"Right here?" Chris asks, looking around at all of the people and car traffic.

The kid points up into the tree that we're standing under. We look up, and there in the high branches is another kid smiling down at us.

Chris and I both start laughing. "Are you serious?" Chris asks.

The kid points up again. "You climb da tree."

Chris just shakes his head. I look up again. And then, maybe because I've had a few drinks, I grab the lowest branch and pull myself up. It's an easy tree to climb, and I quickly make my way up to the other kid and sit on a branch opposite him. I look down at the people walking by, all of them oblivious to us up here. Then, mixed in with the other traffic I see a cop car slowly driving by.

I look at the kid and he says, "No worries brah."

Then he pulls a cellophane bag out of his pocket with what looks like a small amount of leafy buds.

"How much?" I ask.

"Twenty five," he says.

A total rip. But, since we don't have anything, I pull a twenty out of my wallet. "It's all I got," I say.

He thinks about it for maybe five seconds, and then takes my twenty and hands me the bag. I go to climb back down but he grabs my arm. "Wait," he says.

I follow his gaze, and see another cop car driving by. When it's gone he says, "Okay."

I climb back down, and when I lower myself to the sidewalk the passersby don't seem to notice me at all. Chris has been waiting for me, and as we start walking away he says, "Did you get some buds brah?"

I laugh. "Yeah brah," I reply. "Not much, but I figured what the hell."

"That was crazy!" Chris says.

"I know. I wonder how long they've been getting away with this."

We catch up with Andy and Dean, and when we tell them what happened they're both incredulous, but laughing.

"Fucken Ben!" Dean says.

The next morning we don't get to the Manoa State Park parking lot until about eleven. We plan on spending the night, so we each have sleeping bags strapped to our backs. Dean also carries a daypack with our provisions in it, which is a loaf of Drew's homemade bread and sandwich makings.

At first the trail is flat and straight, and it's easy going. But pretty soon it starts climbing up, until we come to a spot where it's virtually straight up. Drew has hiked it before, and he told us about this part of the trail. He told us to keep an eye out for protruding roots that act as handholds. They're easy to spot, and we all make it to the top of this section pretty easily. Up here we rest and take in the view of the lower valley and the ocean off in the distance. We also smoke some of the paka lolo that we got the night before, and this may have something to do with what happens next.

We continue on the trail, which follows a stream. Thinking that this stream ends up at the falls, we stray from the trail and keep following the stream. As much as the four of us are devoted fans of Tolkien, and the Lord of the Rings, you would think that we would remember Gandalf's advice to Bilbo and the dwarves not to stray from the path, but we commit the same error as they did.

The stream is cool and clear, and we refill our reusable water containers. After maybe a half mile we come to a small waterfall, maybe ten or twelve feet high, and it looks to be impassable. It's straight up on either side of the falls, the right side having more vegetation.

Dean tries to scale the left side, with no luck, so I try the right. I hold onto vines and other plants, and manage to find footholds here and there. I slowly make it up and over the top of the falls, but I'm still eight to ten feet above the rocky floor that I'm trying to get to. Then the plants that I'm holding onto rip free, and I fall.

I twist to the right in midair, not knowing what else to do. While my sleeping bag cushions my head, my right hip hits sharp rock, and I get the wind knocked out of me.

I slowly roll over and lay on my back, looking straight up and unable to breathe. My sleeping bag is my lucky pillow; I would probably have a concussion right now if it wasn't for it. I slowly start taking short gasps of air, and although I'm in pain and am struggling to breathe, or maybe because of it, I am hypnotized by the scene above me. Trees shooting their branches and leaves into a perfect blue sky with wispy white clouds.

I become aware of Chris and Andy calling from down below, asking if I'm alright. In between short breaths of air I manage to squeak out, "I'm okay, I'm okay!" But with my difficulty breathing I sound like a chipmunk. And I mean like Alvin and the Chipmunks.

I finally regain normal breathing, and slowly stand to my feet. I look at my right hip and I have a gash about an inch long and a quarter of an inch wide. Strangely enough it isn't really bleeding, but it hurts like hell and I need stitches, or at least a butterfly bandage, but we have no first aid kit with us.

I slowly walk to the top of the waterfall so they can see that I'm in one piece. I take off my sleeping bag and throw it down to them. Then I inch down the rock ledge to the side of

THE BULLET HILL DIARIES

the fall as far as I can, and then jump into the pool below. As I crawl out of the water they all come over to help me out, relief showing on their faces. They look me over, and when they see my hip Dean rips the bottom of his T shirt off and ties it around my waist, a make do bandage. My hip bone is sore too, and that hurts more than the cut.

Now that I seem to be okay, aside from the cut on my hip and a bruised ego, they can hold it no longer. First Chris, and then the other two start laughing uncontrollably. Apparently I sounded pretty comical when I was Alvin the Chipmunk.

Their laughter is contagious, and I start laughing too. I feel pretty lucky, actually, thanks to my sleeping bag. No broken bones, which is unbelievable.

"We couldn't see you," Chris is saying, "and when we finally heard you, you just sounded hilarious!"

They all clap me on the back, happy that I'm not too badly injured.

"Fucken Ben!" Dean says, smiling.

It's late afternoon, and we slowly make our way back down the stream that we came up. After a while we come to the grassy area where we split from the trail, and now that we've found it again, instead of going up to Manoa Falls we just decide to camp here for the night.

We make sandwiches for dinner, and then turn in early, trying to make ourselves comfortable in our sleeping bags. I can't lay on my right side, and we didn't bring 'Insolites', or any other kind of cushioning, so for me it's a night of fitful sleep.

We wake early and rinse ourselves off in the stream, which feels cold in the early morning. It's exhilarating though, and after I dry off I feel great, considering.

It's a beautiful Hawaiian morning, and we're all in good spirits as we head back down the trail. When we get to the car Andy asks me if I want to get stitches for my wound, but I say no. I tell him that I'll be alright, but I'm sure I'll have a scar to remind me of my stupidity. And when we get back to the house, after hearing our story, Drew gives me some aloe vera gel and a butterfly bandage for my hip.

The next day Chris and Andy and Dean like the idea of bodysurfing at Sandy's. Drew's roommate Mike is back from the mainland, and he has a Volkswagen camper van that we all pile into.

The waves are pretty much identical in size as the last time I was here, but it's even better because it's a weekday and there's less people. The three of them are really loving this, just like I did my first time, and they're having a ball. Chris and Andy are always messing with each other, and they continue to do so while bodysurfing, cutting each other off and trying to steal the other guys wave.

The next day Drew informs us that the big swell that we had heard about has arrived, and that we should go check it out. He tells us that he has a friend who lives in Haleiwa, and we can spend the night there. Since we have already dropped my bug off at the port, hoping that it will be on Maui when we get there, Mike lets us take his van. We stop at another one of Drew's friends along the way, so we don't get to the north shore until nightfall.

His friend's house is straight up the mountain a few miles, and when we get out of the car we not only hear the huge surf below us, but we can feel it, like thunder off in the distance.

I wake in the middle of the night, forgetting for a moment where I am. I have to take a pee, and thinking that I might wake someone using the bathroom I decide to go outside. When I get out there I hear and feel the huge waves again. It is an eerie and ominous sound, powerful beyond description.

In the morning Drew's friend and his wife make us breakfast, and after that we're eager to get down to the beach. When we walk out of the front of the house to the van we look down at the ocean, and hovering above the unseen coast is a rainbow, made from the mist of the waves.

While Drew is taking us down the hill he says, "We'll go to the beach in front of Pipeline, see what that looks like."

When we walk out onto the beach we're still unprepared for what we see. Pipeline definitely isn't breaking like the perfect left break that you see in surf films. It's totally un surfable, and just the angriest barrel of water that you can imagine. Huge crushing things that look like death itself.

We continue walking down the beach to a break called 'Off the Wall' and sit in the sand. The name really fits today because these are gigantic walls of water, looking like they're forty feet high. They appear as though they're going to devour us, but then get consumed by the coral reef.

We just sit here for a while, transfixed by these monster waves, and getting wet from the mist.

At one point Dean looks at me and says, "Ben, you said you have the Elmo with you?"

"Yeah," I say, and then I realize the depth of my stupidity. "But it's back at the house."

Dean just shakes his head.

The 'Elmo' is my eight millimeter movie camera.

Pretty soon we notice a guy come out of his house back towards Pipeline, and he's got his Churchills in his hands.

And Dean voices what we're all thinking. "He's not actually going to go out in this, is he?"

"That would be crazy!" Chris says.

He sits down on the beach like us, and we keep an eye on him.

After a while Andy says, "There he goes!"

We look back down the beach just in time to see him dive in the water. He swims out and dives under the first wave coming at him. He keeps doing this for a while, just diving under wave after wave. Finally he takes off on one, slipping down the face until he disappears into the whitewater.

We all run down the beach to where we last saw him. He's nowhere to be seen, until he finally emerges near the shore, walking up onto the beach carrying his fins like it's just another day.

We come up to him and he smiles at us. He's a fairly tall haole guy, about Drew's size but a few years older.

Drew says, "We were worried about you brah!"

The guy laughs, and with a sheepish grin he says, "I just got bored."

The day finally comes for us to go to Maui.

Oahu has been a stepping stone, and now it's time to take the next step. I stepped a little earlier than the other three, and maybe I needed to. I have had amazing help from wonderful people, like Hasani, and Drew and Tom, and Mike. I've had a lot of fun too. And I have done things with questionable judgement, resulting in injury. Hopefully I will learn from my mistakes.

Chris is a good addition to our group, and we're becoming friends. No matter what I was thinking before, now I'm really glad that he came. And actually when I think about it, there was an odd man out. The three of us were an odd number, and now we're even.

Looking out the window of the Hawaiian Air 707 that we're on I start to get my first glimpse of Maui, just a couple of bluish humps at this distance. I get a sudden feeling deep in my chest, a combination of excitement, anticipation, anxiousness, and a little fear.

But the feeling of excitement reigns supreme...

And it's making me smile.

We were the generation between wars. Too young for Viet Nam, too old for Desert Storm. As kids we played with our army men, staging wars with each other. For Christmas we'd get army helmets and real looking fake guns with plastic daggers on the barrel. We saw no shortage of World War II movies on television, and

TV shows like 'Combat!' and 'Rat Patrol' and 'Hogan's Heroes', not to mention 'McHale's Navy' and 'Twelve O'Clock High' were all the rage.

And as we got older, and felt somewhat cheated out of a war, consequently everything we did was a 'Mission'. We loved to become a finely tuned tactical unit and conquer things, like an oil derrick for instance.

Of course, as we were being bred with a love for war, we had no idea of the real terrors of actually being in one. We didn't know the horrors that men in combat saw on a daily basis. The carnage and the death, and the tears. And then we started getting our first inkling of what it might be like when guys started coming back home from Viet Nam. And it was quite a different story from the guys like our dads, who came back from WW II. Those guys won their war. They got the bad guys and came home as heroes. But the Nam guys seemed to come back home in a daze. Coming back from a winless war, wondering how to fit back into a society that had mostly grown to hate the very war that they had risked their lives fighting.

And of course if we could have chosen our war, not that we really wanted one, it would have been something more along the lines of Pearl Harbor, where we were actually attacked on our own soil. And then yeah, most of us would have joined up and been happy to help go kick those sons of bitches asses.

While I was working with Andy at the gas station one night he turned to me and said, "You know Ben, we're really lucky that we didn't have to go to Viet Nam. If we were just a couple of years older we might've had to go." He pauses a second, looking out into the night. He had just been talking to a customer, a dad whose son had died over there. "That was one fucked up war," he finally says. "Just one really fucked up nightmare of a war."

I couldn't agree more.

Some nicknames:

Andy – *Krame*
Dean - *Goob*

Gary – *The Golden Bear*
Richard - *Bone*
Mark – *Min*
Matt – *Von*
Eric – *E*
Scott – *Status*
Ben – *Spin (or Mark would call me Fin)*

'DING DING OUT THERE'

'Leaves are falling all around, it's time I was on my way
    Thanks to you I'm much obliged, for such a pleasant stay
    But now it's time for me to go, the Autumn moon lights my
way

    For now I smell the rain, and with it pain, and it's headed my
way

    Ah, sometimes I grow so tired
    But I know I got one thing I got to do...'

'Ramble On'
Led Zeppelin

Early Summer, 1974
Seal Beach, California

"Hey Beenut, you ever met my little brother?"

That's what Gary calls me, Beenut, and it always makes me laugh. "Which one, don't you have two?"

"Yeah well, Tommy's the youngest, and I have an older brother Ken, but I'm talkin' about Andy."

"I know who he is, but I've never really met him."

Gary stops mopping the floor for a second and looks up at me. "Well, you're gonna get your chance, because I'm getting him a job here."

'Here' is Benny Rapp's Chevron Station, located at the southeast corner of Main Street and Pacific Coast Highway, in our cozy little town of Seal Beach, California. Working here at Benny's could arguably be one of the cooler jobs that young guys such as ourselves could have in this town.

"I'm going back to working days, and I need someone to take my place," Gary says. "And Andy needs a job."

Gary is two years older than me, and we're the 'Night Crew', along with another guy Richard, better known as 'Bone', who is the same age as Gary.

"Oh okay, cool," I reply, not knowing what else to say.

I've only been working with Gary for a few months now, and he almost feels like my big brother. Sometimes he'll say to me, "If anyone ever gives you any shit Beenut, you just tell me who they are, and I'll pop their lips for you."

He takes a boxer's stance and starts punching the air, quick left and right combinations.

And he's making me laugh again.

Good ol' Gary.. He's the 'Golden Bear' and he's rarin' to go. And at about six three and maybe two thirty five he cuts a pretty imposing figure. He's got a short crop of blonde hair on his head, and in fact his entire body is covered with hair. In the summertime, like now, the hair on his back and shoulders turns gold, and so the nickname.

We're mopping and squeegeeing the floors of the service bays, something we do every night. Our shift starts at five and we close up at ten, and it usually takes another half hour or so to record the numbers off of the gas pumps, count up the credit card receipts and cash, and clean and mop the bathrooms and lounge area.

We might be busy for the first couple of hours pumping gas, but then it'll die down, and some nights it will be completely dead. We'll sometimes use this downtime to work on our own vehicles, putting them up on a lift if we need to, changing our oil or maybe changing a tire. And sometimes we'll just talk.

When we get hungry we'll more often than not go right next door to Taco Bell. Or we might dash across Main Street to Jack in the Box, or we might even order up a Johnny's Pizza, one of us jamming over to fifth street real quick in the station truck to pick it up.

Benny Rapp is tall and slender, but strong as a tightrope. With his dark complexion and a kind of sloping forehead, one might think that he has some Native American blood in him. And he's possibly one of the smartest business men in town. His gas prices are the highest around, but he's so good at customer service that people will come in just to get gas anyway.

When a customer drives in to get gas at Benny Rapp's Chevron, even if it's only a couple of bucks worth, they will get their front and back windows washed and their oil and water checked. During the first hour of our shift, we of the Night Crew will work right alongside the day guys, so sometimes there will be four of us on a car, washing windows and checking under the hood, and even checking the air in their tires.

My friend Ron, who is Gary's age, got me the job here, taking his place so he could go to work for a local plumber. I usually work Monday through Thursday nights, and sometimes a Saturday or Sunday day. I'm free to go to Friday night football games at Huntington Beach High School, with my dad and sometimes my brother and Ron if I want to, and I couldn't really ask for a more perfect schedule.

Gary's brother Andy has worked about a week of day's now, so Benny is switching him to nights. And his first night is with me.
The two of us don't know it yet, but both of our lives are about to change. Forever.
We seem to hit it off instantly, talking about all sorts of things while we wash a customer's windows or while we're mopping the floors. And it's weird, Andy is so easy to talk to that I feel like we've already known each other for a long time.
And I soon notice that he's a real natural with the customer service thing.
"Check under that hood for you Ma'am? Or maybe change the air in your tires?"
That last line will always get a laugh, especially with Andy's mock seriousness. He's quite the schmoozer, and he's cracking me up.

I will usually just ride my bike to work, a short ride down 'The Hill' from Crestview, but sometimes I'll drive. My car is a 1959 Volkswagen Karmann Ghia. When I was still fifteen, with only a drivers permit, my dad happened to find the car in an old airplane hangar at Long Beach Airport. It was next to his old airplane hangar, where he keeps his single engine Cessna 210 that he co-owns with our neighbor Russ and another guy, Al.
Apparently the guy who has the hangar next to my dad's keeps more than just his airplane in there. Among other things he has about a thirty foot boat, and tucked behind that was the Karmann Ghia. The only dent on the whole car was a two inch crease on the nose, where it had obviously been pushed into the rudder of the boat. Besides a rusted out floor panel on the driver's side, with a hole the size of a volleyball, the only other thing wrong with it was that the motor didn't run. But

that didn't turn out to be such a huge problem, because my brother has become a Volkswagen mechanic, turning our parents garage into his VW shop.

With his help, and the 'Manual of Step by Step Procedures for the Compleat Idiot', I managed to overhaul the engine in our garage. When I finally started it up and drove it down Crestview for the first time, I definitely felt a little proud.

But I also felt a little funny, because the guy who owned this car before me is dead. Another sad statistic of the Viet Nam War. What was he like, I wonder? Maybe we had something in common, because he was obviously into old Volkswagens. His dad was storing the car in the hangar at the airport so it would be there for him when he came back. But, like so many others, he didn't come back.

This also made buying the car and changing ownership a little complicated, and I remember my dad showing me the thick stack of paperwork required to do it. The sale of the car was listed at fifty dollars, but the guy refused to take any money, so my dad gave him a bottle of 'bubbly'. I don't know how appropriate that was, or if the guy even cared, but that's my dad.

A few of our friends, Andy's, Gary's and mine, will sometimes drop by the station at night to work on their own vehicles. They might change their oil, or put on a new tire or two, or maybe just vacuum out the inside after they've washed it. (The station vacuum really sucks!) This gets Andy going, and now he wants a car of his own. And wouldn't you know it, he wants a Volkswagen.

Word gets out that Andy is looking for a car, and it doesn't take long before he finds one. My brother's friend Ron, a different Ron, has a blue '68 Bug that he's ready to unload. It's in very good shape, and aside from wide tires and flared fenders it's pretty much stock. It runs perfectly, the inside is immaculate, and most importantly it has a great stereo. Andy buys it, really happy that he doesn't have to do a thing to it.

One night I'm working at the station with Bone, and not

long into the night Andy comes in with his new Bug. He's washing the windows inside and out and using the station vacuum. He just bought a new eight track tape, Crosby, Stills and Nash, and he's got it turned up with the doors open.

Bone likes Andy, but he can't help teasing him a little bit. Bone is strictly an American Car kind of guy, and doesn't understand our attraction with Volkswagens. In fact Bone has just bought a new vehicle himself, a bright yellow Ford F-100 4x4, and he claims he could drive it up and over and crush our cheesy little VW's.

And when I say his truck is bright yellow, I don't mean school bus yellow, I mean bright like the sun yellow. I try to tease him back by calling his truck the 'Screaming Yellow Zonker', stealing the name from a popular popcorn snack. The ruse backfires though because Bone likes the name. He even has a custom license plate frame made that says Screaming Yellow Zonker in yellow lettering on a black background.

My good friend Mark, who is my age, starts coming around the station at night. Among other things he's my VW buddy, and drives a really clean white '67 Bug that he customized himself. He likes my Ghia, and talks me into making it 'California Style'. California Style means stripping off all of the chrome, including the bumpers, and filling in the holes with Bondo. It also means beefing up the motor somewhat, lowering it a little bit, and putting on custom wheels with racing radials.

Mark takes a liking to Andy, but teases him about his Bug, and for different reasons than Bone. Andy's Bug, with its wide tires and flared fenders, and all of its chrome, is definitely not California Style. But even with all of Mark's teasing Andy's not about to change it. He likes it just fine the way it is.

Andy has had his new Bug for all of about a week, when fate steps in.

The two of us are coming back into Seal Beach from Westminster, heading towards the ocean on Seal Beach boulevard.

I'm sitting in the passenger seat, and Andy takes a right on Bolsa avenue, which takes us by J. H. McGaugh Intermediate School, the school we both attended as kids.

As we approach the stop sign by the tennis courts we both notice our friend Jeannine and her mom Fanny playing tennis, and we can't help but notice that they both look very cute in their short white tennis outfits. There's a car stopping at the stop sign in front of us, and we're stopping behind it.

And then everything happens so fast it's a blur...

Andy looks in his rear view mirror and says, "Oh my God, this guy isn't stopping! He's looking at Fanny and Jeannine and he's not stopping!"

Andy can't go anywhere because of the car in front of us, and then sure enough, wham!! The guy slams into the back of us. We get out to survey the damage, and since the guy is driving a full size pick-up, it's not good. The whole back end of Andy's Bug is smashed in.

Andy is hopping mad, and even though the guy is bigger and probably a few years older, Andy could care less. After ripping him a new one he says, "I just bought this car! Look at it, it's totaled!"

The guy doesn't try to argue, and in fact he looks downright embarrassed. He readily gives Andy his driver's license number and his insurance information.

Since we're only four or five blocks from Andy's house, instead of bothering with a tow truck we just push the car down Bolsa to Balboa, turn right and park it in front of his parent's house.

Andy does end up having to total the car, and the other guys insurance company pays him the blue book equivalent for it.

Maybe two or three weeks later Mark tells Andy that his cousin Craig has a '64 Bug for sale. Craig has just finished dechroming and painting the car. It's a really nice paint job, even though, as Mark says, it's 'baby shit' brown. Andy buys the Bug from Craig, and now, whether he wanted one or not, he has a

California Style VW like Mark and me.

Lately, while I have been working nights with Andy, his friend Dean has been stopping by on his bicycle, talking to Andy out by the gas pumps. Dean is Andy's age, and just like with Andy, I know who Dean is, but I've never really met him. I do know his older brother Guy though, because he was a drummer in the marching band at McGaugh, and so was I.

One night, after one of these visits from Dean, Andy walks back to the garage. "Dean wants a job here," he says to me. "I'm gonna talk to Benny about it tomorrow."

Dean ends up getting the job, and in a short while he's put on the Night Crew. My first night working with Dean is kind of like my first night working with Andy. We talk easily with each other, and find out that we have a few things in common, like our taste in music. Dean is a little bit on the shy side, which doesn't really make sense to me because he's tall and good looking, blonde haired and blue eyed. He also has a quirky sense of humor, which I like.

Dean lives on fourteenth street, right across from Mark it turns out, and the four of us start becoming good friends.

Late Summer, 1975

"Dean sure is over at Taco Bell a lot lately." Andy is telling me this as we stand by the cash register in the garage. He and Dean are working tonight, and I'm just hanging out.

"He has been over there for a while, hasn't he," I say.

"About twenty minutes," he says, a hint of frustration in his voice.

Just then a car comes in. "Ding ding!"

"Damnit, it's his turn!" Andy says as he walks out to get the car.

"I'll go get Dean," I say, and walk the short distance to Taco Bell.

When I come around the corner I see Dean, leaning on the counter with one arm and chatting it up with the girl at the order window, looking like he's in a saloon in a western movie. The girl is stunningly cute, with short blonde hair and big blue eyes, and a million dollar smile.

Dean's got a smile of his own going, and I silently laugh, because it all makes sense now.

I walk up and Dean notices me.

"Ben!" he says, a little startled.

"Hey Dean," I say. Then I lower my voice. "You better get back over there, Andy's getting pissed."

"Okay, yeah..." Then he turns to the girl. "I'll be seeing you next time," he says, putting all of his charm into it.

"Bye," she says, laughing and flashing that kilowatt smile at both of us.

As we come around the corner to go back to the station Dean practically jumps out of his shoes. "Woo hoo!" he shouts.

I laugh. "Oh my God, you are smitten!"

As Dean starts heading towards the car that Andy is taking care of he turns around, and walking backwards he says, "Can you blame me? Did you see her?"

I did see her.

And I can't blame him.

Now that the gig is up, Dean isn't holding back.

"Her name is Mary Beth, and she's a living doll!" Dean is gushing as he's telling Andy and me this back in the garage.

Andy looks over at me and I nod. "She's very cute."

A few seconds later Andy says, "Well, I am getting kind of hungry... maybe I'll just go over there and see for myself."

As he turns to go he smiles and gives Dean a good natured punch in the shoulder.

Dean laughs. "Go ahead. Just remember that I found her first!"

This time Andy's gone for about twenty minutes.

When he comes back he's all smiles. "You were right," he says to Dean. "She is cute."

Dean takes it in stride, but I'm thinking that we may have

a situation here...

About once or twice a month a couple of executives from Standard Oil will drop by the station and take Benny to lunch at the Wooden Shoe, which is directly across Pacific Coast Highway from the station. They appear to be in their early forties, and they look more like Secret Service Agents than Standard Oil execs, decked out in dark blue suits and mirrored sunglasses.

These lunches always last about two hours, and when the three of them come back they're always laughing and in good spirits. The Wooden Shoe is kind of like a Denny's, except that it has a full bar. So Kim, one of the daytime mechanics who is telling me this, thinks that they're having a few cocktails there as well.

We soon find out one of the reasons for these visits from the Standard Oil 'Big Wigs', and from none other than Benny himself. One evening he tells Andy and I that they want him to make a couple of his islands at his station 'Self-Serve'.

The self-service island at gas stations is a relatively new concept, and a few of the stations in town have at least one. But the very idea of this self-serve thing at all makes Benny cringe. It's about the opposite of what he stands for. He'll be damned if he's going to have us stand around while a customer pumps his own gas and washes his or her own windshield.

Since Mark and I have just graduated High School Mark decides that he would like to work at Benny Rapp's also. He likes to have his nights free though, so he's applying for a day shift. A lot of the daytime gas jockey's come and go, so it doesn't take long before he's hired.

At about his second or third week working at the station I come in at five to start my shift, and work side by side with Mark. Pretty soon we see Benny and Tom, another mechanic, roll out a couple of metal signs towards the Main Street island. They place them at either end of the pumps. Even though I knew it was coming, I was still kind of shocked to see that they said 'Self-Serve'.

Benny clearly isn't happy about it, and it looks like it took him all day to finally do it. He has fought tooth and nail against the idea, but must have been given some kind of ultimatum. He held his ground about one thing though. Instead of two islands, he only agreed to one.

Mark and I are standing just outside the garage talking to Tom and Kim when a car pulls into the Self-Serve island. 'Ding ding'.

Mark and I kind of look at each other, not knowing what to do.

Benny walks up behind us. "Ding ding out there!"

"But it's the Self-Serve island," Mark protests.

"I don't care," Benny says. "Ding ding out there!" And he draws back his foot like he's going to kick us in the ass.

Mark and I both jump and then hastily make our way out to the car. Tom and Kim join us, both of them laughing under their breath. The customer is just starting to get out of his car when he sees the four of us converging on him. He looks puzzled, but climbs back into his car. We proceed to pump his gas, wash his windows, check under his hood and check the air in his tires. All of this at the Self-Serve island, where the price of gas is about five cents cheaper.

When we're done the guy pays and slowly drives away, waving at us with a big smile on his face. And I'm thinking, maybe Benny Rapp really is the smartest businessman in town.

I'm riding my bike to work, and it's Santa Ana conditions all across Southern California. The hot dry desert winds push all of the moisture, and all of the smog out to sea. Overnight these winds have switched the temperature from the mid-sixties to the low nineties.

I'm a little early for work, so I decide to ride on down to the pier and check out the beach and the waves. The first thing

I notice is the smog layer out over the ocean. It lays there like a big flat brown carpet, so perfect and thin in its flatness that I can clearly see the top half of Catalina Island above it.

These warm offshore winds make for perfect surfing conditions, and today the waves are only about two to three feet, which is ideal size for a beginner surfer like myself. The wind is blowing the spray off the tops of the waves as they curl, shaping them and adding a nice visual to the beauty of it all. There's a fair amount of surfers out having fun, and it's really making me wish that I didn't have to go to work right now. Which reminds me...

As I ride into Benny's off of Main Street the first thing that catches my eye is Andy's Bug parked next to the double glass doors of the station lounge. His driver's side door is open and he's leaning against it with Mary Beth in his arms. They're both wearing bathing suits, which still look a little wet, and they've obviously been to the beach. Dean is standing a little apart from them, wearing his Chevron uniform because he's working with me tonight.

"Hey Ben," Dean says as I ride up.

"Hey," I say.

Mary Beth smiles and says Hi, but Andy's in another world, his eyes only for his girl.

Just then Benny walks up, and in the nicest way possible suggests that Andy and Mary Beth get going so that Dean and I can go to work. They hop in Andy's Bug and she waves to Dean and I out the open window as they drive off.

And it's kind of funny how things turned out. The 'situation' that I was concerned about some weeks before luckily ended up not being much of a situation after all.

To his credit Dean did take out Mary Beth first. Took her to a movie at the Bay Theater, which is right next door to the station. I remember working with Gary that night, and Dean driving up with Mary Beth in his dad's Cadillac Fleetwood. He was dressed to the nines, with his light blue slacks and white coat. Mary Beth looked even more dazzling than usual, and they parked at the station and walked next door.

Everything was fine and good, but I guess there wasn't really any major sparks flying.

About a week or two later Andy took Mary Beth out. And the sparks flew.

Later that night when business dies down Dean and I kick back in the garage and get a chance to talk. "I've gotta hand it to you man," I say. "You're taking this whole Mary Beth thing really well."

Dean sighs. Then he says, "They're so in love Ben. When they came together it was like a freight train." He claps his hands for emphasis. "When two people click like that there's just nothing in this world that can stop it!"

"Well, I think Andy's pretty lucky that you're being so cool about it."

Dean laughs. "I'm not saying it was easy at first. Luckily I didn't have enough time to totally fall in love with her."

"Like he is," I say.

Dean laughs again. "Yeah, like he is. Totally and completely."

"I noticed."

We both laugh.

And I silently wish them well.

One night back in May, before Mark and I graduated, we found ourselves down in Bullet Hill drinking some beers.

At one point Mark said, "Hey Fin, have you ever climbed one of those?"

He was referring to the oil towers off in the distance.

"As a matter of fact I have."

"No shit, really?"

"Honestly. But it was like five years ago, with my brother and a few of his friends."

We were sitting in a small clearing next to some of the

biggest eucalyptus trees in all of Bullet Hill, with a full moon shining down and a twelve pack of Coors in between us. We were looking out at the oil towers of Hellman's Ranch, which we could clearly see in the bright moonlight.

"Which one?" Mark asked.

"Which one did we climb?" I slowly flashed back to that night. "See the one furthest to the right, kind of all by itself? We picked that one because it was the farthest one away from the Man's house."

The 'Man' is the oil worker who rides around at night in an old pick-up truck, a big German Shepherd named King always in the back. He slowly makes his rounds to the many oil wells, recording numbers off of the pumps or something, we assume.

"We waited until about midnight before heading out, all of us wearing dark clothing. We turned it into a full on Ninja mission, moving in single file and keeping a sharp lookout for the Man."

Mark laughed, then pointed his beer can at the tower and said, "I wanna climb it... are you up for it again?"

I laughed. "Seriously?"

"Yeah man," he said. "I wanna climb it."

I laughed again. "Okay," I said. "But it has to be on a dark night, not a full moon night like this."

Mark started getting excited. "Cool Fin, we're gonna do it!"

We smacked our beer cans together, making it official.

It's about a week or so later, and Mark and I are crouched down next to the chain link fence that separates us from the private property of Hellman's Ranch and the oil derricks. In the late night darkness we scour the area looking for the Man in his truck, but he's nowhere in sight.

The smell of oil is strong, replacing the scent of eucalyptus that permeated our senses at the beginning of our little trek through Bullet Hill. The sounds of the oil wells are louder now too, and could mask the sound of the Man and his truck if we don't keep an eye out.

Once we climb the fence there is no turning back, I tell Mark. From there we have to quickly make our way the hundred feet or so to the tower and instantly start climbing the first ladder. Our initial goal is to get to the halfway station, where we can lay down on the wide planks and hide if the Man should come.

After one more look around I say, "Let's do it!"

We both start climbing the fence at the same time. There's two rows of barbed wire at the top, but they're easily avoided if you're careful. We swing one leg and then the other over the top, grabbing the wire in between the barbs, and then jump down to the other side. We move fast towards the tower, but I tell Mark to watch out for pipes and things hidden in the weeds.

As we get close to the tower the sound of the oil well pumping directly underneath gets louder still, a slow rhythmic whine that seems to intensify the situation.

Mark reaches the bottom ladder first, so I let him go first. I wait for him to get a good ten or fifteen feet up before I start climbing. I feel the daypack I'm wearing pull slightly at my shoulders. It's got our 'supplies' in it, which is a six pack of beer and a joint and a lighter. This is, after all, a seriously fun mission.

There's three ladders to climb before we get to the halfway station, each of them about twenty feet long. At the end of each ladder is a very small landing where you can rest for a second, before climbing the next one. From the halfway station to the top is exactly the same set up, three ladders with three landings. Of course the tower gets narrower the higher you go, so while the halfway point might be twenty five feet wide, the top might only be about ten.

I look up and see that Mark's making good time. He's a good climber, and I'm glad for that. When I reach the halfway station and pop through the hole Mark is sitting on the planks a few feet to one side. I do the same thing and we sit for a few minutes and take a breather.

From this vantage point we can easily see the Man's house, and notice a few lights on inside. There's a few dim lights shining at some of the oil wells, but for the most part the surrounding area below us is dark. Off to our north about a half mile away is the Haynes Power Plant with its multitude of lights, literally thousands of them, and it casts the most light of anything.

We scan the area below us for the Man's slow moving pick-up, but we don't see it anywhere.

"Should we go for it?" Mark asks.

"I think so… it doesn't get any better than this."

Mark goes first again, and I keep looking for the Man while I wait for him to get to the next landing. This is the second point of no return, from here to the top, and the higher we get the more vulnerable we feel. If someone, anyone, were to look up they would easily see our silhouettes moving up the ladders. So the thing to do now is quickly, but carefully, get to the top.

When Mark reaches the top of the last ladder I hear him say, "Holy shit!"

And then I remember.

One side of the top ladder moves. It swings out about three or four inches until it can go no further. Needless to say, if you're not ready for it, it will scare the crap out of you.

I reach the top and crawl over by Mark. "Sorry man, I forgot all about that last ladder moving."

"Damn!" he says. "That woke me up!"

We sit on the side facing the ocean. "But hey, what a view huh?"

From here we can see over the tops of the trees of Bullet Hill to the oil islands beyond out at sea, their twinkling lights reflecting off the water. To the east is the Naval Weapons Station, many square miles of it, with a few lights here and there. Off to the west are the lights of Long Beach, with the Long

Beach Marina in the foreground.

I pull off my daypack and unzip the top and pull out a couple of beers. "Here you go man. Welcome to the top!"

Mark takes it and laughs. Looking down he says, "We are definitely up here! What would you say it is, maybe two hundred feet?"

"Probably close to that, yeah."

Mark holds up his beer. "Cheers Fin, we did it!"

I hold up mine. "Cheers!"

We don't know it yet but we will be coming back up again soon. And next time there will be four of us.

Only a few nights later, after hearing about Mark's and my little adventure, both Dean and Andy want to climb the tower too. The night that we decide to go Andy and I are working together, so Mark and Dean are meeting us at closing time.

Later that same night, huddling at the base of the tower, we decide that Mark will go first, then me, then Andy, with Dean bringing up the rear.

Mark and I waste no time, and with no sign of the Man we just keep going until we reach the top. Down below us things aren't happening so fast. Andy is moving slowly, and Dean is doing his best to encourage him.

Andy finally makes it to the halfway station and lays down on the planks, frozen in fear. He's not going up or down, he's just staying right where he is for the time being.

After fifteen minutes or so I decide to climb part way back down to see how they're doing. Dean is sitting next to Andy, the picture of patience.

I stop at the landing above them. "Everything okay?" I ask.

"We might not be going all the way to the top," Dean says.

"That's cool," I say, not wanting to push it. Then I add, "But if you do, there's a cold one waiting for you."

Dean laughs, but Andy doesn't make a sound. And I think I understand what he's going through. I have a fear of big waves, sometimes psyching up and then going out, but terrified the entire time.

I climb back up and join Mark at the top, explaining things.

After maybe ten more minutes we hear Dean say, "We're coming up."

Mark leans his head through the opening. He can see Andy about halfway to us, moving a little faster this time. "Yeah Andy! You can do it!"

When Andy reaches the top ladder Mark holds it so it won't move on him. Andy climbs through the opening and crawls to one side, white knuckling the lower handrail.

"This is nuts!" he says, then looks at the two of us. "You guys are nuts!"

We both laugh, and Mark says, "You did it man!"

Andy slowly starts breathing a little easier. "I did do it, didn't I?" He looks around. "I can't fucking believe I did it! Holy shit, look how high we are!"

"Good job Krame!" I say. Then I reach into the daypack. "You wanna beer?"

He lets out a short laugh and shakes his head. "I don't think so."

Just then Dean pops his head up through the hole. "I'll have one!"

Mark and I laugh.

After a while Andy relaxes, even letting go of the handrail. Tonight he's crossed a major threshold in conquering his fear of heights, a fear that none of us knew he had.

"You know," he says, "I wasn't going to go through with it. I was gonna climb back down and wait for you guys at the bottom. But I just couldn't do that. I had to conquer this goddamn thing!"

"And you did!" Dean exclaims, clapping him on the back.

"Yeah Andy!" Mark says.

"Ah hell," Andy says, a little embarrassed. "Gimme a beer!"

I laugh and give him one, and we all clink cans.

What Mark and Dean and I don't know yet though, is that we've unwittingly created a monster.

"Yeah Scott, you heard me right. We're gonna jump the bridge *and* climb the tower."

Andy is on the station phone.

"Why don't you meet us down here around ten thirty?"

The bridge Andy is talking about is the Davis Bridge, which crosses the channel into Naples and Belmont Shore. It's about fifty feet high and, of course, illegal to jump from.

Just minutes before I had told Andy that Scott and I had jumped the bridge a few nights ago, and since Andy is on his 'conquer my fear of heights' mission, he wants to jump it too.

Scott, who is Andy and Dean's age, is about six five and maybe two twenty, and could be half human, half fish. He's captain of the water polo team at High School, has been on the swim team since he could crawl, and can hold his breath underwater longer than what should be possible. Some of us think that he might have gills.

Scott and I were coming back from Belmont Shore the other night, Scott showing off his new Mazda to me, listening to the Who at close to max volume on his new stereo he just installed. Then he pulled into the parking lot at the base of the bridge and stopped the car.

"What are we doing?" I asked.

He just laughed, then opened his door and pulled off his shirt and then his pants. "C'mon, we're gonna jump the bridge!"

I looked to my right, then back at him. "This bridge?"

"Yeah!" he laughed again. "C'mon!"

So, what the hell, I got out of the car, took off my clothes and followed him up the steep ivy covered slope to the sidewalk that leads out to the top of the bridge. He left the car running and the door open, so we could easily hear the stereo still playing the Who.

'Teenage wasteland, it's only teenage wasteland'

We ran along the sidewalk, naked as jaybirds with cars going by, until we got over the water.

"We gotta make this quick!" he'd said, and swung both legs over the rail and looked back at me. "Don't hesitate, just jump."

Then he stepped off the bridge and was gone.

I climbed over the rail, looking from side to side at all of the cars going by, sure that some of these people could see me and wondered what the hell this naked idiot was doing, and then stepped off myself.

It was pretty dark, but I could make out the water below. The fall took a little longer than I expected, but I landed okay. When I came up Scott was already on the dock waiting to help me out. We started running back to the car laughing, and then stopped dead in our tracks. Right next to Scott's car was a police cruiser, two officer's out and looking at Scott's car with flashlights.

There wasn't much else we could do, so we just walked up to them, dripping wet and naked. They shone their lights on us, and one of them, the younger one, started laughing.

The other one shook his head. "If you two could only see yourselves right now." He looked back at the car, the music still blasting.

'No one knows what it's like, to be the bad man...'

The same cop looked from the car to us a few times, dragging it out, seeming to enjoy watching us freezing our naked asses off. Then he finally said, "Just get in your car and get the hell out of here."

We quickly did as we were told, and slowly drove away, trying not to scream.

Then we both started laughing uncontrollably.

"Why didn't they bust us?" I finally managed to say.

In between laughs Scott said, "Didn't you notice? They weren't real cops, they were Marine cops!"

I shook my head. "We are so fucking lucky!"

"It was great though, right?" Scott says, high fiving me.

Oh yeah, it was great, and totally unexpected. And of course I got a major rush because I didn't know what the hell we were about to do. I'm finding out that Scott is the king of surprises, something that he will continue to be for all of the years to come.

Scott cranks the stereo back up.

'I call that a bargain, the best I ever had...'

The wild and crazy times that we will have at Benny Rapp's Chevron Station, both during work and after, will be too numerous to mention. In the coming weeks and months there will be many tower climbs and bridge jumping's, some of them on the same night if Andy gets his way.

And there will also be a 'streaking'.

Five of us, including Dean, Scott, Matt, Dave and myself will go to the Bob's Big Boy restaurant just outside of Seal in Long Beach at around eleven at night and order up all kinds of food. When we're done eating we will all go to the restroom, take off all of our clothes, and carrying them in our arms we will run through the restaurant, out the front door and past the plate glass windows in full view of everyone inside, taking 'dining and dashing' to a whole new level.

Streaking is the new popular gag of the day, and the people in the restaurant will actually stand up and cheer, including our waitress, who just got 'stiffed'. (At least I thought she got stiffed. It turns out that Dave kept his clothes on and paid the tab.) Things will get all the more comical when my Ghia won't start, and a few of us will have to push start it.

We will drive back down Pacific Coast Highway to Seal Beach again and pull into Benny Rapp's, Matt in front of me in his MG. He will pull to a stop by the front door, step out of his car bare ass naked and say, "What the hell did we just do?"

I can't say enough times what a great man Benny Rapp is. Kind and giving, but stern. Compassionate and forgiving, but strong and by the book. Smart and caring, and sometimes funny, even if it might not be his intention.

So I feel all the more guilty when one day he says to me, "You know Beenut, I have a bottle of pills at home that I labeled 'Night Crew'. The doctor prescribed them to me so that I could get some sleep at night and not worry about what you guys are doing down here."

He's telling me this after the previous night's antics, when he was summoned down to the station by someone, we don't know who, because of all of the noise we were making.

Benny had suddenly appeared in his blue El Camino, his wife Lyla driving. He stepped out wearing his plaid pajama's, his black slippers, and his navy blue Chevron Jacket. This is what he saw:

Matt's MG halfway up on a lift, his speakers on top of his car blasting Led Zeppelin. Matt's standing on the adjacent lift, up about three feet with a mop in his hands playing air guitar, Andy slowly spinning him around in circles. I'm playing air guitar myself with a broom, and Dean is standing on the back counter with a shock absorber in his hands for a microphone, pretending to be Robert Plant.

In the back storeroom Benny finds the sink full of empty beer cans.

We're all fired, right?

That's what you would expect from any normal boss. Close up the shop, pack up your shit and get the hell out. But not Benny Rapp.

He just tells Matt to get his car down off of the lift and go. He tells Andy, Dean and I to close up the doors and clean up the mess in the back. Then he gets back in his El Camino and leaves.

Needless to say, we're on our best behavior now, knowing that we're lucky to still have our jobs. The next time that I see Gary or Bone, they just shake their heads.

So, in the coming months we're good boys, staying out of trouble, not partying at work, and keeping our nose to the

78

grindstone. That is until one night, when something kind of unintentional happens.

I'm working a night with Andy and it's dead. It's deader than dead. We get maybe one or two customers the entire night and that's it. Andy is so bored he's looking for something to do, anything to occupy his time. Then in the back storeroom Andy finds a potato bug. He informs me that he really hates potato bugs. He gets a can of motor oil and cuts the top off with a razor knife. He pours out most of the oil, and then puts the bug in the can. He then gets a cigarette lighter and lights it under the can, trying to boil the bug in oil.

It's not really working though, so he gets another idea.

He walks out about halfway between the building and the gas pumps and pours the oil and the potato bug on the smooth concrete driveway. He then gets into the station truck, the 1940's Chevy Step Side pick-up, that has probably been at Benny Rapp's since before we were born, and starts doing burn outs on the bug. The oil is making things real slippery, and the back tires are spinning effortlessly.

Andy is having so much fun now, the boredom obviously cured, that he starts doing donuts, driving around the pumps and then back to the slippery area doing three sixty's. I'm getting worried that he might get out of control and hit one of the gas pumps, so I motion with my hand to slow down. He does one more three sixty and then to my relief, parks the truck.

When I show up for work the following evening the station truck is parked right in front of one of the service bays, which is unusual. The hood is up and Benny, Tom and Kim are standing around it with somber faces.

"Beenut," Benny says as I walk up. "I just want you to know that today I spent close to six hundred dollars rewiring this truck."

My face goes ashen, and I don't know what to say. But I'm also getting the feeling that he seems to know that I wasn't the one responsible. He closes the hood, and Tom and Kim walk back into the garage. Benny then tells me that the battery had tipped over, and all of the wiring in the truck had burned up during the night like a slow fuse.

"We're lucky it didn't start on fire," he says.

I try to think of something to say, but lucky for me nothing good comes to mind.

Just then a car comes in to get gas. Benny bends down and looks me in the eye. Very softly, almost a whisper, he says, "Ding ding out there."

Andy possesses something, a certain quality that I'll call, for lack of a better term, the 'teacher's pet' personality.

Andy and I were in the same physiology class when I was a senior and he was a Junior. He sat across the aisle from me, both of us in the back of the room. Sometimes he'd be talking to me when our teacher, Mrs. Barkley, would turn around from the blackboard and tell me to keep quiet, even though I hadn't said a word. This would happen every time, and Andy would just laugh and make faces at me, hiding behind the long haired girl sitting in front of him. Mrs. Barkley obviously liked Andy, and would never reprimand him.

It turns out that the boys at Heartwell's Shell Station across the street saw and heard the whole thing the night before, probably saw me standing there and Andy driving the truck, and felt it was their duty to tell Benny.

When Andy shows up for work Benny summons him into his little office and shuts the glass door. They're both in there for quite a while, and I don't know what Andy is telling Benny, but I have a pretty good feeling that he's probably leaving out the part about the potato bug.

This could be bad. This could be the last straw. Andy could be getting fired in there right now. But it seems like it's taking too long for that.

I take care of a few cars, and when I walk back towards the garage they suddenly emerge from the office. And they're both laughing!

Another car comes in, 'ding ding', and as I turn to get

it Andy joins me. As we're washing the guys windows I say, "What the hell happened in there? I thought maybe you were cooked!"

Andy half smiles and under his breath he says, "I'll tell you later."

Later that night he finally tells me. He told Benny that he was real sorry, and that he wanted to pay for the electrical work on the truck.

"He's going to take a little bit out of my check each week."

"Wow, okay."

This is all he tells me, and I let it go at that. But I have a feeling that he must have really used one of his best Andy salesman pitches to pull this off. Whatever he told Benny, it worked. And maybe he has the same effect on Benny as he had on Mrs. Barkley.

December, 1976

I'm working a night with Andy, and he seems real excited about something. I finally ask him what's up, but he says he'll tell me later when the day crew is gone. The suspense is killing me.

Later, when we're finally alone he tells me.

"Ben, I'm freaking out!" He pauses a few moments, and then says, "I'm going to Hawaii with Mark!"

I'm stunned. This hits me by surprise. Earlier this summer Mark had told me that he and his mother had gone to his aunt's house on Oahu for the Christmas Holidays, and that he was going again this year. His mom said that he could take a friend this time. Would I want to go?

I remember telling Mark, "Are you kidding? Yeah, I'll go."

So am I a little jealous right now after finding out that Andy's going? Yeah, I am. But the truth is, I had forgotten all about it. And the look on Andy's face is priceless. He's so excited that I can't help but feel happy for him.

"That's great man!" I say. "When are you going?" I already know, but I don't let on.

"In a couple of weeks, during the Christmas Holidays."

"That is too cool! What a great Christmas present!"

At the mentioning of Christmas Andy gets a startled look on his face. "Oh shit! I haven't told my parents yet that I won't be here for Christmas!"

Just then a car comes in, 'ding ding'. I laugh and say, "I'll get it. You'd better call your mom and tell her." I spin around as Andy picks up the phone.

Matt and I end up taking Andy to LAX in Matt's truck, meeting Mark and his girlfriend Dorothy, and his mom and dad at the departure gate. We turn it into a big sendoff, taking pictures and wishing them a fun time.

Of course, none of us have any idea how profoundly this trip is going to change Andy's life. That this is a pivotal turning point in his life.

It's about the second week in January and I'm working with Andy tonight. It will be the first time I've seen him since he's been back from Hawaii.

I come in a little late and the day crew is long gone. I spot Andy sitting alone on the back counter. He's got something next to him, a large book it looks like, and he's got one hand on it. And he looks different somehow. He's got a strange far-away look in his eyes, like he's seeing something outside of the horizon.

I walk up and say, "Hey man, how was your trip?"

He slowly smiles and says, "It was unbelievable Ben."

He doesn't say anything for a few moments, then he says, "You know Ben, we didn't just go to Oahu. Mark and I got to go over to Maui for a few days."

Then he gets kind of choked up, and he can't talk. When he recovers he says, "There's this place..." He trails off and can't talk again.

He picks up the book that's been lying next to him and

cradles it in his hands, like it's the Holy Grail. Then he shows it to me. It's one of those big, expensive looking coffee table books, and it's simply titled, 'Maui'. On the cover is an amazing aerial shot of some pools and some small waterfalls. He opens the book to where he has a bookmark, and it's the same picture that's on the cover. And there's other pictures of the same area, a small bridge in one of them. These are images of lush green paradise like I've never seen.

"They call it the Seven Sacred Pools, and it's just... magical."

I look at the pictures in the book, turning a few pages, mesmerized. "You went here?"

"Yeah Ben," he says, pride coming through in his voice. "We swam in those pools."

I look at him, and he nods. It's so unbelievably beautiful that I'm speechless. I turn back a few pages and there's pictures of a town called Hana.

"That's the town you come to before getting to the pools." He pauses for a few seconds, watching me take it in. "It's on the far side of the island, the jungle side." He pauses again for emphasis. "And the road to Hana Ben..." He trails off, at a loss for words.

I look at some other pictures in the book, then close it and put it back on the counter next to him.

Andy looks up and fixes me with his gaze, a serious smile on his face. "I'm moving there Ben." There's silence while he lets that sink in. Then he says, "And I think you should too."

Being the kind of somewhat ignorant rebels that we are, for Andy and Dean, and Mark and I, college isn't really on our radar. But my parents want me to do something though, so I enroll in a few classes at Golden West College, 'Creative Writing' being one of them.

On the first day of class our teacher, an attractive woman who I can't help but notice looks a lot like Barbara Streisand, tells us to take out a blank sheet of paper. She says she's going to set her watch for fifteen minutes, and to just start writing.

Several people ask, "Write what?"

"Just start writing," she says. "If you can't think of anything to write, then write 'I don't know what to write' until you think of something."

The entire class is at a loss, including me, so I write 'I don't know what to write' just once, and then suddenly, I know what to write. I've had this thing on my mind for the past few weeks, the same thing that's been on my mind every night when I go to bed. At those times I can hear Andy saying, 'I'm moving there Ben. And I think you should too.'

So that's what I write about. My indecision about going, and my growing desire to go.

The fifteen minutes goes by too fast. "Times up," she says.

I wasn't done, but it doesn't matter. I turn in my paper with a smile on my face, because this little writing exercise has just helped me make up my mind.

My teacher doesn't know it, but this has been the best day in any class that I've ever had. And sadly, I won't be completing the course.

The next night that I work with Andy, when we're finally not busy, I tell him.

"Okay man, I'm going."

Andy is so happy he literally jumps for joy. "Yes Ben!" He high fives me and then starts doing a little dance, the famous Krame chicken dance, spinning in circles.

He's still dancing when Dean rides up on his bike. "What the hell?" Dean asks, laughing.

Andy practically pulls Dean off of his bike. "Ben's going Dean! Ben's going!"

I can tell by the look on Dean's face that Andy has already been working on him, and when he looks over at me, I nod.

Then Andy really digs in.

"You gotta go too Dean, you gotta go!"

Then he looks at both of us. "I saw people there, people our age, living and working there, living the life! We can do it too, the three of us, living and working in paradise!"

Andy the salesman, in high gear.

Before Dean gives Andy an answer to that, he's got something else on his mind. In the coming weeks he will buy his first vehicle, a '59 Volkswagen Bus, and he'll be wanting to take a little trip in it.

And he'll be asking me to go with him.

And it's up to the North that we will go...

To the lands of mist and snow...

AS THE CROW FLIES

'So I'm packin' my bags for the Misty Mountains
Where the spirits go now
Over the hills where the spirits fly'

'Misty Mountain Hop'
Led Zeppelin

October, 1976

Sometimes, when I'm feeling a little down, or things seem a bit overwhelming, I try to recall a line that Gandalf says to Frodo in the Lord of the Rings. They're feeling a little down themselves. They're lost, and sitting in the dark, deep in the Mines of Moria.

While smoking his pipe Gandalf turns to Frodo and says, "All we have to decide, is what to do with the Time that's been given to us."

The Time that's been given to us.

If I could just remember that.

My sister introduced me to The Hobbit in grade school, the seventh grade, I think. But I didn't start reading the Lord of the Rings until my senior year in High School. It would definitely be an understatement to say that J.R.R. Tolkien is having a profound effect on our little circle of friends. And Dean is embracing the books just as much, if not more, than any of us. Dean the tree climber, Dean the Elf. We all want to be someone in the Company, and it is pretty obvious that Dean is Legolas, no doubt about it.

Dean and Andy had to hear me ramble on about the Trilogy, because I had to share this stuff with someone, and they're my friends and co-workers. So they started reading the books themselves, if for no other reason than to just shut me up. But they took a liking to them as well, and they in turn got Scott and Matt, and Chris and Mark, and others reading them also.

So now, some nights a bunch of us might find ourselves down in Bullet Hill with usually more than a few beers, and maybe some pipe weed, sitting in some niche in the trees and talking about the books, sometimes even acting out different parts.

If it's cold Dean and I might be wearing our Elven Cloaks. Dean got his mom to make them for us for the upcoming Halloween, and he instructed her specifically how to make the hoods, which are long and Wizard like, the tips almost touching the ground. These night meetings in the trees start forging a new bond between us, a bond that grows stronger each time we come down here.

It's Halloween night, and Dean and I know of two parties on the Hill that we are definitely going to check out. One is on lower Catalina, and the other is on Harbor Way, so they are on opposite ends of the Hill. We also might go down to the boardwalk on the beach, because there's always multiple party's going on down there. This is probably the only night of the year that you can walk right into a stranger's house, drink from their keg or make yourself a cocktail, and they won't know who the hell you are because everyone's wearing a costume.

To complement our Elven cloaks we have both made long swords out of wood, fastening plastic handles to them with tape and colored cloth. Dean has a bow, but no arrows, and some kind of elven sash tied around his waist. I have a similar kind of sash to hold my sword, and a long wooden staff. I also have a chain around my neck with a golden ring on it. The one ring, to rule them all…

Dean meets me at my parent's house, and we decide to go to the Catalina party first. It's early evening, and since we're in no big hurry Dean wants to take the long way through Bullet Hill. We go through my parents back gate and down into the woods. There's a big moon coming up, and it really feels like Halloween down here in the twilight. Spooky cool…

Making our way down the trail, a flock of Crows swoops above us and through the trees, flying in the direction that we're going. None of them make a sound until they get ahead of us, and then we hear them start cawing. Dean, ahead of me on the trail, watches them, and then turns to me with this inspired smile on his face.

"Did you just see that shit Ben? If that's not an omen, I don't know what is!"

We soon catch up to the Crows sitting in the tree tops. Dean holds up his arms to them. "To fly like a Crow...would be so fucking cool!"

Dean and I have also been reading a little anthropology. Carlos Castaneda, and the Teachings of Don Juan, which also include the books Journey to Ixtlan, and The Tales of Power. Among other things, Carlos talks about eating Peyote with Don Juan, and then turning into a Crow and flying around the Mexican countryside. Dean has taken this part of the book to heart.

"C'mon Ben, I know you like to fly. Can you imagine it? Flying over Bullet Hill as a Crow?"

I concede. "Yes," I say. "That would be really fucking cool!"

We continue on, until the trees abruptly stop and the trail winds through a short grass meadow ending at the top of Avalon. Dean turns and faces the broad view of the lights of Long Beach laid out to our right before us.

"The entire fucking world is out there Ben!" Dean says, making a pronouncement. Maybe a little more serious, but still with the mischievous grin. And something else, like he's got ants in his pants. Like he's got a fire underneath him.

When we get towards the bottom of Catalina we can hear the party from three houses away. That is to say we hear the music, which is definitely Pink Floyd, and as we get closer, The Dark Side of the Moon.

'For long you live and high you fly, and smiles you'll give and tears you'll cry...'

We get to the house and turn into the passage way that leads to the front door. There's quite a few Jack-o-Lanterns, and spider webs, and different colored lights. I suddenly realize that this house used to be on my paper route when I was in the fifth grade, but I can't for the life of me remember who lives here. Maybe it's someone new. Whoever it is, this looks like 'the parents are gone' kind of party.

In the front door we go, and the party is in full swing.

There's quite a few people, but it's not over crowded, and they're all in some sort of costume. Taking it all in, I'm noticing that there might actually be more girls here than guys. A lot of these girls are wearing very sexy costumes, like the one dressed as a French Maid, and another one in a leopard skin Cat outfit.

A blonde girl wearing a pretty revealing Toga grabs onto the hood of Dean's cloak, admiring the length of it. Dean throws off the hood and faces her. All of a sudden they recognize each other, and hug. The hug turns into a slow dance, and it looks like Dean is off and running.

I leave them be and make my way to the sliding glass door that leads to the backyard. Just as I suspected there's a keg of beer back here, with a few people standing around it, mostly guys. I grab a red cup off of the table and one of the guys says, "Why it looks like a Hobbit, from Middle Earth!"

I turn to him and bow saying, "Mr. Underhill, at your service."

He laughs and says, "Nice cloak, Mr. Underhill." He grabs the keg nozzle and gives the keg a few pumps. "Here, have some Ale lad," and fills my cup.

He's dressed as Dracula and he looks familiar, but I can't quite place him. He's maybe a couple of years older than me. "Thank you kindly," I say.

Just then a girl dressed as a witch comes over to him and dramatically throws her head back, and he pretends to bite her neck. She moans softly, writhing in faux extasy. She might be his girlfriend, but then again, who knows. They start kissing though, so I leave them alone and go back to the house.

When I get inside I'm just in time to see Toga girl leading Dean to a bedroom and shutting the door. Oh boy. I suddenly feel kind of awkward and alone, so I go back out to the keg again. I have one more beer. Since I don't really know any of these people, and Dean is preoccupied, I decide to leave.

I go out the front door and turn right, deciding right then to head down to the Boardwalk. I cross Pacific Coast Highway and take fifth street almost all the way down to Ocean avenue, but then turn left into the alley, also known as the Ho Chi Minh Trail, and make my way to Main Street. I turn right on Main, and to my left I notice a group of ghouls gathered in front of Clancy's. I then cross Ocean and go down the concrete ramp to the left of the pier, through the beach parking lot to the beginning of the boardwalk.

Just like we thought, there's quite a few parties going on down here. I walk along until I see one that looks fun, and go inside. I make my way through a bunch of ghosts and goblins and witches and vampires, to the front deck overlooking the beach, where the keg is. I might not be much good at picking up girls at parties, but I'm getting pretty good at finding the keg.

I pour myself a beer and just stay out on the deck, watching wild and crazy people go by. I start feeling kind of lonely again, and really wish that Dean was here. I drain my beer and exit the party, and keep walking down the boardwalk. I eventually go left at Dolphin street, deciding to head over to the party on Harbor Way that Dean and I talked about. It's at a girl named Lisa's parent's house, who is Dean's age, and at least I'll know some people there.

I come out to the front of Dolphin Market, which is closed, so that means it's after nine o'clock.

And then I hear... a Crow cawing.

I stand on the corner and look up, and I see the Crow, slowly circling and flying lower, until it lands on top of the stop sign not three feet away from where I'm standing. Now I know that I've had a few beers, and I've been reading Carlos lately, and Dean and I were talking about Crows earlier, but this is weird. It's nighttime, and it's Halloween, and here's this Crow looking down at me, the closest I've ever been to one.

It cocks its head and peers straight at me with one eye, and starts cawing again, loudly. I just keep staring at it, and after what seems like minutes, but probably only seconds, it takes off, and flies down Ocean towards Seal Beach Boulevard, the same way that I'm about to go.

I start walking again, taking the same path that the Crow just did, crossing Pacific Coast Highway again, cutting through McGaugh School, then across Bolsa to Bay Side Drive until I get to Harbor Way, and then turning right and walking the short distance to Lisa's house.

I walk into the kitchen through the garage door and I'm greeted by people that I know. It feels good to be among friends again. Someone tells me that there's a keg out back, and I laugh. They didn't have to tell me, I'd find it.

I walk through the kitchen to the living room, and there standing with a beer in his hand, is Dean! He's not wearing his elven cloak anymore, and when he sees me he says, "Ben!" Then he motions for me to come out back with him.

"The last I saw you," I say, as we walk over to the keg, "you were being pulled into a back bedroom by some girl in a Toga."

Dean laughs. "Well, it wasn't what you might think. There was a few other people in there, and we just kind of hung out for a little while." He hands me a cup and then gives the keg a few pumps. "And then this one guy broke out some hash. We smoked it, and it was way too strong for me, and I ended up passing out."

"Oh wow."

"But wait a minute, listen to this. While I slept I dreamed, and I had the most amazing dream, Ben. A full on Don Juan dream!" He hands me my beer and starts filling his own. "I dreamed I turned into a Crow, and I was flying around Seal at night. I remember seeing the clock tower at city hall, and the pier, and Main Street all lit up." Then he looks at me, getting even more animated. "But that's not all, Ben. I saw you, walking along in your elven cloak. I wanted to get your attention, but I didn't know how. I just didn't know what the fuck to do! So I just flew!"

I almost choke on my beer mid swallow, and spit it out.

"Don't laugh," Dean says, laughing. "It was so lucid, so fucking real!"

"I'm not laughing," I tell him, as soon as I can speak. I can't believe what I'm hearing. No one is going to believe this, because I don't believe it myself. "You'd better sit down man." I say. " I've got something I gotta tell you."

May, 1977

Either Andy or Dean, I'm not sure which, have started this thing where they say 'goon' instead of like 'dude', or 'man'. They might say, "Do it goon!" or "You're not gonna believe this goon!"

Dean and I are working one night, and during a lull we talk a little bit about the 'Crow Incident', as it has come to be known. Then he starts telling me what's been on his mind lately. And it turns out that he just really has the urge to go somewhere, that he absolutely needs to go on an adventure.

"You and Andy took that train to Mazatlan," he says. " You've been to Mammoth skiing, I haven't really been anywhere."

I know that there's been something up with him lately, and I guess this desire to 'flee the coop' is what it is. "Okay," I say. "So where do you want to go?"

He looks at me with that one eye, wiggles his finger in my face and says, "Canada goon!"

Apparently Dean was with Matt and Drew a few nights ago, and Drew and a friend of his had just returned from a road trip up North to British Colombia. Drew really got Dean going, with vivid descriptions of lush pine forests and high waterfalls slicing through granite valleys with icy cold water. He told him about the beautiful Rainbow Trout that they caught and cooked over the campfire. Sleeping under the stars at night, the sky lit up by the Milky Way. Dean already wanted to go somewhere, and now Drew had just made his mind up for him.

So Canada it is.

Dean has just bought his first vehicle to call his own, a

59' Volkswagen Bus. He didn't waste any time cleaning it up, putting new carpet in the back, and installing a brand new Pioneer Super Tuner that plays cassettes too by the way, along with a couple of Jensen Tri-Axle speakers. (Scott will give us two or three cassette tapes recorded specifically for our trip.) And we've decided to put my slightly built up 1740cc engine in his bus, to give us a little more power. We also install a separate oil cooler, with side mounted air scoops.

The next thing to do is get some camping gear, and since we're on a budget we decide to go to the big Army Surplus Store in Belmont Shore. We get sleeping bags and Insolite pads for cushioning, reusable water bottles, cooking utensils, some fishing tackle, and the 'coup de grace', a two man inflatable boat, complete with two plastic oars and a foot pump. What we don't get is a tent, because we've already sort of got one.

I had recently gotten into 'Pyramid Power', and when I told Dean about it he was intrigued. I told him that all you needed was a frame, and if you made it the same angles as the Great Pyramid in Egypt, and aligned it to magnetic north, you could put one over your bed and reap the benefits of better sleep and more lucid dreams. I built one out of three quarter pine and put it over my bed, to the surprise of my mother and funny looks from my brother. Dean went one step further and bought some metal connectors that he found in one of my Pyramid Power catalogs. These connectors were made to fit half inch tubing, (electrical conduit), and you could build it any size you wanted. We made one with an eight foot base, which put the peak at a little over six feet off of the ground.

We didn't know yet about the funny looks we'd be getting from other campers when they would walk by our campsite. They would see two sleeping bags under a metal framed pyramid with no covering of any kind, and scratch their heads. (If it rained we would jump into the Bus.)

Dean and I have told Benny about our plans for our trip up North, and he has agreed to work around it and let us both have two weeks off at the same time. We plan on leaving the first week in June, but our departure date gets delayed...

It's a week before we leave and Dean is chomping at the bit. The two of us are working one night and we decide to get some beers. Dean takes the station truck over to the Drive in Dairy across the street and buys a six pack. But not just any ordinary six pack. He gets a sixer of Schlitz Malt Liquor Tall's, sixteen ounces of horrid tasting high gravity malt liquor, the 'Bull' they call it on the TV commercial.

We're almost through our first beer when Dean gets the urge to climb something. Since we're at the station and there's obviously no trees, Dean goes for the next best thing, which is the high shelves with the new tires on them. He gets on top of the counter and then pulls himself up to the shelf with all of the new tires and starts crawling over them, and even through some of them.

He looks hilarious up there, so I decide to follow him. I get up to the tires and slowly make my way towards him. At the end of the shelf with no place left to go, Dean crawls out onto the glass and metal roll up door, careful to stay on the aluminum frame. He sits for a second on the topmost part of the door, which is horizontal because the door is rolled up. Then he inches his way over to the side of the door, grabs the tire shelf again with both hands and hangs down until he lets himself drop to the counter below next to the cash register. He makes it look easy, but he's taller than me, so I'm thinking that I'll find a different way down. But first I crawl out onto the roll up door where he was and sit in the same spot.

While I'm sitting there I see Andy and Todd drive up at the same time in different cars. They walk in and finally notice me. "What the hell you doing up there Ben?" Todd asks.

Good question. With that I decide to come down. I'm sitting on the frame but my feet are on the window pane, and as I start to move the last thing I remember is the sound of breaking glass...

I've done a few stupid things in my twenty years in this world. Flying off of the jump at Dead Mans in Bullet Hill on my paper route bike when I was nine, without applying the brakes at all, getting a concussion and scraping my face up and spending Easter vacation in bed. Or walking through a drainage ditch on the Navy Base with my friend Pete in the seventh grade, stepping on a broken whiskey bottle and the doctor telling me as he stitched up my foot that I just missed severing a major artery. But this new one, falling through the roll up door at Benny's, definitely takes the cake.

As I come too, I'm looking into the face of a fireman. I'm lying on my back in the waiting lounge of the station, the fireman shining a small flashlight into my eyes. My right hand hurts, and my left knee hurts, but the worst hurt I got going on is in my head. I have one big whopper of a headache, and I realize that I can't see out of my left eye.

The fireman starts asking me questions. "How much did you have to drink?"

For some reason I think that he's asking me how much Dean and I bought. I tell him a six pack of Schlitz Malt Liquor.

He looks over at where I landed not six feet away, nothing but a concrete floor and a steel lift, and says, "You're lucky you didn't crack your head *open*"

I weave in and out of consciousness, and then realize that I'm being loaded into an ambulance. I feel a needle go into my arm, and I'm out cold.

The next time I wake up I feel like I've been transported to the Little Shop of Horrors. I'm on a lower bunk bed, and there's maybe a dozen bunk beds in here, and every one of them is filled with bloody, crying, and moaning people. I go to sit up, and that movement is all it takes for nausea to hit, and I throw up on the floor.

Just then a large black nurse comes into the room, and when she sees my puke on the floor she is not happy. Before I can protest she shoves a needle into my arm, and the lights go out again.

This time when I wake up I'm in a hospital bed in a room next to a window, and the early morning light tells me that it's the next day. I slowly realize that I'm not alone, and a curtain separates me from my roommate. I learn that I'm in Long Beach Community Hospital, situated above the infamous 'Traffic Circle', and I almost laugh at the irony. This is the hospital that I was born in.

Pretty soon a doctor comes in. He's a white male, maybe in his early forties, and he looks at my chart and smiles. "I'm the Bone doctor," he says. "I'm going to take a look at your left knee and your right wrist."

"Okay," I say. "My head really hurts too Doc. Do you think I broke anything up there?"

That smile again. "I don't think so. But that was a nasty fall, so you could possibly have a concussion."

Him and my nurse, another large black woman, but definitely not the one from the night before, get me onto a gurney and wheel me down the hall to another room where he takes x rays of my knee and wrist. The doctor ends up just wrapping my knee with an ace bandage, but he puts a small cast on my right wrist. I don't think to ask him for a fiberglass cast, something that I will regret later.

When they get me back to my room I use the crutches that they left me and hobble to the bathroom. As soon as I get in there I feel nauseous again, and throw up in the toilet.

Later that same day the 'Eye' doctor pays me a visit. He's probably mid-fifties with dark hair turning to gray, and balding on top. He looks at my chart and does not smile, and shakes his head. He gives me a kind of disgusted look and mumbles something about underage drinking. Then he pulls a chair up next to my bed and examines my left eye with a small bright light.

After a while he says, "You're lucky. It looks like your eye is going to be okay. I'll be giving you some eye drops to put in it when the swelling goes down."

"Well, that's good news, thanks Doc. I guess that's where I hit my head huh, on my left eye?"

He nods.

"I've been throwing up too Doc, what's that all about?"

He sighs. "That's from drinking too much. It says here that you drank six, sixteen ounce malt liquor beers, more than enough to give someone your age a hangover."

I think I need to hear that one again.

"Whoa, wait a minute," I say, "that's how much we bought," but I can already see the disbelief in his eyes. "I only had one, and I don't even think I finished it."

Yeah right.

He shakes his head. "That's not what the report says. You told the EMT you drank six of them."

I do remember telling the fireman how much we bought, so I guess in my brilliant state of mind I misunderstood him.

So that's what's going on. Everyone thinks I was wasted. And why wouldn't they? Who in their right mind would crawl up onto that door in the first place? I've really hit the big time now in the embarrassing stupidity field.

While I'm feeling so good about myself I start getting visitors. Dean, and Scott and Von. Sometimes the three of them all at once, sometimes just Dean. They will wheel me or walk with me down the hallways, and I get the feeling that they're trying to speed up my rehabilitation.

Dean will come by almost every day of my nine day stay at the luxurious Community 'Hospotel'. He's still got one thing on his mind, and that's Canada. He's not really trying to rush me at all, but I can tell that as soon as I'm ready to go, he'll know.

One day in the middle of the week I get another visitor, someone who I've just met recently. Dean's friend Kim, from Huntington Beach.

Led Zeppelin Kim. I can still remember Dean describing her to me.

"She might be more into Zeppelin than we are Ben," he told me.

"Wait a minute, are you joking me? A girl, more into Zep-

THE BULLET HILL DIARIES

pelin than us?"

"Wait till you see her," he said. "Her hair, long and brown and kinda curly... it looks just like Jimmy Pages'!"

"Wow. I gotta meet this girl."

And now, here she is. Kim goes for a long walk with me down the halls, and then sits with me in the room for a little while. She never asks me why I did the stupid fucking thing that I did to get here, she just wants me to get well soon. She's been talking to Dean, and knows how pumped up he is about Canada.

"He can't wait for you to get out of here so that you guys can go on your adventure!" she says.

"I know. I really fucked things up."

She squeezes my good hand. "You'll be okay."

Before she leaves she signs my cast, in Tolkien inspired Led Zeppelin script.

"I'll see you again when you're out of here Ben."

I just nod, trying to hide my emotions, and then she's gone.

By my fourth or fifth day I don't need the crutches anymore, and my nurse is in the room when I limp to the bathroom. I feel nauseous and throw up again, and this time she hears it. When I come out she has a concerned look on her face. She helps me back into the bed and then says, "Are you sure you're okay? No one throws up from a hangover five days later."

"Yeah, tell me about it. That's what I've been trying to tell everyone, because I wasn't hungover. I have a frikken concussion, but no one seems too concerned about that because everyone thinks I was wasted!"

I'm kind of pissed off, and I think she's starting to believe me now. She adjusts my covers and makes me comfortable and then says she's going to go talk to the doctor.

The next time that I see the doctor he agrees that I have a concussion. And his advice? 'Don't drink any alcohol.'

No shit.

By my eighth day I'm feeling pretty good. My head doesn't hurt anymore, except when I forget after taking a shower and shake my hair, and yeah, that really hurts. But I haven't thrown up in a few days, and I can walk with almost no limp at all. I can see pretty good out of my left eye, all of the swelling has gone down, but I still have a pretty good shiner underneath it.

So I'm thinking that I really don't need to stay here anymore. But they want to keep me here for two more weeks.

"That's ridiculous!" Dean says when he visits that evening.

I agree.

"Okay Ben, I have a plan. Be ready to go tomorrow morning around ten. I'll see you then!"

I don't know what he has planned, but I'm up for it. I've been in here for a little over a week now and I'm going crazy.

Dean shows up the next morning around ten, which is the perfect time for an escape. Long after breakfast but before lunch. And he's dressed for the part, wearing his white doctor's coat that he sometimes used to wear in High School, complete with a couple of pens in the top pocket. He's also wearing light blue slacks and white shoes, and looks for all the world like a young doctor or intern.

Before he can say a word to me the nurse comes in, and takes a double look at Dean. And before she can say anything Dean says, "Mr. Powers will be leaving today."

She's clearly flustered, and says, "But... he isn't due to leave yet!"

He fixes her with that one eye and says, "There's been a change of plans."

This really rattles her, and she hurries out of the room and down the hall.

Dean turns to me. "C'mon Ben, we've gotta make this quick!"

I get out of bed, grab the bag that I had ready with my clothes in it, and follow Dean out the door, where he has a wheelchair waiting.

I laugh. "What the hell is this?"

"We've got to make this look official. C'mon, get in."

I sit in the chair and he starts wheeling me down the hall towards the elevator, moving fast when there's no one around, and slowing down when there is.

We make it into the elevator, and when the doors close I start laughing. "I won't believe it if we get away with this!"

Dean looks anxious but calm at the same time. "We're not out of the woods yet!"

The doors open and it's everything he can do to push me slowly down the hall towards the double glass front doors. I can see his Bus now, parked right in front of the entrance.

Dean smiles and nods his head at the pretty receptionist behind the front desk, putting all of his charm into it. She smiles and only looks slightly puzzled.

Out the front door we go, and I can't believe that we might just pull this off. He left the motor running, and it's a good thing. His bus has a six volt battery, just like my Ghia, and with my built up engine in it now it's usually not enough power to turn it over, and we would have to push start it, which would be challenging for me in my present condition.

Now he starts wheeling me faster, around to the far side of the bus. He throws open both of the side doors and I climb into the lone armchair that he has back there, an armchair that looks like it came out of someone's Grandma's living room. He shuts the doors and walks as slowly as he can around to the driver's side and gets in. He puts it in first and takes off, squealing the tires.

"Woo hoo!" he shouts as we pull onto Pacific Coast Highway.

I'm laughing now. "I think my nurse really thought you were a doctor!"

Dean laughs too, sweating but visibly more relaxed. He unbuttons his coat as he weaves through traffic, me and the chair sliding around in the back. I feel like I'm in an episode of M*A*S*H, and Dean is my crazy ambulance driver. And man does it feel good to be out of that damn hospital!

He pops in the Who's 'Tommy' on his stereo, and the song queued up just for me, I suppose.

'I'm Free
I'm Free...
And freedom tastes of reality'

And the song gets me thinking. I have a pretty good idea that Benny will not let me have my job back at the station. And there's not much that I can do while I'm one handed for a while. But I'm not going to let that bother me right now. Our trip has been delayed, but it's still going to happen. And the look on Dean's face is priceless. Now that I'm out of the hospital he knows that it's only a matter of days, maybe only two or three more, and I'll finally be ready to go. And that's making him smile...

It's late morning, and the California coast whizzes by us on our left, with small glassy waves breaking on a rocky shoreline. We're somewhere in between Ventura and Santa Barbara, finally out of LA. Dean is alternately sticking his head out of the window with one hand on the wheel, then looking over at me as he comes back in, a huge smile on his face. He's cracking me up, and it's great to see him 'spread his wings'.

It's a perfect sunny day where we are right now, but up ahead we see some ominous clouds. We pull into San Francisco just in time for afternoon rush hour traffic and some drizzly rain. Dean has been driving the entire time, and he's starting to look tired. I offer to take over, but there's really no easy place that we can quickly pull over and switch places, so Dean just keeps trudging on.

The Golden Gate Bridge comes into view, and it's the first time Dean has seen it. The enormity of it commands his attention for a while, temporarily bringing him back to life, but soon he looks tired again. The stop and go of the traffic is what's really killing him, and it's going to be all that he can do just to make it across this bridge.

It's getting dark now, and starting to rain harder.

"Hey Dean," I say, "How about when we get to the other side of this bridge we take the first offramp and just find someplace to crash for the night."

"Yeah, okay," he says, wiping the moisture off of the inside of the small windshield.

The little outside wipers barely do the job of getting the rain drops off. Our visibility factor is quickly deteriorating.

The first few exits don't look that promising, but then we see one that does. "Maybe this one?" I say.

Dean goes for it. From what we can see it looks more like a country road. In the headlights we see tall trees blowing around in the wind and rain. Dean barely slows down, and I have to alert him some times when he gets too far to the right.

It's a two lane road now, and it appears as though we're going up a canyon. The wind and the rain are making the situation that much more dramatic and scary, and now Dean looks positively frightened out of his mind. His eyes are huge and he's still driving too fast.

"Ease up a bit," I say. He does, but veers to the right again and barely sideswipes a tree. We hear a Smack! A plastic sound, like a bucket dropped to the ground. The rear view mirror is still there because I'm looking in it. But where I usually see the scoop in the back, there's none.

"We lost our scoop Captain!" I say, Scotty to Kirk.

Dean slows, and pretty soon I see an area in between some trees. "Pull in here," I say.

Dean gladly does so. We pull to a stop and Dean slumps onto the wheel, completely wiped out.

"We made it!" I say, and pat him on the back.

He lets out a few sighs, breathing hard. Then he just turns around and climbs over the seat into the back of the bus. He curls up into his sleeping bag, and after only a few minutes he's out.

Since it's raining I just crawl over the seat too, and as I get into my sleeping bag I realize that I shouldn't have let Dean drive that long. I decide right then and there that we're going to start splitting up the driving from now on.

I wake the next morning and the first thing that I notice is that it's sunshine and blue skies outside. The next thing that I notice is that Dean is gone. I open the side door to a beautiful Northern California morning, a fresh smell in the air from last night's rain. We're parked in the dirt off of the road in between some very tall trees, and I laugh because we really couldn't have picked a better spot if we tried.

As I'm standing there taking it all in, up walks Dean. He's got a big smile on his face, and the missing scoop in his hand.

"You are shitting me!" I exclaim, laughing.

Dean holds it up for me to see, chuckling. "Yeah, and look at this Ben, it's still in one piece!"

We both laugh. There's some slightly bigger holes where it pulled through the screws, but it is indeed in one piece, and we should be able to fasten it on again somehow.

And Dean's demeanor is the opposite of what it was last night. He looks very confident and sure. He tosses the scoop into the back and says, "Okay Ben, I'm ready to do this!"

"Cool," I say. "Mind if I drive the first leg?"

He laughs. "Just what I was going to suggest."

After a quick breakfast of snack bars and juice, I hop into the driver's seat and shut the door. Dean opens the passenger door but stands there, and then I remember that we'll probably have to push start. But I turn the key, and it starts!

Dean gets in, chuckling again. The 'Goob Chuckle' we call it. And I know what he's thinking. The fact that the car started is an agreement, and a good omen for the rest of the trip.

We make it into northern Oregon by late afternoon, and check into a K.O.A. Campground while it's still light out. Dean likes this campground, pointing out the benefits that K.O.A provides. I laugh, noticing how Dean is embracing the whole camping experience. It's drizzly rain off and on, so we sleep in the Bus again.

The next day our plan is to get to the Toutle River in Washington, and stay at the campground on the river that I have stayed at a few times with my family while on summer vacations. We find the campground easily enough, and get a campsite right on the banks of the river. Dean is really liking this place, and the sound of the river, and he can't wait to try out his new fishing gear.

We set up the pyramid tent for the first time, and before it gets dark we grab our rods and try fishing right below our campsite. We don't catch anything, but we're having fun just going through the motions.

Later we build our first campfire, and have our first beers, some Henry Weinhard's that we brought in our cooler. The stars are out, and you can hear the river gurgling below us, and Dean is just beside himself with how cool the whole scene is.

We sleep under the stars that night, and it's the most stars Dean can ever remember seeing.

The next morning we make our first real breakfast, cooking eggs and bacon and toast on our camp stove. While we're eating at the picnic table, the sun shining and the day looking promising, I tell Dean that we'll take our fishing rods and go upstream to some pools that I remember.

Not far upstream we find one of those pools and try casting into it for a while. It's a beautiful area, but we're not having any luck, so after a bit we decide to go further upstream. While walking along the left side of the bank the plant growth gets thicker, and soon the trail disappears, and we're kind of stuck on the side of the river. It's either turn around and go back, or try crossing the river to the other side where it's wide open and rocky. We decide to cross.

Of course I've got my cast on my right wrist, but I'm thinking that I can hold my rod with that hand out of the water while I steady myself with my left.

Dean goes first, and he's doing fine, but when he reaches

the middle of the river, where it's the deepest and the swiftest, he's suddenly swept downstream. He keeps maneuvering across though, and I see him get to the other side about a hundred feet away.

Can I do this without getting my cast wet? Dean did hold his fishing rod out of the water the entire time, so I'm thinking that I can too. After a few minutes hesitation, I decide to go for it.

I know what's going to happen, so I just get to the middle of the stream without trying to fight it and let it take me. Everything is good until my right foot snags a large rock that spins me around in a circle, and I go under, rod, cast and all.

I swim over to where Dean is and climb out onto the rocky shore.

"Shit Ben," Dean says.

"I know."

I'm not much for fishing anymore, and Dean feels bad about my cast, so we just walk downstream some more and then cross back over the river again. My cast is already soaked so I don't worry about keeping my arm out of the water this time.

Back at the campsite I just want to get the damn thing off, and I let Dr. Dean do the honors, which he does carefully with his fishing filet knife. We have an Ace bandage in our first aid kit, and Dean wraps a stick around my wrist with it. It looks hilarious, but hey, it's keeping my wrist straight, and maybe it'll actually work.

We spend one more night here at the Toutle River, making a fire again and mostly talking about Canada, whose border we will be crossing over tomorrow.

And of course we don't know that in about three years from now Mt. St. Helens will blow her top. And right where we're sitting, in fact the entire Toutle River Valley, will be completely obliterated and transformed.

Luckily, before we left, Drew had prepped us for the actual crossing of the border. He told us how he and his friend were taken into an office and subjected to what he said was like a police grilling, asking them if they did drugs and smoked pot.

"This is not the time to be honest," Drew had told us. "Just say no to everything that they ask, or they won't let you in. And if you have any stash hide it real well, because they're definitely going to search your car."

And yes, we do have some stash, and a pipe. And we have to figure out a good hiding spot. The one we decide on has only one drawback.

Anyone familiar with older VW Buses will know about the interior air vent control located up in the ceiling just behind the split windshield. It has a lever that lets you switch the incoming air either to the sides, or straight back. The under- side panel is held in place with maybe two dozen screws.

When we get about three or four miles from the border we pull over to the side of the road and proceed to unscrew the bottom panel of the air vent, stash our weed and pipe up there, and screw the panel back on.

We're all proud of ourselves with our ingenuity, thinking that no one is going to take the time to unscrew all of those screws, and get back on the road and drive towards the border.

And then we both start smelling something.

We give each other wild looks, because now we can see the border station only about a quarter of a mile away!

I jump into the back and the smell is even stronger, the whole van smelling like a pot den. Dean pulls over. He hops out and opens the side doors, and the passenger door, the back hatch and all of the windows. As we sit and wait for it to air out, we ponder another hiding spot, somewhere in the engine maybe? But we don't want to get into all that this close to the border. We look conspicuous enough as it is.

We just sit there and wait, and after about ten minutes the smell is totally gone. Dean and I look at each other and he says, "I'll just drive real slow."

With nervous laughter we get back in and decide to go for it. We keep the windows open and the wind wings pointing straight back for maximum air flow. I can't help but think that Cheech and Chong would be proud. Or at least laughing their asses off.

Inching down the road at maybe five miles an hour we finally pull up to the border station. It's a brand new facility, and the entrance looks more like a hotel. Dean parks just past the front doors that are underneath a roof canopy. He opens the side doors again, pretending to look for something, but really just airing the inside of the bus out one last time. We grab our wallets with our drivers' licenses, and then shut the side doors but leave the windows open. We take a deep breath and head for the front door.

Just before we reach the doors two men come out. They're wearing dark suits and sunglasses, and look very serious. I can't help but notice that they remind me of the Standard Oil Big Wigs that visited Benny Rapp's. Dean gives them a cheery hello and a slightly overdone smile, but they don't smile back. They take us inside, and just like Drew said, they lead us to separate rooms.

The room I'm taken to has glass walls and a glass door, and the guy leading me opens the door and I'm introduced to another man behind a desk. He's a little older, maybe early fifties, and smiles and shakes my hand. Then he nods to the man that brought me here, and he steps back out of the room, shuts the door and stands outside of it.

We exchange a few pleasantries, and then he goes right in to asking me questions. And they're all drug questions.

"Have you ever smoked marijuana?"

"No Sir."

"Have you ever smoked hashish?"

"No Sir."

"Have you ever used heroin?"

"No Sir."

"Have you ever taken LSD or ingested psychotropic

mushrooms?"

I feel like saying, 'What if I have? Would that mean that you wouldn't let me in to your country?' But I remember Drew's advice.

"No Sir."

"Do you take pills of any kind? Amphetamines or barbiturates?"

"No Sir."

"What are you planning to do in Canada?"

Wow. A non-drug question. Maybe I passed the first part of the test. "Well, my friend and I just recently graduated High School, and we thought we'd come up to your beautiful country and do some fishing this summer before going back home and starting our college education."

That might've worked. "Fine. Good. Okay, well, be safe, and please obey all traffic signs."

"Thank you Sir, we will."

He gets up and comes around from behind his desk and opens the door for me. I try to mask my relief as the guy guarding the door leads me back to the entrance. As I go out of the front door I look back and see Dean approaching. I wait for him, and then we walk back to the Bus together.

The first thing that we both notice is that the side doors are open. When we look inside we can't believe what we're seeing. It's total chaos. Our stuff is everywhere, like a tornado hit. And no attempt had been made to put it back into any kind of order. We both glance up at the air vent, but it looks untouched.

"Those assholes!" I say.

Dean shuts the side doors. "Just get in Ben. Let's get the hell out of here."

Of course it doesn't start, so we push start it and get on our way. We go a couple of miles, looking behind us to see if anyone is following, before we start laughing, and hooting and hollering.

"They may have torn the van apart, but they didn't find shit!" Dean exclaims, laughing.

"Yeah, those bastards! Later on we'll smoke a bowl in their honor!"

We're ecstatically happy. We may have a little clean up to do, but we made it across the border.

After maybe ten miles or so the terrain starts getting mountainous, with thick forests of tall pines. We start to see sections of a high waterfall between the trees right off the side of the road.

"Look at that Ben!" Dean says, and then pulls into a small clearing in between some large boulders.

He's out of the car like a shot, then runs around the front of the Bus and starts climbing the rocks to the side of the waterfall. At first I just sit there and watch him go, noticing how happy he is, how he's totally in his element. He's making good time, moving up the side of the waterfall pretty quickly. I get out of the Bus and walk over to see how hard the climb is, and even though it's fairly steep I notice that there's a lot of solid hand and foot holds. I proceed to follow him slowly, trying not to use my right hand too much.

When I get maybe thirty feet up I come to a flat ledge of solid granite, and Dean is sitting there smiling. There's a little patch of green grass behind him, and from there the rock goes straight up, virtually unclimbable. I sit next to Dean and we're both transfixed by the powerful waterfall not ten feet away from us slicing through a gorge down to unseen depths below.

After looking over the edge for a while Dean looks back at me and shouts, "If I don't see anything else for the entire rest of the trip, it will be worth it just for this!"

Looking at him I can tell that he means it, and we high five each other.

Dean and I have many things in common, and one of them is that we both like to go off of the beaten path.

We're two or three days into Canada, heading into the interior of British Columbia. I was thinking of taking us up the coast, and maybe catching a ferry over to Vancouver Island, where I had very good luck fishing for trout with my dad and my brother on one of our summer vacations. But we decide to keep heading North and inland.

One morning as we're driving along, we notice that every now and then there's a logging road off to our left. These roads look dark and mysterious, and well -traveled by logging trucks.

I'm driving, and Dean is intrigued. "Look at those logging roads Ben. You can tell that they cut right into the heart of the forest." After a pause he says, "We should go up one."

I look over at him, and then look back at that forest. He's right, we should go up one.

I see one coming up, and say, "I'm gonna go for this one"

"Yes, go!" Dean says.

I turn left onto the logging road, which is dirt and just wide enough for a logging truck. It's kind of steep at first, then levels off after a mile or so, then gets kind of steep again. It keeps going like this, except that the road gets wider just before and after the occasional one lane bridge that crosses over a creek. Off to our left and right are huge stands of old growth trees, so thick that the sun doesn't penetrate to the forest floor.

We want to pull over somewhere and check out the forest, but there's not many opportunities to do so. We cross another bridge, and just past it where it's wider I pull over and shut off the engine. We get out of the Bus and stand there for a few minutes, looking at the trees and taking in the quiet.

But soon we hear something, a low rumbling sound. It slowly gets louder, and then we realize that it's an approaching logging truck coming down the mountain. We can't see it yet, but it must be close because the ground is starting to shake. We both stand frozen on the spot waiting for the appearance of this unseen monster. And then, there it is! Barreling down the road at what seems a very high rate of speed for the road that it's traveling on, doing maybe sixty miles an hour. It blows by us, the wind shaking the Bus as all eighteen wheels hit the bridge. It's across the bridge in an instant, and we watch the truck and its load of logs disappear into the tree lined road below us.

Dean and I look at each other.

"If we were on that road, or on that bridge, that truck wouldn't have had time to stop," Dean says. "We would have been smashed to holy fucking hell!"

"You're right."

As we're pondering this Dean says, "Maybe this wasn't such a good idea after all, Ben. I say we turn this bitch around and get on back down the road and out of here."

I agree. Dean hops into the driver's seat and tries turning the key, but it won't turn over. I go to the rear and start pushing while he steers and pushes from up front. He turns it around and back onto the bridge, where we start picking up a little speed. At the far end of the bridge we both hop back in, and when we exit the bridge and start going downhill Dean pops the clutch in second gear and the motor roars to life. He starts driving as fast as he dares while I look behind us for another logging truck.

So far so good, until the motor starts sputtering. Dean puts it in neutral and tries revving the engine, but it slowly dies. We're going downhill and moving pretty good, so Dean tries popping the clutch in third gear a few times, but with no luck.

"We have gas, right?" I ask.

"Yeah, plenty."

"Well, just keep coasting for as long as you can."

That's what he does, until we start approaching another bridge and the slight uphill before it is enough to slow us to a crawl. We just make it up onto the level bridge before we come to a complete stop. We don't even have to say anything to each other, we just get out and start pushing again. About halfway across the bridge we start to hear the sound that we're both listening for, and the sound that we're both dreading. Another approaching logging truck.

We don't look back, we just start pushing harder, like our lives depend on it, because they probably do.

Just as we reach the end of the bridge we feel the truck come onto the beginning of it behind us. And since slowing down or stopping doesn't seem to be an option for the truck driver, he starts blowing his horn, which really scares the piss out of us. We come over the end of the bridge to the downhill part, and Dean hops back into the driver's seat and steers off of the road to the right, and just in time as the truck blunders past, a blur of wheels and logs.

I walk up to Dean, who is half out of the driver's seat and breathing just as hard as I am. After I catch my breath I say, "That was close man!"

"Yeah, too close!" he says, in between breaths.

"Well, I guess the good news is... I don't think that there's any more bridges. And I think it's all downhill from here back to the highway."

"That's great," Dean says. "But what the hell is wrong with the motor?"

"I don't know, but it seems like it's a fuel thing."

We open the back engine hatch and I pull off the air cleaner. Sure enough, when I twist the throttle on the carburetor no gas comes out. "It might be clogged, or it might be the fuel pump," I say.

We both know that the only thing we can do now is coast back down to the main road and try to get a ride to a gas station or something. I put the air cleaner back on and close the hatch, and we get back in the car, Dean in the driver's seat, and we start coasting down the road again, both of us wondering how this is going to play out.

Pretty soon the road starts leveling out, and as we coast slower and slower we can see the highway maybe a half a mile ahead of us. As we finally come to a stop we both notice a house off to our left, about a hundred feet further down the road. It's an older wood frame house with a barn, and here and there next to the barn are cars in various states of disrepair. And they're all Volkswagens.

We both look at each other with wild hope in our eyes.

"You have got to be kidding me!" I say. "Do you remember seeing that place on the way up?"

Dean shakes his head. "No, but it appears as though whoever it is might be a Volkswagen mechanic."

We're both in disbelief, but we get out and push the Bus toward their open gate with new hope. Just inside the gate we stop and then slowly walk towards the house. Before we get there a man emerges from the front door. He's probably early forties, tall with dark hair, and walks towards us smiling.

"Having some trouble?" he asks.

We tell him what we know about our fuel situation.

"Well," he says, "Let's push it over under the shade of this tree and take a look."

Dean and I look at each other hopefully. He helps us push the Bus down his driveway and under the huge tree. Just then a woman comes out of the front door with two small children in tow.

"You two look exhausted. Can I get you some lemonade?"

"That's very nice of you, thank you!" Dean says.

Meanwhile her husband has his head in the engine compartment. After fiddling around for a little bit he says, "Yes, I believe it's the fuel pump." He thinks for a moment and then asks, "What year is the Bus?"

"A '59," Dean says.

"Hmmm." A pause, and then he says, "I don't think I have anything that old, but I might have one old enough that will work."

"We really appreciate this," Dean says.

"No problem at all," he says, and walks towards his barn.

Dean and I are so happy with this turn of events that we don't dare say anything for fear of jinxing our luck. Just then his wife comes back out of the house with a pitcher of lemonade and cups, and sets them down on the picnic bench under the tree. Then her two little ones, a boy and a girl maybe four or five years old, come out of the door each holding plates of sandwiches.

"Won't you two have a seat?" the woman asks.

We look at each other again, and then walk over and accept the lemonade and the sandwiches gratefully. "You really are too kind. Thank you both so much for all of this." It's all that I can think of to say.

While we're eating sandwiches and drinking the best lemonade we've ever tasted, and she's asking us all sorts of questions, the man comes back out of the barn with a fuel pump in his hand. "This should do the trick," he says.

Dean and I glance at each other quickly. Nothing shocks us anymore.

We finish our sandwiches and thank her again, and then walk over to the Bus to see if we can help him in any way, but he has the situation well in hand. While he's installing our new fuel pump we tell him about our logging truck experience. To that he says, "Yeah, you gotta watch out for those damn logging trucks."

He says it with some distaste, obviously not very fond of them.

Dean says, "Well, we probably won't be going up any more logging roads from now on."

He looks back at us and winks. "That's probably a good idea."

Soon he stands up and wipes his hands with a rag. He has a little capful of gas and primes the carburetor with it, then he tells Dean to go ahead and try turning the key. We tell him how that will only work sometimes, but Dean turns the key and it starts! It only runs for a few seconds though, and quickly dies. Dean tries turning the key again, but nothing, so he hops in and the man and I push, and after a few tries it starts, and stays running.

Dean and I are beside ourselves. He walks back to the guy all smiles and asks, "So, how much do we owe you?"

The man shakes his head. "I just want you two to save your money and get back on your trip."

But Dean insists and pulls some cash out of his wallet. The guy finally relents and says he'll take ten dollars for the used fuel pump. Dean tries to give him more, but the man absolutely refuses. Dean gives him the ten dollars and shakes his hand, thanking him profusely. I do the same, and then we walk over and thank his wife for the lunch and lemonade. They smile and wave at us as we get back in the Bus and slowly drive back down their long driveway.

"Ten bucks!" Dean shouts. "That ain't right!"

I agree. When we get to the end of their driveway we both spot their mail box. "Are you thinking what I'm thinking?"

He pulls out his wallet, and I pull out mine, and we each pull out another twenty. Dean makes a makeshift envelope out of a piece of paper, scribbles something on the inside, puts the money in it and stuffs it into their mailbox.

As we head back to the highway Dean says, "That's the least we can do. Look at this, we're up and running again!"

"Yeah man!" I say. "Those people were a God send! I can't believe our luck!"

Dean laughs, then looks over at me. "Maybe it wasn't luck Ben."

I just laugh, and leave it at that.

"This is it!" I say.

We have been looking for this lake and campground on our map for a few hours now, and it looks as though we've finally found it. Dean drives us into the campground entrance and then right along the shore of the lake, which is all rocks and grass and virtually no trees. We pick a campsite right on the lake, which is easy to do because there's not another single solitary soul in here. Even without any trees the place is strikingly beautiful, with a backdrop of tree covered hills on the far side of the lake. We don't know why there isn't any other campers here, but we're not complaining. It's kind of cool to have the whole place to ourselves, even if it is a little eerie.

It's late afternoon, and our camp is made (meaning the pyramid tent is put together) and we sit at the concrete picnic table enjoying a beer. We bought some Canadian beer, Molson's, and some Black Labels.

Way off to the east we notice some thunderheads that weren't there a little while ago. They look dramatic, the late day sun turning the tops of them pink, while the undersides are dark gray to black. Where we're sitting there isn't a hint of a breeze, and the lake looks like polished glass.

Dean suddenly gets up from the table and says, "I know what we need to do Ben!"

He goes to the Bus and pulls out the inflatable boat.

"Great idea!" I say.

We take turns with the foot pump, and our little two man boat is ready to go in about ten minutes. We fit the two plastic oars together and put them in the oar locks. Since this is our first go around with the boat we decide not to bother taking any fishing gear.

I sit towards the front and row while Dean sits in the back, just enough room for the two of us. We each brought a beer, and clink our bottles together toasting the moment. Our first ride in our little boat!

I just row straight out into the lake leaving the shore behind. Sunset is starting to come on, and when we get maybe five hundred yards out I stow the oars and we just drift, mesmerized by the ruddy colors of the oncoming sunset reflecting off of the surface of the lake.

It's all super peaceful. And then we hear a distant rumble... followed by another one.

Those thunderheads that we kind of forgot about are much closer now, in fact they look like they're heading straight for us. A little breeze comes up, from the direction of those clouds, and then underneath them in the darkest part we both see a bolt of lightning. It only takes a few seconds to hear the thunder.

"Holy shit!" Dean says. "We'd better head back in!"

Just what I'm thinking. I turn us around and start rowing back towards shore, but that little breeze that came up has turned into a full on headwind, and it's getting stronger by the second. What was just calm and peaceful a few minutes ago has turned into a gale with whitecaps. With the wind getting stronger I'm forced to row at an angle back towards shore, an angle that is taking us farther away from our campsite.

And then all of a sudden there's a bright flash, followed instantly by an ear splitting crack of thunder, seemingly right over our heads. This is followed by big drops of rain, falling here and there, which quickly turns into a downpour.

I'm rowing as hard as I can, but I'm starting to tire out. Dean notices, so we quickly switch places and he takes over rowing with fresh strength. He's making good time, and pretty soon we can make out the shoreline through the rain. Another flash is followed by thunder, but this time it's a little farther away. We're just hoping and praying that we don't get struck.

After what seems like an eternity we finally reach the shore. But it's not like where we disembarked by our camp-site. It's jagged boulders, piled at an angle going up maybe ten feet, and obviously man made. We manage to get onto the rocks and pull the boat up to us, both of us holding the boat at each end so it doesn't get ripped up by the rocks. We slowly make our way to the top, and there we find rail road tracks.

We're both soaked, but we put the boat upside down over our heads to act as an umbrella and start walking down the tracks in the direction of our campground. The rain starts let-ting up, and after walking maybe a quarter of a mile the train tracks start turning left away from the lake. We can see the Bus and our campsite now, and the pyramid tent. Luckily we didn't put our sleeping bags out.

The storm has completely passed now, and the twilight

seems bright in comparison. When we get back to the camp-site we have another beer, and then a dinner of sandwiches. Then we make a fire and smoke a bowl, marveling at the stars reflecting off of the lake, which is as calm as glass again.

After a while I turn to Dean, "I've been wondering. What did you write in that note to those people?"

"I just said, ' "Thank you for everything, please accept this. You saved our asses." '

I laugh. "They certainly did, didn't they."

We're sitting on top of the picnic table facing the fire. Pretty soon Dean says,   " I've been thinking about those people too Ben, and I get the strangest feelings, weird feelings, like they were put there for a reason. Like they were put there just for us."

"I remember saying how lucky we were, and how you said it might not be luck"

"Think about it Ben. Neither one of us remembers seeing that house on the way up that road, but on the way back down our fuel pump happens to take a shit, and then, Voila! Just as we coast to a stop here's this house, and the guy just happens to be a Volkswagen mechanic!"

I laugh. But I've got to admit that he's making a pretty compelling case, and he's on a roll. I hum the 'Twilight Zone' music.

And he's not done. "Everything was just too fucken per-fect Ben. They just happened to be right off of the road? How convenient! And we're hungry and thirsty, and she brings out sandwiches and lemonade? And oh yeah, he just happens to pull a '59 fuel pump out of his ass!" He pauses for a second. "I mean his hat! His fucking magicians hat!"

I'm laughing hard now, even while I see his point.

"And another thing Ben, how many VW's have you seen since we've been in Canada? I've seen maybe three, tops. And the logging road that we picked to go up just happens to have a Volkswagen mechanic living on it, right when we need one?!"

I'm still laughing, and say, "You should think about be-coming a lawyer man!"

"I'm telling you Ben, those people were phantoms. Guardian Phantoms that were put there just for us. And if we went back there right now and found that road, and turned up it, I swear to you that there would be nothing there. The house would be gone, the barn would be gone, the cars would be gone... Just a grassy meadow and that big shade tree."

"Then who got our money?" I ask.

Dean frowns. "We had to give them that. You know we did."

I'm still laughing while I grab us two more beers. We toast and clink bottles, eternally grateful for the Guardian Phantoms from the Twilight Zone.

It's the next day, a Saturday, late in the afternoon, and we find ourselves cruising through a picturesque little mountain town. We see an old wooden bar/restaurant at one end of what appears to be the main street, and right next to it is a baseball field with a game going on. Dean and I are ready for something different, a diversion of sorts, so we park and walk over to the game.

The crowd is a rambunctious group of mostly thirty and forty something's, drinking beer and having a good time. If the men aren't wearing baseball jerseys they're wearing flannel shirts. And the women are mostly wearing sweatshirts and blue jeans. They're playing slow pitch soft ball, which kind of makes us feel at home because we've been to many slow pitch games back in Seal Beach, watching Andy's brother Gary, and his friend Gary L. (The Gary and Gary Show, we call them) play soft ball while a bunch of us sit in the bleachers and drink beer, cheering them on.

We mingle in with the crowd and sit in the stands that are on the third base side of the field, cheering when they do. We're just a little bit younger than everyone else, with the exception of a few kids running around, but no one seems to notice.

Pretty soon the game ends and everyone starts making their way into the adjacent bar. Dean and I fall in with them, walking across a walkway and up a ramp that takes us inside. The place is bigger than I thought, with a long bar going the full length of the building on one side, and then a few steps going down into a huge open air room with high wood ceilings. The walls are covered with antlers and deer heads and prize fish mounted on plaques. Long wooden tables with wood benches fill the room. Everyone is drinking pitchers of whatever is on tap, so we order up a pitcher also. When in Rome, we're thinking.

We take a spot along the railing that looks down into the big room, in between a group of women on one side and a group of couples on the other. Dean is on the side next to the women's table, and he soon starts chatting it up with the one closest to him, a blonde thirty something smoking a cigarette. After a while she turns on her stool facing him, laughing every now and then and looking at Dean with a twinkle in her eye.

About half a pitcher later I hear a crash coming from the direction of the bar, like maybe a mug hitting the floor. Then I notice a guy trying to make his way through the crowd. He's a big, tall, lumberjack of a feller, wearing a baseball jersey covered with dirt and what looks like spilled beer. He's weaving from side to side, obviously three sheets to the wind. And the prevailing wind is blowing in our direction. One of the women sitting next to us notices him and says something to the blonde girl that is flirting with Dean.

She looks up, and then starts screaming the guy's name, telling him to, "Stop, just stop!"

The guy, only about ten feet away from us now, is looking straight at Dean with fire in his eyes. Then he trips over something, maybe his own feet, and goes down to the floor. I tap Dean's shoulder and make a motion with my head towards the front door. Dean nods and starts moving in that direction. The guy gets up and tries to lunge at Dean, but goes down again. Dean slowly backs up through the crowd, still facing him. When the guy manages to get up again two guys close to his size grab him by each arm and try to calm him down. I see Dean finally go out the front door. Before people start putting two and two together, instead of following him I slowly make my way towards the back.

When I get outside of the back door the sun has gone down, but the parking lot is fairly lit up from the lights of the baseball field. As I make my way to the Bus Dean is already there, sitting in the driver's seat.

"Holy shit!" I say, as I open the shotgun door. "I think we need to get the hell out of here!"

"Yeah," Dean says. He turns the key, but of course it won't start.

We both get out and push from up front by our doors, and then hop in and Dean pops the clutch, the engine roaring to life, and then he punches it out of the parking lot. We're getting better at push starting.

I look behind us for lumberjacks chasing us with long axes and death in their eyes, but I don't see any.

We've been in Canada for about a week now and still haven't caught any trout. I want to try to remedy this situation, so I find Nicola lake on the map, a lake that I fished at with my dad and my brother years before, and we caught the most trout in one day that I ever remember catching. Dean and I are in the 'Kamloops' area, and I notice that Nicola Lake is on our way back down south. We decide to make it our last try for fishing before heading back home.

When we find the campground at Nicola Lake it looks different to me, but it's a big lake so there might be more than one. All of the lake front campsites are taken, but we find one that is a short walk to the lake with a nice set up.

The next morning we don't bother with the blow up boat and just fish off of the shoreline. I end up catching two and Dean catches one, but his is definitely the biggest. All three fish are Rainbows and easily enough for a good dinner. I thought we might catch more, but Dean is more than happy with what we've got, and is really looking forward to grilling them over the fire.

It ends up being the best meal of the trip, complimented with baked potatoes and corn on the cob wrapped in foil, and it's a perfect capper to our last night in Canada.

Later that night we smoke our customary bowl by the fire and talk about what we might do on our way back down south. We should reach the border by early afternoon we're thinking. And then talk of my dad growing up in Washington State reminds me of something.

"Hey man, I just remembered that my uncle has a cabin on Henderson Bay in the Puget Sound. Maybe we could spend one or two nights there. It's right on the water and next to an oyster farm. Have you ever had raw oysters?"

"No," Dean says, "but I've got a new love for seafood now after having that trout!"

"Cool," I say. "I'll call my dad when we get back across the border tomorrow and get Uncle Phil's number, and see if it's a possibility."

We have filled our cooler with Canadian beer, mostly Molson's, because the drinking age in Canada is eighteen, and now we're back in the good ol' USA, where it's twenty one. We were legal up there, but now we're breaking the law down here. It's confusing. Are we adults or not? Maybe people up in Canada mature at an earlier age. Maybe something to do with all of those trees and fresh air.

My Uncle Phil, my dad's older brother, and someone who I've always loved and connected with, has graciously granted us to stay at his cabin on Henderson Bay. He gave me detailed directions, and now that we have found it I'm amazed at how easy it turned out to be.

The cabin is situated at the top of a steep incline thick with berry bushes and small trees. A switchback trail takes you down to the shore of a small lagoon, where at low tide it is completely devoid of water.

The first few times that I came here with my family on summer vacations there was no cabin, just a long, long yellow trailer. The last time that we came here the cabin was just completed, and it still looks to be in pretty good shape.

We park the Bus in the gravel driveway, and before we even go inside the cabin I take Dean down the switchback trail to show him the lagoon, which is about half full of water, but filling with a rising tide. We find my Uncle's wooden row boat down there tied to a tree, and Dean looks at me with a mischievous smile. Yes, I tell him, this will be the boat that we will use tonight to go get oysters. He rubs his hands together smiling. He can't wait. Another new adventure for the new Dean.

We go back up to the cabin, and after bringing some of our stuff in Dean sets up the Pyramid in the living room. He's a firm believer in pyramid power now, and doesn't want to sleep one night without it. I laugh to myself at what my uncle might say if he saw this steel-tubed replica of the Great Pyramid of Egypt taking up a large portion of his living room.

At early twilight the two oyster thieves are ready for their 'mission', that they have decided to accept. If caught the setting sliver of a moon will disavow any knowledge of their actions. Equipped with rubber gloves and a flashlight they make their way back down the switchback trail to their stealth water craft, cleverly disguised as a rowboat.

Dean unties the boat from the tree, and with the high tide helping us it's not much of a push to get it floating. We climb aboard and I take the position of the rower, all of this a flashback to the time I did this exact same thing with my brother, our dad never asking us where we found such big beautiful oysters.

Out into the lagoon and then following the shore to the left, it isn't long before we see signs sticking up out of the water saying 'Oyster Farm-No Trespassing'. To us the signs might as well be saying 'Looking for a sneaky adventure? Come on in!'

After passing the signs we start to see floats with numbers etched into them. Dean pulls up the rope attached to one of them and it has maybe two dozen very large oysters on it, of which we take about half. We do this a couple of more times, and that gives us plenty of oysters for the two of us. We may be thieves, but we're not greedy thieves.

Back in my Uncles kitchen we proceed to have one hell of an oyster feast, steaming some of them just until the shells open, and frying some in a pan. I even get Dean to try a raw one with a little horseradish and a drop of Tabasco, which he quickly chases with a beer. He says he likes it though, and wants another one. Have I created a monster? I guess time will tell. All I know is, it's great to see Dean trying new things, and I can't help but notice that he is a completely different person from that scared driver at the beginning of our trip.

Once again the Golden Gate Bridge looms in front of us, but this time it's a nice sunny day. Dean is driving, and we laugh at our bad timing. It's rush hour again, and the traffic is inching along. It's stop and go, and just past the top of the bridge Dean stalls the Bus coming out of first gear. But we look at each other and laugh. At least we're not on a logging road. We're not going fast enough to restart the engine so Dean just coasts and stops, coasts and stops. As we get towards the end of the bridge the traffic starts moving faster, and as we pick up speed on the downhill he pops the clutch and we're back in business again. I'm looking in the rear view mirror and laughing. We haven't had any more problems with the engine, and we never did put that scoop back on.

We're both running really low on money, and we're just trying to make sure that we have enough for gas to get us back home. We could both use a really good home cooked meal, and Dean has an idea.

"I have some cousins that live on a farm somewhere south of Sacramento. I could call my mom and get directions. We could crash there for the night, and I know that they would feed us good."

Sounds good to me. We stop for gas and Dean uses the pay phone to call his mom. When he gets back in the Bus he looks at the map. "We need to cut across the Bay Bridge into Oakland, and then make our way over to the I-5"

Neither one of us has ever been across the Bay Bridge before, and we can't believe how long it is, feeling way longer than the Golden Gate. We finally hook up with the 5 and don't end up reaching his cousins house until around nine o'clock.

They greet us warmly, all seven or eight kids, I lost count, and his Aunt and Uncle. Dean's mom must've called them because they knew we were coming, and they waited on dinner for us. And what a dinner it is. I've never seen such a spread.

Their extra-long dining room table is filled to capacity with big platters of fried chicken, big bowls of salad and mashed potatoes, corn on the cob and fresh baked rolls, and oh yes, cantaloupe. Bowls and bowls of cantaloupe. It turns out that that's what they've been growing on their farm, and his Uncle promises us more to take home. But right now it's eat up you two! And especially you Ben, it looks like you could use some meat on your bones!

Dean and I are in hog heaven. Never mind the last two weeks, we haven't had a meal like this since the last Thanksgiving!

The next morning as we prepare to leave, Dean's Uncle is true to his word and gives us more cantaloupe than we expected to get, five or six huge gunny sacks worth. We thank them, and after many hugs and goodbyes we finally get on the road, and the last leg of our journey.

With the Bus permeated with the smell of fresh cantaloupe, Dean is in high spirits, singing along with Pink Floyd.

'We're just two lost souls swimming in a fish bowl

Year after year'

He has this sense of accomplishment written all over his face. He finally went somewhere and did something, and now he can't wait to get back home and share it with everyone. And

I'm really happy for him. I just wish that I was as happy as him.

I know that when I get back I won't have a job at Benny Rapp's anymore, and right now I'm at a loss as to what I'm going to do. What I don't know, is that Benny will call me down to the station, not to give me my job back, but to get me another job right next door at the Bay Theater. It will turn out that the new owner of the theater will have plans to install a huge pipe organ, and he'll need the first four or five rows of seats taken out so that he can move the screen up to make room for this colossal organ. He will give me one tool, a pair of vice grips, which I will use to twist off the old bolts holding the seats down to the concrete floor. When I pull up the bolts they will be dripping with a thick black goo that has the consistency of molasses, the product of years and years of spilled cokes and candy. I will go home at night with my fingers smelling like corn syrup.

That job will only last about a week though, and after that I will luckily start working for my Uncle in Costa Mesa, doing construction with my cousins, building a concrete warehouse on their property, and making more an hour than I ever have.

But of course I don't know any of this yet. As we get closer to home I think about the plans that Andy and Dean and I have. Out on the horizon I see a large flock of Crows flying into the sun, only to part, and then in my mind's eye I see coconut palms and waterfalls, and black sand beaches.

LAHAINA

' You're halfway up and you're halfway down
And the pack on your back is turning you around
Throw it away, you won't need it up there, and remember
You don't look back whatever you do'

'Dance on a Volcano'
Genesis

Kipahulu, Maui, Hawaii
February, 1978

We're all at different spots on the rim of a large volcanic pool. Dean is behind the high waterfall that feeds the pool, slowly inching his way into it, daring to feel the full force of the water. Andy is sprawled out on a rock in the sun, and so is Chris. I'm swimming along the pool's outer edge, inspecting every little nook and cranny for hidden mysteries. We're at what we've been told are the Seven Sacred Pools, in Oheo Gulch, and it feels like we've just landed in the Garden of Eden.

We found some 'magic' mushrooms in a cow pasture to the right of the pools that Andy knew about, and now we're all 'shrooming' for our first time. (Except for Andy, it's his second). It's a perfect day, and we're all luxuriating in the blissful feeling of true paradise.

Some months later Dean will name this pool the 'Pool of Death', because it is unjumpable. The waterfall is too high, maybe about a hundred and fifty feet, and the rocks stick out too far to clear them from the top. And we don't even know yet about the trail to the left of this pool, that it continues up and beyond this waterfall to many other pools, some of them long and narrow with overhanging rock walls, and one with two waterfalls that Dean will name the 'Pool of Life'. We also don't know about the bamboo forest, or Waimoku Falls at the end of the trail. But none of that matters right now. We have this pool all to ourselves, and we can't imagine it getting any better than this.

We found our way to this pool in the early morning, and after about four hours of melting in and out of reality, and diving in and out of the water, we slowly start making our way back down the stream, swimming through other pools until we reach the road and the bridge. To the right of the bridge we hook up with the trail again that takes us to the lower most pools, and we ultimately end up sitting next to the pool that dumps fresh water directly into the ocean.

I remember seeing this exact area, including the bridge and this pool, in the 'Maui' book that Andy had showed me back at Benny Rapp's. And now here I am, I'm really here, experiencing it in person.

Sometimes the wave surge will come up and fill the pool with sea water, only to recede, and the flow of fresh water will continue back into the sea, and then the other way again. We all watch this water exchange for a while, mesmerized.

We arrived in Hana in the late afternoon the previous day, and then spent the night here at the Seven Pools on the grassy bluff that borders the ocean. The four of us came here in my red VW Bug that I shipped over here from Oahu, and we all have sleeping bags but no tent. Luckily it didn't rain last night.

After a night and a full day here at the pools, with enough time to relax and really think about things, it seems like we have all subconsciously come to the conclusion that we are not going to move to the Big Island. We don't even have to really say this to each other, (a side effect of the mushrooms?) We just know now that this island, Maui, is to be our new home. This is where we will try to make a stand, get jobs, and get a place to live. And after spending this time in the heart of one of the most magical places on this island, we feel reborn.

Early the next morning we're back in my bug and heading back towards Hana. We again marvel at the incredible valleys that I'm slowly driving in and out of, the denseness of the jungle, and the tallness of some of the trees that spring from unseen depths below. And then after we pass back through Hana we're in for more of the same, in fact close to three hours of driving in and out of even more valleys, each one just as spectacular as the last. No wonder they call Maui 'The Valley Isle'. Two days ago, when we were driving this road the other way for the first time, I remembered Andy saying, 'And the road to Hana Ben...'

Our first plan of action when we get back to Kahului is to get a newspaper and start looking for a place to live. Andy kind of takes charge of this, and after looking in the paper and a couple of rental brochures, he quickly finds out that places in Lahaina, where we can find jobs, are about twice as expensive as places on this side of the island, in Kahului, or say, Wailuku, where jobs are scarce.

Pretty soon he finds something that looks interesting. It's a newly renovated three bedroom apartment in Wailuku for four hundred bucks a month. That's a hundred bucks apiece, and with the security deposit it's eight hundred, but that's okay. We have that right now, and we could move in immediately. And since I have a car we're figuring that we could car pool the twenty five miles to Lahaina.

"This is it," Andy says. "Mamo Place."

We're in the very old town of Wailuku, which we have learned used to be the capital of the Hawaiian Islands. I turn right onto the little street called Mamo Place. Maybe four or five houses down we find the address that we're looking for. It's a two story house with cinder block walls on the first floor, and wood siding on the second. Andy and Chris get out to knock on the door while Dean and I wait in the car. We see a Hawaiian woman maybe in her early forties answer the door, and Andy and Chris go in. Just a few minutes later we see Chris open the door again and wave at Dean and I to come on up.

We're introduced to Lani, who is a strikingly beautiful Hawaiian woman with a very friendly and positive personality. She takes us all out of the back door to the exterior staircase that leads to the apartment upstairs. As we go in she tells us that everything up here is new. The wood paneled walls, the kitchen appliances, the bathroom, the carpet, everything.

We instantly like it. And we like her. She's very nice to us, and seems genuinely interested in us and our situation. Of course she wants to know what we do for work, so we just tell her the truth, which is that we still have to go to Lahaina and find jobs. But Andy tells her that we have the money to move in right now.

Since Andy is in salesman mode, the three of us let him

talk to Lani while we walk around and check out the bedrooms. Looking out one of the windows on the street side we can actually see the ocean. We look at each other, excited that this just might be ours.

We walk back into the kitchen and Andy is shaking Lani's hand and telling her thank you. When Andy sees us he says, "Get your money guys, we're moving in!"

We're incredulous, and happy beyond belief! The rest of us thank Lani heartily, telling her not to worry, that we will be good tenants, and other lies. And we can't believe now that we have a place to stay tonight, and that we can actually take a shower.

Moving in consists of bringing up our backpacks and or daypacks from the car, and then driving to the airport to get other bags that we left in lockers there. The ride to the airport is filled with raucous laughter and a lot of 'Owoooo's!' We actually have an address, a place on Maui, and even though we don't have jobs yet, we're excited and as happy as only happy idiots can be.

We have to celebrate, of course, and Lani tells us about a restaurant in town called 'La Familia'. We go there and have a good time, eating good Mexican food and drinking Mexican cervesa's and shots of tequila, and toasting our new life on Maui.

It's the next morning, and we're on highway 30, finally on the road that will take us to Lahaina, and our destiny.

We're coming up on Papawai Point, which is the 'chin' of West Maui if you're looking at a map. After coming around the Point and going through a tunnel, we emerge on the other side, and it's as if we have driven into another world.

The sea stretches out flat and calm below us, and we see the island of Lanai for the first time, a peaceful mound in an impossibly tranquil ocean. Coconut palms hang out off of a beach that is literally devoid of waves. We can't help but notice that this side of the island is the complete opposite of the

Wailuku side. The sun seems to dominate things over here, making colors brighter and the ocean sparkle.

Way off in the distance, about as far as the eye can see, is an outcropping of palm trees, and Andy tells us that's where Lahaina lies.

Lahaina. To Dean and Chris and I it looks unbelievably idyllic, a paradise town right out of a dream. Is this really where we're going to work, and eventually live? We're getting more and more excited by the minute.

Maybe five miles outside of Lahaina is the Olowalu Store, and we stop there for fruit juices. We don't know yet that in the future this will be our 'leaving town' stop for smoked octopus and Budweiser's when making the occasional trek to Hana or Haleakala.

When we reach Lahaina Andy has me turn left down Prison Street, and just before Front Street he tells me to park. We get out and start walking north up Front Street, and pretty soon we come to the center of town, where we walk up to the infamous Banyan Tree. We've all heard about this tree from Andy and Mark. We're amazed at the tree's size, noting that some of the connecting roots are the size of tree trunks, and we also notice post's here and there supporting enormous branches. The sun barely filters through, throwing bluish shafts of light here and there. From up high we hear Mynah Birds, chattering.

Dean starts chuckling, and looks over at Andy. "Is this where it happened?"

Andy laughs. "Yes, it is."

He's referring to the last time Andy was here with Mark, their first time, and they had their comical run-in with the law. The two of them had just purchased a bag of Paka Lolo, and proceeded to spark up a joint sitting under this very tree. They were approached by two police officers, who were watching them from the nearby courthouse. The cops proceeded to take their bag of buds, fill it up with water from the nearby drinking fountain, and then put it back into Mark's pocket. Then the cop smacked Mark's leg, exploding the bag inside. The officer followed that up by saying, "You two go out in the sugar cane and smoke that stuff!"

Mark would later immortalize the incident, painting a very humorous cartoon-like watercolor.

We continue on through the park under the Banyan Tree and then cross the street to the Pioneer Inn, where we decide to have a late breakfast/early lunch on the patio. Not a good idea to job hunt on an empty stomach. And the Mahi and eggs look especially good.

After lunch we keep walking up Front Street, noticing certain restaurants here and there, until we reach the north end of town and the end of any shops or bars or eatery's. We sit on the seawall next to the Lahaina Broiler, the last place on the water side, right across the street from a place called Longhi's.

All of a sudden Andy gets up and says, "I'll be right back," and walks into the Lahaina Broiler.

The three of us look at each other.

Andy has just made the first move.

About fifteen minutes later he comes back out trying to hide a smile.

Dean says, "You didn't."

Andy laughs. "Yes, I did. I start tomorrow. Prep cook."

We all congratulate him, and then start walking back down Front Street, the way we came. Pretty soon we're in front of Kimo's, and this time it's Dean's turn to say, "I'll be right back," and he ducks inside.

The three of us keep walking until we get to the seawall, where Lahainaluna meets Front Street, and have a seat there while we wait for Dean. Maybe twenty minutes later Dean catches up with us, and we can tell by the look on his face that he has good news.

Chris asks him, "Did you just get a job too Dean?"

Dean's still smiling. "Bussing tables. I start tomorrow too!"

Now it's Chris's and my turn, but for some reason I'm not ready yet. I have got too used to being on Hawaiian Vacation, and now I'm not sure if I want it to end. Neither Chris nor I apply for a job that day.

The next morning the four of us are back in my bug again heading to Lahaina, taking Andy and Dean to their first day of work. After we drop them off Chris and I go to the beach and smoke a joint from the bag that we all went in on.

Pretty soon Chris says, "Ben, don't you feel a little guilty sitting here on the beach and getting high while those two are working?"

I want to ask him if he feels guilty, but his question kind of throws me off guard. In my Eternal Hawaiian Vacation state of mind I hadn't given it much thought. But hearing Chris say it forces me to realize that he's right. I need to get my shit together and get a job.

A day or two later Lani tells me that La Familia is looking for a dishwasher. I decide to give it a try. I go up to the restaurant in the late morning and talk to the manager, who asks me if I can start that evening. I say yes. He shows me the kitchen, which is small, and then he shows me the dishwashing station, which is microscopic. There's barely enough room for one person to stand. Dishes are piled all around from the night before, and all of a sudden I'm getting kind of a bad feeling about this.

"Don't worry," the manager says, "these dishes will all be cleaned up before you get here."

I have a feeling that he's the one who is going to have to clean them. I tell him that I'll be back at five like he asked.

When I show up that night the dirty dishes are gone, but there's already quite a few pots and pans waiting for me. I put on my apron and start in, and manage to get all of them done before the dishes and glasses start to come in.

It's a Friday night and getting busy. The work station is so small that there's not enough room for all of the incoming dishes, so the waiters and waitresses haphazardly stack them on other counters in the kitchen wherever they can. The dishwasher itself is old and slow, and no matter how hard I try I can't keep up with all of the incoming dishes. And this is a Mexican restaurant, so the refried beans are making things even more fun. The cooks are starting to get upset because the dishes are starting to crowd their work space. To top things off there's almost zero ventilation in here, and we're all sweating like pigs.

By around eleven that night, long after the restaurant has closed, I finally get caught up. I'm completely drenched with sweat and splashed water. I take off my apron, which is wringing wet. My manager comes back and assesses me.

"You're not gonna come back in tomorrow, are you?"

It's more of a statement than a question.

I hesitate, then I say, "No, probably not. I'm sorry." Then I add, "You need a bigger kitchen."

"I know," he says, something that he's fully aware of. "Well, let me get you your check."

He doesn't seem mad at all, and in fact he seems like he was expecting it. He gives me my check, which is all of about twenty some dollars, and I thank him and tell him I'm sorry again. I walk out into the fresh air, my shorts and shirt still wet, and tell myself again that it's just not worth it for the little bit of money it pays. But then again it's a job, and maybe I should stick with it anyway. I don't know.

At this same time Chris has talked his way into a salesman job at Sears. It's in Kahului, at the Kaahumanu Shopping Center. He'll be selling tires, something that he knows absolutely nothing about. He basically has to wear a suit; polyester slacks, dress shoes, a long sleeved collared shirt, and he also wears a clip-on tie, something that Andy will find immense pleasure in giving him shit about.

The next morning is Chris's first day at Sears, so I give him a ride there, and then give Andy a ride to Lahaina. After I drop Andy off at the Lahaina Broiler my 'mission' is to apply for a job somewhere on Front Street.

There is one restaurant, after walking up and down the street a few dozen times, that I really like the look of. It's upstairs, next to a park, and right across the street from the Pioneer Inn. It's called the Whale's Tail, and it has nautical looking window shades that are rolled up to reveal people happily gazing out, eating lunch and sipping iced teas.

I drum up the courage, and go up the stairs.

I ask the hostess, a pretty thirty something haole woman with long, light brown hair if I can talk to the manager. She informs me that she is the manager, and after asking her if she needs any help, she says that she is looking for a bus person. I tell her that I have no experience, but she says that's okay, she can train me. She says that I can start tomorrow, and asks me if I have any collared shirts. I tell her no, I don't have any, and she says that's fine, she can loan me a couple. She's extremely nice, and in contrast to La Familia I'm getting a really good feeling about this place. As I go back down the stairs I almost jump for joy. I've got a job in Lahaina!

I go back to my car and start heading back to Wailuku. Since Dean has the day off our plan is to pick Chris up when he gets off work at Sears, and then head back to Lahaina and have a few beers at Kimo's with Andy. Dean gets an employee discount of twenty five cents for draft Beers, and he thinks that he can get all of us the same deal. That would be incredible, because four beers for a buck is a very good deal indeed.

I'm back at Mamo Place with Dean for maybe a half hour when we hear footsteps coming up the back staircase. The door opens, and there's Chris! He's wearing his dress slacks and shoes, but no shirt, and he's covered in sweat. He throws his shirt on the living room floor (we have no furniture) and says, "I quit that fucking place!"

Dean laughs and says, "Look at you! What happened?"

Chris then tells us the story, about one of his customers who happened to be a very large ornery Moke, apparently none too happy that he had to deal with a young Haole boy.

The guy spoke very thick pigeon, and Chris couldn't understand a word he was saying. This made the big guy even more upset, and he really started getting animated and hostile towards Chris.

The only thing that Chris could make out was something that the guy kept repeating. "I need one da kine tire! Haole boy! I need one da kine tire, now!!"

Chris told the guy that he was going to get his manager, and then walked into the back storeroom, where he proceeded to walk straight out of the back door and then break into a run. He tore off his clip-on tie and threw it somewhere along the way, and then hitchhiked, but mostly walked and ran back to the apartment.

On his way here he got to thinking. "Why am I working at Sears in the first place? I didn't move to Hawaii to wear a suit and a tie while those guys are off in Lahaina living the fun life!"

Dean and I can't hold our laughter back anymore, especially after hearing Chris's impersonation of the angry Moke.

Later we head back to Lahaina, drinking twenty five cent drafts at Kimo's just like Dean promised, and Chris telling Andy the Story, which causes Andy to make funny faces.

"And Andy," Chris adds, "You can't give me anymore shit about that clip-on tie, because it's gone! I threw it the fuck away!"

Now Andy laughs.

Maybe a day or two after Chris's four hour stint at Sears, he gets a job in Lahaina at the Blue Max, washing dishes. At about this same time Andy switches jobs from the Lahaina Broiler to the Ship's Wheel, which is at the other end of town, right next door to the Lahaina Shores Hotel.

The pool and jacuzzi at the Lahaina Shores Hotel has become our unofficial hang out, our 'base of operations' when we're in Lahaina. The staff at the hotel must know that we aren't staying there, but for some reason they don't hassle us, and leave us alone.

February twenty second rolls along, and it's my twenty

first birthday. And even though the drinking age is eighteen the boys want to throw me a party anyway. We can't really afford to celebrate in a bar, so they buy a case or two of Lowenbrau's and we party it up at the jacuzzi at the Lahaina Shores. We proceed to have the time of our lives, drinking many beers and laughing loudly, and alternately jumping from the pool to the jacuzzi. We're also celebrating the fact that we all work in Lahaina now, and it feels as though things might be starting to work in our favor.

Back in California I was pretty good at saving my money, keeping a little bit of my paycheck and putting the rest in the bank. But once I got to Hawaii I seemed to have forgotten how. Even though I'm working, once it's time to pay the rent again, I don't have it.

One night just Andy and I are at Mamo Place, and he tells me that my only option is to sell my Bug. In fact he says he knows someone, a couple in Lahaina, who will buy it for two hundred dollars. Right now.

"You'll be able to pay your rent and have an extra hundred bucks," he tells me.

That's Andy, always the optimist. This is the last thing that I wanted to do, but I have painted myself into a corner. So I sell my bug to the couple, and now we are 'car-less'. This means that we have to hitchhike the twenty five miles to Lahaina, which is a Catch-22 in and of itself, because it's against the law to hitchhike in Hawaii. And the way around this funny rule is that you just can't stick your thumb out. But we don't know any of this yet.

We have to walk about a mile and a half from our house to the main road, highway 30, before we can even try. If we all leave at the same time we will split up into pairs, and then, ignorant of the law we will stick our thumbs out. For twenty or thirty minutes we will get 'stink eye' from a lot of locals, and then finally get picked up, usually by some tourists in a rental car who don't know any better, and want information from us.

Finally someone clues us in to the no thumb law, and the

next time we're at our usual spot with our hands by our sides we get picked up almost immediately.

At about this same time Andy has made a new friend, one of the head cooks at the Ships Wheel who goes by the name of Roadie, and he wants us all to meet him. Roadie turns out to be an original Dead Head, usually wearing some kind of a tie-dye T shirt, and long blonde hair always tied back into a pony tail. It so happens that Roadie lives in a kind of quirky apartment, set up above some shops at the Lahaina Market Place, at the corner of Front Street and Lahainaluna.

One afternoon when we're all free Andy has us meet him at the Lahaina Market Place, and then he leads us up the private stairway off of Lahainaluna to Roadies apartment. It's an old wooden building, with wood floors painted red and brown, and we walk through a couple of mostly empty rooms until we come to Roadie's room, which has windows that look out onto the street.

Roadie greets us each in turn, saying some sort of funny one liner as he does so. As he shakes my hand he laughs and says, "Tom!"

I have no idea who he's talking about, so he grabs an album from his extensive record collection, which literally runs from one side of his room to the other, and holds it up in my face. It's the brand new Tom Petty and the Heartbreakers album, and yes, I see a resemblance, especially with the hair. But I'm also suddenly thrown into a Déjà vu memory that I can't quite put my finger on.

Roadie takes out the vinyl disc and puts it on his turntable. Soon we hear 'Breakdown' starting to play, and Dean smiles and gives me a knowing look. "It's like I said Ben, this is who we saw."

He's talking about a band we saw in San Diego, at a Long beach State, San Diego State football game. After the game a band started playing in the parking lot, and Dean and I went over and checked them out. And it was this band, and they played this song.

Roadie is incredulous. "You guys saw Tom Petty and the Heartbreakers in a parking lot?"

"Yeah man." Dean says. "We were right next to them, as close as we are now!"

Roadie looks at me, and I nod.

"Wow, cool!" Roadie says, seemingly appraising Dean and I in a new light.

Dean, Chris and I instantly like Roadie, who has a pretty witty sense of humor. Someone makes the suggestion to get some beers, and we end up drinking a few Budweiser bottles with Roadie and learning more about him.

He tells us that he is from Oregon, and moved to Maui soon after graduating college there. He's obviously into the Grateful Dead, and shows us pictures of the house he rented with friends while going to school. One of his friends was an amazing artist, and painted perfect renditions of Grateful Dead album covers on the doors and walls of their place.

I look at his record collection again and notice that they're alphabetized, with tabs sticking out here and there.

I nod at his records and say, "You have quite an impressive collection man!"

To this Roadie laughs. Then he tells us the story about how he came to own them. The college that he went to had an FM radio station, and Roadie and a friend of his were the sole deejays. He tells us that the school would give them the money to buy four albums a week, and along with their own personal albums they soon built up a sizeable library. Then in their senior year, just as they were about to graduate, they learned that the radio station was going to be disbanded, and pulled off the air. This kind of made Roadie and his friend upset, so they secretly took the albums. And Roadies friend let Roadie have the bulk of them.

So here they are in Lahaina, in Roadies room above the Lahaina Market Place. You can literally think of an album, go to the letter that it would be filed under, and there it will be.

141

Too cool!

We have fun drinking beers with Roadie and talking 'story'. He walks us through the adjacent rooms to the other side of the building where it looks down onto the brick courtyard of the Market Place.

We've obviously been having a good time, because the lights are coming on in the courtyard, and it's starting to get dark.

"We'd better get going," Andy says to us, and thanks Roadie for letting us hang out.

Roadie looks at us, and then says, "You know, you guys can crash here tonight if you want," and he nods at a few of the old couches in the rooms behind us.

We all look at each other.

"But," he says, smiling, "there's one condition..."

It turns out that Roadie doesn't pay rent to stay here. That is, he doesn't pay any money. In exchange for staying here he gets up every morning at seven am and hoses down the courtyard, takes out the trash from the many cans placed around the Market Place, and does a little raking and weeding. Every day, seven days a week.

So we spend the night, sleeping in the spare rooms, either on the couches or on the floor, and then get up at seven with Roadie and help him with his chores. It doesn't take that long with the four of us helping, and we trade off with the hose.

"Push the leaves, not the water," Roadie will say, coaching us.

And so, in the coming weeks and months, this starts becoming a routine. If we don't want to go back to Wailuku after work we can stay at Roadie's, and we'll even pack a change of clothes in our daypacks. But no matter how late we stay up the night before, or how much we have to drink, we still have to get up at seven and help Roadie in the morning.

I'm liking my job at the Whale's Tail, even though I'm not making very much money. I usually work with just one waitress, a Haole woman in her late twenties with shoulder length brown hair. She's a single mom and works all of the hours that she can. At the end of each shift she will give me my share of the tips, but it isn't much, usually five dollars, but never much more.

One day she calls in sick, so my manager tells me that I will be waiting tables. This kind of scares me, because I've never been a waiter before. But she says not to worry, I'll do fine, and she'll help me.

Luckily it doesn't get terribly busy, and everything goes well, and I'm all happy with myself at the end of my shift. And I make some pretty good tip money, about forty bucks. I share this news with my manager, telling her the difference between today and what I usually get when I'm bussing. She then asks me what I usually get, and when I tell her, she frowns.

The next day when the waitress shows up my manager takes her into her office and shuts the door. When they emerge a few minutes later my waitress does not look happy. And I know that I just threw her under the bus, but I want my fair share. At the end of the day she gives me fifteen dollars. Now that's better.

There's a dive rock and roll bar across the street from Kimo's called 'Le Teuts'. It's mostly only open at night, and they serve food also, but none of us have ever eaten there. It seems like the same cover band is always playing, and it also seems like all I ever hear them play is Foreigner songs. And they're actually pretty good at it. The music is easily heard through the open front door late into the night…

'C'mon baby you can do more than dance
I'm hot blooded, I'm hot blooded'

There's always a few shady looking characters hanging out by the front door, hitting up on the cute Haole tourist girls who go in there wanting to have a good time. They're probably trying to sell them some coke or buds. One of these scalawags who hangs out there a lot is known around town as 'Fast Eddie'. He's a medium built Latino guy with a pretty sizeable afro, and he'll try to pass himself off as a Hawaiian.

It's fairly late on a Saturday night and the four of us are up at Roadies drinking beers. Roadie is playing Lou Reed's live album, 'Rock n' Roll Animal' at a pretty good volume, and we're partying it up.

Pretty soon It's time to go get some more beers, so I volunteer to make the run, everyone pitching in and giving me money. The liquor store isn't far, about five or six doors down Front Street. But to avoid the crowd I go out the back and take Luakini Street, which takes me the back way to the store. I get a twelve pack, which is really two six packs of Bud bottles, and then head out the back door again.

It's dark back here, and I'm almost to where Luakini meets Lahainaluna when two guys come around the corner towards me. When they see me they slow down, and then I can tell by the silhouette of his afro that one of them is Fast Eddie. They're both carrying plastic to-go cups, probably coming from Le Teuts.

I hold on to my bag of beers a little tighter, and then Fast Eddie walks right up into my face, and holding up his cup he says, "You like some beer brah?"

Of course my first reaction is to say no, thanks anyway, got some. But I have a sneaky feeling that this will piss him off. Maybe he's actually trying to make a friendly gesture, so with that in mind, and against my better judgement, I accept the cup and start to take a sip. And that's when Fast Eddie cold cocks me in the face.

I fall back on my ass and the beers go flying, and I hear a few of them break. He hit me square in the nose and I start to feel the blood flow. Then they both jump on me, but they don't hit me anymore. Instead they start feeling me up and patting me down, and I realize that they're looking for my wallet, which I luckily didn't bring with me.

I get a sudden adrenaline burst of energy and squirm and roll, and break free of them. They just stand there looking at me, and since I don't have anything that they want, they just

THE BULLET HILL DIARIES

slowly turn, and continue walking down the street.

I gather up what's left of the beers and make my way around the corner to the door of Roadie's stairway. I come in the door and start going up the steps, but I must sound different because Andy and Chris quickly come to the top of the stairs. Even in the dim light of the stairway they can see that my shirt is ripped and bloody, and that my face is smeared with blood. They're both down the stairs in a flash, Andy saying, "What the fuck?"

"Fast Eddie..." I say, pointing towards the back of the Market Place, "down Luakini."

That's all they need to hear, and they're off like a shot, running out the door and down the sidewalk.

Dean comes down the steps, followed by Roadie, and they help me back up with the beers. Dean takes me aside and looks at my nose. "I don't think it's broken Ben," he says.

"He didn't hit me that hard," I say, " he just hit me where it counts."

I clean up my face in the bathroom, and Roadie loans me a shirt. Pretty soon Chris and Andy come back, and we can tell by the look on their faces that they didn't catch up to them. Fast Eddie had given them the slip, living up to his name.

They all sit me in a chair and give me a beer, and treat me like some sort of beer-run hero.

Chris says, "I wish I was there. I would have *killed* that son of a bitch!"

I'm sure he would have. And Chris will soon get his chance, but it won't be with Fast Eddie.

There's a waiter from the Ship's Wheel that comes over to Roadies every now and then. His name is Billy, and he's kind of tall, maybe six two, with toe head blonde hair and pale blue eyes. He's definitely on the shy side, but he's also the nicest guy in the world. The kind of guy that would give you his last dime. He also happens to be the highest grossing waiter at the Ship's Wheel.

Billy has an old navy blue, maybe late sixties Plymouth station wagon. After hanging out with Billy a few times at Roadies he'll sometimes offer to give us a ride back home to Wailuku, as long as he can crash in our living room for the night. We don't have a problem with that, and he'll do this every so often.

Now that it's been a couple of months, Andy, Dean, and Chris and I are itching to go to Hana again. We manage to find a time when all of us have a few days off, and for transportation Andy asks Billy if he wants to go. Billy declines, but being the nice guy that he is, he offers to let us take his station wagon.

We're all excited about going again, this being the first time that we've been back since we've been living and working here. We stop at the Olowalu Store for sealed packs of smoked octopus, sandwich makings and Budweiser's.

Soon we're on that 'road of roads' again, the three hour road to Hana, and we're really taking our time, sipping on Budweiser's, munching on smoked octopus, and smelling the flowers along the way, literally.

When we're almost to Hana Andy tells us that he heard that it's possible to jump the bridge at the Seven Pools. "There's supposedly a red cross painted on the top of the concrete rail that shows you where to jump from," he says.

"That would be one really hairy jump!" Dean says.

Chris and I agree.

Billy's station wagon is nice and big and roomy, and after we pass Hana we find ourselves going in and out of the 'Super' Valley's preceding the pools. This is just such a magical part of the island, and the three of us who aren't driving start 'car riding'. What we call car riding is really just sitting on the door with the window rolled down, your head above the roof getting an unobstructed view.

We get to the pools right around noon and it's perfect conditions again. There's been enough rain so that the pools are flowing, but not too strongly. We've now learned that it can rain too much and that the pools can turn into a brown raging river, or that sometimes it might not rain enough and they can stop flowing altogether. So far, we've been lucky. We've also learned about the trail to the left of the pools, and after parking Billy's car on the grassy bluff we start making our way up that trail for our first time.

After climbing up the trail for maybe ten minutes we come to a sort of lookout that looks down on the valley and a view of the waterfall that feeds the Pool of Death. We laugh now at what we didn't know then. We continue on until we see a cow pasture off to our left, and decide to look for some mushrooms there. We find some, but not a lot. Not like the other pasture to the right of the pools, where they seemed to be everywhere. We definitely find enough though, because back on the trail I feel myself starting to come on.

Colors are getting brighter, and my hearing is becoming more acute. I can hear every bird, every insect. I see the wind in the leaves of the trees as a living, breathing thing. And I'm getting simultaneous feelings of fear and euphoria, of anxiousness and wonderment.

I've got ahead of the others, and stop to call down to them in a voice that isn't my own. I've never heard that voice before. Dean is the first to reach me, and I can tell by his eyes that he is just as high as I am. He laughs and says, "I think these 'shrooms are stronger than the last ones we found."

I think he might be right.

Or maybe, after having lived on Maui for a little while, we're just more receptive.

Andy and Chris catch up to us, and they're both laughing, and it's pretty obvious that we're all on the same page.

We continue on up the trail, marveling at everything, until all of a sudden we're entering the bamboo forest that we've heard about. It's kind of dark in here, and kind of spooky too. When the wind blows, the bamboo trees, shooting so high we can barely see the tops, hit each other, sounding kind of like one big gigantic wind chime. This is the trippiest thing that any of us have ever heard or experienced, and we stand in awe.

Pretty soon Andy says, "Okay, I'm ready to get back to those pools and jump in the water."

We all agree, and follow him back down the trail, until we hear the unmistakable sounds of water falling off to our left. Dean takes the lead from here and we soon come to the top of the most amazing pool any of us have ever seen. The pool is about twenty five feet below us, and is being fed by two waterfalls. It's dark blue water shimmers in the sun.

We've all moved to different spots around the rim, totally amazed. But Dean is beside himself. "Oh my God, look at this!" he says. "This is just the Pool of... Life!"

That's all Andy needs to hear, and he says, "We gotta get into it goon!"

And he jumps.

He hits the water, and when he comes back up to the surface he looks up at us and lets loose with a shout. "Wooohoo!

Our pool jumping days have officially begun.

I jump next, doing a spin to my right, and don't quite make the full three sixty when I hit the water. While I'm underwater I slowly exhale, watching my bubbles stream towards the surface. I just feel like hanging here for a little while, suspended in a sublime inner space that is greenish blue with sunrays penetrating the surface. I look straight down below me into a deep blue nothingness that could be bottomless, but I feel no fear. All I feel is the beauty and mystery that embodies these pools. I come up, and spot Andy standing at the exit of the pool, which is the top of the small waterfall that leads to the next pool, maybe about ten feet down.

I swim up to where he is and climb out onto the rock. Andy says, "Aren't you glad you came to Maui now Ben?"

I'm so glad I'm speechless. We high five each other, Andy saying, "Yes, Ben! Look at this!"

Dean and Chris soon join us, jumping at the same time.

They both swim over to where we are, and climb up onto the same rock ledge. The only thing to do now is go with the flow.

We are, all of us, One with this jungle now... One with this stream, One with the water. We all dive headfirst into the next pool. When I come up from my dive I take a breath and then go back down again, swimming most of the way underwater. I feel like I'm turning into some sort of an amphibian, a Gollum like creature maybe, with webbed hands and webbed feet. Swimming underwater seems easier, and holding my breath for long periods of time seems effortless.

We all reach the other end of this pool at about the same time, and it's a short but gradual fall into the next one. We all just kind of slide down the smooth rocks into this next pool, which is unique in that it is a long narrow channel. Rock walls go straight up on either side, a multitude of flora and fauna clinging to their sides, and guava trees overhang the top. There's a few guavas floating in the water, and every now and then one or two might fall from above, yellow and perfectly ripe, and ready for eating. I grab one and bite into it, tasting not just the guava, but the jungle, this stream, this paradise on earth.

When we come to the end of this pool we've gone as far as we can go. The stream turns into a narrow slice in the rock, and if you keep walking you'll end up at the top of the water-fall to the Pool of Death.

We turn from the stream and it's a short hop and a skip back to the trail. We proceed back down, passing a few hikers on their way up, until we come to the road. Andy turns left on the road and heads towards the bridge, beckoning us to follow him. As we reach the bridge there's a couple of tourists there taking pictures. They soon leave, and we start to inch our way along the ocean side of the bridge. Andy is in the lead, and as he nears the center he starts looking at the top of the rail, looking for the red cross. Just then a Park Ranger emerges at the far side of the bridge.

Andy stops what he's doing and tries to look nonchalant. Which is laughable, because we're all wearing swimsuits with no shirts, and we've obviously been in the water. The Ranger, in his green uniform and green Smoky the Bear hat, starts walking towards us and we think that the gig is up. Then he says, "Yeah, it's right in there somewhere."

Andy gives him a quizzical look and the Ranger laughs. "The spot where to jump from. That's what you're looking for, right?"

We all can't believe what we're hearing. The Ranger walks up to the rail and looks closely, then says, "Yeah, here it is."

We look where he's pointing, and there on top of the rail is the barely perceptible shape of a small red cross that was painted there probably years ago. I look over the side at that point and it does look like it's in the center of the slow moving stream below. And then I remember what Dean said, that this would be one 'hairy' jump.

The Ranger continues walking and says, "Just be careful."

This is unbelievable, that we actually have permission to do this.

I look over the side again and notice that it looks about as far down as the Davis bridge that we jumped back in California. But instead of jumping into a large body of water we're jumping into about an eight foot wide stream.

This was Andy's idea, so he steps over the rail first, standing on the four inch wide ledge on the outside. Looking down he says, "Holy shit!"

Then he nervously clears his throat, and steps off...

We watch him fall, which seems to take a long time, until he hits the water and disappears. The three of us hold our breath, and then he surfaces. He does another victory shout, and gives us a thumbs up.

Who's next? I'm thinking about it when Dean beats me to it. He steps onto the outer ledge and holds the rail behind him. "This is fucken crazy!" he says, and wasting no time, he steps off.

Chris and I watch him land, and then Chris turns to me and says, " Well, it's just you and me Ben."

I just nod, and then step over onto the ledge, holding the rail like Dean did. I look straight out at the ocean and then slowly back down below me. Dean and Andy are looking up expectantly, all smiles and shouting something to me that I can't hear. It's not going to get any better the longer I wait, so I take a breath and step off the ledge. I try to keep my arms close to me and straight down so that they don't slap the water. The fall takes even longer than I thought, and when I hit the water and go under I spread my arms and legs to slow my descent, but the pool is obviously plenty deep.

When I come up I swim over to where Andy and Dean are. I got some water up my nose, but other than that I'm okay. "Wasn't that cool Ben?" Andy asks me.

"Oh yeah," I say, trying to clear the water from my nose. Dean laughs.

"Okay Chris!" Andy yells up at him.

Chris is perched on the ledge in position. "You can do it Chris!" Dean shouts.

After a few more seconds Chris jumps. He hits the water, and when he comes up he looks a little dazed but says, "What a rush!"

The only way to go from here is to jump to the next pool, which is very large and doesn't look as high as the bridge. Hell, after jumping the bridge anything else looks easy. We all make our way to the right of the waterfall and jump in quick succession. As I'm in the air I realize that this just might be as high as the bridge!

We swim to the side and hang out on the rocks for a little while, soaking up the sun. After a while Andy tells us that he has been talking to Drew on Oahu, urging him to come over to Maui for a visit. He can't wait to bring him here and show him the new places that we've found.

"And we'll get him to jump the bridge too!" Andy says, smiling.

This has been a trip of firsts, what with going up the Waimoku trail, seeing the bamboo forest, finding the Pool of

Life as well as the other pools, and of course jumping the bridge.

And it appears as though we might be back soon.

The Blue Max, where Chris works, is one of our favorite places to have a beer or catch some live music. It's laid out in dark mahogany's and brass rails, with a large model of a biplane up in the rafters. And it's upstairs across the street from the seawall, so it has an unobstructed view of the ocean and the island of Lanai. Every now and then some top name talent will be in town, and even though they might be on vacation, they might do a surprise performance, and it will likely be at the Blue Max. Here we will see the likes of Linda Ronstadt, members of Fleetwood Mac, Cheech and Chong, and Jackson Browne, to name a few.

One late morning the four of us, Andy, Dean, Chris and I, find ourselves walking down Front Street after leaving Roadie's, and it's a particularly quiet and uncrowded day. Some of us have the day off and some of us work tonight, and we're just taking a leisurely stroll. When we get in front of the Blue Max this guy suddenly comes down the stairs and onto the sidewalk. He's got a white T shirt tucked into faded blue jeans, and he looks strikingly familiar. Then we realize that it's none other than Jackson Browne. He also happens to have a lit joint in his hand, and as we stop and say hey to him he sits down on the curb.

He looks up at us and says, "Times are changin' boys." He hands one of us the joint. "They used to let me smoke up there, but now they tell me that I have to take it outside."

Andy says, "You're kidding! What's up with that?"

We all laugh, and he laughs too. And it looks as though we're witnessing the end of the Wild West days in Lahaina.

Pretty soon Jackson gets up and says, "Well, you guys have a great rest of the day."

We say the same back, and watch him walk on down the

street.

Dean looks back at us laughing. "No one's gonna fucken believe this!"

Chris tells us that Linda Ronstadt is playing at the Blue Max tonight, and he has the night off. All four of us decide to go and see her, and the word must have got around town pretty quickly because when we get there the line to get in is most of the way down the stairs. We get in line, and I'm squeezed in between Andy, Dean and Chris one step below me, and a very pretty girl in a short skirt one step above me. After standing there maybe thirty seconds, quicker than lightning, Andy reaches his hand through my legs and pinches the girl's ass.

She whips around, looks me in the eyes for a second, and then slaps me hard across the face. This commotion brings the bouncer down from the top of the steps, and after she says a few words to him he grabs my arm and escorts me down the stairs and out the door, not bothering to listen to my protests of innocence.

I walk across the street to the seawall and sit there, realizing that this is as close as I'm going to get to Linda tonight. Then I hear the music start and Linda's unmistakable voice drifting out of the restaurant. She sounds very cool, and perfect for this town.

'I'm going back someday, come what may, to Blue Bayou'

Pretty soon I see Andy, Dean and Chris crossing the street towards me. Maybe Andy felt too guilty about going up there after I got kicked out for something that he did.

"It's too crowded up there anyway Ben," he says. "She almost sounds better out here."

I look at him, and then the laughter starts.

Chris is in hysterics. "You should have seen your face Ben! Right after she slapped you!"

"Yeah, really?" I say, but then start to laugh myself. I put my hand to my face. "It's still numb."

More laughter.

And Linda does sound really good out here. And we're soon joined by more people on the seawall.

We seem to be spending more time in Lahaina and less time in Wailuku these days, but a lot of times either a couple or all of us find ourselves back there at the same time. One day, as Chris and I are walking up to our stairway, a captivatingly beautiful girl comes out of Lani's back door. Her long dark hair hangs down to the bottom of her shorts, and her green eyes sparkle in the sunlight. She introduces herself to us, saying that she's Lani's daughter Lydia. She looks to be in her mid to late twenties, and she's the epitome of the classic Hawaiian beauty. She tells us that she has just split up with someone, and is moving in with her mom for a little while.

After getting to know her a little better and talking to her more, we also learn that Lydia has forty eight acres of land Up Country somewhere near Makawao. It turns out that she grows her own Paka Lolo up there, and sometimes, usually in the early evening, she will come up the inside staircase, unlock the door and say "Yoohoo," and throw a joint into our hallway.

I've always noticed an old VW Bug in the carport next to the house, and an engine in pieces on the workbench, and we soon find out that it's Lydia's. One morning Chris and I are down there talking to Lydia, and I casually tell her about my '59 Karmann Ghia. And that's my first mistake.

Then Chris says, "Hey Bennett, didn't you rebuild the engine in your Ghia?"

At that Lydia's eyes go wide and hopeful. I tell her that yeah, I did, but I had my brothers help, and the 'Manual of step by procedures for the Compleat Idiot'. She laughs, and then walks over to the bench. After rummaging around a little bit she comes up with the same manual. I can't believe what I'm seeing.

She holds the book out in front of me and says, "Do you think that you could try to rebuild mine? I'll pay you for it."

After some hemming and hawing, and Chris urging me on, I foolishly accept the challenge. And I also agree to let her pay us (Chris says he'll help me) in buds. Lydia gets all happy and gives us a quarter ounce down payment, and I'm already feeling guilty for taking this on.

It gets very busy at the Blue Max pretty much every night, and Chris really has his work cut out for him washing dishes. They like him there though, and sometimes during the night a waiter or waitress will bring him a complimentary shot or a beer. They even have a small hole cut into the wall for him, about two foot by one foot, so that he can see the stage and the band that's playing.

Chris is getting tired of washing dishes though, so he soon gets a part time second job at the Pioneer Inn, bussing tables. He's on his way back to Roadie's place from this new job when he starts getting hassled by some young locals.

On Friday and Saturday evenings the corner of Front Street and Lahainaluna becomes a hangout for the younger locals, mostly high schoolers and maybe a few twenty somethings. If we're on our way to Roadies place we might have to walk by them, and we'll always get a little stink eye from the guys and occasionally some taunting looks from some of the girls.

Chris finds himself in the middle of them, and his response to something one of the girls said to him causes the stink eye to go one step further. Chris isn't one to back down, and now probably a dozen guys are getting hostile and starting to surround him.

This whole affair is not going unobserved however. Directly across the street from Roadies door is a little hole-in-the-wall bar called 'Moki's Inn'. You will only see older locals, or 'Mokes' in there, and they're kind of a rough looking bunch. But they don't bother anybody, and they keep to themselves.

The circle of angry guys around Chris is getting tighter, and it's not looking good for him. But then he somehow convinces them to keep it fair, and asks them to send out their one best guy. They reluctantly agree, and the guy they send out is almost a head taller than Chris. What they don't know is that Chris is somewhat of a boxer, along with his brother Mike. Back home in their parents garage they have a couple of heavy bags, a speed bag, many pairs of gloves, and they spar with each other fairly often.

Now I wasn't an eye witness, and I don't know how long the fight lasted, but the fact is that when it was all said and done, Chris took the big guy down in no uncertain terms. Would've made Clint Eastwood proud.

This outcome of course infuriated the little crowd, and they started moving in for the kill.

And that's when a few of the Moke's at Moki's came out of the bar and stepped in, putting a stop to anymore fighting. They saw the whole thing, saw Chris beat the guy fair and square. This was stopping now.

We celebrate Chris's victory that night, and he definitely has some new respect.

And the young locals don't seem to give us as much stink eye anymore.

Drew and his roommate Mike are coming over for their first visit to Maui. They will be staying at our apartment on Mamo, and they will have the place mostly to themselves because we're hardly ever there. They will be getting a rental car, which will also make our lives easier.

When they get to Lahaina they will delight in taking us out and buying us drinks and Pu Pu's. Their like of Maui is already turning into love, and that goes for both of them, but especially Drew. He is loving everything about this place, and there's something on the tip of his tongue, but he can't say it yet.

Andy and I have the honor of riding with Drew and Mike to the top of Haleakala and pulling an all-nighter at the observatory to watch the sunrise. We've brought along some beers, and munchies and Paka Lolo. Andy and I have only been up here one other time with Dean and Chris.

Drew is checking out the many pictures and maps of the Crater on the walls inside of the observatory. Pretty soon he says, "It shows trails going down into the Crater." He turns and faces Andy and me. "Have you guys hiked down into it yet?"

Andy and I look at each other. "No," Andy says. Then he looks back at Drew smiling. "But I have a feeling that's gonna change."

The sunrise is of course at its most dramatic when it first spills it's fire over the rim. But then after that colors start to materialize in the Crater that you didn't see before. And as I'm looking down there, I'm seeing separate craters within the big Crater, and how it really looks like the Moon, or even Mars. And I really want to go down there now. But that will be another time.

Andy will end up taking Drew and Mike to Hana, and the Pools. The two of them will experience the area for their first time, and Andy will even get them to jump the bridge. When they come back to Lahaina for their last night before going back to Oahu, those words that Drew couldn't voice before are rolling off of his tongue now.

"Maui me!" he will say, about every ten minutes.

And he indeed plans on making the move to Maui. He and Mike will be back in less than a month, and this time they will be bringing Mike's VW Camper Van with them. That is to say, they will ship it ahead of time so that it will be here when they get here. They only stay a few days, but now Mike's Van is ours to use as we please, and his generosity completely blows us away. We're assuming that it's really here for Drew when he finally makes the move, but it is obviously much appreciated until then.

Due to some stupid reasoning on my part, I will lose my job at the Whale's Tail. I don't really lose it, but after missing a few days because of the Hana trip that Andy, Dean, and Chris and I took, I assume that I'm fired, and don't go back. (The truth is, my manager was very nice and probably would've taken me back, but I was too embarrassed to face her.) But luckily I will quickly get another job bussing tables at a new Mexican restaurant called Los Caballeros, which is in a small shopping complex walking distance from Roadie's place.

Los Caballeros is maybe one notch above casual, with red tablecloths and red candles. After each table is vacated I have to put on a new tablecloth, put a pitcher of ice water on the table, along with silverware and glasses and chips and salsa. And doing all of that can get pretty hectic when it's busy.

The owner, who is also my manager, is a late thirty something Italian, with long curly dark brown hair. He looks like somewhat of a body builder, probably with help from some steroids, and most times he's dressed in short shorts and fishnet tank tops. And it is also pretty common knowledge that he is a cokehead.

Nothing that I ever do is fast enough for him, and he is constantly on my ass to move faster. One afternoon when I show up for work he is in the little storeroom next to the walk-in. He has the attic access ladder pulled down and is surrounded by at least a dozen cases of bottled Mexican beer of various kinds. He wants me to help him get the cases of beer up into the attic, and while I'm thinking that it can't be a good idea to store beer up in a hot attic, he climbs the ladder to the top and says, "Okay."

I grab a case of beer and start going up the steps to hand it to him when he shouts, "No, throw them to me!"

It takes most of my strength to throw that case of beer up to him, and by the fourth or fifth case I'm starting to tire. "Faster!" he says, and by the time I get that last case up to him I'm covered in sweat and breathing hard.

He comes down the ladder and says, "Okay, now get out on the floor and get those tables set up, and be quick about it!"

I walk back out of that storeroom, and what relatively little Irish blood that I have in my veins is starting to boil. I'm this close to telling the son of a bitch to fuck off, but I need this job. So I get to work setting tables, and at the same time curse myself for losing my job at the Whale's Tail. My manager over there was so nice and fair and cool, while this guy is a Vinny Barbarino wannabe prick.

The next day before work I come up with a plan to speed things up. Roadie has a coffee maker up in his apartment, so I make a pot and proceed to drink cup after cup, drinking most of the pot in about a half hour. When I show up for work I'm all jacked up, and I have to piss every five minutes. Everything is okay at first, and I'm practically running from table to table, and from the walk-in where I have to refill plastic pitchers with salsa.

It's a Friday night and getting busy, and I think I'm doing okay, until my manager pulls me aside and tells me that I have to move faster. Is he shitting me!? If I go any faster I might as well be wearing track shoes! And to top things off I'm feeling really weird from the coffee, and starting to get the shakes.

One of the waitresses, a cute short haired blonde about my age, sees me in the walk-in drinking ice water from a pitcher, and tells me that she overheard the owner talking to me. She says that he is a bastard, and that I'm doing fine, and to try not to let him get to me. It's very nice of her to tell me this, and I appreciate her concern, but not ten minutes later he yells at me again.

I'm sweating profusely, and shaking like a leaf on a tree from the caffeine. And I'm definitely a little angry. I go into the walk-in again to get more salsa, and I leave the door open. I'm squatting down refilling my pitcher with salsa and feeling the cool air of the walk-in on my skin, when I get a sudden un-expected feeling of 'total relaxation.' I look out of the door of the walk-in and see the back exit of the restaurant, and I get an image in my mind of Chris, going out of the back door at Sears.

And that's all it takes. I calmly set down the pitcher of salsa on the floor, get up and walk out of the walk-in and straight out the back door. And then, just like Chris, I break into a run. I run all the way to Front Street, and not wanting to stop I turn left and keep running, after a while realizing that I'm heading towards our first hang out, the pool and jacuzzi of the Lahaina Shores Hotel.

Just then I hear a voice calling my name from behind, and when I turn around I see that it's Dean running up to me. He has the night off and must have seen me running by the Market Place, wondering where the hell the fire is.

When he catches up to me he says, "Holy shit Ben, you're white as a ghost!"

I briefly tell him what just happened and how much coffee I drank. We get to the Lahaina Shores and he tells me to go sit in a chair by the pool, and that he'll be right there. When I get to the pool I'm thinking of jumping in with all of my clothes on, but then decide against it and grab two lounge chairs and take them out onto the beach. I lay back on my lounge chair, and that's when I feel my heart thumping about a thousand beats per minute. Silly me had no idea that you could O.D. on caffeine.

Dean finds me out on the beach and he's clutching a brown paper bag from the store. He reaches into the bag and pulls out a Miller Tall Boy and hands it to me. He also has one for himself, and sits in the chair next to me. I open my beer and take a long pull from it.

And Dean's a lifesaver, because this beer is hitting the spot, and bringing me back down from my self-inflicted caffeine nightmare.

Now I'm thinking about what I did, and tell Dean that I feel bad about leaving that waitress there with all of those tables.

"Don't worry about it Ben," he says. "And you'll find another job."

Good ol' Dean. A true friend to the rescue.

I do find another job, but I'm forced to fall back a notch and wash dishes again.   It's at the Banyan Inn, right across Front Street from the Banyan Tree.

The Banyan Inn from the outside looks very Polynesian,

with lava rocks and palm trees. But on the inside it's basic-ally one big dining hall, with linoleum floors and long tables placed end to end, looking more like a cafeteria. It takes me a few minutes to realize that the Banyan Inn isn't a normal restaurant. It caters to retirement age tourists who show up all at once in two or three tour busses. One minute there's no one in the restaurant, the next minute it's filled to capacity, probably close to two hundred people. And the domino effect is that one minute I'm standing there with nothing to do, and then the next minute the dishes start coming in 'en force'.

At least this kitchen is nothing like La Familia. It's huge, with a big dish washing station that is set up to handle the large quantity of dishes to be washed. And usually when I'm about half way through those dishes, the cooks start bringing over all of their stuff.

And that's where I am right now, up to my elbows in pots and pans. Soaking some of them, trying to loosen the long rice, sticky white rice, and teriyaki sauce that is caked to their sides. I silently curse myself *again* for losing my job at the Whale's Tail. I was on the way to becoming a waiter there, but now here I am washing dishes at the Banyan Inn.

One of the cooks feels sorry for me and comes over to help. She's a middle aged Japanese woman, one of about seven or eight who prepare all of the food. She starts loading dishes and glasses into the dishwasher for me while I work on the pots.

I didn't think to wear dishwashing gloves when I first started, and now that I'm wearing them it's like it's too late. My hands sweat inside of the gloves, which would have been okay if I hadn't already ruined my hands by not wearing gloves in the first place. All of that moisture and hot water for four or five hours made my hands crack and peel when they dried out, and now the only way to remedy the situation is to not get them wet, or let them sweat.

I go to the local clinic one day to see if they can help, and there in the waiting room is three or four other dishwashers with the same condition as me. The doctor gives us some kind of oil to put on our hands, which temporarily makes them feel better but doesn't solve the problem. The only cure at this point is to quit washing dishes.

It's after work on a payday, and after cashing my check I decide to have a beer at Longhi's. I've only been in here once before with Andy, and the bartender was very cool, a woman probably in her mid-thirties named Cyndi. There's only a few people at the bar, and I grab a stool and order up a draft beer. In a little while a cute blonde comes in and sits down about four stools over, and she looks familiar. Then I realize that she's none other than the waitress from Los Caballeros, the one that I left stranded when I quit.

She hasn't noticed me yet, and I find myself wishing that I could turn invisible. Since that's not an option I decide to try something else. I call Cyndi over and ask her to please put that girl's drink on my tab. Cyndi hands the girl her cocktail, and then says something to her and points down at me. When the girl looks my way slow realization comes over her face.

"You!" she says, and sets her drink down. She looks like she's about to get up and leave, but then she says, "Do you realize what you did to me?"

"I do," I say. "And I'm sorry. I'm really, really sorry."

She starts to get up. "Wait," I implore her, " do me a favor and please accept the drink, and hear what I have to say?"

The other people at the bar are starting to look over at us, and she senses this and looks a little embarrassed, and sits back down. I don't want to shout at her from four stools away so I move over and ask if I can sit next to her. She just nods.

"You know," I say, as I sit down, "I didn't take your advice, and I guess I just let that asshole get to me. I worked as fast as I could for him but it was just never fast enough. I finally reached my breaking point, and I just bailed."

She's listening, but not saying anything.

"And you probably won't believe this, but I thought about you later, and what I did to you, and I felt bad. And all I can say is that I am really sorry."

She looks me in the eyes for a few seconds, and then softens. Pretty soon she says, "I can't really blame you for bailing. We needed two bus persons there, but he was too much of a cheap bastard to hire another one." And then she looks at me and actually smiles. "I guess it doesn't really matter anymore anyway. He's gone. The restaurant is history."

I look at her wide eyed. "The restaurant is history?"

"Yeah," she says. "And he split the island. He wasn't paying his bills. Rumor has it that he was doing all the profits up his nose."

"No kidding?" I say. "Well, I guess it's a good thing that I went over there the next day and got my check."

Now she looks at me wide eyed. "You got your check?"

"Yeah, he made it out to me right there on the bar, with his big bouncer goon hanging out nearby. And you know, now that I think about it, he seemed different, kind of mellow and sad. And he didn't even say anything to me about running out on him."

She's giving me a look that I don't even know how to decipher. "If you really did get your check then you're the only one who did. He bailed on the rest of us."

"Wow, I'm sorry."

That smile again. "It's okay," she says. "At least I got my tips at the end of each shift, and that was a hell of a lot more than his measly little check would've been."

Now I'm starting to wonder why I didn't try to get better acquainted with this girl back when I was working with her, and I feel like even more of an idiot for letting her down the way I did. I mention something about my caffeine OD and she actually laughs, and it's really good to hear.

She turns slightly in her stool and holds up her glass to mine. "Apology accepted."

I nod my head in thanks, and we drink to it.

She sets down her empty glass and gets up to leave, and then turns and gives me a quick peck on the cheek. "Thanks for being honest," she says, and I watch her walk out.

I'm kind of in a daze from that simple peck on the cheek, and then I start thinking, wait a minute, what just happened here? Wait, come back! When will I see you again? Maybe we could go to dinner sometime! Maybe... but it's too late, she's gone.

When I swivel back towards the bar Cyndi is handing me a fresh draft. "This one is on me," she says.

I look at her smiling. "What's this for?"

"You did okay there. You handled that pretty well."

I laugh. "I did? But I just let her get away!"

Cyndi smiles. "Like I said... you did okay." I thank her and take a drink of my beer, thinking, we need more people like Cyndi in the world.

THE MAUI WOWIE POTATO CHIP FACTORY

'Anyone who's ever had a dream
Anyone who's ever played a part
Anyone who's ever been lonely
Anyone who's ever split apart
Sweet Jane
Oh, sweet sweet Jane'

'Sweet Jane'
Lou Reed

I'm in the last hour of my shift at the Banyan Inn. All of the dishes are done, and I'm about half way through the pots and pans, when Andy walks into the kitchen. He smiles at the Japanese cooks and says hello, and they smile and say hello back.

Then he comes around the shelves to where I am, and in a lowered voice he says, "Hey Ben, how would you like to get out of this place and come with me and cook potato chips for seven bucks an hour?"

I look at him in a kind of questioning state of shock. "This is a joke, right?"

He stifles a laugh. "Not at all. When you get off work meet me over at the Pioneer Inn. We'll have a beer and talk about it."

I nod and say okay. He smiles, then turns back to the cooks and says, "Bye ladies."

"Bye," they say, and he walks out.

As I'm scrubbing these pots I'm trying to process what Andy just told me. Cooking potato chips? For seven bucks an hour? That's almost twice as much as I'm making right now. I don't know where he heard about this, but for seven bucks an hour it sounds like a no brainer.

When I get off work I go out through the front door, cross Front Street and cut through the park under the Banyan Tree, then cross the side street to the Pioneer Inn. I soon spot Andy sitting at one of the small tables next to the rail in the Patio area. He notices me, and then I see him signal his waitress. I circle around the back, and by the time I reach his table she meets me there at the same time with a draft beer and sets it down in front of me. I sling my daypack around the back of my chair and settle in. I grab the beer and take a good long swig, and when I set it back down Andy is laughing.

"That must taste pretty good after washing all those dishes."

"Yes it does!" I reply. "Thanks."

He picks up his own beer, clinks it off of mine, and then takes a good long drink himself. When he sets it back down he says, "If you agree to what I'm about to offer you Ben? You'll never have to wash dishes again."

He says this with a twinkle in his eye. And I'm intrigued, to say the least. I pick up my beer again. "Okay man, I'm all ears."

Andy and I are sitting in the back of an extended Chevy van, somewhere on Waiehu Beach Road in Wailuku, skirting Kahului Bay. We're sitting on the floor because all of the seats have been taken out of the van, with the exception of the shotgun seat. There's two guys riding with us, local Haoles about two or three years younger than we are, and then there's our driver Al, whose name fits him perfectly because he looks like a bearded Al Pacino, a la Serpico. He's our new boss, and seems very cool. Just how cool, we're about to find out in the coming days.

Al pulls the van up to the front of a 'Quonset Hut', or a warehouse built by the military back during World War II. It's made out of corrugated steel, and looks like a small airplane hangar. It was built to store weapons and ammunition, but that's not what's in here now. Instead there's potatoes. About three hundred sacks, weighing approximately one hundred pounds apiece.

Al backs the van up to the large double doors of the hut and shuts off the motor. We hop out and Al unlocks the padlock on the doors and opens them, and we all get our first look inside. Shafts of sunlight stream down onto the sacks from roof vents up above. The potatoes are stacked in fairly neat rows on either side of the hut. It's warm in here, and now we can smell the potatoes, which have obviously started to rot. Al tells us that there are two other locations just like this one, with more potatoes to be transported to the new factory.

It never ceases to amaze me how Andy can strike up a conversation with a total stranger, get on their good side, and then turn the situation into his benefit. Or in this case, our employment.

Andy had met the two owners of this potato chip factory

while he was working a night at the Ship's Wheel, and after talking with them for a short while they asked him to meet them over at the Whaler's Pub, the bar across from the restaurant, when he got off work.

Later he meets up with them, a couple of surfer looking Haoles in their early forties, and they buy him drinks and tell him their story. Apparently they had a potato chip factory somewhere in Lahaina, and it was an old wooden building and caught fire, and burned to the ground. They used the insurance money to lease a brand new warehouse in an industrial park in Wailuku.

Then they told Andy that as soon as they were up and running they would need some cooks, which was the job they were offering him, and anyone else he knew of who might be capable. Good ol' Andy came to me.

Then they told him the new name, the 'Maui Wowie Potato Chip Factory', and they even had one of the new bags to show him. It was done up in bright colors, and had a cartoon character of a guy on it, who looked completely zonked out of his brain on... potato chips.

Now Andy learns that the first thing they need to do is get a bunch of potatoes from a few locations in Wailuku over to the new factory.

So here we are, in an old Quonset Hut, humping rotting sacks of potatoes into a van and getting slimed in the process. And I'm talking about the most slipperiest, slimiest, most foul smelling sticky goo that you can imagine. It takes two of us to tackle one sack, and you have to grab underneath it, so your whole upper and lower body gets slimed. We get ten, maybe eleven of these sacks into the van each time, and the van sags under the weight. Then it's about a twenty minute ride to the factory, where we unload them.

On the ride back to get more potatoes the slimy goo on our shirts and shorts is starting to solidify. Al is wearing a nice red Aloha shirt, and he pulls it out from his chest laughing, saying, "I wore the wrong fucken shirt today!"

He really is Al Pacino.

As we start to get freshly slimed again, one of the kids makes the crack that maybe they should use this batch of potatoes to make Vodka instead. We all laugh, not yet realizing the profound implications of his statement.

We manage to get five or six runs in by lunch time, and not only have we been getting a workout, we've been getting supremely slimed. We're quite a sight. That is to say, we're a total fucking mess! We are, all of us, now covered from head to toe in various stages of slimy and hardening potato goo. One of the younger guys has even slimed his hair into a Mohawk, and our laughter threatens to suffocate us.

Al pulls into the parking lot of a Pizza Hut, parks the van and shuts off the motor. He turns and faces us. "Okay now, listen. We all look like holy fucking hell, and if they get a good look at all of us they might not let us in. So here's what I want you guys to do. When you go in the front door, just go straight back to the tables and get one in the back, preferably in a dark corner. I'll go up front and order the pizzas. Pepperoni good with everyone? And maybe a Canadian bacon and pineapple?"

We all chime in, "Yeah!"

Al goes in first, then we follow and go straight to the dining room like he said. We do find a large table that is kind of all by itself, in a darkened corner. Andy and I make a beeline for it, and the other two follow.

Pretty soon we see Al heading back to our table, and he has two pitchers of beer in one hand, and as many mugs as he can carry in the other.

Andy kicks me under the table. "I like this guy!"

Andy gets up and helps Al with the mugs. "Al, you are the Man!"

Al laughs but puts a finger to his lips. "Keep this nice and mellow and we might be cool."

We all nod and say okay, and he fills up our mugs with the Foamy Golden Goodness. After lifting all of those bags of stinking rotten potatoes, the beer is looking mighty good indeed. Pretty soon Al is taking the empty pitchers back for more. After a few more pitchers and a couple of pizzas we're all in good spirits, laughing at the hardened slime on our clothes and body.

Almost two hours later we thank Al for the lunch, and then we all hop back into the van to go get slimed again. It takes us four or five days to transfer all of the potatoes from the three locations to the factory, and Al takes us to Pizza Hut every one of those days.

The following Monday the owners are ready to show Andy and I the cooking procedure. Well, they're almost ready. They're having problems with their bagging machine, a towering conveyer belt contraption that we have nicknamed T-Rex. While they're tinkering with it they decide to go ahead and have us cook up a couple of trial batches.

It is important to note that the two Quonset Hut locations had the bad, rotting potatoes, but the third location was climate controlled, and these potatoes still looked fine and were not rotting at all. But they want to use the old ones first, which causes Andy and I to scratch our heads.

The potatoes are first put through a spinner, which looks like a small washing machine on spin cycle, except that it has sandpaper on the inside. This gets most of the skin off, and some of the bad spots. Then they are dumped onto a table where about a dozen middle aged local women are sitting with paring knives, who cut out the rest of the bad spots. These women, who are constantly chattering and laughing, really have their work cut out for them with this first batch of bad potatoes.

From there the potatoes are put into small plastic trash cans on wheels and brought to us. The cooker is a large stainless steel vat, three feet by four feet, and three feet deep. It is filled with cottonseed oil and brought up to three hundred degrees. We put a certain amount into the slicer, which is mounted to a wooden platform that is also on wheels, and it spits the raw chips out onto the hot oil. We then use steel garden rakes to stir them.

These first batches, made from the older potatoes, do not look good. As soon as the raw chips hit the oil they start turning dark brown, and later when we scoop them out they look greasy and chewy, not crisp. These results obviously do not make the owners happy, and that's when Andy glances over at me, and then suggests to them to maybe try cooking some chips out of one of the newer sacks, see how they compare.

Not surprisingly (to Andy and I anyway) there's a night and day difference between this batch and the first. These chips come out white and crispy, and they look beautiful. The two owners have mixed reactions to this outcome. One of them seems happy, but the other one definitely does not, and I guess understandably so. He doesn't want to have to shit-can sixty thousand pounds of potatoes that he has already paid for. But the answer seems obvious to us. Do you really want your first chips, the first bags to hit the stores, to be anything but the best?

Life at Maui Wowee starts becoming routine. At first Andy and I work together, cooking chips eight hours a day. But after a few weeks they add a swing shift, and split us up so we can train the new cooks, who are older local teenagers. They hire more to do various other jobs, like loading trucks with chips and cleaning the place. These kids seem to be a good bunch, and we don't get any bad vibes from them for being Haoles.

It's early evening and Andy and I are sitting on our kitchen floor (we still have no table or chairs, or any other furniture for that matter) and eating yet another potato dish that Andy has prepared. He made it out of the hundred pound sack of potatoes that we stole from the factory. (One of the good sacks.)

He wants to be the potato chef, so I'm letting him. And he's really getting quite good at it. This dish that he's making now is kind of like potatoes 'au gratin', with melted cheese and sour cream. But he's made other things, like 'Baked Potato Supreme', with sour cream and green onions and grated cheddar cheese, and hash browns, and French fries, and even scalloped potatoes.

One potato, two potato...

Andy takes a few bites, then looks over at me with a funny look on his face, and then proceeds to throw his dish across the kitchen, making a pretty good sized mess of the floor and the cabinets next to the fridge.

Still with the funny face he says, "I'm fucking sick and tired of goddamn potatoes!"

I slowly start laughing, and then on impulse I throw my dish across the room too. This seems to cheer him up.

"C'mon Ben," he says as he gets up. "We're going to the store. We're gonna get a bottle of tequila, and we're gonna get drunk."

I look back at our mess, then follow Andy out the door and down the steps. We still have Mike's van, but Andy has recently acquired a little Honda 70 trail bike, which I think is a loan from somebody who owes him money. He wants to take the bike, so I hop on the back.

The closest store to the house is about a mile away, and Andy tears through side streets and alley's getting us there. It's situated at the peak of a triangle corner, and Andy pulls right up onto the sidewalk by the double glass front doors and parks. I wait on the bike while he goes inside.

When he comes back out he hands me the bag. "I got limes too. We have salt, right?"

I kind of laugh and say, "That's one of the few things that we do have. Besides potatoes of course, and a little cheese, butter, and sour cream."

Andy gives me his 'don't be a smart ass' look, and then, inside of two seconds, gives me a multitude of faces that are too numerous to count. He hops on the bike and takes us back the same way we came.

Biting into my third lime, I glance at the bottle and notice that it's already half gone. After Andy's third lime he gets up and starts trying to clean up the mess we made, but then says fuck it, and sits back down. We commence to passing the bottle, the salt shaker, and the plate of limes.

In no time at all the small bottle is gone. Andy jumps up and says, "I should've got a bigger bottle. C'mon Ben, let's go get another one."

Last time it was kind of like a chore to go. This time it's fun! The breeze feels great on my face, and I'm holding my arms out like I'm flying while Andy races along just about as fast as the little bike can go. As we reach the front of the store Andy realizes that he's going too fast, so when we hit the sidewalk he just lays the bike down, and we continue to slide right on in the open front doors, the motorcycle crashing into the first row of display shelving, which just happens to be... potato chips.

Andy jumps up like nothing has happened, and walks up to the counter and asks the Japanese man for another bottle. You can probably imagine the man's reaction.

He's one notch below shouting at Andy. "No, you go! You crazy! You drunk! You go!"

I pick the bike up and wheel it back out onto the sidewalk. Then I come back in and start picking up bags of chips off of the floor, and that's when the Japanese woman comes over.

"You just go!" she says, as she starts picking up bags too. "I fix. You get friend and go."

I feel bad now. These are nice people, and they don't deserve this. I put the bags that I have in my hands back on the shelf, and then slide the shelf back to its original position, to which she almost nods her approval. But when I walk out of the door it takes a supreme effort to not start laughing. The way Andy just walked up to the man like nothing happened! Only *he* could do something like that.

I straddle the bike and start it up, and pretty soon Andy comes out with another bottle in a bag, and hops on the back.

"Go Ben, go."

I put it in first and take off, and when we're about a block away I shout back at Andy, " How'd you talk him into selling you another bottle?"

Andy shouts back, "I paid way too much for it!"

We're sitting on the floor again, but we've moved into the living room. From our vantage point out of our living room window we can see the top of one lonely coconut tree, gently swaying in the breeze. Andy is gazing at that palm tree right now, but at the same time he's looking far beyond it.

Pretty soon he says, "I'm sorry I got you into this, Ben."

I know what he's talking about, but I say, "Into what?"

"You know, the potato chip factory. And that's just what it is, a factory. We're doing fucking factory work now, and it's boring the hell out of me." He does another shot and bites another lime. "It was kind of fun at first, even when we were humping all of those old bags of potatoes and getting slimed. But now it's just the same old dull routine every day. The hours just drag by, and it seems like the only thing we do anymore is work and come home."

He glances over at me, and then looks back out the window. "We didn't come all this way to work in a damn factory. We could do that back home." He turns and faces me. "We need to get back to Lahaina Ben. Back to the restaurants, back to the fun life!"

Andy has just thrown me into a Psychedelic Tequila Moment of Awareness.

I suddenly see the truth of it!

Of course we have to get back to Lahaina! What the hell are we doing here? This sudden influx of intelligence is almost too much to handle. I hold it in check by doing another shot and biting another lime.

Andy laughs at my response, or maybe at the lack thereof. "I'm gonna get my job back at the Ship's Wheel," he proclaims, holding up the bottle. He faces me again. "I know they'll take

THE BULLET HILL DIARIES

me back. And I'll get you a job there too, Ben. They could use some more help in that kitchen, especially on Luau Wednesdays. I'll talk to Walter, the manager. I'll talk him into it. He likes me."

I laugh. And hearing the conviction in his voice, I have no doubt that he will make good on his word. I know now that when Andy puts his mind to something, he usually gets it. And I also have to agree with him that the potato chip factory has been getting pretty dull. I've been bored to tears lately, but I keep thinking that I'll do it for just a little while longer, and maybe even save a little money. But now with Andy's talk of Lahaina, and the Ship's Wheel, I can't wait to make the change.

"On my next day off," Andy says, "I'll take the van to Lahaina and start working on Walter."

We shake hands on it, excited about going back to Lahaina again.

And we're definitely drunk. Drunk on tequila, and intoxicated with the knowledge of our new plan.

Andy jumps up to his feet, but a little too quickly I guess, because he promptly falls back down. He rolls over on the carpet laughing, and then manages to stand. "I'm starving!" he says. " I'm gonna make some French fries!"

"That sounds great!" I say, laughing at the fact that potatoes sound good again.

It's a few days later and I'm at the end of my shift. I'm talking to a co-worker by the name of Kaleo, and he's giving me a ride home, which he has done a few times now. Kaleo is just a year or two younger than me, which makes him older than most of the other guys. He is kind of like their ringleader, and I notice that they all look up to him.

I ask Kaleo if he'd like to come up for a beer. He says sure, and when he comes in he remarks that he likes the apartment, but laughs at the fact that we have no furniture. As we sit on the living room floor and drink our beers I turn on the stereo to KAOI-FM.

Kaleo laughs and says, "At least you got a nice stereo brah!"

I laugh, and I tell him how I convinced my mom to ship it over.

Then he says, "And you got a nice big kitchen too." After a pause he says, "And that's something I wanted to talk to you about."

He explains that him and a few of the other guys at the factory grow small amounts of Paka Lolo in their parents back yards, and right now it's the 'off season'. During this time they will trim a bunch of leaf off of their plants and have a 'Leaf Party'. This consists of baking brownies and cookies out of the ground up leaf, and drinking beer and eating large buckets of fried chicken. But they can't do this at their parent's house, so Kaleo is asking me if I would consider letting them have their Leaf Party here.

The whole thing sounds kind of hilarious, like a Cheech and Chong party. After a while I say sure, okay.

"Cool Brah!" Kaleo says. "And you won't have to pay for a thing. We'll buy all of the beer and the chicken, and bring all of da kine."

We clink our beer bottles and drink to it.

And I have no idea what I'm getting myself into.

Meanwhile Andy has done what he said he would do, and has got his job back at the Ship's Wheel. He's quit Maui Wowie, and works at the restaurant full time now. He says he's one hundred percent sure that he can get me a job there too. He tells me that the dishwasher is leaving soon, and that I can take his place. But he says not to worry though, it won't be anything like the Banyan Inn. He says I'll be prepping too, and doing all kinds of different things on Luau nights.

This sounds great, and I'm getting excited about going back to Lahaina with everyone else.

It's Friday, and the night of the Leaf Party. I work until six, But Kaleo and most of the other guys who are coming have the day off. I lent Kaleo the key so that they could get into the apartment and get 'cooking', and I'd meet them later.

I have Andy's trail bike, and when I turn down Mamo Place and then up our driveway, I can hear my stereo playing upstairs. The last thing I want to do is piss Lani off, so when I get up there I'm going to have to turn it down a little. At least, that's what I think I'm going to do.

When I walk in the door the scene isn't too far off from the Cheech and Chong party that I had envisioned the other day. To start with, the smoke is so thick that I can barely see into the living room. There's two guys in the kitchen baking brownies and cookies, with plates of each covering the counter tops. They offer me a plate, and I take a cookie. I walk into the living room to find Kaleo rolling oversized spliffs on our 'coffee table', which is really one of the boxes that my stereo came in. He's rolling them out of the big rolling paper from his Cheech and Chong 'Big Bambu' album that he brought along with him.

When he sees me he flashes me the 'Shaka' sign, then shouts into the kitchen. "Get Ben a beer!"

One of the 'cooks' brings me a beer, and as I take a swig and munch on my cookie I can't help but wonder how Andy, Dean and Chris would react if they saw what I'm looking at right now. Our little apartment is completely overrun with almost a dozen local Hawaiian's, some of whom I've never seen before. They're passing around two or three of the Big Bambu leaf J's that Kaleo has rolled, and there's plates of fried chicken, brownies and cookies, and full and empty beer bottles scattered everywhere. One guy that I do recognize from work is passed out in a corner.

They've got my Dark Side of the Moon album cued up on the stereo.

'Breathe... breathe in the air
Don't be afraid to care...'

The boys start treating me like a King, making a spot for me on the floor by the window. They bring me another beer, and a plate of fried chicken, and a plate of brownies and cookies, and pass me one of the giant spliffs. I have to laugh, because that's really all I can do.

And I totally forget about turning the stereo down.

I slowly wake up and realize that I'm in my bedroom. I try to peel my eyes open, but they want to stay shut. It's obviously the next day, and I don't know what time it is, but it's bright outside. I force my eyes open and look at my alarm clock, and see that it's almost noon. Shit. I was supposed to be at work at eight.

I sit up and my eyes will only open to slits. I don't really feel bad, but I feel fuzzy, and still sleepy. I guess I have a pot hangover, although up until now I didn't know there was such a thing.

I get up and go out into the living room, and what a mess! Plates of half eaten chicken, beer bottles, and half smoked leaf joints seem to cover every square inch of the room. There's only two guys left from the party sleeping on the floor, and I recognize both of them from the potato chip factory.

I manage to find my sunglasses and then head down the stairs to the motorcycle. We don't have a phone, so I've got to get to the payphone in front of the little store about a mile away and call work. I don't know what's going to happen, but I've got a pretty good idea that I might be fired. And I'm also thinking that if that is the case, it won't be the end of the world.

I get a hold of one of the owners and just tell him the truth. I tell him that we had a party at my place last night, and that I overslept. He's incredibly cool, and just wants to know if I can still come in. I tell him that I can, and then he asks me if so and so is at my place. I say that yeah, he is, but he's passed out on my floor. He tells me that if I can get him up and get him to come in to work too, that we'll be okay for the day. I tell him that I'll try and do that, and hang up.

When I get to the potato chip factory, the day has that laid back Saturday feel to it, and the owners don't seem mad at all. In fact they start joking about the party, saying that they heard it was a pretty wild one. I laugh, thinking that a really 'wild' party would have been one with some naked girls dancing around. But one of the owners tells me not to let those guys take advantage of me, saying that they might get used to the idea of crashing at my place all of the time. I tell him not to worry, that I don't plan on having anymore parties. What I don't tell him is that I probably won't be working here for much longer. And I'm thinking that I need to talk to Andy, soon.

My replacement shows up at five, and I'm grateful for only having to work a half day. When I get back to the apartment I just want to clean the place up. There's plenty of leftover beer, so I crack one and start in. And it takes me two solid hours to complete the job.

The next day, Sunday, Andy shows up at about mid-morning. He tells me that it's all set, and that I can start tomorrow at the Ship's Wheel if I want. Unbelievable! Or maybe not so unbelievable. He made good on his word, as usual, and I thank him and shake his hand. It all seems to be happening so fast now, and I'm excited about going back to Lahaina. But I tell him that the owners have been really cool to me, and that I at least need to work there one more day, and give them some kind of a heads up. I owe them that, I say.

Then he looks around the apartment and says, "Wow, did you just clean the place?"

I just laugh.

I'm with Andy, Dean and Chris, and the four of us are eating a late breakfast at possibly one of the coolest places to eat breakfast in Lahaina. It seems to hang out over the water, and it's the first place off the seawall where Lahainaluna meets Front Street. And that just happens to be kitty corner across the street from the Lahaina Market Place, where I'm living now.

Roadie has moved into a condo, and he has let me take his place, which means that I'm officially out of Wailuku, and it also means that I have to get up at seven every morning and hose down the bricks. But that only lasts about a week, because this guy named Steve, who lives in the Market Place also, has taken over that job completely.

There's one other guy who lives above the Market Place, and he occupies the biggest room in this little complex. His name is Marco, and he is a somewhat overweight Cuban, (or so he says) and keeps to himself. We all met Marco a while ago, and we could never quite figure out just what it is that he does here. But he seems to be in charge, and evidently he got Steve the job here and the place to stay. Marco is a strange one, to say the least. I've never seen him leave the grounds, and in fact he hardly ever comes out of his room.

Now that I'm totally moved in, I'm wondering what's going to happen next, because I know that I can't live here rent free. And so one evening Marco knocks on my door, which is at the other end of the building from his room. I'm listening to my stereo, and I turn it down a little and let him in.

Marco sits down and gets right to the point. "I just wanted to tell you that I'm willing to let you stay here, but on one condition."

And I'm thinking, okay, here it comes.

He looks over at one of my speakers and says, "You've got a nice stereo." Then he looks back at me. "And that's my proposition. I'll let you stay here if you let me keep your stereo in my room."

Talk about the last thing that I thought he was going to say! This completely throws me for a loop. I love my stereo, but at the same time I know that I should definitely take advantage of this. And I like it here. So I reluctantly agree.

A pretty sweet deal, one might say. But sometimes late at night, when I'm lying in my bed, I'll hear the music coming from Marco's room... and it kills me.

We're done with our breakfast and taking our time with our coffee, and Andy says, "My brother Ken is on Summer vacation from college right now, and he's in Seal Beach visiting my parents. I'm gonna call him up and get him over here. I know he'd love this place."

We react to this news with raised eyebrows.

"That's pretty funny timing Andy," Chris says, "because Dean and I have some news of our own."

They both proceed to tell us that they are planning to move back to the mainland soon, and for different reasons. Chris says he has had an 'epiphany', and as much as he likes Roadie, he doesn't want to end up like him, still working in restaurants in Lahaina ten years from now. Dean says he misses his girlfriend Sara, and his plan is to get her to come back to Maui with him.

Two completely different reasons, but they both take Andy and I by surprise. I look out at Lanai, and I get kind of a sad feeling. We've been on Maui for just shy of a year now, and with Chris and Dean leaving it feels like the end of an era.

The day has come, and Andy and I are taking Dean and Chris to the airport in Kahului. We're in the camper van, so there's plenty of room. Chris and Dean are looking out of the windows and saying goodbye to the now familiar places.

So long Olowalu Store, with your big beautiful Monkey-pod trees. And see you later white sand tranquil beaches. As we go around Papawai Point Chris mentions something about the first time we drove around this Point on our way to Lahaina, and how long ago that seemed. Just over ten months ago, but we were different people then, unsure of everything except our intentions. Since then we've learned a little bit about ourselves, and a little bit more about how the world really works. Ten months ago, but to us it feels like a lifetime.

And their goodbye's continue. To Haleakala Crater, House of the Sun. And to Hana, and the Pool of Life. It's emotional for them, and at some point I see both of their eyes glass over. It can't be easy, leaving the Islands of Aloha.

We get to the airport and Andy and I walk with them to

their gate, and even out onto the tarmac as they board. They go up the steps, and just before they enter the aircraft they turn and give us the Shaka sign. And then Chris yells, "Aloha!" One last look, and then they both disappear into the plane.

It's hard to describe the mood Andy and I are in as we head back to Lahaina, but it's definitely a little somber. And Andy soon puts an end to that.

As he's driving along he gives a sudden shout out of his window, and then grabs my arm. "We're still here Ben! We're still here!" he shouts. "We've got this van now, and we can go anywhere we want!"

His enthusiasm is contagious, and I'm feeling his energy.

"Ken's here now," he says, "And Drew's gonna move here soon. A whole new Maui life awaits us!"

And yes, with Dean and Chris gone it's the end of an era, for sure.

But, like Andy says, it's also the beginning of a new one.

In my dream I'm at work, framing a house in Arizona. It's a somewhat complicated floor plan, and I'm framing a section of the roof. Pretty soon I hear my foreman calling to me from down below. "Hey Ben, there's someone down here wants to see you." I look through the trusses and see Andy standing there and talking to my boss. So this is what he's done! Instead of calling me, he's decided to come all of the way out here to the desert and tell me exactly what happened, and why. I get a smile on my face, because I know I'm going to have to tell my boss that I'm taking the rest of the day off, and that Andy and I are gonna go to some dark cool bar, and have some tall cold beers, and he's going to tell me everything that happened, and why. But, as dreams go, none of this ever comes to pass. We never even make it off of the jobsite. I can't find my keys, but wait a second, I think I left them in my tool pouches. No, they're back in the car. But wait, these aren't even my keys, they're Nancy's keys! Oh fucking hell! C'mon Andy, we've got to get the fuck out of here! We've got to get out of this heat and into that dark, cool bar and have those tall, cold beers.. so that you can tell me everything that happened, and why...

THE SHIP'S WHEEL

'Awake again
  I can't pretend
  That I know I'm alone
  And close to the end
  Of the feeling we've known'

  'Late for the Sky'
   Jackson Browne

I'm in an elevator on my butt, with half of a three hundred and fifty pound dead pig on top of me. I should say we, because the other half is on top of my co-worker, Theresa. It's a Tuesday afternoon, and this is when the pig is always delivered in preparation for our Wednesday Luau's. The local farmers bring it to the parking garage on the basement level, and then help us wrestle it into the elevator, where we take it up to the kitchen. But when they let go of this particular pig Theresa and I promptly fell down under the weight, with the dead pig in our laps.

So here we are, in the elevator with this exceptionally large pig, in fact the biggest one that either one of us can remember, on top of us. I'm back in the corner of the elevator with the ass end, while Theresa is in front of the doors and closer to the buttons. She reaches up and stretches with all of her might and pushes one. The doors close and we start going up, but she must have pushed the wrong one because we pass the first floor and continue on up to the second. A comical situation just made funnier, we both start laughing uncontrollably. And laughing isn't especially easy with all of this dead weight on top of us.

We reach the second floor and the doors open, and Theresa abruptly stops laughing and looks up open mouthed. Someone is standing there, but I can't see who it is.

She gives a little wave with her hand and says, "Hi Don!"

A voice says, "Well, I can see that you've got your hands full, so I'll just take the stairs."

"Okay, sorry," she says, and reaches and pushes the button again, and the doors close.

As we're going back down I look over at her. "Was that who I think it was?"

"Mmm hmm," she says. "Don Drysdale, big as life, looking down at me with a huge dead pig on top of me."

We both start laughing again, and when we get to the first floor and the doors open it's all we can do to quit laughing and get out from under this pig. Theresa gets help from the kitchen, and it takes four or five of us to get the pig in there and into the walk-in.

With Don Drysdale's Whaler's Pub right next door to the Ship's Wheel Restaurant, it's not uncommon to see Don once or twice a year. But the timing of this appearance was just a little bit of a surprise.

The end of our pig escapade causes Theresa and I to high five each other. Theresa is about five foot five, with long blonde hair that is usually tied back into a pony tail. She's cute, and somewhat of a tom-boy, and is always upbeat and quick to laugh. She's a prep cook, and she recently moved to Maui from Carlsbad California, along with her friends Gina and Maureen, who are both waitresses here at the restaurant as well.

Gina is a tall, leggy blonde with a kind of quirky smile that really works for her. She's just a little shy, and has a sweet, reserved personality. Maureen is tall also, but not quite as skinny as Gina, and definitely not shy. She has long, thick reddish brown hair and tanned skin sprinkled with freckles. Her eyes light up like two crescent moons when she smiles and laughs, which is what she manages to do most of the time.

And don't think that it hasn't crossed my mind that I might not be here right now, working alongside these really cool cute girls from Carlsbad. Oh no no.. I could be back at that damn potato chip factory, cooking fucking potato chips, and being bored out of my mind. I silently thank Andy once again. Even though he got me into the potato chip factory in the first place...

Luau Wednesdays at the Ship's Wheel are easily the busiest day of the week at the restaurant, even overshadowing Friday and Saturday nights. I will work about fifteen hours, starting at eight in the morning and then finally finishing with the clean-up at around eleven. Andy and Roadie will work about eighteen hours, starting at six in the morning to get the pig ready to cook.

The pig is cooked out on the beach in front of the restaurant in an open steel box, about three feet by eight feet by three feet deep. The pig has a long stainless steel pole running through it, which connects to a chain driven motor, and is slowly rotisserie cooked all day long over coals of Kiawe.

The first thing that Andy and Roadie do when they get to the restaurant in the morning is get the pig onto one of the large tables in the kitchen, and then get the stainless steel pole through it. They literally run the pole up its ass and out of its mouth, and then tie wire the pig to it. The pole is about ten feet long and two inches in diameter, and it has holes drilled through it at different angles every foot or so. Andy and Roadie will criss-cross the tie wire in an X fashion, and it takes them about two hours to complete this task. When they're done they will take the front and the back and hoist the whole thing to their shoulders, with a towel for a cushion, they will very ceremoniously carry it out to the pit on the beach. There it will slowly cook for about ten hours.

And I seem to remember two additional waiters helping them to carry out this particular pig.

I find out from Andy that this whole Luau event is our manager Walter's idea, and he is no dummy. As the pig cooks during the day the aroma will start wafting up and down the beach. Curious tourists will walk up, and the cook tending to the pig will pull off small pieces of pork rind and give it to them to sample. Then they will inevitably go up to the restaurant and buy their tickets for that evening. Fifteen dollars will get them all they can eat, and all the Mai Tai's they can drink.

Maureen is in charge of mixing the Mai Tai's, and she laughs every time she does it. She grabs the biggest pot in the kitchen, fills it with ice, and then starts pouring the bottles of mix and rum in, and she makes them strong.

"Plenty of rum!" she'll say, as she's pouring in the bottles. "Walter wants them good and buzzed!" And her laughter is contagious.

After preparing food all morning we spend the afternoon

setting up tables and benches in the grassy area in between the restaurant and the beach. The tables all get plastic tablecloths and candles and flowers. Then on the beach side, with the ocean and the island of Lanai for a backdrop, we set up a stage for the Hula Dancer Show. It's put on by a large Hawaiian family performing classic Hawaiian favorites, complete with drums and ukuleles, and grass skirts. The show's finale is a very talented fire dancer, the climax of the Luau.

A Lahaina sunset is coming on, and all of the tourists are at their seats.

It's Mai Tai time.

This is definitely the funnest part of our job. All we have to do is dip our plastic pitchers in the big pot and walk around filling and refilling the eager tourist's cups. It's kind of relaxing after working all day, and definitely funny watching the tourists get drunk.

Pretty soon the finished pig is brought to a table and separated, the meat literally falling off of the bone. The happy tourists line up to fill their plates with slow cooked pork, long rice and chicken, an assortment of Hawaiian fruit, and little cups of poi. When they return to their seats our work is finally done for a while.

At this point a lot of us will go up to the second floor and sit on the Lanai and watch the show. A joint might be passed around, and we'll laugh and do nothing until the show is over. Then we'll go back to work, cleaning up and putting all of the tables and benches away. We're usually not completely done until around eleven thirty or so, at which point we'll all go next door to the Whaler's Pub and have a much anticipated beer or cocktail. Walter will usually pay for the first round, and we will toast him, with raucous cheers and laughter.

My days at the Lahaina Market Place are coming to an end. Marco is leaving, and rumor has it that all of our little upstairs apartments are going to be renovated and turned into office space. And of course I don't know where I'm going to go, or what I'm going to do. But then Gina, Theresa, and Maureen come to my rescue.

The three of them live at the 'Huea House', a three bedroom rental house on Huea street, a short walk from Front Street on the north side of town. Gina and Theresa share one bedroom, Maureen and her boyfriend share another, and a cook from the Ship's Wheel, Mike, has the third one. But there is also a single bed in the living room that I can rent for seventy five bucks. It's all done on the sly of course, so every morning I have to make my bed up to look like a couch so the landlord won't know. He will sometimes pop over unexpected to check on things, and if I happen to be there Gina and Theresa will hide me in their bedroom.

There's also a guest house in the back yard, a one bedroom with a kitchenette, and a waiter from Longhi's by the name of Craig lives there. There is absolutely no room in the main house for my stereo, so Craig says that he will be more than happy to keep it back there in his place.

So yeah, here we go again. And just like with Marco, I will sometimes hear my albums playing late at night.. and it kills me...

There are two other Haole girls that we know in Lahaina that are worth mentioning. Their names are Vicki and Joyce, and they seem to be attached at the hip, because we never see them apart. Occasionally they will pop by Roadies place to smoke a joint, and I'm finding out that Roadie is the King of assigning people funny nicknames. He calls them Sticky Vicki and Moist Joyce, and for reasons that I can't quite put my finger on, the names seem to fit them perfectly. Vicki is real cute but almost anorexic thin, with shoulder length straight brown hair. Joyce is not real thin, but healthy looking, and cute also, with long curly light brown hair and a lot of it. Joyce is a waitress at the Ship's Wheel, and that is the only time you will ever see Moist Joyce without Sticky Vicki.

Sometimes while she's working she'll come into the kitchen with a complaint, saying, "Roadie..."

Roadie will bow his head low like he's Japanese and say, "Yes, your Moistness..."

As Andy had said on the day that we dropped off Dean and Chris at the airport, 'we have the van now, and we can go anywhere we want'. We get a rare day off together, so we decide to go to McKenna Beach. I'm driving, and when we get close it's a dirt road that takes us in.

I'm turning this way and that through the Kiawe bushes, and when we start to see the beach Andy sees a spot. "Pull in here."

I do as he says, but it's really soft sand and when we come to a stop I feel the back tires dig in and drop down. I put it in reverse just to see if I can back out, but it just digs down more. We look at each other, and we're both thinking the same thing. Screw it for now, we'll worry about this later. We just want to get out on the beach and into the water. I shut off the motor and we head out.

The sand at McKenna is blindingly white and soft, and it 'barks' as we walk through it. It's a nice day here, not too many people, and the wave surge is next to nothing. Down at the far end of the beach to our right, next to the rocks that lead over to the 'nude' beach, is a cluster of maybe twenty little tents. We realize that it's a young girls scout troop, the Hawaiian equivalent of Brownie Scouts, and all of the little girls are in the water in front of their campsite, splashing around and having a good time.

Andy and I take off our shirts and run and dive in the water. And man, does it feel good! The water is crystal clear, and it gets deep and over our heads just a few feet from shore. We swim out another twenty feet or so since there are no waves, and after cooling off a bit we head back in and plop down on the sand.

Maybe five minutes later we both notice a large shadow

in the water, moving straight towards the beach. When it gets about ten feet from shore it turns parallel to the sand, and we see it very clearly in all of its glory. A shark. A big one. About nine to ten feet long, with a wide dorsal fin that is slowly cutting the surface of the water.

"That's one da kine Tiger Shark," says a voice just behind us. We turn to see a large Hawaiian man, holding a big rod and reel in one hand, and a five gallon bucket in the other.

Andy and I turn back to the water and we are frozen on the spot, mesmerized by the size of this shark that is swimming very slowly, almost lazily, in the exact same spot where we were just cooling off.

The shark then does a complete three sixty and starts heading down the beach the other way, towards the rocks, and straight towards the girls in the scout troop, all of whom are still in the water.

We're on our feet now, watching the shark very closely. And all of a sudden it seems to sense something, and slightly quickens its pace. Out of nowhere a woman appears, and she starts running alongside of the shark, waving her arms frantically and screaming at the girls in the scout troop to get out of the water. She finally attracts the attention of the troop leader lady, who realizes what's happening, and then hastily starts getting the girls out of the water and up onto the beach.

The last little girl runs up onto the sand just seconds before the shark reaches that spot. The shark seems to realize what it just missed, and instantly turns around and starts heading back down the beach towards us again.

Andy and I both know that there are sharks in Hawaii, but we never wanted to believe that they got this big, or came this close to shore.

Still swimming slowly, the shark is directly in front of us again. Then, out of the corner of my eye, I notice the fisherman moving up towards the water. He drops the five gallon bucket, then reaches in and pulls out a dead octopus. He quickly hooks it to the end of his line, then swings the rod back and casts it out, a perfect cast, the octopus landing maybe five feet from the shark's head. The shark swims over, takes the octopus in his mouth in one gulp, and starts heading out to sea.

The line starts peeling off of the man's reel, and this is a big reel with thick line. The shark is moving faster now, maybe because he knows that he's hooked, and the line is really singing as it comes off of the man's reel. Andy and I are transfixed, watching the shark getting smaller, and watching the spool of line on the fisherman's reel, which is really getting smaller.

The guy tries tightening down his drag, but it doesn't seem to have any effect one way or the other. The end of the spool comes, and the man plants his feet firmly in the sand and holds on with all he's got. And then, snap! The last of the line flies out and is gone, and he falls back into the sand on his ass.

Andy and I help him to his feet, and then all three of us look out to where the shark just was moments ago. But it's just empty blue water again.

"I've seen a lot of da kine," the guy says, motioning towards where the shark just was, "but he's definitely one of the biggest."

Andy and I look at each other, and Andy shudders.

We say so long to the fisherman and plop down in the sand again. After a while Andy wants to get going, but I want to jump in the water one last time.

He gives me his quizzical, comical look. "Are you crazy?"

"I know, but that shark is long gone. And look at that water, it's so clear you can see anything coming."

Having talked myself into it, I run and jump in the water. And the second I go under, in my mind I can see that shark again. See it for all of its power, for all of its terror. I'm in his world again.

I turn around and start scrambling straight back out.

As I come up the beach Andy's laughing. "You're a real brave man, Ben."

"Oh yeah," I say. "Real brave."

We're sitting in the tiny Windsock Lounge at Kaanapali Airport, Andy and I, sipping Bloody Mary's and waiting for Andy's flight to Honolulu. There he will catch a flight back to LAX. He's going back to Seal Beach for a little while, says he's got a few things he needs to take care of. He doesn't really talk about what those things are, so I don't ask.

"I'm gonna miss you man," I say, and we clink glasses.

He kind of shrugs it off. "It won't be for long," he says. "I'll be back before you know it."

But I'm already feeling isolated. I take another drink of my Bloody Mary, which seems to be helping. They are reportedly the best on the island, and now that I'm having one for myself I totally agree with that assessment. Made by our bartender Harry, 'High School Harry', as he is known, in what has to be one of the smallest bars in the world. We climbed a spiral staircase to get up to the lounge, which has two tiny tables and a hammock strung in between. Business cards from all over the world cover the walls.

Andy heard about this from someone who had left Maui a couple of times before. He told Andy about flying in the twin engine Cessna seven seater prop plane, and how the pilot takes the scenic route to Oahu, flying along the backside of Molokai, which is sheer cliffs and home to the highest waterfalls in the Hawaiian Islands.

"He said it's the best way to leave the island," Andy tells me. "More up close and personal. You should do it too Ben, when you leave."

When I leave.

I notice that he didn't say 'if', but 'when'. And I don't have any idea when that's going to be. But I'm already starting to feel alone, and Andy hasn't even left yet.

"I hear your plane coming," Harry says. "You'd better suck 'em up."

He must have amazing hearing because I don't hear a thing. Or maybe I just don't want to.

We toast again in silence and drain our glasses. We tell Harry Mahalo and Aloha, and go back down the spiral staircase. We don't say much as we watch the plane taxi up. After a little while the other passengers start boarding, so Andy and I shake hands and hug.

He gets on last, and when he reaches the top of the little steps he turns to me and says, "Take care of my favorite island for me Ben."

"You can count on that brah," I reply. "Aloha!"

"Aloha!" he says back, his eyes looking all around, saying it not just to me, but to all of Maui.

The door shuts, and I wait for the plane to taxi out to the runway and take off. I watch his plane fly away over the sea, getting smaller and smaller. And the world starts looking blurry through watery eyes.

I start thinking about how I came to Hawaii alone, waited for Andy, Dean and Chris to arrive, then came to Maui, lived our lives and worked our jobs and had our little adventures. And now they've all gone back, and here I am, alone again.

I realize that I'm feeling a little sorry for myself, and on the way back into Lahaina I slap myself in the face, and remember that I'm not really alone. I have some great new friends now that I care about, and they seem to care about me. And even though Andy's coming back, I know that it's really the end of an era. And it already feels different.

It's pretty common knowledge in Lahaina that singer/songwriter and phenomenal jazz guitarist George Benson is a Maui resident and lives in nearby Kaanapali. He will sometimes perform at different venues in Lahaina, and just like with Jackson Browne and Linda Ronstadt, and Cheech and Chong, the only way we'll hear about one of these shows is by word of mouth.

I'm working a day at the Ship's Wheel and Gina and Theresa come in the kitchen on their day off. They're kind of excited because they had just run into George Benson on Front

Street, and he invited them to his gig tonight, saying that he would put their names on the guest list. He's playing at Nimble's, a new restaurant across the street from Kimo's. Gina tells me that their little dilemma is that Theresa has to work tonight, so she asks me if I want to go. This takes me by surprise, and I say 'what about Maureen?'. But Maureen's working too. She says she'll feel more comfortable if a guy goes with her, and practically begs me, so, you know, I say yes.

We arrive a little late that night, and we can hear George playing as we come up the steps. The small dining rooms at Nimble's are just that, small intimate rooms that kind of make you feel like you're in someone's house, and the room that George is playing in is no exception.

A host greets us inside the front door and Gina whispers something in his ear. He checks his list and then leads us back to the room where George is playing. Every table in the small room is taken except for the one right in front of the stage, and I notice a 'reserved' placard visible on top. The host leads us to the table and pulls out Gina's chair for her, and we sit down. He smiles, and as he removes the reserved placard, I look around and see that everyone is pretty dressed up. And now I feel a little goofy, sitting at the best table in the house wearing shorts and flip flops. But it's Lahaina, and at least I'm wearing my button down Aloha shirt.

At one point in between songs George actually acknowledges Gina and her 'friend'. And then another surprise. A bottle of champagne on ice is brought to our table, courtesy of George, of course, and as the waiter is opening the bottle I'm remembering that this was supposed to be for Gina and Theresa. Two girls getting champagne from George. And now I get the feeling that the people around us are starting to wonder just who we are.

Gina is all smiles as she sips her champagne, and we both bask in our brief little time of glory. We both know that things like this don't happen often, and we might as well enjoy it while it lasts.

George ends the night with an extended version of his hit 'Masquerade', and the words seem to fit the night.

'Are we really happy here
With this lonely game we play
Looking for words to say
Searching but not finding
Understanding any way'

When he's all done Gina goes up and gives him a hug and a kiss, and thanks him for the table and the champagne. We then go across the street to Kimo's for a beer, and she tells me that George wanted her to stick around, but she politely declined.

"Damn, girl," I say. "You turned down an after party with George Benson?"

She laughs. "I think he had ulterior motives."

I pause, and then say, "Have I ever told you that you are an amazing, smart girl?"

She laughs again. "Yes, you have. But I don't know if I believe you."

"Well, you'd better believe me, because it's true."

She gives me one of her famous smiles and says, "Thank you Ben."

So, why aren't I going for Gina?

I swear that the fact that she's about three inches taller than me has nothing to do with it. I get the feeling that she's hiding something in her past, an abusive relationship maybe? I sense that she's been hurt, and I don't want her to get hurt again. And I'm afraid that's just what I might do, if I was to have sex with her. I really like her, but I would feel like I was just using her for my own gratification. And I know that she deserves better.

And then things get even more complicated. Or maybe less complicated. Theresa has announced that she's going back to Carlsbad.

I happen to be working the night before she's due to fly out, and Gina, Maureen and Theresa come into the kitchen after a going away party on the town. They're all wearing nice skirts and they've all obviously been crying, as is evident by their streaked makeup, and they keep hugging each other. Pretty soon Theresa comes over to me and I hug her as well.

As she pulls away she manages a smile through teary eyes and says, "Well Ben, this means that you don't have to sleep in the living room anymore. You can take my place in Gina's room."

I give her kind of a funny look and she actually laughs. "It's okay, Gina's fine with it. And it's a big bed!"

We both laugh at that.

And now I'm almost feeling pressured. How many more signs do I need? There was the unexpected night out together with George Benson, and then the whole thing turning romantic with the champagne and all. And now I'm moving into her room.

So of course everyone thinks that we're sleeping with each other, because, well, we're sleeping with each other. And no one will believe it, but that's all we do. Somehow we're managing to keep it platonic, and so far it's working just fine.

It's only been about a month since Theresa left, and now I'm thinking about leaving too. About actually leaving Maui and going back to California. I'm sure that Andy, Dean and Chris being gone has something to do with it. But it also just feels like things are stagnating.

Another reason is that I miss snow skiing, one of my absolute favorite things to do. This is the first winter that I haven't skied since I learned how, eight years ago. And in a conspicuous place low on the list, I'm also actually thinking about college, although I haven't thought about where I'd like to go, but it's something I could talk to my parents about.

Then one day I get a letter from my brother at the Huea House. He must have got my address from our mom, and for him to send me a letter means that it must be something fairly important.

He tells me that he's getting married to his girlfriend Jeannine this coming summer, and he wants me to be in the wedding.

I take this as an omen, or maybe an agreement to what I've been thinking, and this letter is the catalyst that makes me decide to go. It's not an easy decision though. It can't be easy leaving the islands of Aloha, and I don't imagine it gets any easier the longer you stay.

A few days later Gina and I get off work at the same time, so we decide to go next door to the Whaler's Pub for a beer. After we've been there for a little while I tell her about my decision to leave. And then she surprises me by saying that she's been thinking about leaving too.

"Really?" I say.

She leans forward in her chair. "Maybe we could go together."

I'm trying to figure out how that would work, her living closer to San Diego and me living closer to L.A. But I say, "That's an idea." I take a swig of my beer. "So you've really been thinking about leaving?"

"I have, Ben." Then she says something about Theresa, and in that moment I realize that she misses her friend just like I miss mine.

She takes a drink of her beer, and when she sets it back down she says, "I have to warn you Ben, if we do this, I'm gonna be an emotional wreck. You know, like, crying and stuff."

I laugh. "That's okay. I'm gonna be a little emotional myself. Maybe we could help each other."

She holds up her beer and says, "It's a deal!"

We drink to it, but with definite hesitation, because neither one of us really wants to leave.

Her eyes glass over, and she looks out at the ocean and the island of Lanai. "Oh my God," she whispers. "It's already starting."

Gina is laying in the hammock in the Windsock Lounge,

sipping on a Blue Hawaii and determined to make every last minute count. I'm sitting at one of the small tables with my Bloody Mary, smiling at Gina when she looks over at me. And just like she said, her eyes fill up with tears about every five minutes or so.

When I told her that I wanted to take the small plane out of Kaanapali like Andy did, and asked her if she would be up for that, she got kind of excited, and said yes, she would love to do that. So here we are, up in this tiny bar, having our last Hawaiian cocktails before we leave Maui.

A fortyish couple is at the other remaining table, trying to give Gina some encouraging words. She smiles at them and says thank you, but I can tell that it isn't really helping. Because there's really nothing anyone can say that would help. She climbs out of the hammock and joins me at the table.

"I can't believe we're doing this Ben."

"I know. I can't believe it either." I try to lighten the mood by talking about some of the things that have happened since I've been here. The Hana trips, and the potato chip factory, and the Leaf Party, and the Luau's at the Ship's Wheel, and... Oops, this isn't helping, because Gina's eyes are glassing over again.

I grab her hand. "Sorry, I wasn't thinking."

She squeezes mine back. "It's okay."

"I think that's the one," I say to Gina. We're both looking out of the same little window of the plane, looking at the backside of Molokai. This side of the island is sheer cliffs, and we can see a few waterfalls streaming down their face, but they look more like thin wispy threads of mist falling in slow motion. One of them is so high that the top of it is hidden in the clouds. I tell Gina that it could be Kahiwa Falls, the highest waterfall in the Hawaiian islands.

"Wow," Gina says.

My sentiments exactly.

We keep looking out of the little window for as long as we

can, until Molokai is gone from our view.

We settle back in our seats. Next stop, Honolulu International Airport, where we will board our Jumbo Jet to California. Gina talked me into flying with her to San Diego, and then spending the night in Carlsbad. Then the next day she's going to drive me up to Seal Beach in her car. She insists that it's no big deal.

We both doze off for a couple of hours during the flight back home. When I awake Gina is sitting up and looking out the window, and it's dark outside. I lean over and look out the window too, and then I see the lights. Lights, lights, everywhere. I forgot how many lights there were.

As we start our approach into San Diego I think about what Gina told me concerning the guy who is picking us up and giving us a ride to Carlsbad. She said he is 'sort of' an ex-boyfriend, whatever that means. And she did tell him that I was going to be with her, but she warned me that he might be a little 'cold'.

After we get our bags and my backpack from baggage claim we go out front to meet him, and it isn't long before he pulls up in a 240-Z. Yeah, a two seater. Great. He hops out and gives Gina a big hug and a kiss, and I notice that he kind of looks like a cleaned up version of Jerry Garcia, with longish thick curly brown hair and a short beard. And in contrast to our shorts and flip flops he's wearing a three piece suit. He somehow manages to cram our bags and my backpack into the back of the car, and then I sit in the passenger seat with Gina sitting half in my lap, and half on the center console.

Jerry pulls onto the freeway and starts hauling ass, doing close to ninety at times. Pretty soon he reaches into his top pocket and pulls out a 'Bullet'. He does a snort and hands it to Gina, she takes a hit and hands it to me. I do a hit and, whoa... Welcome back to the fast lane.

It doesn't take him long to get us to Carlsbad, and Gina's parent's house. And just like Gina said, 'Jerry' doesn't seem too crazy about my presence, and hasn't said one word to me. In fact the only time I heard him talk the entire drive was when he asked Gina if she was going to spend the night at his place. But she declined, said she was really tired, and just wanted to sleep in her own bed. He definitely didn't seem too happy about it.

After he unloads our stuff in the driveway he gives Gina a quick hug, then he hops back in his car and does a burnout, squealing the tires down the street. It's about midnight now, and I'm sure that he must have woke up Gina's parents, if not the whole neighborhood. But as we go in the front door she tells me that her parents are out of town.

Even after doing that coke we're both totally exhausted. Gina leads me to a spare bedroom right off the kitchen with a soft comfy bed. I say goodnight and sink into that bed, and am gone to the world quickly.

The first time I awake the next morning it takes me a little while to remember where I am, but then slow realization comes over me. It's starting to get light out, but I don't know what time it is, and I fall back asleep. I wake again maybe a couple of hours later and this time I hear voices coming from the kitchen. As I become a little more alert I can tell that it's Gina talking to someone. But for some reason I don't want to move, and fall back asleep again. The next time I awake I have to pee, but I still don't want to move. Why am I so reluctant to leave this room?

I slowly shake the feeling off and open the door, and there's Gina and Theresa sitting at the dining room table drinking coffee, just as if they're back at the Huea House again.

"Good afternoon, sleepy head," Theresa says.

"Afternoon?" I say.

She laughs. "Well, it's twelve thirty."

"Wow, I guess I was tired."

She comes over and gives me a hug. "You can take a shower if you want while Gina makes you breakfast."

I laugh at that. It's really lunch time, but we ate a lot of late breakfast's back in Lahaina. "It's good seeing you again."

"Good seeing you too, Ben."

I take a shower and then eat the big breakfast that Gina has prepared, wolfing it down like I haven't eaten in days. Pretty soon Theresa has to leave, so we hug again and say our goodbye's. It's a little emotional, because we both seem to know that we probably won't see each other again.

In a little while I'm ready to go, and we load my backpack and my Aspen bag into Gina's little Toyota. We start driving North, and I thank Gina again for taking me home. It's a perfectly sunny Southern California day as we head up the coast, and we don't talk about Maui the entire drive. Maybe because it would be like grieving, and neither one of us wants to grieve right now.

"Welcome to Seal Beach," Gina says, reading the sign after we've got off the 405 Freeway and turned left onto Seal Beach boulevard.

I can't believe I'm back. Everything looks familiar, but different at the same time. And I can tell that things will never really be the same again.

As we get closer to my parent's house I notice the back side of Bullet Hill off to my right, and suddenly remember the nights down there with Andy and Dean, drinking beers and talking about moving to Hawaii.

I tell Gina which streets to turn on, until we're finally on Crestview, and she pulls into my parents driveway. We sit there for a few moments and don't say a word. Then her eyes well up with tears and we hug. We finally break loose, and then we both get out and get my stuff out of the back, which I just drop on the driveway.

We hug again, and then she says, "Bye Ben. Call me sometime."

"I will," I say.

As she drives off her hand comes out of the window making the Shaka sign, and I barely hear her say, "Aloha!"

"Aloha," I say back, but it comes out low and hoarse. I

watch her car until it turns the corner, and then she's gone.

I turn and look at my parent's house, and realize that I'm at a crossroads in my life. Whatever direction I go from here is a mystery. And aside from my big plan of going skiing, I have no idea what I'm really going to do. I know that I'm feeling a little more than melancholy, and I have no control over the tears that I can't hold back anymore.

It *isn't* easy leaving the Islands of Aloha.

1979

'Let the stories be told
Let them say what they want
Let the photos be bold
Let them show what they want

Let them leave you up in the air
Let them brush your rock and roll hair
Let the good times roll'

'Let the Good Times Roll'
The Cars

Early Summer, 1975
Seal Beach, California

"Hey everybody, I'm Jim Ladd, and this is the Mighty Met, 94.7, KMET. And I've got a pretty good idea that most of you know who this is..."

The unmistakable intro into Led Zeppelin's 'Ramble On' starts playing.

I'm sitting in my room, idly looking at the fish in my fresh water aquarium, and listening to my brand new stereo. It's a Kenwood, with a separate amplifier and tuner, and it's the new favorite thing in my life right now.

Matt has let me borrow a pair of very high quality headphones, because he feels bad for me, since he knows that I haven't bought any speakers yet. In fact all I can do is listen to the radio, because I don't have a turntable yet either. But that's okay right now, because Jim Ladd is throwing down some Led Zeppelin, and I'm loving it.

With the volume on four, which is fairly loud, I feel my Mom tap me on the shoulder. As I pull off the headphones she says, "I hope you're not ruining your eardrums with those things."

"No, Mom," I lie.

"You have a phone call. It's Matt."

"Oh, okay.. thanks Mom."

Matt and I have been hanging out quite a bit together lately. In fact he's the one who turned me on to the Kenwood stereo, which I really liked, and ended up buying. But I haven't heard from him in about a week.

I pick up the phone. "Hey Matt."

"Hey Ben. What're you doin'?"

"Oh, you know, listening to my new stereo."

"I had a feeling," he says. "And actually, that's what I wanted to talk to you about. Do you still need a turntable?"

"Oh yeah," I say.

"Well, I've got one. It's a Garrard, worth about two hundred and fifty bucks new."

"And you're gonna let me have it for..."

"Your drum set."

I'm momentarily stunned. My drum set? I haven't played it in.. I don't know how long. It's a Gretsch three piece kit, with a bass drum, a bass tom, and a snare. I also have a hi-hat and one ride cymbal. I could sell it all for maybe two hundred bucks. But why does Matt want it?

Now I'm curious. "Are you gonna start playing the drums?"

"Maybe..." he says.

Hmmm. "So you want to trade this turntable for my drums."

"Yeah man. And the turntable comes with a brand new stylus, a good one."

I believe him. When it comes to music he only buys the best. I think about it a little more. My drum set is just sitting there collecting dust, and I really want this turntable.

"Okay," I say, "It's a deal."

"Cool Ben! I'll be there in about twenty minutes."

I laugh. He's wasting no time. "Okay man, see you soon."

About a week later Matt calls me again. "Hey Ben, what're you doin'?"

"Nothing much. What's up?"

"Well, if you're not really doing anything, why don't you come over?"

"Okay," I say. "I'll see you in a little bit."

I'm glad he asked me over. I was getting a little bored, and was thinking about maybe going over there anyway and seeing what he's up too. Besides, I like getting out of Seal Beach sometimes and driving to Huntington. Matt's family moved there right about when Matt and his brother Eric started High School, Huntington Beach High School, where we all go. Well, Eric and I just graduated, but Matt will be starting his senior year in the fall. Drew is a couple of years older than Eric, and Dirk is a couple of years older than Drew. They're the Band of Brothers, and they used to live right down the street from me, on the same side of Crestview, with Bullet Hill at their backyard also.

I pull up to the front of their house in my Karmann Ghia, and shut off the motor. Matt's room faces the street on the second floor, and I can hear music. This isn't really unusual, because Matt has a killer stereo and he likes to play it loud sometimes. But something sounds different.

As I walk up the brick walkway to the front door I realize that what I'm hearing is not Matt's stereo. Those are electric guitars.

Before I can knock on the front door Matt's Mom opens it. "Hi Ben," she says, opening the door wide for me. "Go ahe on up to Matt's room. They're both up there playing their rock and roll."

I assume she means Matt and Eric. I thank her, and start heading up the stairs, listening as I go. When I get to Matt's bedroom door I hesitate before going in. They actually sound pretty good! That's got to be Eric, I know he's been playing guitar a lot lately. But who is the other one? Is that Matt? I can take it no longer, so I open the door and go in.

It's Matt and Eric of course, with electric guitars and amplifiers that I've never seen before. When they see me they instantly stop playing. They've both got huge, shit eating grins on their faces, and they don't say a word. I close the door behind me, and then something catches my eye to my right. There, kind of in the corner under the window, is my drum set. It's all polished up, and Matt has even added a few new cymbals.

I look back at them, and they just look at me, and look at the drums.. Then it hits me. The sly bastards, they had this all planned out.

And I realize that there's really only one thing for me to do, so I walk around and settle in behind the drums.

Matt looks at Eric and says, "Eighteen?"

Eric nods his head, and then Matt looks at me and says, "Eighteen Ben?"

"Sure," I say. Alice Cooper. This should be interesting.

They go into it, and I start drumming, definitely a little rusty at first. But I love this song, and I've heard it a million times, and I slowly start getting in the groove. Then, in no time at all, we connect, and it's almost like we've played this together before.

But we've never played anything together before. In fact this is the first time that I've ever played with live guitars, and I'm pretty sure it's the first time they've ever played with a drummer.

We finish the song, minus vocals of course, and Matt shouts, "Yes!!" He comes over and high fives me ecstatically. "That was great Ben!" Then he looks back at Eric. "We're a fucking band, man!!"

We all break out laughing.

And we're definitely a little excited. We play three or four more songs that they've learned, some Led Zeppelin, and some Eric Clapton, and I'm actually amazed at how it sounds. But then we stop, deciding not to push it with Matt and Eric's Mom.

But our excitement does not go away. We start talking about getting a PA system, and microphones, and a bass player. And oh yeah, who's gonna sing?

I look around Matt's room at the posters on the walls, mostly Led Zeppelin, and many of them exclusively Jimmy Page, and I start to wonder. Did Jimmy and the boys have a day like this in their lives? In someone's room or garage, bashing it out for the first time, getting all excited when it actually sounded good?

In this one afternoon in Matt's room my whole world has changed. I didn't really know if I would ever even play the drums again, but now I'm actually loving them again, thanks to Matt and Eric.

Later, on my ride back to Seal, I'm screaming along with my eight track, the volume about as loud as it will go. More excited than I've been in a long time.

And the future is wide open...

January, 1979

Matt and I are traveling North on route 395, approaching Red Rock Canyon, California. We're headed to Mammoth Lakes, and we're driving separate vehicles. He's in his '73 Capri, and I'm in 'La Bamba', my dad's '63 Impala that he bought exclusively for a Mammoth skiing car.

I've got my 'Elmo' Super eight movie camera with me, and I'm filming as I'm driving. The next day I'll have footage of Matt and the Capri in front of me, the Sierra's and Mount Whitney out of my window to the left. We'll have breakfast in the very picturesque little town of Lone Pine. I'll film a close up of the green and white highway sign bearing the towns name, and then Matt standing next to a black '30's era sedan that throws us into a state of timelessness. The car is in really good shape, but not exactly 'show' quality, and it fits the towns ambience perfectly.

So even though it's still early afternoon, we've decided to spend the night in Red Rock Canyon, because we both love the place. We love the dramatic colors, the contrasts between white sand, yellowish limestone, red rocks and blue sky. We also love the weird looking canyons, crevices and caves. I've ridden dirt bikes here a few times with my friend Ron and his Dad. Many movies have been filmed here, and the one that always comes to my mind is 'Beneath the Planet of the Apes', when they're filming scenes in the 'Forbidden Zone'.

So I'll be filming too. Matt sitting in the Capri with a long wooden pipe in his mouth that he named 'Roseburner', La Bamba behind him. Views looking out of shallow caves at white puffy clouds and blue sky. That night I'll wish I could film the stars above us as we lay in our sleeping bags, the Milky

Way bright and clear.

About two or three weeks earlier, Matt had pulled into my parents driveway one evening while I was hanging out in the garage with my older brother and a few of his friends. Well, I should say we were hanging out. My brother was always working on a car, usually someone's Volkswagen. He has become a mostly self-taught Volkswagen mechanic, and there is always at least three or four VW's in the driveway or parked on the street in front of the house. Our parents garage has turned into a hangout for his friends, and there is always plenty of Coors in the old Hotpoint garage fridge, thanks to a guy named Willy, and KMET is always playing on the radio.

Matt pulled into the driveway in his Capri, and after saying a quick hello to everyone he turned to me and said, "Hey Ben, hop in."

He wants to go somewhere, anywhere, because he has something he has got to talk to me about. He drives down Crestview, past his old house, and then turns right on Avalon which leads to the entrance of Gum Grove Park, or Bullet Hill. He stops, still on the high side of the parking lot and shuts off the motor. In front of us is a panoramic view of the lights of Long Beach and the Marina. A little to the right, mostly shrouded in darkness, are the oil derricks.

Matt turns down the radio just a little bit. Pretty soon he says, "I've got the fever now, Ben."

He looks serious, but excited, and I just let him take his time. I can only guess what this is all about.

Still looking straight ahead he says, "I've gotta get out of here and go do something somewhere. You guys have been to Hawaii, you and Dean went to Canada. Now I need an adventure."

Speaking of Dean, this whole thing is sounding very familiar. So I ask Matt the same question. "Okay, so, where do you wanna go?"

"You know me, Ben. I'm a mountain man!" Then he turns

in his seat and looks straight at me, and even holds up one finger like Dean did and says, "Tahoe goon!"

We've had a good night's sleep in Red Rock, and a great homestyle breakfast in Lone Pine, and now we're turning right off of the main highway into Mammoth Lakes Airport, which is only four or five miles outside of town. From here we have a clear view of Mammoth Mountain to the North, solitary in its grandeur.

On one side of the small steel airport terminal building is a row of about twenty five or thirty cars parked alongside the fence. They're mostly older American cars, equipped with snow tires, ski racks, and if they're smart, Die Hard batteries.

I pull La Bamba in and back it up to the fence next to the last car in the row. I take my stuff out and lock it up. Here it will sit until my dad flies up with my brother and some friends to go skiing, eliminating the need for a rental car.

Whether Dad dummied into it, or he had more vision than I gave him credit for, the '63 Impala is the perfect car for the job. With its two huge bench seats it sits six people pretty comfortably. And all of our skis, boots, poles and luggage will actually fit into the more than spacious trunk.

Al, one of the co-owners of the plane, likes to ski also, and he and his girlfriend fly up with us sometimes. Al is a very successful realtor who grew up in L.A., and he's the one who named the car 'La Bamba'. On his first ride into town in the Impala Al went into his perfected Cheech and Chong mode, joking that the car needed dingo balls, and fuzzy dice hanging from the rear view mirror, and "oh yeah Gordon, maybe lower it, and put on some twice pipes, and re-do the seats in pink and purple tuck-n-roll, and maybe paint it candy apple red man, and keep a bottle of Spanada in the back man..."

Al had us in stitches all the way to the cabin.

So, it's no more La Bamba. I load my stuff into Matt's Capri, which is somewhat of a challenge, because besides my bag of clothes I have my skis, boots and poles. but we manage to cram everything in. We turn right out of the airport and head into town. Steve lives here now, so our plan is to stay with him for a few days and maybe go skiing, before continuing on to Tahoe.

It doesn't take us long to find Steve's house, a small rental cabin with the classic mountain style A frame roof, and big gable windows on the living room side. Steve gives us a grand welcome, and then later takes us to happy hour at a place with a killer view of the mountain called the Cask and Cleaver, which Steve tells us it's referred to as the 'Crotch and Cleavage.' And he's really got this happy hour thing down, telling us that there's a different one each night, you just have to know where.

We meet a lot of Steve's friends there, guys and girls, most of whom work on the mountain like Steve does. They're a great bunch, and we have a good time talking and laughing with them.

The next evening we go to a different happy hour, and the guy at the door is checking everyone's I.D. Matt doesn't turn twenty one until August, and since he can't get in we decide to say screw it, and go pick up some beers and some munchies and take them back to Steve's cabin, where we turn up the stereo loud and have our own little happy hour.

By a funny coincidence my friend Ron, the same Ron that I went dirt bike riding with in Red Rock Canyon, happens to live here in Mammoth also. Ron and Steve grew up on Crestview in Seal Beach too. Steve right across the street from me, and Ron on the same side as me, also with Bullet Hill at his back yard.

Ron has heard that Matt and I are in town, and he wants to take us cross country skiing out to Mammoth Hot Springs. Matt has never skied before, but he's an avid hiker, so Ron's thinking that Matt shouldn't have any trouble. Ron has all the gear we need, and when we set out in the afternoon it's sunny and bright, almost feeling warm.

What we didn't foresee is that Matt is a lot bigger than Ron and I, and probably has at least fifty pounds on both of us. Ron and I are gliding along effortlessly, but with each step Matt takes he breaks through the top crust and sinks down about a foot. It's excruciatingly slow and hard for him, and I feel bad and ask him if he wants to turn back. But he says no way, and trudges on. But luckily it gets a lot easier for him in the shadows where the snow is harder, and as the shadows grow longer he starts having an easier time.

We reach the hot springs around sunset, and we all strip down and get in the water. There's really hot spots and there's cooler spots, and Ron shows us how to move around to find the perfect spot. It really feels good, and Matt is especially loving it.

Ron brought a 'Bota Bag' with him that we pass around, and pretty soon we see a big bright full moon coming up over a rise. (Ron purposely had us go late in the day, knowing that the moon would light our way back, not to mention make the trip that much more spectacular.)

We could sit here all night under the moon and stars, but we're starting to get hungry for something more than trail mix. We don't want to get out of the water though, and Ron jokes that the only thing missing is three naked women.

On the way back the moon is high in the sky, and lighting our way perfectly. The snow has hardened, and Matt is gliding along easily. A sharp contrast to his trip out, where for a while he was welcomed to hell. Now he has the biggest smile on his face out of all three of us. Back at the car we thank Ron for a truly memorable experience.

The next day Matt and I decide to go skiing on the mountain, his first time. I'm going to try and teach him how, something that I'm wholly unqualified to do. We go up chair six and I take him down Broadway, showing him how to snowplow, and telling him to just follow me and do what I do. Weight on the downhill ski, I say, and he gets that, and then switches his weight to his other ski and makes a turn.

"You're doing great!" I say, and after a few more turns I stop.

He keeps coming and then says, "How do I stop, Ben?"

While I'm fumbling for something to say, he crashes into me, and we both fall down. It's pretty comical, and we're both laughing. Even with my terrible instruction Matt gets the basics down that day, and has a great time.

We've been staying with Steve for almost a week now, and I can tell that Matt's getting a little restless. He's ready to get back on the road and get to Tahoe, and so am I.

It's Saturday, and Steve asks us if we want to go to a party at a friend's house. It's an outdoor afternoon affair, with a big fire ring and twenty or thirty people, some of whom we met at the Cask and Cleaver.

There's also a guy playing acoustic guitar, and he's pretty good. As Matt and I move a little closer to give him a listen, he goes into a Neil Young song. But he's tweaking the lyrics a little bit.

'You can't be twenty, on Mammoth Mountain
Though you're thinking that your leaving there too soon
You're leaving there too soon'

Matt and I look at each other, the irony of this not lost on either one of us.

'Now you say you're leaving home
'Cause you want to be alone
Ain't it funny how you feel
When you're finding out it's real'

Matt moves in close to me. "Did you hear that Ben? That guy is fucking bagging it!!" He pauses, and then says, "I say we leave tomorrow."

I laugh. And I also agree, and we shake hands on it.

We mingle around the party, having a good time, happy with our decision. Everyone is really engaging with us, and it almost feels like this party was solely for our benefit.

The next morning we say goodbye to Steve and thank him for everything. He tells us that if we have any problems we're always welcome back here. We thank him again, and get on the road.

We're tooling along somewhere between Mammoth Lakes and June Mountain, and I'm filming again. It's a picture perfect postcard day, and out the passenger window I film some small herds of sheep, and a little further on, what I want to believe are wild horses.

Not too long later Matt tells me that Mono Lake is coming up, and I definitely want to get some footage there. I end up getting some shots of some salt formations, trying to recreate the postcard in my Pink Floyd 'Wish You Were Here' album, but not with very good results. I do record a pretty spectacular sunset though, and some seagulls flying around. It's weird seeing seagulls here, hundreds of miles from the ocean, on the backside of the Sierras. We spend the night here in our sleeping bags, the stars even more dramatic than the night we spent in Red Rock.

The next day we hit Reno, Nevada at around noon and decide to eat lunch there. We go into one of the Casino's and get a table at the restaurant. Neither one of us knows what 'Keno' is, but we notice the Keno pads on all of the tables, and even in the restroom. Matt picks one up and checks it out, then pulls off a couple of sheets and slides one over to me with a pencil.

"Pick some numbers Ben," he says. Then he looks at the different scenarios that you can possibly win. "Wow," he says. "If you bet a buck, and get three out of five, you win a thousand bucks!"

We decide to bet a buck a piece and pick twelve numbers, thinking that our chances of winning might be better. During lunch our waitress brings our tickets back, and to Matt she says, "Congratulations!"

She leaves and Matt looks at his ticket. Then his eyes go wide.

"What?" I say.

He laughs, and then says, "I just won a hundred and eighty bucks!"

He shows it to me, and indeed he has hit six or seven numbers out of twelve. He pushes it over to me. "You cash it in Ben. I don't want to take a chance getting I.D.'d again."

When I come back with his cash he hands me a dollar and says, "Let's play one more time, see if this was just beginners luck."

We both lose the second time and decide it was. On the way out to the car we joke about writing a song.

'Little did we know
When we got to Reno
We'd have some luck at Keno'

Yeah, pretty bad.

Winding through some beautiful mountain country, with tall fir trees and massive granite outcroppings, we finally get our first glimpse of North Lake Tahoe. We're next to Crystal Bay, and we decide to stop there and go down and check out the water. It really is crystal clear, and we can easily see the bottom in the shallower parts of the bay. We walk down to the water's edge and stick our hands in, feeling just how cold it really is.

"The water only gets a few degrees warmer in the Summer," Matt tells me.

I look out onto this huge expanse of water, and I have no way of knowing that in about ten years from now I will be coming back up here with Andy. We'll be in my Dads truck, towing a boat, a small Donzi that Andy is returning to its owner. It will be the heart of the winter then too, and our destination will be the Sunnyside Inn, also in North Lake Tahoe, and a restaurant that Andy had helped open.

While we're coming around the north side of the lake Andy will say, "You know Ben, the name Tahoe, it's a Native American word. You know what it means?" I'll shake my head, and he'll spread his arms wide and say, "Big!"

We'll both laugh.

Matt and I are standing on a boulder next to the bay, and he says, "I'd really like to stay up here on the North Shore, but I know that we have a lot better shot at jobs and a cheaper place to stay in South Lake."

I remember Steve suggesting to us to try and get work at Heavenly Mountain, the sprawling ski resort in South Lake Tahoe. We climb back up to the Capri and start to make our way south along the shoreline. At one point Matt starts humming the tune to the TV show 'Bonanza', and I soon realize why. Off to our left is the 'Ponderosa', where they would film from time to time. Filming quit in 1973, so now it's just a tourist attraction.

We go through a tunnel at Zephyr Point, and then descend into Stateline. High rise Casino's suddenly jut up into the air around us, and then abruptly stop at the border. We pass through them and then suddenly we're in California again.

It's late afternoon, so we decide to find a cheap motel room for the night, and then go back to one of the Casino's to eat. We noticed a few of them advertising 3.99 all you can eat buffet's. Sounds like the ticket to us.

"This must be it," Matt says.

It's the next morning, and we're in front of the Black Rock Inn, which is obviously an old motel that has been turned into rentals. Matt found it in the 'rooms for rent' section of the paper. It's actually walking distance from the lake, easily less than a quarter of a mile, and it's also walking distance from the border, and the Casino's. There's a one bedroom available for two hundred and fifty bucks. It's furnished, with a Queen size bed in the bedroom, and a 'hide-a-bed' in the living room, and the rest is very worn looking, Old American style tables and chairs. The kitchen is small but adequate. Weighing the pro's and con's, we decide to take it.

That evening just before sunset we celebrate our new place by getting a six pack and walking down to the lake. We reach the shoreline, and the long flat beach is covered in about four inches of snow. Just to our left are about a dozen two-seater pedal boats chained together and looking out of place, waiting for summer. We walk over to them, and then notice that the one on the end is unchained from the others. Matt and I look at each other, and then grab the boat by the bow and drag it the short distance to the waterline. We hop in with our beers and start pedaling straight out onto the calm lake, which is a perfect mirror of the sunset above.

We get maybe two or three hundred yards out and stop pedaling, taking in the serenity of the oncoming twilight. Then Matt looks down and says, "Oh shit Ben.. we're taking on water!" He looks back at the shore. "If we sank right now we probably wouldn't make it back. Hypothermia would set in before we reached the beach."

That's all I need to hear, so I start pedaling, and so does Matt, and we do a slow one eighty and start heading back to the shore. We make good time and pretty soon the bow of the boat bumps onto the snow covered beach.

Matt looks down again and says, "We hardly took on any more water. Lucky for us it's a slow leak."

The following morning we go to the main lodge of Heavenly Mountain, on the California side, to see about jobs. After finding the administrative office, a woman gives us applications to fill out. When we're done she takes us down a short hallway and knocks twice before opening a large door. We hear a man say 'come in', and she ushers us into a large office room with high vaulted ceilings and big plate glass windows looking out onto the slopes. A man maybe in his early forties sits behind a huge oak desk, the windows behind him, and stands and shakes our hands and motions for us to have a seat in two high back leather chairs. He thanks the woman and she leaves, shutting the door behind her.

After a little small talk, asking us where we're from and other things, he asks if we both know how to ski.

Matt looks at me, and I say, "I do."

The man looks at me and says, "Are you at least an intermediate skier?"

"You bet," I reply.

"I have an opening at the East Peak Lodge on the Nevada

side, bussing tables, flipping burgers, stuff like that. I see on your application that you worked at some restaurants in Hawaii. Does this sound like something you'd be interested in?"

"Sounds great!" I say, trying not to sound too excited.

"The East Peak Lodge is up on the mountain," he continues. "You'll take a chairlift up to it from the Nevada Base Lodge."

"Okay," I say.

Then he looks over at Matt. "I also have an opening at this same base lodge. If you two are riding together it might work out quite nicely for you."

"Sounds perfect," Matt says, looking over at me with hilarious disbelief.

"Good. Great." He pauses for a second, and then says, "Can you guys start tomorrow?"

"Sure, we can do that."

"Okay, great!" he says. "Just be at the Nevada Base Lodge tomorrow morning at seven thirty."

"No problem," we both say. We stand and thank him and shake his hand again, and then go back out that huge door and make our way back to the car.

When we're outside Matt says, "Can you believe that Ben? That was almost too easy. We've got fucking jobs!"

We high five each other, and I say, "And we've got the whole day off! What should we do?"

"I'll tell you what we're gonna do," Matt says. "We're going to drive all the way around this entire lake! And we're gonna check out Emerald Bay!"

We get in the Capri and start driving around the lake, happy as loons.

The next morning after driving to the base lodge I say so long to Matt, and he goes inside the lodge to find his new manager. I go out front and get on the chairlift with a co-worker I just met named Paul. He's my age, a few inches taller than me with curly brown hair and blue eyes. He tells me that this is his second season working at Heavenly, his first at the East Peak Lodge.

"The East Peak Lodge is brand new," he's telling me, as the chair whisks us up through the trees. "And it's real nice. It's probably the best place to work on the mountain. You're lucky you got on here."

As I'm looking around, I'm feeling pretty lucky.

"The first thing you'll probably be doing is helping to make burger patties," Paul's saying. "Then later on we grill them out on the patio if it isn't snowing. Then we'll be bussing tables, which is easy and fun."

"Sounds cool," I say. Then looking down I ask, "What's this run below us?"

"Oh yeah," he says, "that's the run we'll be taking back down at the end of the day. It's called Olympic, because the downhillers trained on it for the 1960 Olympics at Squaw Valley."

The 1960 Olympics. I was turning three.

"Some of us like to race each other down to the bottom. It's pretty fun."

I look at his skis. They're at least 205's, long and fast. I've got 185 Rossignol Freestyles, definitely not downhill racing skis, but I can still move along pretty good on them.

"That does sound fun," I say. "Does everyone have long skis like you?"

He laughs. "A few of us do. We're into speed."

About half way up we see a snow cat below us, slowly winding its way up the mountain. It's loaded down with all kinds of supplies.

"That's Bo," Paul says. "He brings up everything we need for the lodge. We'll be helping him unload."

I already feel kind of sorry for Bo. It's a round trip for him, so he doesn't get to ski back down at the end of the day.

We finally reach the top, and just before we get off Paul points behind us. "There's the lodge."

It's not far away at all, maybe a couple of hundred yards,

and we ski down to it and around to the back. We take off our skis and Paul leads me to a room with lockers to store them. I take off my daypack and pull out my Sorel's. I obviously can't be walking around in my ski boots all day.

Paul introduces me to anyone that we bump into, and then takes me to meet Frank, our manager. Frank looks to be in his late thirties, and has shortish brown hair and a stocky build. He's wearing jeans and a flannel shirt, and looks more like a construction contractor than a lodge manager. He comes off kind of gruff, but nice, and shakes my hand with authority, releasing it just before the point of serious pain.

Then he smiles and says , "Good to meet you," and that's when I notice a hint of mischief in his eyes, and realize that he's light heartedly fucking with me.

After a few words he says, "Get with Paul here, and he'll show you how to make burger patties."

It's a beautiful sunny day, and at around ten thirty or so we wheel two big grills out onto the huge front deck. They get loaded up with real hardwood charcoal and promptly lit. By 11:30 the aroma of char grilled burgers is rising up from the lodge and into the trees. Skiers by the dozen start filing in, lured by the smell of the grill that is drifting up into the mountain.

And then it hits me. Maybe Frank might just be as smart as Walter. Because this whole thing is reminding me of the Luau at the Ship's Wheel.

By the end of day I've met the three friends of Paul's that like to race each other back down the mountain, and they encourage me to join in. I ride the chair up with Paul, and I notice that his friends have long skis too. When we get to the top they all take off, and I do my best to keep up with them, but they're pulling away from me. The mountain is closed now, so there's no one else on it, and we're the last one's down, free to go as fast as we can. And I'm really loving this speed thing, just pointing them downhill and going for it. When I catch up to them at the bottom, I decide right then and there that I'm getting longer skis as soon as I can.

After saying so long to Paul and the others, I meet up with Matt at the base lodge and ask him how his day was.

"It was okay," he says. "Spent most of the day making sandwiches. We make sandwiches for pretty much the entire mountain, including your lodge."

Now I feel kind of guilty. While I was up there having fun, Matt was down here in a kitchen all day making sandwiches. And no matter how hard I try, I'm not doing a very good job of hiding the fact that this is looking to be the most fun job that I've ever had.

"Everyone talks about you guys up at East Peak," Matt says. "How it's the best place to work on the mountain." He looks at me. "Looks like you really scored, Ben."

Damn. Now I really feel bad.

The end of our first week comes, and with it, our first pay-check. Everyone tells us not to cash our checks at the bank, but at one of the Casino's instead. Depending on which one you go to, they might give you a couple of free drink tokens, or maybe a pull on a handle.

Matt and I get in the Capri and follow a few of our co-workers to 'Park Tahoe Resort and Casino,' which looks to be brand new. We go inside and make our way through the lights and the bells, the black jack tables and the craps tables, past the many different themed bars, with pretty cocktail wait-resses wearing short black skirts and white sleeveless button up tops, until we finally reach a cashiers booth.

When we cash our checks we receive two drink tokens and a free pull on a slot machine. But this isn't just any slot ma-chine. It's up in the bed of a brand new four wheel drive truck. And this isn't just any four wheel drive truck either. It's a truck the likes of which neither Matt nor I have ever seen.

Just shy of a monster truck, it's impossibly high off the ground on huge off road tires. It's got double roll bars with a multitude of lights, and triple shock absorbers all the way around. It's super high gloss paint job, a two tone dark blue down low into a tannish brown up above, sparkles in the Casino's bright lights. And it's also got a powerful sounding stereo system that's turned on and thumping out of the rolled down windows.

There's a red carpeted staircase that leads up to the open tailgate and the huge slot machine in the bed. I climb the stairs and walk up to pull the handle, which has got to be four feet long. This machine has four 'wheels', and if they come up Truck-Truck-Truck-Truck, I'm the big winner. I pull the handle and then stand back and watch, but of course it comes up nothing. Matt comes up behind me and pulls the handle too, and then starts laughing.

On our way back out we notice a few people we know from work sitting at one of the bars. A girl I work with named 'Sunshine' sees us and invites us over.

I look at Matt and say, "Well, what do you say we use up these free drink tokens?"

Matt agrees, and we sit at the bar next to Sunshine and order up a couple of beers. Pretty soon I notice a guy sitting at one of the tables, another co-worker, and he doesn't look so good. He's got kind of a blank, vacant expression on his face, and slowly sips his cocktail.

Sunshine sees me looking at him, and then whispers to us, "He just lost his whole paycheck at the black jack table."

Matt and I look at each other. Wow, that was quick! An entire weeks work gone with the flip of a few cards. This is our first glimpse into the dark side of gambling.

On about our third or fourth payday Matt and I are back in Park Tahoe again. We have just cashed our checks and we're about to pull the handle in the back of truck. The fact that the truck is still here tells me something about the odds.

Matt goes up the stairs first this time to try his luck. After pulling the handle with the usual result he comes back down the stairs, muttering something like, "No big surprise there!"

Then I go up, and not expecting anything different I go

through the motions, pull the handle, and then turn to leave.

But then something happens.

I look back at the slot machine, and it's going crazy. All of its lights start flashing, bells start ringing, and a siren goes off. I'm frozen in shock, and my legs suddenly feel rubbery. There's no way... Did I just win the truck? Then I look at the wheels of the slot machine and they say 75-75-75-75. I slowly realize that I didn't win the truck, but I did win seventy five bucks. Which is nothing to sneeze at. But man, what a come down...

That evening after dinner, since it's a calm clear night, Matt and I grab a few beers out of the fridge and walk down to the lake. It's the end of twilight, and the stars sparkle on the glassy surface of the water. We drag the pedal boat to the waterline and hop in. We know now about the slow leak, so we just keep it in mind and don't pedal out too far. We stop and float, awestruck by the scene all around us.

After a little while Matt looks over his beer at me and says, "Correct me if I'm wrong Ben, but for a second there today you really thought you won that truck, didn't you?"

I laugh. "You're not wrong. For a second there I thought I did win that truck. I almost fainted on the spot."

Matt laughs. "I thought so. But you did win seventy five bucks, which is better than nothing."

"Yeah, but can you imagine it? If one of us were to win that truck? We could just sell the Capri, and then when we finally headed back home we would ride back into town in style!"

Matt laughs again. "That would be pretty cool."

"Can you see us pulling into Seal Beach in that thing? All of our friends drooling over it and wanting a ride? And maybe going to Benny Rapp's and making Bone and Kim jealous? That thing would dwarf their little F-150's! And then, after a while we could just sell it and split the money. What do you think that truck's worth?"

"I have no idea," Matt says. And then after a pause, "Yeah, that would be nice, but..."

"Probably not gonna happen," I finish for him.

"Probably not. It's a nice fantasy though."

With that thought in mind, we start pedaling back in.

A week or so goes by, and it's one bright and beautiful sunny day after another. It feels nice, but Heavenly needs some more snow. If this keeps up it could be a short season.

With short notice our friends Scott and Todd show up from Seal Beach for a visit, and Matt and I manage to get a day off together. We decide to take advantage of the weather and take them around the lake to Emerald Bay. We've got the little inflatable boat with us, the same one that Dean and I took to Canada, and our plan is to paddle out to the little island in the center of the bay.

On the drive there Todd asks, "So you guys know of a spot at the bay where you actually jump in the water?"

"That's right Todd," Matt says. "It's one big rock area that slowly angles into the water, and once you dive in it's easy to climb back out."

Scott looks at Todd and says, "And that water is..."

"Freezing ass!" Matt continues. "But on a day like today, sunshine and no wind, it feels amazing when you get back out!"

"Quite the rush," I add.

Todd laughs. "That's why I like you guys. You're both crazy!"

We reach the bay and park the car. We grab the inflatable boat and the foot pump and walk the short distance to the rock area that Matt was talking about. It's on the left side of the bay, and looks straight out to the little island.

Todd is not about to jump in the water until he sees one of us do it. But he doesn't have to wait long, because Scott has already stripped down to his shorts and is running down the rock towards the water. He dives in head first like he's in a swim race, and he should know how because he's been in many.

Scott slowly climbs back out of the water, stands up and lets out a shout that echoes around the bay. "That was great!" he yells.

Matt and I follow suit, although not quite as gracefully as Scott.

Todd knows that he has to go now, or risk being thrown in by Scott. He's already down to his shorts, and runs and jumps in, and in one fluid motion he's out again, like he's part seal or something.

Matt's laughing so hard he can barely breathe. "That was awesome Todd!" he says, trying to regain some composure. "I don't think I've ever seen anything go in and out of the water that fast!"

Todd's laughing too. "It does feel great now though!" he says as he towels off in the sun.

After we get the boat inflated we take turns in pairs rowing out to the little island. Scott and I go together and take our time exploring the island, and the little 'castle' on top. It's such a nice day, and we just relax there for a little while soaking up the sun.

On the way back to town I notice that we all got a little bit of a sunburn on our faces. I look at Heavenly Mountain off in the distance and notice brown patches here and there on Gun Barrel.

"Man, we really need some more snow."

"That we do," Matt replies.

Early the next morning I'm walking up to the chairlift to go to work when Bo, the snow cat driver, intercepts me. Bo is about five six, with a stocky build and closely cropped blonde hair.

"Hey Ben," he says, "Wanna ride up with me in the snow cat?" He flashes a joint real quick in his top pocket and smiles.

I laugh. "Sure," I say.

We walk up to the snow cat, which Bo has already loaded. "Just throw your skis and poles in the back somewhere."

I stow my skis and poles and then climb into the cabin. I've never been in a snow cat before, and it's actually a lot roomier than I thought. It's really quite comfortable, and as we get going I notice that the heater really cranks. I think of the occasional windy mornings when the rest of us were all freezing our asses off on the chairlift, and realize that Bo was in here, all toasty warm.

We slowly make our way up the mountain on a road that is a series of switchbacks. I'm seeing parts of the mountain that no one else can see, unless they were to hike up this road. There's tall stands of pines, and then all of a sudden a stunning view of a valley.

Bo sparks up the joint and passes it to me, then does a sweeping motion with his hand and asks, "How do you like it so far?"

"I love it," I say, passing the joint back. "But I've got to ask you though. Don't you ever miss skiing back down at the end of the day?"

"Actually, I do get to. Every now and then, maybe once or twice a week, Frank will offer to drive the snow cat back down so I can ski."

"Wow, really? I didn't know that."

"Yeah, Frank's pretty cool. Plus, I think he likes driving the snow cat sometimes."

After a little while Bo asks me, "So, have you had your paid ski-day-off yet?"

I look at him. "Paid ski-day-off? I never heard about it."

"Oh. Well, we're all on a rotation, and each day someone gets the day off paid and can go skiing. Of course you could just go home if you wanted to, but most everyone takes advantage of the free skiing."

"Yeah? Well, I know I would!" And I'm thinking, this

really is the coolest job ever.

After about an hour or so we reach the lodge, and I help Bo unload all of the supplies. I then stash my skis and poles at my locker, but I can't stop thinking about that paid day off.

One Friday after work Matt and I are sitting a few seats apart in the Keno area, at the Park Tahoe Casino. Right now we're actually really playing, betting a dollar and picking some numbers. But sometimes we'll just pretend to play, because either way a waitress will come around and give us a free cocktail of our choice. We're starting to learn little tricks of the trade.

At one point Matt gets up and walks by me, throwing his ticket on my desk. Then he keeps going and walks out of the room. This means that he has a winning ticket and he wants me to cash it in. I take it up to the cashier lady, and she counts out three hundred and twenty bucks and hands it to me. Holy shit! Matt has really hit the jackpot this time! He is now officially the Keno King!

I meet up with him by the front doors, and when I give him his money he says, "Ben, we're gonna celebrate tonight. We're gonna have a real nice dinner, and then we're gonna see a movie."

Across the street from Park Tahoe is Harrah's Casino, which is right on the lake. On the very top floor is a bar/restaurant with a fantastic view. Later that night we go there and order up steak dinners with all of the trimmings. Then we go downstairs to their theater, and this is one cool idea for a theater. Instead of regular seating it has comfortable couches with end tables, and reclining chairs.

We settle into one of the couches, and lo and behold, here comes a waitress! We can order a cocktail, and even play Keno while we watch the movie! I've got to hand it to these Casino guys, they think of everything.

The movies aren't new releases, but we don't care. Tonight it's 'Butch Cassidy and the Sundance Kid', and there's no

THE BULLET HILL DIARIES

previews to sit through. When it's time, they just start the movie.

We kick back with our cocktails, and pretty soon it's, 'I'm sorry, I can't help you Sundance.'

And then, 'I didn't know you were the Sundance Kid when I said you were cheatin'.

And then, 'Hey Kid, how good are ya?'

'Bam, bam, bam-bam-bam!'

And later on, 'You just keep thinkin' Butch, that's what yer good at.'

'Man, I have vision and the rest of the world wears bifocals!'

Early one morning at the beginning of my shift I'm stuffing my daypack into my locker, when Paul approaches me. He kind of looks around, then opens his hand and says, "Check this out."

In his hand is a tiny little piece of paper with an image of Mickey Mouse, the Sorcerer's Apprentice on it.

A hit of LSD.

"Sunshine gave it to me," he says. Then he starts grinning. "You wanna split it with me?"

I look at him. "You mean like, now? While we're working?"

He laughs. "Yeah man, it'll be a gas!"

While I'm thinking about it he pulls out a pocket knife, and then very carefully cuts the hit in half on the bench seat. He takes one half and puts it on his finger, and then puts it on his tongue. He hands the other half to me.

"This is just a little bit crazy," I say. Then I put the half hit to my tongue, and swallow. No turning back now.

Paul starts laughing. "This is gonna be one hell of a day!"

Little do I know how true his statement is.

Maybe half an hour later I feel myself starting to come on. In that same instant one of the girls passes me, then stops and turns around. "Oh hey Ben, Frank wants to see you."

I suddenly freeze in unnecessary terror. Frank wants to see me? What the hell does he want to see me about? I gather my wits as best as I can and make my way up to his office.

When I get up there I notice that the door to his tiny office is open as usual, and he's sitting at his desk under a dingy light doing paperwork. I feel certain that if he takes one good look at me he'll know something's up.

But without even looking up he says, "It's your turn, get outta' here."

"Huh?" I manage.

Then he spins in his chair, looks straight at me and smiles. "It's your turn to go skiing. Go! Get the hell outta' here! And have fun!"

Sometimes, just sometimes, things like this happen. Just sometimes, the planets all line up, the timing is perfect, and everything falls into place.

I'm doing everything but peeing my pants as I get on the chairlift in front of the lodge. The sendoff I just got was unbelievable, everybody cheering me on, making me feel like I'm in a movie or something. And Paul, sitting there at one of the booths, looking at me with kaleidoscope eyes, saying, "Have a great day Ben, you lucky bastard!"

While I'm riding up the chair I reach into the inside pocket of my jacket and pull out a map of the mountain. Without unfolding it I look at it and laugh, and then stuff it back into my jacket.

I don't need a map.

I'm just going to go up every chairlift on this mountain, and ski every run that I possibly can.

I meet all kinds of interesting people riding the chairlifts. I talk to a college professor who says to me, "Yes, have fun now! But think about what you really want to do with your life, and plan for the future." I ride up with another guy, probably five years older than me, who says, "Just live for today, you could die tomorrow." I ride with a business man in his fifties.

"You never know what's going to happen. I got to college with one major in mind, and after my freshman year I ditched that for something completely different." I ride with kids younger than me, and also with retirees, and I learn something new from every one of them.

I make it over to the California side and ski Gun Barrel, the big mogul run that you can see from town and across the lake. I'm sure I didn't ski every run on the mountain, but by the end of the day it feels like I have. I just make it back to the Nevada side and then down to the base lodge where Matt works by closing time.

As I'm climbing into the Capri with Matt I remember what Paul had said this morning. 'It's gonna be one hell of a day!' And indeed it has.

While Matt pulls us out of the lodge parking lot he says, "How was your day Ben?"

I start laughing. "You remember that time when we went to the movies and saw Fantasia, with Mickey Mouse as the Sorcerer's Apprentice?..."

It's snowing. We've needed this for a while, and now it's finally really snowing. It's been snowing most of the day, and after we get off work it snows into the night. Matt and I pick up some beers and take them back to the apartment. We start throwing them back and occasionally check on the snowfall out front.

But then, something goes wrong. We get into a quarrel about something trivial, I don't even remember what. What I do remember is, while I'm getting angry, Matt is staying calm. My anger won't subside, and I can't seem to snap out of it.

At one point I grab the car keys off the table and head out the door. I get into the Capri and start driving, no destination in mind. The snow is still coming down really heavy, but I don't give it a second thought. The Capri has chains on it, the new plastic kind, and they work okay, but not as well as real chains.

I drive through town heading south, just aimlessly driving. Before I know it I'm heading up the mountain pass, the town of Stateline far behind me. I suddenly come to my senses and realize where I am. What the hell am I doing? I've got to turn around. But now there's no easy place to do it.

Pretty soon the road starts curving to the right and seems to get a little wider. I decide that this is as good a place as any, and whip the wheel to the left. The front of the car just touches the snowbank and I throw it into reverse, but the tires just spin. Damn these plastic chains! Just then I see headlights approaching from around the bend, and the ass end of the Capri is sticking straight out into the road. The approaching car slams on their brakes, but this just causes them to lose traction, and the car rams into my right rear fender. This causes me to spin around, and I'm momentarily free, but I do a complete three sixty and then nose back into the snowbank, stuck again.

The car that hit me slowly comes to a stop a short distance down the road. I get out and look at the Capri, and there's a small dent in the right rear fender, but nothing major. I walk down to the other car and notice that it's a newer Volkswagen Bug. Two girls get out, a blonde and a brunette, both of them gorgeous and about my age. The brunette is the driver, and she's taking it pretty well, but she doesn't know what to do because her severely smashed front fender is pinching down onto her tire, preventing the car from moving at all.

The ass of the Capri is still sticking out into the road, and I'm worried about another car coming around the bend, and this whole thing happening again. My adrenaline is up, so I put my right foot on her tire and grab the damaged fender with both hands and pull up with all of my might. I manage to bend the fender up a couple of inches off the tire, so now at least they can drive. This really makes them happy, and they both thank me heartily. I caused this accident, and they're thanking me.

The brunette and I exchange information, and then she notices the Capri and asks if I need help. I feel bad accepting their help, but I sure as hell can't get it out by myself. So I feather it in reverse while they push from the front, and soon I'm free and facing in the right direction. These are some good girls, and I find myself really wishing that we could have met under different circumstances. I thank them and say so long. And all the while the snow continues to come down.

When I get back to the apartment I go in and apologize to Matt. Then I tell him that I met a couple of cute girls, and even got an address and a telephone number. But there's something he needs to look at, and I take him out and show him the Capri...

It's been about three weeks since the snowstorm, and the car crash incident. The snowfall did some good for a little while, but now sunshine and warmer temps are creeping back in. It's early March, and it seems as though Spring just can't wait to get its foot in the door.

There's no more snow on the roads, and we take the well-worn 'chains' off of the Capri. Heavenly starts closing down parts of the mountain, mostly on the California side. Lay-offs start happening, a few at East Peak, and a lot more at the base lodge where Matt works. Matt decides he's had enough of making sandwiches, and quits. And I don't blame him.

We start talking about leaving and heading back down South. But Matt doesn't want to go home yet, and starts talking about Mexico. Maybe driving down Baja California all the way to Cabo San Lucas. I don't really want to go home yet either, and now he's got me thinking about warm beaches, and fishing, and taco's and margarita's.

After another week or so we decide it's time, and I quit my job at East Peak. I say goodbye to Frank and Bo and everyone, but Paul tells me that his parents are out of town and he wants to have an 'end of the season' party at his house.

"Sound's cool," I say. "Matt and I will be there."

Paul lives in a nice part of South Lake, in a big three story mountain home among the trees. In fact one big pine goes right through the house, and another one through a hole in the deck. This is because of an ordinance that prohibits cutting down any trees, so they had to build around them.

When Matt and I get there the music is playing, and there's a few people from East Peak that we know, and more people that we don't. We mostly hang out on the deck, drinking cocktails and admiring the house. It's a pretty mellow party, and the talk seems to be mostly about the lack of snow and the early spring. But it's a nice way to say goodbye to these people, since we know that we will probably never see each other again. And the whole thing seems a fitting end to our little Tahoe adventure.

The next morning we turn in the key to our apartment, and then start making our way South out of Stateline, South Lake Tahoe. And no, we're not leaving in the fantasy 4x4, riding high above everyone else like kings. No, we're still in the Capri, which has a new dent in the right rear quarter panel, and basically looks like it's been through hell.

We start heading up the mountain pass and soon reach the spot where I got into the accident. "Right about here," I say, cringing.

We keep climbing in altitude, and the higher we get the more snow there is on the ground, and it starts looking like winter again. We drive by the Kirkwood Ski Resort and see people parking and walking to the lifts with their skis, and I get a sudden pang of regret, and wonder if we're leaving too soon. I want to get out and go skiing one more time, but I don't say anything, and soon the feeling passes, along with the mountains and the snow, and everything else.

And it's not that we *really* feel like we're leaving the mountains too soon. It's not that I'm already missing the most fun job that I ever had, or the friends I made while working there. It isn't the look on Matt's face when he hands me a winning Keno ticket and walks away, or the spectacular sunsets on the lake as seen from the leaky pedal boat, that slowly turn to a dazzling array of stars. It isn't even the thrill of racing my co-worker friends down the mountain at the end of the day, or the full moon Friday night that we partied in the lodge, skiing down at midnight with Mr. Moon lighting our way. Or the occasional ride up in the morning with Bo in the snow cat. It's not the salt formations at Mono Lake, or Steve's hospitality at Mammoth, or cross country skiing with Ron to the hot springs, or La Bamba, or even Red Rock Canyon. It's not even that there seems to be a second recurrence of a gas shortage going on, with long lines at the pumps, making us decide that it's probably not a good idea to go to Baja right now.

It's none of these things.

Or maybe it's all of them at the same time.

Whatever the reasons, when we reach Southern California neither one of us wants to go home to our parent's house yet. When we get back to Huntington Beach, Matt takes Golden West street to Huntington Beach Central Park, pulls in and parks by the big library.

"Let's just hang out in here for a little while, okay Ben?"

"Sure," I say.

We grab our sleeping bags and walk a short distance into the park, plopping down in a grassy area next to a pond under some big eucalyptus trees. It's late afternoon and kind of foggy and cool, but it feels warm to us. We're still used to the cold mountain air.

We lie in our sleeping bags and talk a little bit about our trip, but we both nod off after a while, tired from the drive.

When we wake it's getting dark, and the reality of being back is weighing on us. Neither one of us really knows what our next game plan is, and we're in no mood to go home to our parents and answer questions on the subject.

It's well into the evening, probably eight or nine o'clock, when we finally decide it's time to go, and quit putting off the inevitable. We gather up our sleeping bags and slowly make our way back to the Capri. Matt drives me to Seal Beach and drops me off at my parent's house. He helps me get my stuff out of the car, and then shakes my hand.

"It was great Ben!"

"Yeah, it was," I say.

"I'll talk to you soon. Take it easy."

"You too man."

So here I am again, in my parents driveway with my luggage again.

At a crossroads, again.

May, 1979

I pick up the phone in my parent's house. "Hey Ben, it's Dean."

Hey Goob, how's it Brah?"

He laughs at my pigeon. "It's good Brah." He pauses a second, and then says, "I was just wondering what you were doing tomorrow. Are you going to the Pancake Breakfast?"

"Yeah, actually I was thinking about going to that."

"Okay, cool. Sara and I are going too. Will you be riding your bike?"

"Yeah man, it's all I got right now. Well, that and La Bamba, when it's here."

He laughs again. "Okay, good. Sara and I will be on our bikes too. We'll meet you down there."

"Okay man, see you then."

The Seal Beach Pancake Breakfast, hosted by the Lion's Club, has been a local tradition for many years. Our family started going when my sister and brother and I were quite young, back when my Dad was still a member of the Lion's Club. It's usually held on the first Saturday in May, and they close off part of Central Avenue where it meets Main Street in between John's Food King and the Bank of America and set up tables and chairs. You can smell the bacon and sausages cooking from blocks away, and you're sure to see 'Big Dave' Stangeland, owner of 'Dave's Other Place', behind one of the many grills.

The next day dawns sunny and warm, a picture perfect day, and feels like the beginning of the Summer to come. I'm in shorts, a T shirt and flip flops, and ride my bike downtown and park it next to the Bank. I look around for Dean and Sara, but I don't see them anywhere. I might be a little early, or they might be a little late, so I go ahead and get my breakfast. Along with my heaping plate of pancakes, bacon and sausage, I also get about four or five little cups of orange juice.

I see and talk with many people, friends and neighbors, and parents of friends. After about an hour or so it's getting kind of crowded, so I decide to walk around and look for Dean and Sara. I end up back by my bike, and there they are! Dean, Sara, and another girl, a cute brunette talking with Sara. They've all got their bikes next to mine, and I figure that Dean must've spotted my bike and decided to wait there for me.

Sara sees me first and says, "Ben!" She's all smiles and comes up and gives me a hug.

"Hey Sara," I say, hugging her back.

Then she kind of steps back and says, "Ben, I want you to meet someone. This is my friend, Jacki."

Jacki gives me a shy smile and the hint of a blush, and says, "Nice to meet you Ben."

"Nice to meet you too."

Then I look at Sara, and she and Jacki look at each other, and they both look a little guilty, like they've just been caught with their hands in the cookie jar. Then I look over at Dean, and he's got a big smile going, and gives me a quick wink. Now it's my turn to blush, because I finally realize that I've been set up.

I look back at Jacki again, and I'd be lying if I said that my heart didn't skip a couple of beats. Jacki's got a terrific figure, and she's definitely not hiding it, wearing Dolphin shorts, and a halter top that is barely containing her more than ample breasts.

Dean steps in at the perfect time and says, "So hey, what do you say we take a little cruise, go down to the boardwalk, check out the beach?"

We all agree, and get on our bikes. As we slowly cruise down Main Street I start thinking; that ol' sly Deano. He obviously worked this all out with Sara. They've both been on me lately, telling me how I need to get a girlfriend. And since I haven't really shown any results in that department, they've decided to take matters into their own hands. And I'm not complaining.

We get to the end of Main Street and cross Ocean avenue, ride down the concrete ramp next to the pier, then left through the parking lot and over to the beginning of the Boardwalk. We ride to about fourteenth street, park our bikes and then walk out onto the beach and sit in the sand facing the ocean.

It's a fantastic day, warm with only a slight breeze. (The 'May Gray's' haven't settled in yet.) We all sit close together, and Jacki and I are very comfortable talking with each other. I soon learn that she knows our friends Tim and Troy, who have a place together nearby on twelfth street. Troy now plays guitar with Eric and Matt and I, (still no bass player) and we sometimes jam in a back room of theirs.

After a while we get back on our bikes and start cruising again. We stop at Dolphin Market and get some sodas, then make our way over to the greenbelt, and eventually end up back at Dean's place. It's just off of Pacific Coast Highway on thirteenth street, and he shares the two bedroom apartment with Todd.

We ride to the back and park our bikes next to Dean's truck. Dean always uses the back door, which opens directly into his bedroom. We all go into the living room and relax on the couch. Dean goes up to the stereo and puts on Todd's brand new Cars album, our new favorite right now. We sit and talk and laugh, Jacki and I sitting so close that we're touching. And I can feel the electricity. Every now and then we look into each other's eyes, and there's definitely something happening.

After an hour or so Sara gets up and says it's time for her

and Jacki to get going. We all get up and make our way out the back door, where Dean and I load Sara's and Jacki's bikes into the back of his truck.

Before she climbs into the cab next to Sara, Jacki turns to me and says, "I had fun today Ben."

"I had fun too."

Then she leans in and gives me a quick kiss on the lips. She pauses for a second, looking into my eyes, and then we kiss again, a little more passionate, both of us throwing in a little tongue this time. We finally break it off, and she smiles at me as she gets in the truck.

Then Sara leans forward and says, "We'll get together again next weekend Ben! Maybe go to a movie!"

"Okay," I say, still in a trance from that kiss.

Then Dean shouts out the window as he's pulling away, "Hang out here if you want to Ben. I'll be right back."

"Okay," I say again.

Needless to say, I'm pretty excited right now. I go back into the living room, and the music has stopped. I go up to the stereo and put the needle back to the beginning of the Cars album.

Let The Good Times Roll.

It's the following Friday, and it's an official double date to the movies. But it's not quite what you might think. We're going to the Drive-in, and Dean has a whole new take on the experience.

Dean and I grab each end of the couch from the living room and load it into the back of his truck. We have to leave the tailgate down, so we strap it in so it doesn't go anywhere. Then we grab the two end tables, a boom box, some blankets, and of course a cooler. In it will be beers for Dean and I, and a big bottle of Chablis for the girls to split.

On the way there Jacki and I will ride in the back on the couch, and Sara will ride up front with Dean. When we get to the Drive-in Dean will pull up to the first row, and we'll unload the couch and put it on the berm facing the screen. Then we will place the end tables on each side, one with the boom box on it. Dean will then tune in the truck radio and the boom box to the AM movie station, and now we have mono surround sound at its finest, if there is such a thing.

There's plenty of room for the four of us on the couch, under the blankets, laughing, and kissing, and making out, and occasionally even watching the movie.

Halfway into the night the theater attendant is making his rounds on his golf cart. He pulls up in front of us and stops, and stares at our little set up. The girls give him their best smile and wave, and he just drives on, shaking his head.

Jacki and I are getting along famously, and the four of us go on many double dates, usually to the Drive In, because it's always a winner. But we also might walk the short distance over to Zoeter Field to watch a Slow Pitch game, seeing Andy's brother Gary and his friend Gary L. playing. Or we might ride our bikes down to the beach and spend a few hours, and then maybe later on go back down there again to watch the sunset.

So, after a couple of weeks of dating each other, on a very summery Saturday morning, this arguably not so green green-horn will lose what is left of his innocence, with the stereo playing in the background...

'Ooh my little pretty one, my pretty one
When you gonna give me some time Sharona?
Ooh you make my motor run, my motor run
Gun it comin' off o' the line Sharona'

Tim and Troy's place on twelfth street has become the official 'Animal House' for our little circle of friends. Complete with Toga parties, a poster of John Belushi as Senator Blutarsky on one of the doors, and the four of us as the house band. These parties are the first time we actually play in front of people, if you can call it that, because we're crammed into a back bedroom. And we discover a humorous shy side to Eric. As girls start showing up, Eric starts slowly moving into the bathroom as he's playing. We joke about calling these the 'Bathroom Sessions'. Then we start doing some daytime parties outside, and there's no place to hide.

The previous Halloween, exactly two months before I got on a plane and flew to Oahu with a backpack and a duffel bag, the band was set to play at a party at our friend John R's parent's house. It's on the Hill in Seal, basically right around the corner from my parent's house. Since I had moving to Hawaii on my mind, I kind of let the band slip to the back burner. I hadn't shown up for any rehearsals, and the night before the party I decided to go to John's house and see if I could still be a part of it. But I was too late.

They had already worked out a set with Matt drumming, so I was out.

This crushed me, but I only had myself to blame. I'm forced to remind myself that when you snooze, you lose.

And now, with all of this fun that I'm having with Jacki and Dean and Sara, I'm forgetting about the band again.

July fourth, 1979

"Let's walk out to the lifeguard tower first," Dean says, as he and Sara and Jacki and I get out of the car.

We're in Sunset Beach, and on our way to a party in Surfside, which is a private community on the beach. It's at a friend of Drew's, and it's an outdoor rooftop party. And Eric and Matt and Troy are playing at it.

The four of us walk out onto the beach. We're headed to a lifeguard tower, that for some reason, on a warm, sunny fourth of July has no lifeguard at it. We all climb the ladder and sit on the ocean side with our backs against the tower. Dean pulls four beers out of a bag and hands us each one. We're doing a little pre-party partying.

After a while Dean asks me if Matt is playing drums at the party.

"I don't think so," I say. "I heard that Matt is playing guitar, and that Eric found a drummer somewhere."

Dean gives me a quick, knowing look.

I laugh. "I'm okay with it, I really am," I lie. "Besides, I kind of blew it with them."

Pretty soon we all finish our beers, and then climb back down off of the tower and walk through the sand to the party. As we go in the front door on the bottom floor we can hear the muffled sounds of the band up on the roof. We pass a few people here and there on the way up, and when we reach the top floor we try to squeeze our way out onto the deck. There's quite a few people up here, but Dean manages to get us to a corner by the keg where we can see the band.

They sound good, but something is a little off. Then I notice that the drummer doesn't seem too sure of himself, and isn't quite keeping up with the rest of them. I instantly feel bad for the guy. He probably didn't get one night to practice with them.

They finish the song, and Troy notices the four of us. He says something to Matt and Eric, and then I hear my name being called over the P.A. I look over at them, and all three of them are motioning me over.

"Go for it Ben," Dean says.

I walk over and the three of them converge on me. "Ben, Ben, play a few songs with us, will ya?"

Then Eric adds in a half whisper, "He's a jazz drummer, and he can't really rock."

Then Matt turns towards the drummer. "Hey dude, you mind if our friend plays a few songs?"

He doesn't seem to mind at all, and gets up to hand me his sticks. I don't feel entirely comfortable with this, so I shake his hand and say, "Hey man, are you sure you're good with this?"

He insists that it's okay, and even looks a little relieved. I take the sticks from him, and then take his seat. And he's got an awesome drum set, a red metal flake Ludwig kit with many cymbals and double floor toms. Worlds better than the cheesy kit Matt got from me.

Matt turns to me and says, "Eighteen Ben?"

I laugh. Here we go again. "Okay."

They go into the song, and it's definitely different from the first time. There's three of them now, with Troy singing the vocals, and they're all warmed up. I am so ready to bang the drums again, so ready to just fucken rock, and end up having the time of my life. Whatever tension that I've had is flowing out of me like a flood. We do a couple of more songs before they decide to take a break, and I'm stupid happy right now! I just kind of walked into this unexpected jam session, and what a blast!

"That was fun!" I say, as E High fives me. But it was more than fun. Something might've just happened here.

I go over to Jacki and Dean and Sara, and Jacki gives me a big hug and a kiss. Dean and Sara are all smiles.

"Way to go Ben!" Dean says.

Then Drew comes up and shakes my hand. "Awesome Ben!"

Everyone's treating me like a rock star, and I almost feel like I'm having a Keith Moon moment. Except that I haven't exactly 'thrown the drummer off his throne'. I look over at the drummer, and he's sitting alone by his drums.

I go over and sit next to him. "Thanks for letting me play, man."

"For sure, for sure." He pauses a moment, and then says, "You really click with these guys. How come you're not playing with them?"

I sigh. "It's a long story." I look over at the three of them having a beer by the keg and talking to Dean and Sara and Jacki. "But maybe all of that is about to change."

I thank him again and then walk back and join the others. After a while the four of us exit the party and go back to Seal. We have a really fun rest of the day, riding our bikes down to the beach and partying at a few places on the boardwalk.

And that night of course, there's, uh… fireworks.

A couple of weeks before I met Jacki, I'm with Matt in his car, (he has a Volvo now), and it's a Saturday afternoon. We decide to go see what Dean is up to and Matt pulls in the back next to Dean's truck, right behind the bathroom window. The small window in Dean and Todd's bathroom is actually in the shower, and we notice that it's all steamed up. Suddenly we see a girls blonde hair and tanned shoulders against the glass. Then she slides to the left, and we see Dean's face. He sees us and smiles, and then disappears from view.

While I'm thinking that that wasn't Sara, Matt looks at me and says, "Did you see that Ben? Goob is having sex with that girl right now!" Then through gritted teeth he says, "Goddamnit Ben, we have to get laid!"

That was a while ago, and I had forgotten all about it. I had forgotten all about the intense peer pressure that Von and I used to endure for being virgins. We would joke that we were the last known virgins in Orange County, but now the joke was getting old. And now Dean and Sara are 'on the rocks', and might be breaking up, because I think Sara found out about Dean's little affair with the blonde girl. This all comes to light right after Dean and Sara and Jacki and I were talking about actually moving to Maui together, but now things are uncertain.

At this same time I get a phone installed in my room above my parent's garage where I'm staying, and this is my first phone, and my first monthly bill. One evening in late September I get a phone call, and it's Andy calling from Maui.

"Aloha Benoit!" he says, using my dad's nickname for me. He heard my dad call me that once, and thought it was the funniest thing, so he calls me that all the time now.

"Aloha Brah," I say. "What's happening over there on my favorite island?"

"A lot is happening over here," he replies. He pauses for a second, then says, "I don't know what you're doing right now Ben, but I think you should get back over here. I can get you a job right now where I'm working, which is at the Hyatt Regency Maui in Kaanapali."

"Really. What are you doing there?"

He kind of laughs. "I'm working for Oahu Interiors. They're installing all of the drywall on this job, and I mostly drive a forklift around, taking stacks of drywall here and there. I could get you a job for sure, maybe spraying popcorn on ceilings."

"No shit," I say.

"No shit Ben. And this job is huge. There's three main buildings, and they're also building a pool that's gonna be one of the biggest in the world when it's done. It'll be guaranteed work for some time."

I have to laugh to myself. Here's Andy getting me a job again. In Hawaii. If I want to. And he knows deep down that I want to.

"Okay, listen," I say. "I don't know how my parents are going to react to this, but let me talk to them and then get back to you."

"Cool Ben!" he says, all excited, like he already knows that it's in the bag.

And somehow, he does know.

Jacki is my first real girlfriend, and my first time dealing with a relationship, and after some time passes I'm not handling it very well. I'm getting jealous too easily, and my insecurities are showing. We have a couple of small fights, and then I don't see or hear from her. We don't officially break up, but the whole thing just sort of slowly ends.

And what I don't know, is that in the coming weeks Jacki and Sara will move to Maui by themselves. Dean tells me that he's moving back to Maui, and I assume that he's going with Sara. But Sara has broken up with him, and unknown to me, Dean is chasing after her.

To make things even more complicated, Jacki's mom had got both of us a one way ticket to Maui, I think through a travel agent that she knows. We were set to leave on October 31st,

Halloween morning. But now that we've broken up, Jacki has moved up her departure date and gone with Sara, but I have no knowledge of this.

In early October Mark calls me. He says, "Hey man, I got a call from Andy last night at two in the morning."

I laugh. That means it was eleven there, and he was probably in rare form. "What did he have to say?"

"Well, among other things, he said that you're going back over there."

"Yeah, that's right," I say.

"Well, when are you going? Because I'm thinking about going too."

I laugh again. "He really put the screws to you, didn't he?"

Mark laughs too. "Yeah, well, you know how persuasive Andy can be."

"Do I ever!" I say. "Well, this is great news, because I was gonna go with Jacki, but that's all over now. I'm going on the 31st, the eight am flight. United Airlines."

"Okay cool," Mark says. "I'm gonna try to get the same flight. I'll let you know as soon as I can."

It's October 31ˢᵗ, about seven thirty in the morning, and Mark and I are standing off to the side at the loading gate in LAX, because there's nowhere to sit. Then Mark nudges me. "Take a look at who's sitting over there Ben."

He motions with his chin to a man with long, light brown hair and a beard. He's wearing bright purple satin pants, a red Aloha shirt with a white tie, and he's sitting next to an attractive blonde woman. He looks a little disheveled, but there's no mistaking him. It's Kenny Loggins.

Just then they announce that our flight is ready to start boarding. It isn't until then that I look at the row of seats nearest us, and I don't believe what I'm seeing. There's Jacki, and her mom, and it looks like they've both been crying. In my silly mind I thought for some reason that she wouldn't be going anymore, but here she is. And I don't know that she's already been, and come back, and is now going again. I'll soon find out why.

It takes Jacki a couple of minutes, but then she finally notices us. Her expression changes, and she starts getting a big smile on her face. She gets up and hugs and kisses her mom goodbye, and when her mom turns to leave she comes over and gives me a big hug and a kiss.

She hugs Mark too, then stands back and says, "We're all going to Maui!"

Soon it's time to board the plane, and the three of us are arm in arm, Jacki in the middle, and we feel like the three happiest people in the world, skipping down the Yellow Brick Road.

We're on a 747, and it isn't totally full, and we manage to get three seats together. The mood on the plane is festive, and understandably so, because we're all going to Hawaii. (A night and day difference from return flights to the mainland, which are definitely somber in comparison).

When the drink service starts we all order cocktails. Jacki isn't twenty one yet, but she's getting served. Soon she tells us her story, which takes Mark and I by surprise. She tells us that about a month ago she had moved to Maui with Sara, and was working at an import gift shop on Front Street in Lahaina. Sara had bought a Mo-ped, and the two of them were riding on the highway and got into an accident. Jacki had scraped up her hands real bad, and to avoid getting a staph infection the people next door to her work paid for a round trip ticket so that she could heal up safely on the mainland. Somehow her mom worked it out so that she would be flying back the same day as me, a total surprise to Jacki. And me.

This news shocks me, and I look at her hands, but they look totally healed. Then she surprises us again, and pulls out a multi colored pack of Halloween makeup. We notice a few people on the plane wearing costumes, so Mark and I take the makeup to the bathroom and paint up our faces. Mark does horizontal stripes on his face, so I do vertical ones. When we

come back to our seats Jacki is talking to one of the steward-
esses, and they both take one look at us and start cracking up.
And the cocktails keep coming.

The whole plane seems like it's partying now, and we're
drinking and having a good time. And was there ever food? Did
we ever eat? I sure don't remember it.

Hours later we're making our approach into Hilo, on the
big island of Hawaii. We're definitely buzzed, and we're the
last ones off the plane, or so we think. We come up to the baggage carousel and retrieve our luggage, the last ones left. But
wait, there's two more suitcases. I look at the tags and they
both say K. Loggins.

And then here they come, Kenny and his wife or girlfriend, arm in arm and slowly making their way to where we
are. Mark suddenly grabs both of their suitcases, one in each
hand, and takes them over and plops them down in front of
them. They both laugh, and Kenny thanks him.

Mark comes back to us and says, "That's my buddy,
Kenny..."

And then things become a blur..

I don't remember the inter-island flight to Maui. And I
sure as hell don't remember if someone picked us up at Kahului Airport, or how we got to Lahaina. I find out later that
Jacki called a 'friend', and he picked us up and took us to
Lahaina in his Chevy Nomad station wagon. I also find out
later that Mark bought the car off of the guy the next day.
Apparently when we got to Lahaina, since I couldn't walk too
good, Mark was pushing me down Front Street in a shopping
cart, the make up on my face streaked and smudged.

I finally wake up, and realize that my head is in someone's
lap. I look up and see Sara's smiling face looking down at me.

"Hello Ben," she says. "Welcome back to Maui."

I sit up, slowly, because my head is a fuzz ball. I have a
dry, sick taste in my mouth, and realize that I had thrown up,
somewhere. Sara gives me a cup of ice water that she has next
to her. I thank her, and drain the cup. I look around, and see

that we're sitting on the seawall at the edge of town, across the street from Longhi's. It's nighttime now, and the Lahaina Halloween partyers are in full swing.

I look at Sara again, and feel ashamed. "Thank you for taking care of me Sara. How long have I been here?"

She laughs. "Oh, a little while."

Just as I'm about to ask her where Jacki and Mark are, Dean walks up. "Ben!" he says. "You're alive!"

"Barely," I say.

"Welcome back Brah!"

"Thanks man. Only this isn't exactly the way I wanted to come back."

Dean laughs. "C'mon man, Sara and I will walk you to Andy's condo just down the street. He says you can crash on his couch until you find a place."

"So, Andy still has that condo?"

"Yeah," Dean says. "He shares it with Ken. And there's more news. Drew's here too, and he's brought along his friend Rick from Huntington. They're staying at the Huea House"

"Wow," I say again. "Sounds like there's a lot of us starting a new life on Maui. The beginning of a new era?"

Dean claps me on the back. "That's exactly what it is Ben. That's exactly what it is."

MAUI, TAKE TWO

'We got somethin' we both know it
We don't talk too much about it
Ain't no real big secret all the same
Somehow we get around it.'

'Refugee'
Tom Petty

The windows are down, and the tropical wind whirls around the inside of the car as Andy drives us to the Hyatt Regency Maui, in Kaanapali Beach. There's a purple glow to the early morning twilight, and it's Drew's, and Rick's, and my first day of work.

I inhale the smells of the island, most prominently the sugar cane. I love the smell, and it alone contributes the most to making me realize exactly where I am. Back in the Islands of Aloha.

"The first thing I want to do," Andy is telling us, "is introduce you to the boss. We call him 'Idi Amin', because that's who he looks like."

He's referring to the infamous dictator, known as the 'Butcher of Uganda'. I hope this isn't an omen.

Just then an ambulance whips by us, with its siren blaring and its lights flashing. Andy ends up following it into Kaanapali Beach. "Uh oh," he says. "Something is going on."

When we pull onto the jobsite, it appears as though every fire truck, ambulance, and police car on the island are here. And they've all got their lights flashing.

Andy pulls up to a little trailer and stops. "I'll be right back," he says, and hops out. In a few minutes he returns. "Oh my God," he says, "this is tragic. Someone fell from the top floor of the Atrium Building, and impaled themselves onto a piece of re-bar sticking up."

Drew and Rick and I look at each other. Rick says, "Wow, that's terrible."

Andy gets back in the car. "They want me to go get the welder and send him back here. I guess to cut the guy down." He looks back at us. "Sorry guys, I know this isn't the best way to start your first day."

I try to picture the guy skewered to a piece of re-bar. And then I try not to.

Andy drives on until he sees a group of guys hanging out by a welding truck. He stops the car. "This won't take long."

Drew and Rick and I get out of the car and stand around

it. We watch Andy talk to one guy in particular, and the guy is looking down at his shoes, and occasionally kicking the dirt. He shakes his head, then he looks up at Andy and nods, and then goes to get in his truck.

Andy comes back and joins us. "Damn!" he says. "I'm glad I'm not in his shoes!"

Drew and Rick and I look up at the top of the building, the 'Atrium' building, the biggest one of the three that make up the hotel. Falling from that height to the ground would more than likely be fatal. Make that, it would definitely be fatal. But to spear oneself onto a piece of re-bar is downright horrific.

After a few minutes Rick says, "I guess this means we should be real careful."

Amid nervous laughter, we all agree.

Our boss, 'Idi Amin', is nowhere to be found, so Andy has us fill out applications and tax forms. Then he introduces me to my two new co-workers, Willy and Jose. Their job is spraying 'popcorn' on the ceilings of the rooms. Willy is fairly tall, six foot two or three, with a medium build and short sandy hair. Jose is closer to my size, five foot nine or so, and is obviously Latino. He was born in the islands though, grew up on Oahu, and talks like a local.

It turns out that Willy is from Sunset Beach, California. When I tell him that I'm from Seal Beach he laughs. "What're the odds?" he says, and seems really happy to talk to someone from back home.

"The first thing we have to do," Willy is explaining to me, as we walk through a cave, which is part of the pool, "is to get the mixer from the seventh floor and into the elevator, and take it up to the eighth."

When we get to the bottom of the stairs Willy stops, and pulls out his wallet. He hands a few bills to Jose, who turns and takes off through the building. Willy and I start climbing the steps to the seventh floor, which is somewhat of a hike, because we have to go up three flights of stairs before we even reach the first floor. This gives the bottom floor and the lobby a dramatic high ceiling effect.

We finally reach the seventh floor, and walk out to the concrete rail. Now I see why they call this the Atrium Building. It's really a triangle, and the doors to the rooms surround a courtyard on three sides. They've already begun to landscape the courtyard, and have installed a few coconut palms, tall ones, the tops of them just below us.

Walking along the open walkway, I look up to the ninth floor and see yellow caution tape blocking off one of the rooms. Willy notices me looking and says, "Yeah, that's the room where the poor guy fell from." Then he adds, "Gives me the shivers just thinkin' about it."

We continue on to the room where the mixer is, and when I see it, it's bigger than I imagined. It looks like an ordinary cement mixer, with two full size tires and a trailer hitch to pull it.

"This thing fits in the elevator?" I ask.

Willy laughs. "Barely, but yeah, it does."

Willy pulls and I push, and we wheel it down the hall towards the elevator door. This is a service elevator, a little bigger than normal, and the only one in operation in this building. Meaning whoever has to use it has to take turns. No one's using it right now, so we're in luck. Willy pushes the button, and in a few minutes the door opens. We wheel the mixer into the elevator, the tongue of the tow hitch cramming all the way to the corner, the back end just making it inside the door.

We go up one floor to the eighth, and wheel it out and down the walkway to the first room. Jose is there waiting for us, back from wherever it was that he went. While Willy hooks up a garden hose down the hall, Jose and I start ripping open bags of popcorn and pour them into the mixer.

Willy gets the sprayer hose ready, and Jose and I mask off the tops of the concrete walls with paper and masking tape, with the aid of a roller device that applies the tape to the paper. Then we get out of the way while Willy comes in with the sprayer hose, dressed from head to toe in white protective coveralls, complete with a hood and goggles over his eyes.

When he's done spraying the ceiling, Jose and I come behind him with large scrapers and scrape some of the overspray off of the walls. We then pull down all of the paper, and then wheel the mixer down to the next room. It takes us almost an hour to do one room.

We get a couple of more rooms done by lunchtime, and then the three of us head out to the lunch truck which has pulled onto the jobsite. It's operated by a couple of Haole women, and they make very good Hawaiian style plate lunches.

As soon as we all have our lunches in hand Willy says, "Follow me."

I follow him and Jose to one of the other buildings that is mostly completed. Willy leads us to a ground floor room, and after taking a quick look around to make sure no one sees us, he opens the door and we duck in. The room is totally finished, just no furniture yet, so we sit against one of the walls on the brand new carpet. As I start eating my lunch Jose pulls out a cooler that he had hidden in the bathroom. Willy opens the lid and pulls out an ice cold bottled Budweiser and throws it to me.

"You want a cold beer with your lunch, yeah?" and laughs.

Now I know where Jose went earlier when Willy gave him some money. The closest store is a Party Pantry, and Jose tells me that he just cuts across the golf course on foot to get there.

We take about an hour eating lunch and drinking beer, Willy telling non-stop jokes that have Jose and I laughing. This will be our daily routine, each of us pitching in a few bucks for the beers, and sometimes Jose producing a bud J from his cigarette pack. Welcome to 'work lunch' Hawaiian style.

A few weeks into the job on a Monday morning, Willy and I are heading up the stairs to where we left the mixer on Friday. A Haole kid on his way down recognizes us and stops. "Oh, you guys."

We give him a questioning look, and he says, "Yeah, you might want to be careful, because you have really pissed off a couple of very big and mean looking Tapers. Your mixer is stinking up the entire floor."

I look at Willy, but he just shakes his head and says, "Shit!"

The kid continues going down the stairs, and we continue going up.

Towards the end of our shift on Friday, Willy had mixed up a batch to do one more room, but then we got called off to help 'scrap out' a room on another floor, and we ended up just leaving the full mixer there all weekend.

As we're making our way up the stairs I ask him, "What the hell makes it stink?"

Willy sighs, and then says, "Believe it or not the popcorn bags have milk and egg in them."

I can't believe what I'm hearing. Milk and egg?

We reach the floor where we left the mixer, and yes, it reeks. It smells like a combination of rotten eggs and poopy diapers.

We walk down the hall and are confronted by two very large Mokes, and they are giving us some serious stink eye. Willy tells me to hang tight, and then he goes up to talk with them. Soon I hear him say, "We'll take care of it right now."

We walk over to the mixer, and the stench is pretty overwhelming. No wonder these guys are pissed.

What are we gonna do with it?" I ask, the sixty four thousand dollar stupid question.

Willy walks into the nearest room with a double door and out to the lanai and looks down. Seemingly satisfied, he comes back and says, "Help me wheel it into this room and over to the lanai."

We squeeze the mixer through the doorway and maneuver it over to the other side of the room, positioning the ass end as far out onto the lanai as we can get it. With the drainpipe sticking over the edge of the deck, Willy looks down one more time, and then flips the drain cap open.

And there it goes!

About thirty gallons of heinous, foul smelling liquidy goo, cascading down in a yellowish stream all the way to the ground, about a hundred feet below. God forbid if it were to hit anyone down there. We would most assuredly get our asses kicked!

When it's empty we quickly wheel the mixer back out of the room and down the hallway to our next room to be sprayed. I grab one of the bags of mix and flip it to the backside. And sure enough, there listed on the bag with about fifty other ingredients are the words 'milk', and 'egg'.

While I'm helping Willy and Jose spray popcorn on ceilings, Drew and Rick are delivering sheets of drywall to the installers. Andy drives the forklift, bringing these sheets to wherever they are needed next, and Drew and Rick offload them onto a handcart and take them away. But sometimes they have to 'scrap out', which means getting all of the leftover pieces of sheetrock out of the rooms and down to the dumpster. And sometimes I'm called to help them.

I'm finding out that Rick is a pretty funny guy. Always upbeat and positive, he manages to find humor in just about everything, and has the ability to turn any situation into something fun. He's just a wee bit shorter than me, but built like a middle weight boxer.

The three of us are on the sixth or seventh floor of the Atrium building, and although we're supposed to load the pieces onto a hand cart and take them down that way, Rick has figured out that the dumpster below us is close enough to the building for us to just throw them down.

So here we are, frisbeeing large and small pieces of drywall down to the dumpster, most of them making it in, but some of them not. There's a few full sheets as well, so we send those down too, and watch them zig-zag back and forth like a giant paper airplane, and if they actually make it in we all let loose with shouts of approval. Wasting time and material was never so much fun.

Each morning, after being dropped off by Andy at the back of the jobsite, my usual path to the Atrium building is down through the pool (no water in it yet) then through the cave with the swim up bar (I vow to have a drink there someday when the job is completed), then into the building and up the steps to whatever floor I'm working on. I will go up a set of ten or twelve steps until I reach a landing, and then go up ten or twelve more. At every landing there is some sort of graffiti on the wall, most of it done in black felt marker.

At one of the floors the writing on the wall is very extensive, written very neatly and eloquently. It's like the page out of someone's private diary, and it is obviously the work of a love struck Haole. The script is about his heartbreak, and he goes on and on about the love he once had, and lost. At the end of this 'narrative' is an equally eloquent response, obviously written by a local.

It goes something like this:

'You, the stupid fucking Haole that write this stupid fucking thing, you one stupid fucking guy! You no cry, no ask why!'

And right after the word 'why', in a completely unrelated message is the word 'whore!'

Drew and Rick, and maybe especially Rick, have taken great interest in this response to the whining Haole from this local. Many times I have been with the two of them, and some other people, and if the situation presents itself Rick will say, "You no cry, no ask why!" And then both of them will shout, "Whore!"

The person this is directed at will usually give them a look like, what the hell are you guys talking about? If pressed, Drew will just tell them that it's an 'Inside Stairway', instead of an inside joke. This, of course, will just confuse them even further.

My days at the Hyatt Regency are coming to an end. Andy, Drew and Rick have already been laid off and are working in Lahaina now. Andy is working at Kimo's, and part time at Longhi's, where his brother Ken is a cook on the front line. Drew and Rick are waiting tables at Nimble's, the same place that Gina and I had our George Benson night. This coming Friday will be my last day of work, my last day of spraying ceilings with Willy and Jose.

It's the following Saturday, around eleven am or so, and I'm just waking up. As I'm taking a shower and brushing my teeth, I'm thinking about where I'm going to work next, and I have no idea. And I'm also thinking that I've been crashing on Andy and Ken's couch for too long, and it's high time I found another place. Yesterday was my final day of work, and my final paycheck. And now I'm thinking about more immediate goals, like where I'm going to have breakfast, or maybe lunch.

I come out of the bathroom to find Andy and Ken sitting at the dining room table, a bottle of Jose' Cuervo between them. They've each done a shot, and offer me one. I know that it's the last thing I should do, especially on an empty stomach. But I do one anyway. And then we all do another, and another one after that...

My mind on tequila can go one of two directions. Either intense celebratory pleasure, or straight to the dark side. It can also make me forget things that shouldn't be forgotten, and remember things that should.

I thought I was over Jacki, but I guess not. The tequila has brought underlying feelings to the surface, and in the worst way. Not knowing or remembering what I'm doing, I start screaming and yelling, and to no one in particular. After some time passes, I don't know how long, I finally start snapping out of it. I can hear my voice trail off, like it's someone else's, and I have no idea what I've been saying.

I suddenly become aware of my surroundings. I'm standing at the top of the stairs with the front door open, and two large Hawaiian's in their twenties are coming up the stairs with one thing in mind; to kick my ass.

Ken is standing behind me, and lucky for me he has noticed a change in my demeanor. He brushes by me and stops the two guys before they reach the top of the stairs. He tells them that it's okay now, and that he can handle things from here. He pulls me back inside and shuts the door, then leads me to the couch and we sit down. I'm speechless, and hang my head and look at the floor.

Finally Ken says, "Andy's down in the parking lot. He punched a block wall instead of you. I think he might've broken a knuckle."

I can't believe what I'm hearing, and I don't know what to say.

Then Ken looks me in the eye. "Ben, I'm sorry man, but you gotta leave."

I just nod my head. I slowly get up and start grabbing my clothes and things and stuff them into my backpack. In a daze I make my way to the front door, telling Ken that I'm sorry, but knowing it's too late for that. I slowly head down the stairs, not caring if the two Hawaiians are around or not. They can kill me for all I care, put me out of my misery. There's no sign of them though, and I walk through the parking lot, tentatively looking around for Andy, but he's nowhere in sight either.

I start trudging down Front Street towards town, not really knowing where I'm going. It's another bright and sunny day, and there's shiny happy people all around me. But I feel like I'm invisible, and continue on alone, maybe more alone than I've ever felt before, in my own dark hell.

I pass Longhi's, and then Nimble's, then the jewelry store where Sara works, and a little further on the gift shop where Jacki works. Right then I realize that I have alienated my best friend, and Ken too for that matter, by turning into a tequila monster. And for what? This girl that seems to want nothing to do with me anymore? I decide right then and there that I'm done with her. For real this time.

I pass the Pioneer Inn and walk under the Banyan Tree. I sit on one of the benches under the tree and try to figure out my next plan of action. About twenty feet away I notice some familiar homeless guys sitting in a circle on the grass. 'Dirt Bagger's' we call them, and they're smiling and laughing, looking like they're sharing some secret that the rest of us will never know. I recognize one guy in particular, 'Coconut Man'. He's very dark complexioned and has dark shortish brown hair turning to dreads, and I've never seen him wear anything but a speedo. He earned his nickname because he can literally run up a coconut tree with a knife in his teeth, and cut down coconuts. While I'm thinking that I'm definitely no better than him right now, he suddenly looks up at me and smiles, like he's reading my mind. I smile back, then get up and continue on my way.

I pass the school that's on the water side, and think of the lucky kids that get to go here, and then pretty soon I'm in front of the Whaler's Market Place, where the Ship's Wheel and Don Drysdale's are. I keep walking until I'm in front of the Lahaina Shores Hotel, and look up at it. It's the tallest building in Lahaina, and I remember that this is where it all started, almost two years ago. I think of my birthday celebration, the four of us drinking Lowenbrau's around the jacuzzi, and this makes me think of Dean. Then I remember that him and Sara and Mark live at the 'Haole Camp', an old cane house that's down a private road just across the street.

I decide to go down there. I could really use the companionship of a friend right now, and Dean has always been good at helping me in time of need.

I've been here once before, so I know that it's at the end of this little road. As I get closer I see the screened in porch at the front of the house. This is really the front door, but Dean has converted it into his and Sara's bedroom, so everyone uses the kitchen door around back. Just then Dean walks into the screen room and sees me.

"Ben!" he says, good naturedly. I say hey, and then he says, "Go around back, I'll meet you there."

I walk around back and there I see Sara with Tracy, one of their roommates, sitting at their little back yard hang-out area, talking and drinking coffee.

Sara sees me and gets up. "Hey Ben," she says, and gives me a hug. Then she really looks at me. "Are you okay?"

Dean comes out of the kitchen door and says, "Howzit Brah?"

I look at him and sigh. "It's been better."

The Haole Camp is a three bedroom, one bathroom plantation house from back in the old days. Entirely made of wood, it's painted sugar cane green on the outside, while inside the floors are painted red and the walls white.

The large kitchen has an old box style fridge in it, with the circular cooling unit on top, and it looks very small in this big kitchen. They call it R2-D2, and someone has written it with a felt pen marker on the circular part. We walk by it and into the spacious living room, and sit in chairs and on the couch.

I know that Tracy and her boyfriend Jeff have the room closest to the kitchen, while their friend Max has the middle room, Sara and Dean have the front screen-room, and Mark and Dorothy have the bedroom next to theirs. Tracy and Jeff and Max are all from Cape Cod, Massachusetts, and Jeff and Tracy in particular have the Boston accent in spades. There's another guy George, who lives somewhere else in Lahaina, and they're all known as the 'Codfish'. They're basically here doing the same thing that we are, which is living and working in Lahaina, and having as much fun as they can in the process. They just happen to be from the opposite coast.

I tell Dean and Sara and Tracy my story, about my horrible start to the day. When I'm finished Tracy looks at me and says, "So, you need a place to stay then."

I look at her and nod.

She looks at Sara and Dean, then motions toward a single

mattress in the corner of the living room with pillows on it, a makeshift couch. "You can have that bed right there for... seventy five bucks."

I'm caught unaware. "Seriously?"

Tracy laughs. "Yeah."

This is too good to be true, and don't know what to say. But I know what to do. I pull out my wallet and count out seventy five dollars and hand it to Tracy.

"All right!" she says, and takes the money to her room for safe keeping.

Sara gives me a hug, smiling. Dean shakes my hand. "It was meant to be, Ben! Welcome to the Haole Camp Brah!"

I'm so happy with this turn of events that I'm getting a little choked up. Earlier today I was in a living hell, and now all of the sudden I have a place to stay, all on account of good people and friends coming to my rescue. And this definitely reminds me of when I moved into the Huea House with Gina and Theresa, the whole thing very similar. And it's funny, it's like I was being drawn here, and I didn't even know it. Like Dean said, maybe it was meant to be. All I know is, I'm one lucky son of a bitch.

Later that same day I meet Max. He's tall and good looking, with red hair that is bleached almost blonde from surfing all the time. He's recently returned from a little surfing excursion to Bali, and he took a bunch of pictures, which he's showing me now. Bali looks really beautiful, and he tells me that, believe it or not, it's more beautiful than Maui. I can't believe it. I can't imagine anyplace topping Maui. But he also says that the surfing is better there too, so I'm thinking there's a pretty good chance that might be influencing his opinion.

A few days after moving into the Haole Camp I run into Drew on Front Street. He's on his way to work at Nimble's, and tells me that they're looking for a new salad bar person. He knows that I'm looking for work, and suggests that I go there with him right now and apply, before the position gets filled. This sounds like another lucky break, so I follow him up the stairs and into the restaurant.

Drew introduces me to Peter Nimble, who invites me into his office and shuts the sliding glass door. He sits behind his large desk, and I'm thinking that he's probably in his early forties. He has shoulder length grayish curly hair and wears glasses, and is very congenial. He's also very obviously into music. Behind him are large tinted glass cabinets with all kinds of state of the art stereo equipment, including a couple of reel to reel tape decks, two turntables, amplifiers and tuners, and God knows what else. There's all kinds of different colored lights flashing everywhere, and one of the reel to reel decks is playing right now. I can easily hear Willie Nelson crooning softly out in the restaurant, and he is obviously one of Peter's favorites. Among other photos of famous musicians on the walls, I spy a black and white eight by ten of Willie, and it looks like it's been signed.

After some small talk Peter asks me what my interests are. Since he's obviously into music I tell him that I play drums, and that I'm in a band back on the mainland. (I'm not anymore, but I figure, what the hell). He seems genuinely interested, and asks what kind of music we play. I tell him a few of the artists that we cover, and he nods his head and smiles. Then he tells me some of his favorites along those lines, and we're having so much fun talking music that I'm wondering if he's ever going to ask me about my restaurant experience. But he never does, and finally just hands me a job application and says that I can fill it out at one of the empty tables in the back of the restaurant. I thank him, and go to an empty table in a room by the salad bar.

By all accounts it's a normal job application, except for one thing. Inserted randomly here and there are off the wall questions that have nothing to do with the job. Like 'Who is your favorite musical artist, and why?' Or, 'What was the stupidest thing you did in High School?' Towards the end of the application is another one. 'What is one of your favorite fantasy's?' I decide to have fun with this one.

I'm a pretty big Fleetwood Mac fan, and Stevie Nicks in particular, and seeing her that time in the kite shop on Front Street might've influenced my answer:

'Spending the night with Stevie Nicks in Hana, in a tent full of plumerias'

I end up getting the job. And someone tells me it was because of my answer to that fantasy question.

It's really fun to believe that.

My first day is Monday evening, December 31st, New Year's Eve.

It's gonna be busy, and it's gonna be crazy.

And ready or not, here come the eighties.

My first day of work at Nimble's. It's only around five o'clock but the mood in the restaurant is already festive. My new manager is showing me around the kitchen, and he seems pretty cool. He shows me where all of the food is, which cutting boards I'm supposed to use, what size to chop different things, what pots and bowls to use. He shows me around the walk-in cooler, and then shows me the ice machine. He opens the door and then points to the back corner.

"There's the tequila, and there's the grapefruit juice." He looks at me with a little smile and adds, "Have fun, but keep it under control."

He shuts the door and we both laugh. I don't tell him that I probably won't be drinking tequila again for a while. He then shows me the salad bar, where to put everything, and to keep it stocked and clean. He also tells me that all employees are allowed to eat anything from the salad bar for free, and that I might want to come in a little early to take advantage of that.

By around eight pm the restaurant is totally packed. Anticipated excitement is in the air, and we're all basically partying while we're working. Waiters, waitresses, cooks, just about everybody has a beer or a cocktail stashed somewhere in the kitchen, hitting it when they can. Peter has had speakers

THE BULLET HILL DIARIES

installed in the kitchen also, and the music is pumping.

I go into the walk-in for something and find Rick in there downing a beer. "Spin!" he says, and hands it to me. I laugh, and help him finish it. I go back to restocking the salad bar, and Rick goes to check on his tables. Every now and then I'll see Drew, either taking a tray of food out, or bringing empty plates back into the kitchen, and each time he'll smile and say, "80 me!"

At one point during the evening another waiter, Tim, pulls me around a corner and asks me if I want to split a Quaalude with him. Tim is a tall, funny guy, and we all tell him he should be a stand-up comedian. He's always telling jokes, and getting everybody to laugh. I decide to pass on the Quaalude, so he takes the whole thing himself.

Maybe an hour or so later Tim comes back through the kitchen doorway, losing control and then dropping a large tray of plates and glasses, most of them breaking and the pieces flying everywhere. He slowly slides down the wall to the floor, laughing uncontrollably.

The witching hour finally comes, and just when I thought that it couldn't get any crazier, at the stroke of midnight the place goes ballistic. The sound of noisemakers fills the restaurant, and confetti seems to come out of nowhere in every direction. The entire kitchen staff is out on the floor now, and everyone is hooting and hollering, and hugging. Multiple bottles of champagne are being passed around, and 'Auld Lang Syne' starts playing on the stereo, courtesy of Peter.

We're ringing in the 80's, and if this night is any indication, it's going to be one hell of a decade.

Mark and I are with Drew and Rick in the 'Midnight', which is the name that they have affectionately given their old Rambler that they bought together. They have put in a new sunroof, which is literally a hole cut in the roof, and a piece of linoleum countertop that they got from the Hyatt Regency, that can be through bolted into place when you need to cover the hole. Like right now, because it's starting to rain, and Mark and I are beginning to get soaked in the back seat.

Drew pulls over and he and Rick quickly bolt the countertop into place, held tight with a couple of wingnuts. They wrapped the cut metal edge of the roof with black plumbers pipe insulation, also courtesy of the Hyatt, and when the wingnuts are tight it's actually waterproof.

We get underway again, and Drew deftly operates the windshield wipers with his left hand, pulling them back with a piece of nylon cord that runs through a couple of eye bolts that have been screwed in above the windshield. For some reason the wiper motor only works in one direction, so when the blades go down Drew simply pulls them back up again. It's all very comical, but it works, and Mark and I laugh at his ingenuity.

We're on our way to 'Slaughterhouse Beach', on Maui's north shore, and soon it stops raining, so we pull over and they take the top back off again. When on Maui it's much more fun to go topless whenever you can.

When Drew and Rick bought the Rambler there was really only one major thing wrong with it; it needed a new starter. This is why they got the car for so cheap, somewhere in the neighborhood of seventy bucks. And let's just say that they got very creative in acquiring a new one.

And if anyone ever said that they saw someone fitting my description outside of the Lahaina Junkyard late one night, keeping watch, and then saw two other figures dressed in dark clothing with a flashlight, eventually emerging from the Junkyard carrying something wrapped in a towel, it's all a viscous rumor. But the next morning a 'new' starter was installed, and the Midnight was officially in operation, ready for new adventures.

We're all sitting in the backyard of the Haole Camp sipping coffee. Dean, Sara, Jeff and Tracy, and Mark and Dorothy. It's one of those typical perfect Lahaina mornings, and since most of us work nights we get to enjoy these mornings together quite often.

There's a small table out here, and five or six unmatching lawn chairs. Our neighbors behind us and to the sides are Japanese, and our fence is actually their screened in greenhouses. You can see orchids and other potted flowers arranged in neat rows on narrow wooden tables. Our little sitting area is partially shaded by a tall Mango tree, and a papaya tree grows right next to the back door.

An older VW bus pulls into the backyard and parks. I'm about to meet George, the other Codfish, and friend of Jeff and Tracy. George turns out to be a real character, and in later years he would be called a 'hoarder'. His bus is full of odds and ends that other people are throwing away. There's old radios and clocks, various kitchen appliances in need of repair, small furniture, fishing rods and reels, and a few battered surfboards. George will fix whatever he can and then sell it in the want ads. He always seems to have a gleam in his dark brown eyes, ever on the lookout for a good deal and more stuff. He's funny, and a little bit quirky, and I immediately like him.

Sometimes on these mornings we'll all pile into Mark's Chevy Nomad station wagon, which he has named the 'GoMad', and go to Kaanapali Beach to go boogie boarding. Sometimes George will go too, like this time, and I will ride with him and ask him questions about Cape Cod, and he will ask me questions about Seal Beach.

Riding along and listening to the familiar hum of his Volkswagen engine, I think of Dean's old bus that we went to Canada in, the one that I put my engine in, and then with a jolt I think of Lydia back on Mamo Place in Wailuku. I never did rebuild that VW engine for her, and I suddenly realize with a shock of shame that we never paid her back for the buds that she gave us. It now seems like such a long time ago. I'm sure she thinks the world of me now... what a knucklehead.

It's another morning, and Mark and I are on a mission.

We're in the GoMad heading north, in search of a blow-hole we've heard about. It's somewhere up past Slaughterhouse, where the road turns to dirt, but that's all we know. When we get to the dirt road we go maybe another mile or two, and Mark parks the car.

We make our way down rocky grass slopes, up and over little hills and down through valleys, heading towards the ocean. As we get closer to the water we see that the coast-line is dramatically volcanic, and the ocean beyond is choppy with whitecaps further out. The waves disappear under a ledge of rock, and we can hear them crashing below.

We come to an area where the rock flattens out to a kind of rough floor, about the size of a basketball court. A solid wall of volcanic rock borders the north side of it. We walk to the edge of this rough flattened area and stop, watching and listening.

After a few minutes we hear something. A deep, hollow sloshing sound, like a giant toilet flushing, but we can't make out exactly where the sound is coming from. While we're scanning the area the sound turns to a soft hissing. A few seconds later, from close to the center of the rock floor, a thick stream of seawater suddenly shoots straight up into the air, probably twenty five feet high, before it cascades back down. Mark and I look at each other smiling. We've found it!

We keep our eyes on that spot and slowly start walking towards it. Then, without any warning sounds, water suddenly gurgles out of the hole again, but only a couple of feet high this time. We stop and wait. We look out at the wave surge, but it's impossible to judge just when the hole is going to blow. Another small gusher erupts, but then goes back down very quickly. We're only about ten feet away now, and decide that this is our chance. We quickly run up and look down the hole, and it's like looking into another world.

Maybe two feet in diameter, it's almost perfectly cylindrical. We see clear blue water maybe ten or twelve feet below us, sucking out towards the sea. Surprisingly the walls of the hole are mostly pink, with some red and green thrown in. The moving water at the bottom is bright from sunlight here and there, but we can't make out where the source of the light is coming from. It all looks so peaceful right now, but we know that can change in seconds.

Suddenly the water at the bottom reverses direction, so we step back. Then we hear that hissing sound again, so we retreat even further. In another second it shoots up, really high again, and we stand still and let it shower down on us. It feels refreshing, and we look at each other and laugh.

When the water goes back down we move in again to take another look down the hole. Bad decision. Without warning a ten foot high gusher spews out, drenching both of us, and knocking Mark off of his feet and onto his back. As the water recedes I go over to Mark and help him up.

"Are you okay?" I ask.

"I think so," he says, and then turns around. "How's my back look?"

Below his left shoulder and towards the middle of his back is a half inch wide and four inch long white stripe. Just the top layer of skin is gone, like it's been removed with a potato peeler.

"You've got a pretty good scrape, but it's not bleeding yet."

We hang out for a little while longer, but then decide to head back and get Marks wound cleaned up. We both know about the possibility of a staph infection.

When we get back to the car Mark eases into a T shirt. On the ride back to Lahaina we have the radio tuned to the FM station, KAOI. In between songs we hear about a hurricane that is a couple hundred miles off of the Big Island, and moving north. They're saying that there's a possibility of it impacting Maui.

Back at the Haole Camp Dorothy cleans up Mark's wound with some antiseptic spray and puts a big bandage on it. She tells Mark, "You'll be okay, but you're probably gonna have a scar."

"Something to remember the blowhole by." I joke.

Mark grunts.

Dorothy laughs. Then she says, "Did you guys hear about the hurricane?"

"Yeah, we just did on the way back here," I say.

"It's not supposed to hit us head on, but it could get pretty stormy around here."

Less than a week later, it's 'pretty stormy'.

A lot of wind, and occasional rain squalls, and the surf is starting to pile up in Lahaina Harbor. And that's not a good thing, considering all of the boats that are moored out there.

It's a Saturday morning, the wind is blowing, and Lahaina is not waking up. Almost all of the business's on Front Street are closed, including the restaurants that some of us work at. Storm shutters are put in place on most buildings, and everyone is 'battening down the hatches'. Lahaina literally looks like a ghost town.

With nothing better to do, Mark, Jeff, and Dean and I decide to take a stroll down Front Street. We bring along a six pack of beer and take our time, amazed at how different our little town looks. Hardly anyone is to be seen, except for a few bored tourist's, who are probably out and about because they've got nothing better to do either. We reach the Banyan Tree and hang out there for a while. We feel like we're in an old Western movie, drinking our beers in the center of this deserted town with leaves and branches blowing all around us.

Pretty soon the beers run out. Jeff stands up and says, "Well, what the hell. We might as well keep this Hurricane party going."

We hear from someone that the liquor store down the street is open. Jeff volunteers to make the run, so we all pitch in a few bucks and send him on his way.

While he's gone Mark and Dean and I notice a little vendors shack across the street next to the Banyan Inn. It's only about eight feet wide, with a low counter top and palm fronds for a roof. It looks like something out of Gilligan's Island, and for some reason we've never noticed it before. We decide to walk across the street and take a closer look. Behind the counter there's three folding chairs and a small chest of drawers off to one side. It's obviously not being used today, so we hop the counter and take up residence. Today, this little shack is ours.

Pretty soon we see Jeff coming back down the street, a twelve pack of Bud's tucked under one arm. He doesn't see us at first, and when we call to him he looks at us and laughs. He comes over and hands the beers across the counter and then climbs over the counter himself. We each crack a beer and toast the storm.

A little while later, while we're enjoying our beers, a couple of guys probably in their forties approach the counter. They're obviously tourists, with their golf shirts and sun burned faces. "How much for a beer?" one of them asks.

Jeff winks at me and then turns to the guy. "One dollar sir."

The man puts down two bucks and Jeff hands him a couple of beers. Word seems to get around, and we get a few more 'customers'. I laugh to myself. If we keep this up we could almost double our money. Or at least drink for free. Since the bars are closed today, we have become the only bar in town. As soon as we get enough money Dean makes another beer run. We drift through the afternoon this way, selling a few more 'Hurricane beers,' but probably drinking most of them.

By mid-afternoon the wind has picked up even more, and the rain is starting to blow in on us. We decide to grab what beers we have left and head back to the Haole Camp.

If anyone were out there they might have seen us, weaving along shoulder to shoulder, and maybe even heard us singing...

"Yo ho, Yo ho, a Pirates life for me"

That night I fall asleep to the sounds of the wind and rain rattling the windows and doors of our old plantation house.

The next morning dawns sunny and bright, the storm completely gone. Dean comes back from the Lahaina Shores Hotel with today's newspaper. He tells us that almost two dozen boats washed up on shore during the night, most of them sailboats that broke from their anchor lines.

Not too long later George pulls into the backyard, his Bus completely stuffed with all kinds of new 'junk', including a Yamaha twelve string guitar, which he wants me to put strings on. Apparently he was up early this morning, 'beachcombing'. It appears as though some people's mis-fortune has turned into his fortune.

With the storm gone, like some kind of unwanted relative, causing chaos and then finally leaving, life in Lahaina quickly gets back to normal.

The new talk of the town is the opening of a new restaurant, Blackbeard's, located in a new shopping plaza sandwiched in between the Whale's Tail and the Banyan Inn. Blackbeard's is on the top floor, and they reportedly have a Sunday brunch that is good and affordable.

And that's just what Sara and Tracy and Dorothy want us all to do, and they're making a party of it. Dean and Sara, Jeff and Tracy, Mark and Dorothy, and Dean says Andy is going to meet us there.

Andy.

I haven't seen him in about a month. Not since that fateful day when I let the tequila get the better of me.

It's funny, but I'm kind of nervous about seeing him. Is he still mad at me for making him punch that wall? I guess I'm going to find out.

The layout at Blackbeard's is smart and cool. It's got an open air feel, and there's plenty of seating in the bar area. Right as you walk in the front door there's a display case with various things on ice, including a few fish, some fruit, and a couple of bottles of champagne.

We all sit at a big table, and Mimosa's and Bloody Mary's are ordered. Soon the waitress returns with our drinks, and someone is right on her heels, kind of sneaking behind her. Then I see that it's Andy, and he already has a Bloody Mary in his hand.

We all laugh at his antics, and then he comes straight over to me and cheerfully greets me. "Ben!" he says, and I stand up to shake his hand, but then hesitate. He notices me looking at his hand and says, "Ben, Ben, forget about that shit! Look at this!" He flexes his hand in front of me. "My hand is fine!" Then he leans in close and in a lowered tone he says, "Let's just chalk that up as a bad day, and put it behind us. It's history now."

I smile, incredibly relieved, and shake his hand, but not too hard. "Thanks man."

"Grab your drink," he says. I pick up my Bloody Mary and he leads me over to a side bar. After we sit he looks at me and says, "I've gotta tell you something Ben." He pauses a second and looks down. Then he looks back up at me. "Ken is dating Jacki now."

I give him a blank stare. I'm definitely a little shocked, but then again, not in total disbelief. It all makes sense, actually, and I should have seen it coming.

Andy puts his hand on my shoulder. "Forget about her Ben, she's not worth it." Then he smiles. "She's a wack job man! Wacky Jacki I call her."

He laughs, and I laugh. And I know that he's trying to make me feel good. And I also know that Jacki is a lot of things, but 'wacky' isn't necessarily one of them.

We both take a drink, and when Andy sets his glass back down he says, "They're driving me frikken crazy, the two of them, all lovey-dovey and shit all the time. It's just killing me! She lives there now, moved into Ken's room. I feel uncomfortable, so I just leave all the time. Go downtown, go anywhere!"

"Like out to brunch," I say.

"Yeah, that's right!" he laughs. "Like out to brunch!"

We toast again and drain our glasses. "C'mon Ben, let's get back to the table and get in on some of that complimentary champagne."

During omelette's and potatoes, and bacon and mango's, and whatever else we can gorge ourselves on, our waitress makes the rounds with the champagne bottle. But it's not fast enough for Andy.

He winks at me and says, "I'll be right back."

He nonchalantly walks over to the display case, then returns with a bottle of champagne tucked half under his shirt. He quickly sits down and starts fiddling with it under the table. Dean and Mark had their eye on him, and they're already laughing.

Andy's attempt at being incognito suddenly comes to an end when we all hear a loud pop! And now the whole table erupts with laughter.

Everyone takes turns sliding their glass over to him, and Andy does his best to fill them up under the table. And if our waitress has any idea of what we're up to, she doesn't say anything. But the next time we go to brunch at Blackbeard's, they're a little wiser. The bottles of champagne in the display case are empty.

It's about a week or so after our little brunch party, and most of us are in the backyard of the Haole Camp enjoying our customary morning coffee. And then from behind us we hear someone say, "Aloha!"

I turn around to see who's walking up, and then I slowly turn back around. It's Ken and Jacki, arm in arm.

I get a sudden urge to get up and go inside, but then I think, fuck that, and sit back in my chair.

Dean and Sara greet them, and everyone says hello, except me. They don't acknowledge me, like I'm not even there. Like I'm invisible. And that's just fine with me.

Ken is all smiles, but Jacki doesn't look so good; maybe a wee bit hungover? She clings to Ken and doesn't ever meet my eyes. She tries to smile with everyone, but she's clearly uncomfortable. And I have to admit, I'm kind of enjoying it.

And then, all of a sudden, I feel sorry for her. I'm getting the feeling that coming over here was probably Ken's idea, and that maybe she had to be talked into it. Her armor is down right now, and she looks a little vulnerable. I try not to stare at her, but it's hard. I was in love with this girl once. But love comes and goes, and with her, maybe it's finally gone.

To my relief, they don't stay for very long. Ken says goodbye, and I try not to watch them walk away. Only then do I realize that Jacki never said a word.

After they're gone Dean looks over at me and says, "How you doin' Ben?"

I just smile and nod.

Sara comes over and sits next to me. "You handled that well Ben."

Did I? I'm not so sure.

She takes my hand and gives it a squeeze. I smile and squeeze hers back.

All is okay with the world.

Oftentimes, change is good. And a lot of things have changed in a relatively short time in our little world here in Lahaina.

I have quit my job as salad bar person at Nimble's, and now work at Longhi's as a prep cook, and making a little more money. Andy still works at Kimo's and Longhi's, and he talked me into making the change. Dean works at Longhi's too, mostly bussing tables, but sometimes he cooks on the frontline with Ken.

And speaking of Ken, the most amazing thing has happened. We've become really good friends. He apparently had a falling out with Jacki, and ended up buying her a plane ticket back to the mainland. It's unbelievable how things turn out.

Soon after Jacki was gone Ken and I started talking more with each other. And it just so happens that he loves snorkeling just as much as I do, and we'll sometimes go on snorkeling missions together in Mike's van, going to a new spot each time.

It's mid-summer in Lahaina, and it's hot. The word Lahaina means 'merciless sun', and it's an accurate description. During the summer there can be little or no breeze, and with the mercury hitting the low to mid-nineties it can be pretty sweltering. Like I was shown a few years ago by some co-worker friends, this is the time of year to take a little road trip to Wai'anapanapa State Park and jump in the cool waters of the cave pools.

I mention this to Mark and he likes the idea. So much so that he buys a couple of small flashlights and a large bag of votive candles. We've heard that there's some dry caves there, in addition to the water caves. "We're gonna go spelunkin' Fin!" Mark says.

Andy hears about it and he absolutely has to go too. In fact, he tells us that he has our ride all lined up with expenses paid. A total Andy. He met a guy at the bar in Kimo's, a fisherman from Alaska. Bob is his name, and he's willing to pay Andy to be his tour guide. He sounds like a work hard, play hard kind of guy, and he insists on paying for everything. He gives Andy some money to buy a bag of bud's, a couple of cases of beer, and some munchies. And we're taking his rental car, a brand new VW Bug convertible.

All four of us are in the water of the cave pool, and we have the pool to ourselves. And we're trippin'... It turns out that fisherman Bob brought along some LSD with him from Alaska, and we each took a hit somewhere back on that road of roads.

I've been underwater and slowly come up to the surface and look around me. Andy is showing Bob the backside of the cave where the ceiling comes down to within a few feet of their heads. Their faces are pictures of wonderment, reflected in their eyes, which are huge and dilated. I look to my left, just in time to see Mark's feet go underwater. I know where he's going. He's headed to the 'secret cave', so I go under myself and follow him.

The only way into the secret cave is a short swim through an underwater channel. I surface inside the cave and barely see Mark at the far end clinging to a rock. The only light in the cave is reflected from outside, through the underwater channel that we just swam through. It's an eerie bluish light, which one can only describe as ethereal.

Soon Andy pops up into the cave, followed by Bob.

Bob's about to say something when Mark says, "Shhh... listen."

As soon as we're still, all we can hear is a soft drip, drip, drip, here and there. It's rainwater from up above, filtering through the rock and dripping from the ceiling.

Bob finally breaks the silence by whispering, "This is fucking unbelievable!"

The smile on Andy's face is epic. He just loves showing new people places like this, and seeing how much it blows their minds.

After a little underwater exploring, we're back out of the cave pool and standing on the trail that brought us here. Right now it's sunny and not raining, which is pretty rare in Wai'ana-panapa. The colors are staggering, especially in our present state of mind. There's sort of a circular wild garden of thick tropical growth off and down to our right, and Mark goes down there, somewhere that we wouldn't normally go, but this isn't normally, so we follow him. The area is enclosed on all sides by walls of thick vegetation, and we make it to the far wall and stop. Mark seems to sense something, and gets down on all fours and inspects the bottom of the wall.

He looks back up at us and says, "There's an opening here."

He lays down and then rolls over onto his back. He slithers and rolls under the opening, and is gone. I'm about to lay down and do the same when he slithers back out.

He looks up at us. "There's a full on cave in here... you can stand up in it!" Then he gets up and says, "Hold on, I'll be right back."

He runs back up to the trail and takes off back to the car. I know what he's doing. He's going to get the flashlights and the candles. It looks like we really are going to go 'spelunkin'.

When Mark gets back we all take turns squirming through the skinny opening into parts unknown. The opening itself is about seven or eight feet long, but only about a foot and a half high. Little ferns and things hang from the top of it almost to the ground, concealing it perfectly.

I roll under and then slowly stand. My eyes adjust pretty quickly, for obvious reasons. Mark and Andy turn the flashlights on, and the three of them are silhouetted in the dark. And just like Mark said, the cave is standing room, six or seven feet high and totally dry. It's a natural tunnel, as we can now see, and we start following it.

The volcanic rock that makes up the walls of the tunnel is very uneven, with all sorts of bumps and ledges. Mark hands me the light and then pulls the bag of votive candles out of his pocket. He hands me some of them and a lighter, and we both start lighting candles and place them on little rock ledges here and there as we make our way along the tunnel. The flickering candlelight transforms the cave into another world, like we've walked back in time and straight into an old 1950's horror movie.

Then thoughts of Bilbo, when he gets separated from the wizard and the dwarves in the Goblin Caves comes to mind. And it's easy to believe that we suddenly are in Middle Earth.

While Mark and I have been busying ourselves with the candles, Andy and Bob have gotten ahead of us. Soon we hear them, and it sounds like they've found something. Mark and I quit lighting candles and then hurry to where they are. We're both unprepared for what we see.

It's the end of the tunnel, and the flashlights reveal a room. A big circular room, roughly thirty feet in diameter and about eight feet high. And the entire room is a pool.

And that's not all.

A little off center in the pool is a small island.

We all stand at the edge of the pool and no one says a word. Once again all we can hear is the drip, drip, dripping of drops at different spots in the pool.

And now we really are in Middle Earth, because this is Gollum's pool, to a tee. This is where Bilbo told riddles in the dark, trying to buy his way back out. The only thing missing is Gollum's little boat.

And Andy is picking up on it too. "Bless us and splash us, my preciousss..." he whispers.

Mark and I both let out a chuckle, but Bob is clearly in the dark. He has no idea what Andy is talking about.

Mark slips into the dark water of the pool with the candles and the lighter held above his head. He slowly starts swimming the perimeter of the pool, lighting and placing candles as he goes. Andy and I both slip into the water at the same time. We swim the short distance to the island and crawl onto it. Having gone around the entire pool, Mark swims up to the island and joins us, placing a few lit candles on it as well.

Big, fearless Bob, who literally risks his life everyday fishing for Halibut in the dangerous seas off the coast of Alaska, is having a little bit of a hard time getting into the water of this pool. He finally takes the plunge though, and is swimming around us with a big smile on his face.

We all admire Mark's handiwork with the candles. The whole room is lit up now, the flickering light casting water devils onto the ceiling and surrounding walls. The ripples Bob is making accentuate the effect.

We spend an unknown amount of time here, because time is something that is hard to gauge in this place that seems frozen in time. I slip off of the island and slowly swim around the perimeter of the pool like Mark did, and at one point I take a deep breath and let myself sink down about four or five feet. Looking up I can see the flickering candlelight above the surface, and notice that the water is crystal clear. I spin around and look down, and all I can see is a black void. I know that if I let it, fear could overwhelm me right now. Especially if I let my imagination run wild, and let it conjure up images of things that could rise up from the deep dark below. But for some reason I seem to sense that there is absolutely nothing to fear from the depths of this pool. Nothing alive, anyway.

I slowly rise back up to the surface, and then swim back to the island, and then back to shore. We decide that it's time to leave, but before heading back down the tunnel we all take one long last look. I would like to show this place to Dean, and other friends, but I have this feeling that I will probably never see this Gollum pool again.

We turn and start back down the tunnel, and we don't need the flashlights yet because of the candles that Mark and I left. But further down the tunnel the candles have long since burned out, so Mark and Bob lead the way, switching on their flashlights.

Maybe halfway back Mark discovers a side tunnel branching off to the right. He and Bob want to investigate, so they take both flashlights and leave Andy and I in the dark. We see them turn a corner, and soon all light is gone.

Just like Bilbo, I open and close my eyes, but there's no difference. I hold my hand in front of my face, but I can't see a thing. The darkness is complete.

Andy, who is also pretty fearless, is not liking this one little bit. He'll bodysurf fifteen foot waves at the Wedge, or jump a sixty foot bridge in Hana, but he clearly doesn't like being left behind in this pitch black cave.

I feel him move closer to me. Pretty soon he says, "Those motherfuckers better not take too long. And why did they have to take both flashlights?"

Good question. And Mark has what's left of the candles with him, and both lighters. We know which way the exit is, and we could probably feel our way to it if we had to. But what if we accidentally veered off into another side tunnel? No, our best bet is to just sit tight and wait for them.

Andy suddenly yells down the passage that they took.

THE BULLET HILL DIARIES

"Hey, you assholes, get the fuck back here, Goddamnit!"

The last syllable of that last word ended on a high note. I'm expecting an echo, but there's none. Instead, his shout just seems to fall flat, swallowed into nothingness.

"I'm gonna kill both of them with my bare hands," he mutters softly.

Andy is definitely a little tense, but he's cracking me up, and I try not to laugh.

After what seems an eternity, we finally see their flickering lights in the tunnel.

When they reach us Andy says, "It's about time! Can I have the light now?" He grabs Bob's flashlight and takes the lead towards the exit.

As we follow him I turn back to Mark. "Did you find anything?"

"Hell no," he replies. "It just sort of dead ended."

Pretty soon we see light coming from the low gap that we slithered through. It appears as though Andy and I could have made our way back out after all.

Andy is the first of us to lay down and squirm back to the outside world. I go next, and when I emerge and stand up I see Andy on all fours kissing the ground. When Bob and Mark join us Andy says he wants to see the ocean, so we all follow him out onto Black Sand Beach.

Once we're out on the beach we all kick off our flip flop's so we can feel the soft sand between our toes. A light rain starts falling.

Andy wades out into the ocean up to his knees and then spreads his arms wide. "I love you!" he shouts to the sea. I join him, and he turns to me and says, "I started getting a little claustrophobic in there Ben. I kind of lost my cool."

"Totally understandable," I say. "It got pretty hairy there in the dark."

"Yeah, but you didn't seem frightened at all."

I shrug. "We're all afraid of different things," I say. I look out at the ocean. "I'm afraid of big waves, and you're not."

He laughs. "Well, it was definitely worth it to see the Gollum Pool."

"Yes it was! I'm glad you think so."

We all slowly make our way back off of the beach and through the trees and back to the car. The rain stops, and the sun starts peeking through the clouds. We all grab a beer out of the cooler, put the top down, and start driving towards Hana, and the Seven Pools, of which Andy is already giving Bob the complete rundown.

Good ol' Andy, back in his element. And it's great to see.

My first job in the morning as prep cook at Longhi's is to make the fresh squeezed orange juice. Slicing the oranges in half, juicing them in the juicer, filling up pitchers and putting them in the walk-in. It's something that I look forward to, because I always have a few glasses while I'm making it. If Andy happens to be working the same morning he'll usually come back and bum a glass or two off of me. One particular morning, both of us hungover from the previous night's partying, the pitchers weren't getting filled up because we were both drinking it as fast as I could make it.

Cyndi the bartender, a sweetheart if there ever was one, peeked around the corner and laughed at us sympathetically. "Aww, you poor babies. Let me make you a couple of my special Bloody Mary's."

Maybe she feels a little guilty, since she was the one serving us the night before.

Peter Longhi, son of Bob Longhi, is the restaurant manager, and he's the one who trained me. Taught me everything I know, like how to make the marinara sauce, ('you can never use too much butter or garlic') and the fruit salad dressing, and the regular salad dressing, how to make a Greek salad, ('plenty of grated Feta cheese') how to prep squid, what size to cut breakfast steaks as opposed to lunch and dinner steaks, and literally everything else in between.

It's Peter's birthday today, and he's turning the ripe old age of nineteen. It's a rainy day in Lahaina, looking like it's not going to let up anytime soon, which is pretty rare in this town. And there's practically no lunch business.

Around two o'clock or so the quiet of the dining room is disrupted by some boisterous laughter. I peek out of the kitchen and see Andy and Peter, their arms around each other and ambling up to the bar. They've obviously already started celebrating Peter's birthday somewhere else. I duck back into the kitchen, but soon Andy and Peter come back there.

"Ben!" Andy says, "It's Peter's birthday, and we're gonna have some champagne!" He turns to Peter. "You don't mind if Ben joins us, do you Peter?"

"Of course not!" Peter says. "C'mon Ben, lose that apron and join the party!"

Peter rounds up the two waitresses that are working, (they're not really doing anything anyway) and leads us all over to the biggest table in the restaurant, a large circular booth.

Cyndi brings Peter the wine list. After looking it over he says, "Cyndi, let's start at the bottom and work our way up. Bring us the forty dollar bottle please." He turns to us and says, "We're gonna do a little research, a taste test to find out which bottles of champagne really are the best."

The girls kind of giggle their approval, and Andy gives me a light kick under the table. "This is gonna be way better than Blackbeard's, huh Ben?"

One of the girls says, "What happened at Blackbeard's?"

Andy waves it off. "Oh nothing, nothing."

She's about to press him on it when Cyndi brings over the first bottle and glasses. She pops the top and starts pouring.

When she's done Andy raises his glass and says, "To Peter. Happy Birthday!"

We all raise our glasses. "Happy Birthday Peter!"

After a second sip Peter peruses his glass and gets a thoughtful look. "Not bad, not bad. What do you guys think?"

We all agree. Not bad. Peter refills our glasses, and that's the end of that bottle. He calls Cyndi back over to the table. "Okay my good lady, let's give the sixty dollar bottle a try."

Cyndi returns with the second bottle and fills all of our glasses again. After tasting it a couple of times Peter sets his glass down. "Wow!" he finally says. "That is really good!"

Andy agrees. "That *is* really good."

The girls agree. I more than agree. In fact, this is the best champagne I've ever tasted. Can it possibly get any better than this?

As we drain our glasses, this time Andy takes the liberty of refilling them. "Suck 'em up, Birthday Boy!" He says, the bottle hovering over Peter's glass. Peter laughs, and drains his glass. Andy refills it. Bottle number two gone.

Pretty soon Peter has Cyndi bring the eighty dollar bottle. He pours and we raise our glasses high, toasting him heartily. We all drink and set our glasses down.

Peter once again looks thoughtful. "That's pretty good, but I think the last bottle was better. Whadda you guys think?"

We all agree, the second bottle was better. We slow down a bit, taking our time with this one. Spirits are definitely high now. And I'm definitely buzzed. If the girls were giggling earlier, now they're straight out laughing. Soon they start singing a raucous version of Happy Birthday, and Andy and I join in. When we're done we raise our glasses high, all of us cheering.

Without even waiting to finish this bottle, Peter has Cyndi bring the last one. The crème de la crème, the top of the line, the most expensive bottle on the list... The Dom Perignon.

At a hundred and twenty dollars a bottle, this is turning into an expensive party. I try to do the math in my head, but I'm having trouble. I taste the Dom Perignon. Or, is this still the wine from the last bottle? I've lost track. And at this point it doesn't really matter. We're all laughing loudly and cheering Peter.

And that's when Bob Longhi walks into the room. He's barefoot, and wearing his 'whathefuck' T shirt.

We all freeze.

Bob takes in the situation, then looks at Peter. "Birthday Party huh?" He looks us over, then back at Peter again. "Well," he says, "Have fun, but be careful." Then he turns and walks back out.

We all exhale.

"Well," Peter says, like nothing happened, "This stuff is pretty good, but I still say the second bottle was the best."

We all agree. And then we proceed to finish all of the champagne that is left on the table.

The party slowly breaks up. The girls give Peter a hug and go back to work, although their shift is about over. I go back to the kitchen, definitely a little tipsy, and Andy follows me in. I put my Apron back on and try to remember what I still have to do. Did I cut up the tomatoes yet?

I pick up a knife and Andy says, "Remember what Bob said Ben. Be careful!"

We both laugh.

And then I put the knife back down. I'm done for today.

And then Dean walks in, a little early for his evening shift. He takes one look at us and says, "What's going on around here?" He gets a funny smile, and then points out towards the dining room. "Those girls out there are wasted!"

Andy puts his arm around him. "Hey Deano, it's Peter's birthday! Let me buy you a glass of champagne!"

He's kidding, of course.

Or, is he...

When you're sitting inside of a lava bubble, your perception of the world goes deep. It's making me think of the earth's super-hot core, and of the many volcanoes all over the world, and how these volcanoes seem to me to be pressure release valves. The pressure that was released by this particular volcano, Haleakala, where Andy and I find ourselves now, must have been a massive eruption indeed. Haleakala, Hawaiian for

'House of the Sun', is very aptly named. It seems to hold the sun in its stony canyons and red cinder cones.

We're sitting in 'Bubble Cave', a lava bubble roughly twenty five feet in diameter and about six feet high. It rose to this height and then for some reason, it froze. Indirect sunlight streams through the hole in the top center of the bubble, casting a soft, grayish light. Little ferns hang from the ceiling, motionless.

Andy breaks my reverie with a question. "Can you imagine what it must've been like right here when this bubble was formed?"

He looks around the interior of the cave, trying to picture it.

When he looks at me I say, "Pretty hot, for one thing."

Andy laughs. Then he says, "You know Ben, they say Haleakala could become active again someday." And with a grin he adds, "What if it started happening right now?"

I look him in the eye. "We'd be toast!"

He laughs again. "Yeah, you're definitely right about that." He pauses for a second. "But what a way to go, huh? Like it was meant to be."

I think about the odds of that happening. Yeah, definitely meant to be.

This is only the second time that we've hiked down into the interior of the Crater. The first time Chris was with us, and we hiked all of the way through, down the Kaupo Gap, with Dean picking us up at the bottom in the VW van.

We've been to the top many times to witness the sunrise, usually coming late at night with many beers and a joint or two, partying with strangers in the warmth of the observatory well into the wee hours, until the sun makes its dramatic appearance.

But this time we have our backpacks and sleeping bags with us, and we're hiking all of the way through again. And this time Ken, who dropped us off at the top this morning, will be picking us up tomorrow at Kaupo. It's about a seventeen mile hike altogether, and luckily downhill most of the way.

We slowly climb out of the hole in the top of the bubble. We're eager to see other lava formations in the area, such as 'Pele's Pig Pen', a semi-circular wall of lava that looks like another bubble that exploded and then also froze. And there's also the 'Bottomless Pit', a scary looking hole that you would definitely not want to fall into. But there's also a lot of other very wild looking lava formations that remain unnamed.

For instance, this strange array of tubes that we are looking at right now, tubes that are arranged sort of like bowling pins in a bowling alley. And then Andy and I come around a corner of rock to see what looks like a regiment of 'Minute Men' soldiers that appeared to have been marching by, and then were suddenly turned to stone. Some of them even appear to carry rifles and flags.

I look up at one point and notice the moon, a white crescent in a turquoise blue sky. And that's exactly where it feels like we are, walking on the surface of the moon. But a magical moon, with blue sky and air to breathe.

"Wow, look at that Ben." Andy diverts my attention to a wisp of fog like clouds that are creeping over the Crater wall to our north, looking like white luminous snakes. They're slithering their way through crevices in the rock and sliding down into the Crater itself. And somehow the sun is hitting them at such an angle that at the top is a short prism, a small section of a rainbow.

"Unbelievable," Andy says.

My sentiments exactly.

We plan on spending the night in Paliku, which is at the far end of the Crater, and back down to normal Hawaii clime's. But I tell Andy that I want to spend the night here, on the moon.

"Can you imagine what it must be like right here at night?" I say. "All the stars? We'll feel like we're in outer space!"

Andy starts chuckling. He knows about my fascination with astronomy, and the moon in particular. 'Ben and his moon', he will sometimes say, when I point it out to him in a clear blue sky. Kind of like right now.

"That would be cool Ben," he says. "But it will make for a really long hike tomorrow, and then we might be late meeting up with Ken."

He's right of course, so I have to agree. But someday...

After spending some time milling around the moon, which actually looks more like Mars with its red rocks and red sand, we start making our way along the trail again, towards Paliku. Ever so slowly the landscape around us begins to change. The red lava rock that crunches under our shoes starts to take on a darker brown color. And we start to see more plant life here and there.

Nothing like the Silverswords that we saw up at higher elevations towards the beginning of our hike. One was in full bloom, its burgundy flower stalk shooting up almost three feet from its base. And since it was flowering that means it could be close to fifty years old. But, this also means that it will die.

The plant life that we're starting to see down here is not near as dramatic, little weeds and grasses that signal the end of the lunar landscape that we've been traversing.

Another hour or so and we reach Paliku. Now we're surrounded by actual trees and bushes, and soft thick grass to pitch our tent on. Except that we have no tent. We're betting that it won't rain, which is a pretty stupid bet on most of Maui. In that respect, we're lucky that there's other people here as well. Not a lot, maybe a dozen at most. Some of them have a few tents pitched, but the rest of them are staying in the 'Cabin'.

There's a series of cabins sprinkled here and there in different parts of the Crater. They sleep twelve, with four rows of bunk beds three high, and they can be reserved in advance for a small fee. But of course Andy and I didn't do that. We suffer from being way too spontaneous.

Just before sunset it does start to rain, and the people who have the cabin let Andy and I duck in there until it passes. In fact they invite everyone inside, and this impromptu gathering of strangers turns into a little happy hour. Someone has a bottle of whiskey, and that gets passed around. Someone else has a joint, and that gets passed around as well. Everyone's in high spirits, sharing stories about all of the incredible things that they saw earlier in the day. Andy is totally in his element, chatting it up and remarking about what a fantastic and wonderful place that Haleakala truly is.

And maybe there's a good reason why all of us are getting along so well. We, all of us, do have one thing in common. Tired of just looking down into the Crater from the observatory with the other tourist's, we've all opted to hike down and through it, longing to experience its secrets and marvels up close.

The rain starts to go away, and we all walk out of the cabin and into a twilight that can only be described as magical. Andy and I walk out of the camp to some higher ground and survey our surroundings. Looking back up into the Crater we see that it is partially obscured by a purplish mist. The trees in our immediate area have turned an electric gold. We look up, and behind a rainbow a few stars have started to show themselves. We feel like we're in one of those retouched post cards, where the artist accentuates the colors to make it more dramatic. Only now it's really happening all around us.

"Unbelievable," Andy whispers, the word of the day.

The twilight seems to hang on longer than what should seem possible, but then things slowly start to darken. From the direction of the cabin and off to the right we see an orangish glow. Someone has got a campfire going, and Andy and I head towards it. We join the half dozen or so people sitting around it, basking in its warmth.

After a while we say goodnight and head to our sleeping bags. There we have 'dinner', which is sandwiches made up of what's left of our bread and sandwich meat. After that we turn in.

Looking up now the stars are complete in a jet black background. The Milky Way dominates the sky, looking like a band of multi-colored jewels. I slowly drift off to sleep, my last thoughts wondering what it must be like right now back up in the lunar landscape of the Crater.

We got lucky. It didn't rain anymore, and we both slept soundly through the night. We have a couple of snack bars for breakfast, and except for the water in our water bottles, that's the end of our supplies.

We have no idea what time it is, but it feels early, maybe six or six thirty. We roll up our sleeping bags and put on our backpacks. We bid farewell to a few of the other hikers that are up, and then we get on the trail.

It's a beautiful morning, with just a few clouds and little or no breeze. We're in luck again, because we've heard that it can get pretty windy up here, and all through the Kaupo Gap.

The trail is uphill at first, not too steep though, with a series of long slow switchbacks. We go down and up again a few times, until we reach a summit. Here we are met with a breathtaking view of the ocean laid out before us, and way off in the distance, a barely discernible 'pitcher's mound', which is actually Mauna Kea on the big island of Hawaii.

It's all downhill from here, as they say, with eleven solid miles of mostly grassy and rocky terrain ahead of us. The immensity of Kaupo Gap, and the wide view of the ocean is humbling. We feel really small in the great scheme of things.

After an hour or two my calves start aching from constantly going downhill, and I find myself wishing that the trail would actually go uphill for a little while. Andy feels the same way, so we decide to take a little break. We sit on a couple of boulders and drink some water from our water bottles.

Andy gestures at the sweeping view in front of us. "Look where we live, Ben."

Look where we live, indeed. "Thanks man," I say.

Andy looks over at me.

"For talking me into making the move to Maui."

He smiles. "It really wasn't that hard." Then he adds, "Both times."

We both laugh.

After a little more talking and resting, we realize that we better keep moving. We've still got a long way to go.

As I walk along, slowly descending towards the sea, I think about how many lives Andy has affected by moving to Maui. Starting with me and Dean and Chris, and then Sara and Jacki, and then Mark, who in turn brought Dorothy, and before that his brother Ken. And then of course there's Drew and Rick, and later Scott, so yeah, a lot of people changed their lives since Andy decided to move here. Andy the salesman, I laugh to myself. He's pretty damn good at it.

Our legs are begging for a change, anything but this constant downhill motion. But the only way to change is to stop, and we have to keep moving. And did I mention that we're both wearing flip-flops? They're good ones, Lightning Bolts, but flip-flops just the same. I'm thinking that some hiking boots, or even just some tennis shoes might've made things a little easier. Next time, I say to myself. Next time.

Finally the trail starts to flatten out. We're in a long meadow, and we're not going downhill anymore. Even though we're both totally exhausted, it feels so good that we both let out audible sighs of relief.

After maybe a mile of this we come around a corner of trees and we see a few cars parked. And then, not too much further we see the van! Ken has the side door open, and he's sitting leisurely in a lawn chair. Andy lets out a shout, and Ken walks up and greets us, and helps us with our packs.

I'm completely wiped out, and crawl into the back of the van, half sitting and half laying on the bench seat. Andy seems to have more energy than me, and he's emphatically telling Ken how 'unbelievable' it was.

"You've gotta do it sometime, Ken. You've just gotta do it!"

Andy climbs into the shotgun seat while Ken gets behind the wheel. "So, after that long hike you guys must be really thirsty!" Ken says with a smile. Without waiting for an answer he turns his head back towards me and says, "Hey Ben, why don't you open the lid to that cooler that's next to you on the floor."

I hadn't really noticed it until now, and I reach over and open the lid. I'm greeted with a beautiful sight; about a dozen Heineken's packed in ice. It looks too good to be true. I open one and hand it to Andy, then open one for myself.

Andy leans back and extends his bottle towards me. "Cheers Ben! We did it! We hiked the whole Crater again!"

We clink bottles and drink, nothing ever tasting so good.

Andy screams out of his open window, thanking Pele, the Hawaiian goddess of fire and volcanoes, for seeing us safely through her Crater.

Ken and I are laughing.

Andy thrusts his beer towards me again, the second of many toasts to come.

I'm just so totally relaxed right now, and can't believe that I'm sitting in a moving vehicle. I've got the most exquisite one beer buzz going, and by the look on Andy's face, talking and laughing with Ken, I can tell that he does too. I can't hear what they're saying, but it doesn't matter. I look out of the window at the desert side of the island going by, and it looks beautiful to me.

Andy reaches back and hands me his empty bottle. Ken says he'll have one too now, so I open two more and hand them up to them. I open another one for myself, and we all hold our beers high, toasting the moment.

All is definitely right with the world...

I'm sitting in Dean's VW Squareback behind Longhi's. We both have the day off, but we're working just the same. But not at Longhi's.

In the months before he moved back to Maui, Dean landed

a job through his dad with a company that manufactured and installed Sun Rooms, or 'California Rooms'. He helped another installer for a while, learning the tricks of the trade, until they sent him out on his own, and I would sometimes help him. Made of aluminum and composite wall panels, and aluminum windows, we could usually install one in a day or two.

And now the same company is expanding their business to Hawaii, and Maui in particular. Dean's installer from California got a hold of him through Dean's dad, and Dean has already done a couple of jobs with him here on the island.

This is his first job alone, and to help coax me into helping him on my day off, Dean has promised breakfast. So, not to draw too much attention, I'm sitting in the car while he's inside preparing our food to go. And he's not holding back. Sausage and cheese frittata's, fruit salad, fresh squeezed orange juice, toast and coffee. Good ol' Dean, he never does anything halfway.

The job is in Kihei, about twenty miles away. As we enjoy our gourmet breakfast, coconut palms sliding by on our right and Monkeypod trees gliding by overhead, Dean talks about our possible future.

"This could really be a cool thing Ben," he says in between bites. "We stand to make a lot more money than we do at the restaurant. And they might send us to jobs on Oahu and the Big Island, all expenses paid, of course." He looks over at me and smiles.

He's definitely got my attention. More money, and a chance to check out other islands, and get paid for it? Yeah, this really could be a cool thing.

"I know you gotta work tomorrow," he says, "so we'll just get as much done today as we can and I'll finish up tomorrow by myself."

Sounds good.

We're sitting outside on a picnic bench behind the Sun Room that we almost completely finished, drinking cold Budweiser's and enjoying the view of the ocean a few miles in front of us. We talk about possible trips to the Big Island, excited about our new prospects as Sun Room installers. The sun is setting, and the ocean starts to take on a rosy pink hue. Will our future be rosier too? I sincerely hope so.

I'm almost at the end of my shift at Longhi's, cutting and tenderizing some squid. Ken shows up for his evening shift, and he looks happy. His hair is still wet from the shower, and he looks like he's probably been at the beach all day.

Not long after he's been here there's a knock at the back kitchen door. Ken goes back to answer it, and it's a couple of Filipino fisherman with a fresh Ono for sale. The transaction is quickly made, and Ken puts the fish on the big cutting table in the center of the kitchen. He needed the big table, because this is a big fish, about six feet long and probably sixty or seventy pounds. Known as Wahoo in most other places, the Hawaiian name Ono is very apt, meaning 'Da best'.

It's a sleek missile of a fish, obviously built for speed. This is the biggest one I've ever seen, and maybe Ken's too, the way he is excitedly hovering over it. His eyes gleam like an anxious kid on Christmas morning.

I've never seen an Ono alive in its ocean habitat, so I can only try to imagine the colors that graced it before it was caught. It still has silvery vertical stripes running the length of it, and one big eye stares up at the ceiling.

Ken selects a knife and sets to work filleting the fish, carefully starting at the tail and getting as much of the whitish flesh as he can off of the bone. I'm watching him closely, impressed at how good he's got at doing this.

He looks up at me with a sparkle in his eye. "You want to try some of this, Ben?"

I nod eagerly, and he cuts off a generous piece from the thickest part of the fillet and takes it around the corner to the cooking station.

I finish cleaning up, and about five minutes later Ken comes back around the corner, lavishly presenting me with the finished product like a waiter, setting the plate down in front of me and bowing. The huge fillet takes up the entire plate, and it looks and smells amazing.

Each bite melts in my mouth, and I thank Ken profusely, telling him that this could be the best fish dinner I've ever tasted.

He comes back a little later with a piece for himself, and we sit on the cutting table and eat, thanking the Hawaiian God's for this gift from the sea. And thanks to Bob Longhi too, of course.

We came to the Islands, Andy, Dean, Chris and I, looking for adventure. To live a new life on our own terms, to experience new things and meet new people, and, let's face it, to just plain have fun.

And Dean isn't having fun anymore.

The two of us are sitting in the backyard at the Haole Camp having a beer. It's early evening, and Dean has just got home from working with the Sunroom guy. He's telling me how he misses the restaurant life. And he misses Sara. She's working nights waitressing at Longhi's now, so when Dean gets home she's working, and when she gets home he's sleeping.

"I don't know, Ben," he says. "The guy is pushing me harder now, says we have to finish every job in one day. And we're taking shorter lunches and working longer hours." He pauses and drinks some of his beer. "The money's good, I've even saved a little. But this isn't what I came over here for." He looks over at me. "I want my old Lahaina life back."

This is sounding a lot like Andy and I at the potato chip factory, so I can't really blame him. And from the look in his eye, I can tell that he's already got his mind made up. Ah well, there goes the paid trips to Oahu and the Big Island.

"Have you told him yet?"

"Not yet," he says. "I tried to tell him the concept of running on 'Hawaiian Time', and to not be in such a big hurry all the time, but he laughed in my face. I've got a job with him tomorrow, and when we're done I'll tell him."

I don't really know what to say. I'm thinking of opportunities lost. But Dean is the one that found this opportunity in the first place.

I raise my beer. "Well, welcome back to the fun life!"

Dean laughs, and raises his.

"Spin!" Rick greets me with a smile and a handshake, and hands me a beer.

Mark and I are at the Huea House for a Bar-B-Que. Drew invited us over for grilled Mahi and chicken, and we'll always accept an invitation for a good free meal.

The Huea house is actually split in two. Drew and Rick live on the side where I used to live with Gina, which has three bedrooms and a small kitchen. A breezeway separates them from the other section of the house, which has a much larger kitchen and dining room. And this happens to be where Jacki used to live.

The dining room has a large round table, and that's where the four of us are sitting now, enjoying a cold beer while the coals slowly burn to readiness in the backyard.

"So..." Drew says, setting down his beer. He looks at Mark and I with a funny smile. "We have a bit of news for you two." He glances over at Rick, then back at us again. "The Midnight is goin' down boys. The transmission's starting to go."

"She's on her last legs," Rick chimes in.

Drew leans in for effect. "She's gonna die."

It's a sad moment, indeed.

"What're you gonna do with it?" Mark asks.

Drew looks over at Rick again, then back at us. "Rick wants to cliff it."

What was that again?

Mark and I start laughing.

"Cliff the Midnight!" Rick proclaims, holding up his beer.

After the laughter dies down Drew says, "We're thinkin' about maybe somewhere on the backside of Haleakala... you know, somewhere on the bad road."

I've seen a few abandoned cars on the island, in funny places, usually upside down and unidentifiable. And I always wondered what happened, and how they got there. And now they're talking about contributing to the mystery.

"Cliffing the Midnight," Mark says, absently.

"That's right brah," Drew says to him. "And we were hoping that maybe you could help us out. We're obviously gonna need a ride when the deed is done. We'll be in need of your services with the Go-Mad."

Mark laughs. "I thought we were crazy!" He laughs again and says, "Okay, yeah, sure. I'll give you guys a ride."

"Excellent!" Rick says, and we all raise our bottles to the demise of the Midnight Rambler.

We're on that idyllic section of road between Hana and Oheo Gulch. Mark's driving the Go-Mad, and Andy and Dean and I are 'car riding', which means that we are sitting on our doors with the windows rolled down, and our heads above the roof. We get an unobstructed view this way, and on this part of the road in particular the views are extremely dramatic.

We're following Drew and Rick in the Midnight, Drew driving and Rick sitting out of the sunroof. After a few stops we finally reach the pools. Rick wants to jump the Bridge, but it's one of those rare times that it is unjumpable. There's been a lack of rain, and the lower pools are not flowing. It's a strange sight to see the water just sitting there, and not hear the falls above and below the bridge.

But a few of us have been here before under these conditions, and we know from experience that the upper pools might still be flowing. We take the Waimoku Falls trail that bypasses the lower pools and head straight to Dean's Pool of Life. When we get close we can hear the falls, and we're happy to see that they're still flowing.

We all make the jump at different times, and then proceed to float on down the stream, through the 'guava pool' with its sheer rock walls, until we come to the top of the Pool of

Death, which is barely trickling. Rick, in his normal state of fearlessness wants to jump it. We laugh, and tell him that it's not possible, but he goes out to the edge anyway and leans way out to look down. He's just messing with us, but he's making us nervous at the same time. He comes back and joins us, reluctantly agreeing that we're probably right.

Drew tells us that there's a full moon tonight, and he wants to come back up here to watch it rise. Of course I'm totally up for that, as is everyone, but later that evening it's just Drew and Rick, and Mark and I.

If I had to pick three places in the world to watch the full moon rise, this would definitely be number one. And on this night we happen to get a little Hawaiian special effects thrown in.

On the latter part of the trail up here we get rained on, and do our best to take cover under the trees. When it lightens up we continue on out to the top of the falls where we were earlier today. Only now it's a different picture on the big screen.

Sunset is coming on, and pinks and purples are bouncing off of the rain squall that's passing through. In the valley below the lush foliage lining both sides is glistening like jewels on fire. Arcing across the entire valley is a rainbow, framing the picture.

We're in one of those postcards again, and we're speechless.

And then, as the colors start to fade and the rainbow goes away, through it all we see the full moon rising in all of its glory. It's low, so it's huge, but amazingly bright at the same time. This is one of those scenes that you might try to describe to someone, but words just don't do it justice.

I think this is Rick's second time to the pools, but definitely the first time he has seen anything like this. He's clearly in awe of the spectacle in front of us, and stands in silence at the top of the fall.

"Unbelievable," Mark finally says.

There's that word again.

THE BULLET HILL DIARIES

It's the next morning, and after a dip in one of the lower pools we get on the road. Drew and Rick are in front of us again, and we follow in the Go-Mad. It doesn't take us long to notice that the Midnight is leaking transmission fluid. Badly.

Just as we start getting out of the intense jungle terrain and into more open grassy plains, we see a local Paniolo standing by his pick-up in front of his property. Drew pulls into the guys road and we follow him. We park and get out of the car while Drew and Rick go up and talk to the local. It turns out he doesn't have any transmission fluid, but he has some motor oil. Used, dirty brown motor oil. Thinking that this might be better than nothing, the guy lets Drew and Rick borrow a funnel, and they pour it in with their fingers crossed.

We get underway again but only go in and out of a couple of valleys before the Midnight can go no further. In forward, that is. They find out that it will still drive in reverse, so they follow us now, driving backwards on this really tricky dirt road.

Knowing that reverse probably won't last too much longer, Drew and Rick are desperately looking for a cliff. But the road has turned from cliffs to ravines. They know that this is the end, so at the crest of a fairly deep ravine they stop.

We all get out and help to turn the car around, and get it positioned at the top of the hill. Rick decides to do the honors, so he climbs in the driver's seat and shuts the door. I'm thinking that he's going to pull the emergency brake and hop out, but that's not his style.

He pulls the brake alright, but is still inside as the car slowly picks up speed, just twenty feet or so to the top of the ravine. About halfway there we see him stand up and climb out of the sunroof, then maneuver himself onto the trunk lid. He stands up on the trunk lid and rides the car like a giant skateboard, shouting and jumping off at the last minute.

We all rush up to see the car crash through some bushes and rocks, going about thirty or forty feet before settling in to its final resting place.

Rick landed on his feet, but then took a tumble, skinning up one of his knees. He doesn't seem to care though, and we all stand there for a while, paying our last respects, and then slowly pile into the Go-Mad.

We stop at the Kaupo Store and get munchies and beer, and then a lot of us car ride the remainder of the bad road back to civilization. Before long we come to Ulupalakua, and the end of the desert terrain, and the beginning of lush green Hawaii again.

I know that Rick would rather it had been a real cliff that he could have sent her off, but I'm kind of glad that it didn't happen that way. The only real cliffs they had to choose from went down to the shoreline, and to me somehow that would have been a worse crime. Because we have definitely committed a crime, something like littering in the first degree.

So there the Midnight will lie, probably until she rusts into oblivion.

Before Sara started waitressing at Longhi's she worked at a jewelry shop on Front Street, and she was bored to tears. When Dean informed her that there was an opening for a waitress, it took some coaxing to talk her into applying for the job. Sara is definitely on the shy side, but she was ready for a change, and went for it. And now, wouldn't you know it, sweet little shy Sara has become the highest grossing waitress at Longhi's, bringing home more money than Dean now, and she loves to tease him about it. But Dean is super proud of her, and she positively glows with her new found self-confidence. And it's a beautiful thing to see.

And speaking of Dean, he has quit the sun room job like he said and is working full time at Longhi's again. He is bussing tables, and occasionally cooking on the front line with Ken. And when you bus tables at Longhi's, it's you, not the waiter or waitress, that gets to take out the homemade desserts on a tray, enticing the customer's at the end of their meal. Dean really gets into this, meticulously arranging the desserts on one of the large trays, sometimes even placing some flowers here and there.

One night when both of us are working, Dean comes up to me in the kitchen with a big smile on his face. "I've got a four top of middle-aged women out there Ben, and I've been working the 'Goob' charm on them. They're already in love with me."

Dean the Dream Machine, doing what he does best.

When it's time for their desserts Dean goes above and beyond, placing them just so on the tray and going all out with the flowers.

A little while later he comes back in the kitchen positively glowing. Along with the huge grin on his face he has a bill in his hand, and puts it in my face. A hundred bucks! For serving dessert!

The rule is that whatever tips the bus person makes for serving dessert, they get to keep them, and in this case Dean made more than the waiter, who is none too happy about it. But Dean is high as a kite, telling me that he's buying me drinks after work, and that we're gonna celebrate!

Today is a pretty special day in paradise. Bob Longhi has closed the restaurant for the day, and has rented out the Windjammer Cruise's three masted Schooner for all of us employees. Dean and Sara and I are pretty excited.

We've often watched this boat in the evening on its sunset dinner cruise, either from the beach or from a bar, and always dreamed of going out on it someday. And now, here we are.

We will take our time cruising across the channel to the island of Lanai, about nine miles away. We will be able to indulge in an impressive spread of food, all we can eat, and all of the beer, wine, and booze we can drink. And oh yeah, we'll also have a live rock band playing for us on the way there.

It's about ten am when we depart from the dock. Dean, Sara and I grab our drink of choice and take up a place in the middle of the boat, looking down towards the stern where the band is set up. As soon as we exit the harbor the band starts playing, and their opening song is 'Cocaine'.

I laugh to myself, because I used to play this song with Flurry. That was before they started playing at Mormon dances, where they were told they could only play the song if they changed the title and the lyrics. So they came up with 'Solarcaine'.

'If you don't wanna get burned

You've gotta take a turn, Solarcaine'

Hilariously pathetic.

I've never been on a moving vessel with a live band before, and I have to admit that the overall effect is pretty cool. We seem to crash through the small swells to the beat of the music, and everyone is rocking and rolling, and smiling with the promise of a fun day ahead.

After playing some Stone's, and some Bad Company, the band takes a break, and then it isn't long before we start getting close to Lanai. The boat pulls as close to shore as it dares and then anchors. Most everyone jumps in the water and swims the short distance to the beach, with its blinding white sand.

Dean and Sara and I plop ourselves down on the beach, this being the first time that any of us has been to Lanai, an island that we see from Lahaina every day. We look out at the boat that brought us here, and the West Maui mountains behind its three tall mast's.

And then Dean says what we're all thinking. "Look where we fucken live man!"

Sara shouts, "Woohoo!"

We all laugh.

And we all feel pretty 'fucken' fortunate.

We're on the island for almost an hour before they call us back to the boat. The 'Pineapple Isle' they call it, although we can't see any from where we are.

After we get back aboard and get underway the three of us

take advantage of the complimentary buffet, filling up on deli sandwiches, shrimp cocktails and fresh fruit.

About halfway back to Lahaina they stop the boat and drift, so that whoever wants to can jump in the water. The sea is an azure blue, and you can just make out the bottom, which is probably fifty feet down. Sara says No way, there's sharks in there! But Dean and I go for it, along with about twenty other people. It's calm and serene, and it feels just a little cooler than the shallow water back at the beach. Dean and I swim around the boat, diving under and checking out the hull before we climb back aboard.

Dean and I grab a beer and join Sara on the bow, and not long after we're underway a small school of dolphins swims up and keeps time with us, occasionally surfacing for air. Everyone on the bow is loving it, watching the dolphins play with our boat before they swim off to wherever it is they are going.

It's a perfect finale to a perfect day, and the three of us toast the dolphins, and Lanai, and the boat, and especially Bob Longhi for making it all happen.

I have loaned Drew my super eight movie camera, the Elmo. He has been back to California and has enrolled in a couple of college classes, and he has to turn in some kind of a report for one of them. He has decided that his report is going to be a movie, The Maui Movie, he's calling it.

The only way to edit this movie is to pull the trigger, film something, and then let off the trigger. Then when he's ready again, pull the trigger, film, and let off. There's no second chances, no erasing and re-filming. And even with these constraints Drew will create, in my opinion, a masterpiece.

We're in Haleakala Crater again, doing the full hike all of the way through again. Only this time it's Drew and Rick, and Mark and I. This is Drew and Rick's first time down into the interior of the Crater, and Drew is periodically filming. I've got my elven cloak with me, and Mark has borrowed Deans, and

Drew wants to film us walking along the rim of one of the large cinder cones, a crater within the Crater. He positions himself above us and as close as he can get to the cinder cone, and films us walking along the rim with our cloaks on. When I see this footage later, I can't help but notice that Mark and I look like a couple of Hobbits, like Frodo and Sam, somewhere in the depths of Mordor.

Drew wanted to film the sunrise before we started our hike, so most of the previous night was spent in the observatory. During the early morning hours, still dark and waiting for the sun to show itself, Drew tells me about the first frames of the Movie, the 'opening credits'.

"I got lucky Ben," he says. "I wanted to start the movie with a nice beach, so Rick and I decided to check out Honokawai and Napili. We found a beach with lots of cool looking coconut trees, just what I was looking for. I wrote 'The Maui Movie' in the sand with a stick, and as I'm filming it, maybe ten seconds later a small wave comes up and washes it away. It was perfect!"

"Wow!" I say, "I can't wait to see that."

"Yeah well, I'm hoping to get some more cool stuff on film down in this Crater."

"I can guarantee you that you will, brah,"

After the filming of Mark and I on the red cinder cone, we proceed on and down into the lunar landscape, where I wanted to spend the night the last time I was here with Andy. Pretty soon we find Pele's Pig Pen, and the Bottomless Pit, and Bubble Cave. Rick climbs to the top of Pele's Pig Pen, and Drew gets him on film. We spend a little bit of time here, Drew getting some cool footage of weird volcanic formations, and then we continue on, and my chance to spend the night on the moon slips away once again.

We don't reach Paliku until almost dusk, and there's about a dozen people here and they've already got a fire going. Soon after introducing ourselves things turn into another 'happy hour'. Someone produces a bottle and we pass that around, and I laugh to myself, because here it is, happening again. Talking and laughing with strangers in this very special place.

After we eat we return to the fire. Late into the night, to the surprise of all of us, out of the darkness a Paniolo rides up on a large horse. He hops off the horse before it even stops, and he has a large bottle of Cuervo in his hand. He's a big guy, and very jovial, and everyone greets him like he's King Kamehameha himself. He has a big hearty laugh, and without knowing who he is or where he came from, (does he live up here?) we accept him into our circle, and we pass around his bottle of tequila.

It's a full on party in Paliku now, and we're all getting plenty buzzed. The fire roars, the burned wood crackling and sending sparks high into the sky, where they blend with the stars.

The nearby Cabin has been reserved by four twenty something girls who have been partying with the rest of us. One by one they start turning in, and the thought of crashing in one of those bunks is making me feel tired, so I decide to turn in myself.

I guess I should've stayed up just a little while longer though, because the next morning Mark tells me a funny story. Later on that night the Paniolo got on his horse, actually rode it into the girl's cabin, and *lassoed* one of the girls. All in fun, of course. I'm assuming she wasn't hurt, or dragged off to his lair, wherever that might be.

Apparently not, because now I notice the girls calmly eating breakfast and packing things. And there's no sign of the Paniolo, his appearance last night seeming more like something out of a dream. But dreams like that only seem to happen in places like this, special places that take some effort to get to. And to get out of.

Knowing that we have this arduous hike ahead of us down the Kaupo Gap, I find myself wishing that *I* had a horse.

Things seem to be coming to an end. That's the feeling I'm getting anyway, as I awake in my bed at the Haole Camp. I think I know why I feel this way, but maybe it's the dream I just woke up from, a dream that I'm trying to recollect. But the harder I try the quicker it slips from my memory.

I'm thinking that it had something to do with the band, and playing music. Or is it that I really do miss playing music, and so that's what I think I dreamed. It doesn't really matter, because I know what brought this on...

I was finishing up my shift the other night at Longhi's, around five o'clock or so, and a few of the waiters and waitresses were talking about the band that played upstairs the night before. They couldn't believe how good they were, and asked me if I had seen them yet. I said I hadn't, and they told me that they were playing again tonight if I wanted to check them out. They got my curiosity going, so I decided that I would.

I went back to the Haole Camp and showered and changed. No one was around, not even Jeff, who works days driving the Sugar Cane Train. I was hoping that maybe Mark would be there, but I guess he was working too at the Pioneer Inn. So, I headed back to Longhi's alone.

When I got there, after saying hello to Dean and Ken in the kitchen, I went upstairs and sat at a small table near to where the band was set up. The band wasn't playing yet, so they had some music on. It was Supertramp, and at one point during the song this guy near me, about my age and alone also, suddenly stood up and started singing along:

'Take a look at my girlfriend
    She's the only one I got
    Not much of a girlfriend
    Never seem to get a lot'

It was kind of a makeshift, impromptu karaoke thing, and the guy quickly sat back down, obviously pretty buzzed. He looked kind of sad too, and I figured that maybe he just broke up with his girlfriend. Or perhaps he just didn't have one, something that I could relate to. Then I kind of laughed to myself, thinking that if Rick was here right now he might go up to the guy, maybe buy him a beer, and then tell him to 'No cry, no ask why'.

Soon after that little bit of entertainment was over, the band took the stage. They were a four piece, with guitar, keyboards, bass and drums. They went into their first song, and after listening to it for a little bit I guessed that it was an original. It was kind of a jazz-rock fusion thing, and all four of these guys were very good. Weaving their melodies around a solid bass and drums rhythm, the guitar and keyboards accentuating each other perfectly. No one was trying to play over anyone else, all of them just contributing their part to make one cohesive sound.

After playing one more song that I didn't recognize, they went into something that at first I couldn't put my finger on, then slowly realized that they were starting to play 'Breathe' by Pink Floyd. I'd never heard any band try to cover any part of Dark Side of the Moon before, but these guys were doing it, and doing it well. If I was in the other room I would've sworn that David Gilmour and Roger Waters and Nick Mason were in here. They were that good.

As I was sitting there, happily getting lost in the song, I slowly started to have a kind of a revelation. (Not quite a 'psychedelic tequila moment of awareness', but close). I started realizing that I wanted to do this. I wanted to play music again, and I mean really try to make it a serious goal.

And there's a band back home that I might be able to step back into, if they'll have me.

I started thinking about this more and more, getting myself all worked up, and actually worrying that the boys back home might not wait around for me and get another drummer.

The band took a break, and since I was kind of riled up now I decided to take a break too, and went downstairs and crossed the street and sat on the seawall. For the first time in my life I really knew what I wanted to do, and I was getting kind of emotional about it, because I knew what that meant.

It meant leaving this place.

I thought of the drunk guy who was singing along with Supertramp earlier, and I laughed to myself. Because now I was being the sensitive one, having the emotional moment.

Upstairs in Longhi's I heard the band starting to play again, their music drifting out into the night. And I silently thanked them.

They'll never know what their music has done for me.

Andy, Mister Surf Safari lately, wants to go snorkeling. And it's funny, because he knows that I'm not very good at surfing, but he also knows that I love snorkeling. Maybe he's doing this because of what happened a few weeks ago.

He came by the Haole Camp in the morning knowing that Dean and I had the day off, and talked us into going surfing with him. He's caught the surfing fever, and wants to spread it to us. There's plenty of surfboards here at the Haole Camp, courtesy of George and Jeff, and Andy has his own board. He said it was breaking two to three foot in Lahaina Harbor, thinking that that's not too big for us, and that we could just walk there.

We ended up having a really fun time, and I actually caught a few waves and stood up. We were out there a long time, and towards the end of the day I managed to scrape my shin on some coral. Just the top layer of skin, kind of like Mark's back wound at the blowhole, but I ended up getting a staph infection.

So here we are, the two of us in the van heading to Slaughterhouse, where Andy has been surfing a lot. But there's no waves today, and Andy's thinking that the snorkeling might be good there.

When we get there Andy parks in the dirt off to the side of the road. We grab our gear and make our way down the trail to the beach. The bay is super calm, like a sheet of glass, and it's perfect snorkeling conditions. In fact I've never seen Slaughterhouse this calm, and when I look over at Andy he's hiding a smile. Then I remember seeing his surfboard in the van.

"You wanted to go surfing today, didn't you?"

"I did," he confesses. "But then I heard that there weren't any waves, so I had to do something."

I look out at the water. "Well, I'm glad you came and got me."

We wade into the clear water and put on our fins, then our mask and snorkels. We start following the shoreline to the right, where soon the beach ends and it becomes rocky. We stay as close to the rocky shoreline as possible, diving down occasionally and checking out little niches in the rock. Among a lot of other fish we soon see a pretty good sized Parrot Fish, and Andy dives down to see how close he can get to it, but the fish stays just out of his reach, teasing him.

We continue on around the bay, taking our time and exploring different areas. Before long we come to the end of the rock outcropping, and the beginning of open ocean. We both stop and spit out our snorkels. Andy says, "I don't really want to go all the way back the way we came. Why don't we just cut straight across the bay back to the beach?"

I say sure, and we put our snorkels back in our mouths and start heading across. The bottom drops away quickly, the sand turning from white, to grey, to gone. Now we're just swimming in a blue void, and I feel really vulnerable. I try not to think of big killer sharks, like the one we saw at McKenna's, appearing out of nowhere.

Just then something brushes my left arm, and I twist suddenly in fright. To my relief it's just Andy, and then I almost laugh when I see his face. He's just as scared as I am!

We stick close to each other, kicking harder now, and I wonder if Andy is thinking about that Tiger shark at McKenna's too. I try to tell myself that it's an irrational fear, that the odds of seeing another shark like that here at Slaughterhouse are slim. But out here in this void it's pretty easy to justify irrational fears.

We're both still kicking as hard as we can, occasionally looking off to the sides and behind us every now and then. It seems to go on forever, and I don't remember the bay being this big.

Then finally, I slowly start to see a change in the color of the bottom. First grey, then whiter, then the unmistakable contour of sand.

Wonderful, beautiful sand.

We slow down a little, instantly feeling safer. The sand turns even whiter as we near the shore. It's silly though, this sudden feeling of safety. If there were sharks around they could still attack us, no problem.

We crawl up onto the beach, totally exhausted. We flip off our masks and kick off our fins, and just lay there catching our breaths. Finally Andy says, "Holy shit Ben, for a while there all I could think of was that damn shark that we saw at McKenna."

"Yeah, me too,"

We look over at each other, and then we both start laughing. The kind of laughter that only comes from exhaustion and relief. When we regain our composure we walk into the water again to rinse the sand off our bodies, and then grab our gear and head up the trail back to the van.

When Andy turns the key he says, "Whaddya say we go to Leilani's and have a couple of beers?"

"That sounds great," I say.

Leilani's, on the beach in Kaanapali, is the newest addition to the expanding Kimo's franchise. Since Andy is the kitchen manager, they sent him to Leilani's to help open it. On the beach side of Whaler's Village, Leilani's is a beautiful mix of traditional Hawaiian décor and modern luxury. Lots of tropical plants and Koa wood, with bamboo seats and bar-stools. And behind the bar are a couple of large screen TV's.

The bartender slides two tall glasses of beer in front of us, on the house. When you're on a micro-budget like I am, it's great going out with Andy.

Andy raises his glass. "To Maui Ben."

I raise mine. "To Maui."

After he sets his glass back down, in a lowered tone he says, "You know, we don't really have to tell anybody about how scared we got swimming back across the bay."

I laugh. "You're right. We don't."

"It's just crazy though, you know?" he says. "If we never would have seen that shark at McKenna's we probably wouldn't have given it a second thought. When I go surfing I never even think about sharks."

"Yeah, that is crazy. But when we were in the middle of that bay, nothing but blue water all around us, I felt so defenseless."

Andy raises his glass again. "To never worrying about sharks again!"

I raise my glass.

The bartender comes down the bar to us. "What's all the toasting going on down here?"

Andy doesn't hesitate. "Oh, Ben and I had a great day snorkeling at Slaughterhouse. Have you ever snorkeled there? It's awesome! Lots of fish, and it was really calm…"

Andy gives me a quick wink, and I try not to laugh.

"Okay…" the bartender says, slowly.

"We'll have two more," Andy says, quickly.

After the bartender leaves us with a fresh round, I turn to Andy and say, "There's something I gotta tell you brah."

Andy looks at me and waits.

"I'm thinking about leaving, going back to Seal."

Andy's mouth drops, and then his face narrows. "I had a feeling you were holding something back. I thought maybe you met a girl or something."

I laugh. "No, no, nothing like that."

When I don't say anything more he says, "So, what brought this on?"

I briefly tell him about the band I saw at Longhi's, and my little epiphany.

Pretty soon he says, "Well, I guess this means that you've got your mind made up."

"Yeah man, I really do."

"Well," he says again, "We're gonna have to give you a good send off." He drinks some of his beer, then says, "I'll think of something."

I laugh, knowing that he will.

"Well, shit!" he says. "I guess there's no way I can talk you out of this. I'm supposed to try though. That's what friends are for, you know."

"I appreciate that, and I'd do the same for you. But like you said, I've got my mind made up."

We drink our beers, and I look out at the ocean, and the islands of Lanai and Molokai. I look at the coconut palms in front of us on the beach, barely ruffled by a light breeze. "Yeah, I'm really gonna miss this place."

Then Andy goes in for one more dig. "It'll haunt you Ben, you know, leaving the islands."

"Thanks brah."

He laughs. "You know about how, if you live here you're not supposed to leave. And if you do leave, you'll be haunted by the spirit of the islands until you return."

"Yeah, I have heard that. Thanks for reminding me."

He laughs again, and holds up his hands. "Hey, just doing my job here."

I laugh too. "Right."

We both drink our beers, and then he says, "Well Ben, when you guys hit the big time maybe you can stop here when you're on your world tour."

"Now that's funny!"

We both laugh, and drain our beers.

Soon, not long after Andy's and my snorkeling day, Dean shows me an ad in the paper for a plane ticket. One way from

Honolulu to LAX for a hundred bucks. Even though it's a Red Eye flight, all I have to do is get myself to Honolulu, and then I can use it whenever I want. I decide to buy it. Right after I do, Mark informs me that he has decided to go back home too, and he still has half of his round trip ticket from when he and I came here. He's already sent Dorothy home, using the other half of her round trip ticket.

When Mark's departure day comes, it's Dean and Sara and I that take him to the airport. We leave early though, and take in a movie in Kahului. It's 'Apocalypse Now', a movie that we've been wanting to see. I can't help but notice that some of the jungle footage looks like Hawaii, and Dean says that he heard that some scenes were filmed on Kauai. Fire and destruction in paradise.

When we drop Mark off at the airport it's a little emotional, like it always is. Sara has tears in her eyes, and gives Mark a long hug. Dean shakes his hand and gives him a quick hug, saying, "Aloha brah!"

I shake his hand too, and Mark says, "I guess I'll be seeing you pretty soon, Fin."

"Yeah man. In about three weeks."

"Well, let me know, and maybe I can pick you up at the airport."

"Okay, sure." As I say this I realize that I'm really going to be leaving soon myself. And now is it really starting to hit me.

On the way back to Lahaina I marvel at how powerfully the Hawaiian Islands affect us, and how hard it is to leave them. And then I remember what someone told me, Andy maybe, about how the Islands lie in the almost exact center of the Pacific Ocean, the largest ocean on the planet, three thousand miles from anything. And before anyone got here, before the first Polynesians made their truly heroic journey, it was a true paradise. Not only were there no people, among other things there were no Kiawe trees lining the shore. No wild pigs in the jungle. No snakes, and no mongoose to get rid of the snakes. And my favorite one, no mosquitos!

Being so far from any human civilization, the Islands seemed to be saying, 'Here we are, try to find us. Try to reach us, if you dare. But you're going to have to work for it. And if by chance you do find us, Ye shall be rewarded.' And those first Polynesians, after unimaginable effort and hardship, were rewarded, with an island paradise like no other on Earth.

Andy was right when he was teasing me the other day, about the spirit of the islands haunting me. It's definitely already started, and I haven't even left yet.

Maybe a week after taking Mark to the airport I come back to the Haole Camp from lunch downtown. There I find only Jeff, sitting by himself in the backyard. He has a twelve pack next to him in a cooler and throws me one.

As we're sitting there having a beer he says, "I heard a rumor that you're leaving too."

"Yeah, um, I'm afraid the rumor is true."

He peers at me over his beer. "The Haole Camp is turning into a ghost town."

I laugh. "I'm truly sorry about that." I look around me. "I'm really gonna miss this place, and you and Tracy and George."

With that he gets up and grabs the cooler. "How about we go finish these beers somewhere else Ben? Someplace cool that I know of."

I've got nothing else to do, and it sounds kind of fun. "Sure," I say.

Jeff drives a classic old 60's era MG, a two seater with no top. If it rains, you get wet. It's not in the best of shape, but it's not in really bad shape either. The white paint is fading, and it has a few Hawaiian rust spots, but it looks very cool just the same.

Jeff's the one who drives the Sugar Cane Train in Kaanapali, a tourist train that I've never been on. His uniform is blue and white striped overalls with a matching engineer Bill's hat. How he got this job I'll never know, but he must know what he's doing because this is an authentic old steam engine train, with all of the bells and whistles.

We're heading up towards Kaanapali now, talking and laughing with our hair blowing in the breeze. When we get up past Kaanapali, close to Kapalua and its world class golf course, Jeff turns off of the main road and onto a dirt sugarcane road. Up we climb, speeding along and kicking up red dust that flies into the air behind us.

Jeff knows this area well, (the tracks of the Sugarcane Train are somewhere nearby.) We keep climbing, turning this way and that, tall stands of sugarcane whipping by on either side of us, that smell that I love strong in the air.

We finally emerge out of the sugarcane and onto... perfectly manicured green grass!

Jeff stops the car and looks at me smiling. "Do you know where we are?"

I look around. To my left down a grassy hill I see the ocean off in the distance. To my right, up the hill and over a little rise, I see... a flag. "You're shitting me!" I say with sudden realization. "We're on a fairway!"

"Not just any fairway," Jeff laughs, "but a Kapalua fairway, one of the nicest in the world!"

Before I can say another word, Jeff punches the gas and turns right, and we fly straight up the middle of the fairway, straight towards that flag. We come up over the rise, (I swear we get air) and onto the green.

Jeff instantly whips the wheel and pulls the emergency brake. We spin in circles probably three times before coming to a stop, perfectly facing the ocean. (I shit you not.)

Jeff's laughing so hard he's about to bust, and I start laughing too. "You are fucking crazy!" I finally say. "What if some golfers come along?"

"They won't," he says. "The course is closed today. I think there's a tournament coming up."

Still laughing, Jeff reaches behind the seat and grabs us both a beer out of the cooler. We pop our beers and take in the view, which is pretty amazing. The green that we're on is a plateau, giving us an unobstructed view of Molokai off to our right, Lanai off to our left, and the ocean all around.

I raise my beer to Jeff. "I really have to hand it to you man. This is one hell of a cool spot!"

"Not bad, huh?" he says.

I take a drink of my beer and then look over at him. "You planned this all out, didn't you? Checked out this green, knew that the course was gonna be closed?"

He laughs. "Yeah, I knew the course was gonna be closed. And I found this fairway and this green a while ago."

"Well, mahalo again my friend!"

"My pleasure brah!"

We soon drain our beers and then both of us get out to take a leak. I'm afraid to look at the green, knowing that we must have scuffed it up pretty good doing those 360's. But try as I might I can't see any damage done, which is hard to believe. Then I notice that the grass is wet, so it must've rained earlier, or they watered it. The green being so hard and slick explains why the car spun around so easily without doing any damage.

"I can't believe this. It doesn't look like we hurt the green at all," I say.

Jeff just laughs while he's peeing, like maybe he's done this before. And I get the feeling that he has.

We just hang out and drink more beers, and pretty soon a classic Hawaiian sunset starts coming on. I tell Jeff that this is my last one, because I'm leaving tomorrow morning. And the sunset is a good one, especially from this vantage point, and I like to believe that it was custom ordered just for me.

We finish our beers and Jeff starts the car, signaling an end to it all. He drives us over the green and back down the fairway the way we came, but slowly this time. He turns left on the sugarcane road and I smell it again, that smell that I love. I breathe deeply, inhaling it. Knowing that it's my last time.

True to his word, Andy has lined up a pretty good send-off for me. He had recently met a couple of haole guys about our age, Masons that live on Oahu but have been working on Maui. It also turns out that they're huge Tom Petty fans, and plan on seeing him at his upcoming gig in Honolulu. Andy figured that I could use my ticket on a redeye flight at midnight, the same night as the concert.

And that's not all. Andy also found out that his favorite musicians in the world, David Crosby and Graham Nash, are playing earlier that same day at an outdoor venue. So, we're going to both. And the Mason guys have an apartment in Honolulu, so we can hang out there in between time. Just your typical Andy, in charge of the festivities.

"Wow, talk about spicy! Do you think you used enough Tabasco Andy?"

Andy has made us all Bloody Mary's, and one of the Masons, Greg, is commenting about the heat factor. Or should I say complaining.

Andy looks at me for support. "How's yours Ben?"

"It's good," I say, trying to be helpful. "Really spicy, but good."

Andy frowns, and takes a sip of his own. "Damn! I guess I did go a little overboard with the Tabasco."

"A little?!" Greg jeers.

I look at Andy and shrug my shoulders. He kind of laughs and grabs the Vodka bottle. "Maybe this will help cool them down." He walks around to each of us and pours a 'floater' on top of all of our drinks.

"I don't know if it'll cool it down," Greg says, "but it might help kill the pain!"

We all laugh.

We're on Oahu, in the Mason's Honolulu apartment, and it's much more than I expected. They have the penthouse suite on the top floor, with big picture windows that look out onto the city and the ocean off in the distance.

We took the morning flight out of Kaanapali, mainly because that's the way I wanted to leave again, but also because
Andy wanted to see the look on the Mason's faces when they
saw the backside of Molokai. And it worked, because they
were all but freaking out.

Later that afternoon, after Crosby and Nash's second encore and a perfect finale to their set, Andy and I are climbing
into a cab. "That was a great show!" I say. "Thanks for doing
this man!"

Andy claps me on the shoulder. "Of course Ben! My pleasure brah!"

Just the two of us went to the Crosby and Nash concert,
and now we're headed back to the Mason's apartment. We've
got about four hours until Tom Petty.

Suddenly, Andy decides a change of plans is in order. He
leans forward. "Driver, could you take us to Waikiki instead?
Anywhere on Kalakaua is fine." He looks over at me. "We can't
go back to that apartment yet. This is your last day! We gotta
have a going away drink!"

I just laugh, because I'm not really surprised.

We get dropped off somewhere in the middle of Waikiki,
and decide to go into the Outrigger Hotel. We walk up to the
bar and grab a couple of stools facing the beach. (Ironically,
this bar in later years will become 'Duke's', part of the Kimo's
franchise).

Andy orders us up a couple of Mai-Tai's. "You gotta have a
Hawaiian drink Ben, this being your last day in Hawaii."

I smile. "Whatever you say brah."

We sip our Mai-Tai's, laughing about the last time we
were here with Dean and Chris, and the pot dealer in the tree,
and the Manoa Valley hike. Pretty soon Andy is talking to
the couple sitting next to him, and I soon hear him telling
them about Maui, and the beautiful pools and waterfalls, and
Lahaina, and Haleakala, and 'you two just have to go there.'
He's in super salesman tour-guide mode, and he's getting so

THE BULLET HILL DIARIES

good at it that I would be really surprised if this couple didn't go out and buy two tickets to Maui as soon as they finished their drinks.

As he's telling them tall tales about what we've done on Maui, I start re-living certain times in my head, smiling at the memories, until emotion threatens to well up, trying to reach my eyes. I somehow hold it in check though, saying to myself, 'not now, not yet...'

We finish our Mai-Tai's and Andy orders us up a couple of draft beers. The Mai-Tai's were good but the beer is hitting the spot. I thank Andy and he says, "Yeah, enough of those foofy drinks."

We clink glasses and take long pulls on our beers. Pretty soon Andy says, "How you holdin' up Ben?"

"I'm doing good," I say, not so truthfully. "But when you were talking to that couple next to you I started thinking about Maui, and all the things we've done there. Some great memories man!"

"Some real great memories Ben."

"And speaking of that couple, what do you wanna bet that they'll be on Maui tomorrow? You know, you have a career as a Hawaiian tour guide, if you ever wanted to go that route."

Andy laughs.

And I laugh.

And we both laugh again.

And Goddamnit, it's almost the end.

Andy and I and the Masons are finally at the Blaisdell Arena. The concert is festival seating, so Andy and I have maneuvered pretty close to the stage. Tom is telling us that 'baby you don't have to live like a refugee', and I totally agree.

Watching Tom and the band play amidst the colorful stage lights, partially obscured by a thin haze of Pakalolo smoke, I lament on how this whole Tom Petty thing has come full circle. From that San Diego State football game that Dean and I went to, Tom and the Heartbreakers playing a free gig in the parking lot at games end, Dean and I dancing with girls in our elven cloaks, not even knowing who the hell this band was, to moving to Lahaina and meeting Roadie, and him calling me Tom, and producing the album cover to prove it, and putting the record on, and Dean and I realizing that yes, this was who we saw in San Diego. And now this, my final send-off from Hawaii climaxes with a Tom Petty concert, just because Andy met a very cool group of guys that just happen to be huge Tom Petty fans!

I'm ecstatic, and shout, "Thank you Tom!"

The Heartbreakers play their last song, and while we're waiting for the encore Andy taps me on the shoulder and points to his watch. It's time to go to the airport.

Damn.

I nod okay, and reluctantly start following Andy through the throngs of screaming people. Just as we're about to exit the arena we hear the crowd go wild, meaning that the Heartbreakers are coming back on the stage. I grab Andy's arm and make him stop. I'm pretty sure I know what song they're going to play, because they haven't played it yet, but I have to know. And sure enough, they go into 'Breakdown'. And now I'm forced to hear it in the background as I'm being rushed out of the arena.

Sometimes life isn't fair...

The cab gets us to the airport with just minutes to spare, so Andy and I say quick goodbye's, and I'm off running to make my flight with my backpack strapped to my back.

After checking in my backpack I'm off running again to my boarding gate. I just make it, literally the last person to board, the door shutting behind me. My seat is in the absolute back of the plane, next to the window. It's not a full flight and the aisle seat next to mine is empty, so I raise the middle armrest and collapse into both seats, out of breath.

As we start taxiing out I belt myself into the window seat, gazing absentmindedly at the multi colored runway lights. Just after take-off I watch the lights of Honolulu and Waikiki twinkle until I can't see them anymore. I continue looking out of the window until there is nothing but darkness.

And finally, the emotions that I have been holding back relentlessly come to the surface. And this time I just let them come, silent tears streaming down my face.

It's never easy... leaving the Islands of Aloha.

You look up into the sky and see that it's a crow, flying alone. He enters the forest from the east at treetop level, carving around the topmost branches like a slalom skier. It's obvious that he's just playing, just having fun.

Then, suddenly, you become the crow, looking through the crow's eyes. The first thing you notice is that the color spectrum has switched. Dark colors are light, and vice-versa. The dark green eucalyptus leaves are now a luminous yellowish white, and by contrast the bleached white dead branches at the tops of the trees are charcoal black. You're also amazed at how exquisite your eyesight has become. You see things far off in the distance that you would have never noticed before, like the small cottontail rabbit hiding under that bush a quarter mile away from the trees. And you can't believe how effortless flying is, how fun.

Presently you approach the middle of the forest, and looking down you see two figures on the trail below, hooded and cloaked. They make their way to a small clearing and sit, facing the oil towers off in the distance.

You keep flying along, enjoying your new found freedom. Before long you come to the end of the trees, and also you sense, the end of something else. You don't want this flying fantasy to be over just yet though, so you fly higher, straight into the setting sun that is turning the sky and the waters of the marina ahead into gold.

Then, in the blink of an eye, you're on a tropical island, standing at the top of a high waterfall. It's sunset here also, and straight in front of you is a lush valley, with bamboo and other foliage glistening from a recent rain squall. Framed in the center of the valley, out over the ocean, is a full moon rising. Twilight comes on, quicker than normal it seems, and then, slowly, it all fades to black.

BULLET HILL

'Shivering under lampposts, shivering under glass
    You're standing on charisma again
    God knows it cannot last
    What's the difference?

    So I lied to you once again
    So I painted over you once again
    So I died before you once again
    What's the difference?

    Clear up what you are
    Burn out these eyes
    Rip up this place and scream
    I am your slice of life'

'Slice of Life'
  Bauhaus

Long before we were building tree forts in Bullet Hill, before we were digging ground forts and making the roof out of eucalyptus branches, before we were riding our Schwinn Sting Ray bikes on the trails, getting air and getting hurt on steep jumps with names like 'Dead Man's', before we were shooting BB guns down here, or playing spin the bottle in the fourth grade, kissing girls for our first time, and then later, drinking our first beers, and even later still, climbing the oil towers out beyond the trees in the 'Forbidden Zone', in fact, before the Hellman's purchased the hundred and ninety six acre estate, even before the Mexican 'Ranchos' inhabited the area, long before all of these things, someone else lived here, calling it their home for thousands of years.

You can go online and find all kinds of negative reviews for Gum Grove Park, Seal Beach. How dirty it is, how it's sandwiched in between a barbed wire fence and people's back yards. The not so great view of Long Beach out past the ugly sandy wetlands with the dead bushes, and you know what? They're right.

At the present day, especially during the summer, when any green ground cover from the winter and spring months is dead and brown, it's not a very pretty sight. In fact, it's the worst its ever looked.

But I'm here to tell you that it wasn't always like this... not by a long shot.

Having grown up in one of those 'people's back yards' on Crestview Avenue, I came to know and love Bullet Hill at a very early age. In 1962, during Christmas vacation of my kindergarten year, my family moved from thirteenth street, a stone's throw from the beach, up to Crestview on the 'Hill'. We moved into our brand new house that my dad designed and my uncle built. And because of Bullet Hill it was kind of like moving from the beach to the country.

As a kid it was a mysterious place, with its steep grade and its tall trees. It is less than a hundred feet wide in parts, but close to three quarters of a mile long, about ten acres. We would soon find out that this 'slice of life' is really an earthquake fault, a branch of the Newport-Inglewood fault line. At five years old I fell in love with the forest, and the strong gum tree scent of the eucalyptus. In later years that strong scent would always remind me of home.

Back then, and even into the late seventies, not only were there more tall 'old growth' trees, some of them close to a hundred feet high or higher, there were just a lot more trees, period. In between the large trees it was thick with young ones of all sizes, and looking from the top of the hill to the bottom you absolutely could not see through the forest like you can now.

The trees were full of life, with all kinds of cottontail rabbits, skunks, opossums, King snakes, blue belly lizards, and even racoons. Looking up, you might see a dozen Red Tail Hawks all gathered in one tree. And in winter months, if you were lucky, you might see hundreds of migrating Monarch Butterflies clustered on a branch, camouflaged like brown leaves. In the fall the crows would move in, taking up a noisy residence.

At the bottom of the trees, on the other side of the dirt road, there was no barbed wire fence. The landscape flowed seamlessly into grassy fields, where Jack Rabbits and Foxes lived. To the east on the hilly section, where homes now stand, in the spring it would be thick with yellow flowered mustard plants. In this same area, right about where the police station is now, stood the Hellman's Ranch House and barn.

I loved the grassy fields, especially in late winter and early spring when the new grass would grow tall, and we would crawl through it making tunnels and grass forts. Sitting in the trees on a breezy day the wind would make waves in the grass, and I imagined it to be thousands of rabbits running through it unseen.

We finally got our first dog, a big Irish Setter named Tanker, and man did he love running through those grassy fields! Sooner or later he would scare up a Jack Rabbit and pursue it with everything he had. He never caught one, but he still loved the thrill of the chase.

Sometimes the rabbits would lead him all the way out by the fence that enclosed the oil fields, and he would get into patches of oil in the ground. We assumed that this was from some kind of run-off from the oil wells, but whatever it was, it was nasty. By the time we would get Tanker back home his oil covered legs would also be covered with a multitude of stickers. It would take close to an hour to clean him up before he could come in the house.

And of course we didn't know, that the days of the grassy fields were coming to an end.

Sometime, 1968 I think it was, I came home from school to hear bulldozers behind our house. I ran down to the bottom of the trees and couldn't believe what I was seeing. All around the perimeter of the field, approximately a hundred acres, the bulldozers were pushing the earth into dikes. Days later the entire area was flooded with salt water and sand, the result of a dredging operation out of the nearby San Gabriel River. Seeing all of that water where the grassy fields used to be was strange, to say the least. And disheartening, to say a little more.

My brother and I tried to make the best of this sad turn of events by taking one of our canoes down there and paddling around, but it only made us realize the extent of the damage that was done. We knew it would never be the same.

When the water finally dried up there was nothing left but a sandy desert wasteland. Over the years, of all the things that happened (and didn't happen) at the Hellman Ranch Estate, in my opinion this dredging operation was the worst. And it seems kind of funny that they never had to do it again.

In the mid-seventies another catastrophe was found to be happening in the trees themselves. A lot of the trees were turning brown and dying prematurely, and after some research was done the cause was reportedly due to the infestation of a small Boll Weevil. Certain trees were tagged with red spray paint, and these trees were selected to be cut down. Most of the trees they tagged were the dead and dying ones, but I noticed that some of them were big, healthy looking trees. Why would they cut those down?

Whatever the reason, this selective cutting didn't seem to work. More and more trees kept turning brown and dying, and it seemed that the only real solution would be to just cut down all of the trees. Kind of like cutting off your nose to spite your face.

But during the rainy years the forest looked healthy and green again, making some people think, including me, that maybe this was mainly a drought problem.

During the time that I lived on Crestview there was no shortage of rumored proposals to develop the Hellman Ranch Estate. One developer wanted to build homes and condos, and pretty much everyone in town disagreed to that, citing the obvious increase in traffic and congestion. Still another developer wanted to build an eighteen hole golf course along with some large custom homes. I remember thinking that if something had to be built, the lesser of two evil's might've been the golf course. At least it would've been a lot of green grass and trees, instead of just homes and condos and parking lots.

There was a lot of controversy and drama over the years, and it wasn't until 2002 that Hellman finally agreed to let a developer begin construction of seventy custom homes on the eighteen acre 'hilly section'. Bordered by Seal Beach boulevard to the east, and the Seal Beach Police Station to the north, it was to be a gated community called Heron Pointe.

Construction started in late September, but very soon some human bones were found, and on September sixteenth of the same year a cease and desist order was issued by the California Coastal Commission.

Some archaeologists were called in, and the bones turned out to be the remains of the Gambrielino Tongva Tribe, Native Americans that lived here approximately five thousand years ago. The Gambrielino's lived throughout the greater Los

Angeles area, and were known historically as the San Gabriel Mission Indians.

Some twenty sets of remains were found, and a Tongva representative considered the site to be a *sacred burial ground*. Even though construction had been halted, some Native American activists picketed the site, objecting to any further development. But after no more bones were found, construction continued.

There is a small park and nature trail that the developer built, with markers explaining the regions history with the Gambrielino Tongva Tribe. I'm sure this seemed like a small concession to the current Tongva's, but maybe better than nothing. At least people can read and learn about these Native Americans that lived here so many years ago.

And I sometimes wonder if any of the residents of Heron Pointe ever saw the movie '*Poltergeist*'.

Entry
Bullet Hill Diary
December 24ᵗʰ, 1977

It's afternoon on Christmas Eve and Andy and I were just down in Bullet talking about Hawaii. I told him my flight is on the 30ᵗʰ, and I think it really hit him how soon that is. I told him that I already sold my Ghia and that I just can't wait around anymore. But he said, "That's good Ben. Dean and I will be right behind you... two weeks, maybe three."

We planned on going at the same time, but they're not ready yet and now I have ants in my pants. I'm afraid that if I don't go soon the whole thing might not happen, and I really want it to happen. Mom and Dad know that I'm going, but they don't know when. I need to tell them, but I also know that as soon as I tell my Mom she'll just start worrying. I'll try not to wait until the last minute...

Entry
Bullet Hill Diary

December 29th, 1977

I can't believe it, it's finally here! Tomorrow is the day I leave for the lands West of West! I think I've taken care of everything... My backpack is packed, complete with my sleeping bag, my insolite pad, and most of my clothes. I'm also bringing my Aspen ski bag, stuffed with more clothes and my snorkeling gear. I can't wait to go snorkeling in the clear waters of Hawaii! I've converted about half of my cash into traveler's checks, and keeping the bulk of it in the secret compartment of my backpack. I still haven't told Mom and Dad yet... I've waited too long... Dean is going to take me to the airport in his Bus, and then he's going to sell it. This is unbelievable... it's finally really happening!
Aloha!

Mid July, 1981
Westminster, California

It's a Friday evening and the four of us, Eric, Matt, Mark C. and myself are all here at the 'Abbey' for band practice. This is our good friend John R.'s house, and Matt is his roommate. And Matt is the one who named it the 'Westminster Abbey'. Situated on a corner, It's a small old wood house with an even smaller and older separate wood garage, and a large surrounding yard. This is where we practice every Friday night, and it's kind of like Animal House number two. We can store most of the band equipment here, including the drums. There's a good buffer zone on all sides to the neighbors, and it's walking distance from a Warehouse Records and a liquor store. In other words, it's perfect.

Things happened pretty quickly band wise when I got back from Hawaii, but not necessarily in the way I thought they would. Troy ended up going to another band, a Christian band from his church, so that meant that Matt could play rhythm guitar full time now. And just like I hoped, the drumming position was wide open. I was sorry to see Troy go, but at the same time I was excited to be back in.

So, on this Friday night, before we even play a note, Eric faces us and says, "Okay look guys, we need to talk about somethin'... He pauses for a second, and then says, "what I'm trying to tell you is, I don't want to sing anymore. I'm getting tired of singing all of the songs, and we need to get a vocalist."

We all look at each other, and Mark starts taking off his bass. "Okay, maybe we should talk about this."

Matt takes his guitar off too. "Yeah, maybe you're right."

I come around from behind the drums and sit on the couch.

Eric, already seeming somewhat relieved, says, "You know, I just want to concentrate on my guitar playing and not have to worry about singing all the time."

Matt says, "Actually, it's a great idea, getting a vocalist."

We all agree. In fact, the more we talk about it, the more we like it.

"Hey, we could even get a chick!" Mark says.

We all laugh. But at the same time we realize that that's not such a bad idea. It might give us a 'leg up' on all of the other guy bands.

So that's it, no practice tonight. We all go our separate ways to think it over. I drive back to Seal not really knowing where I want to go, and then I remember that Mark (Min) is getting married in a couple of weeks. I decide to go by his apartment on tenth street and see what he's up to.

As I'm walking up the walkway to his place I hear his stereo, and girls laughing. I open the gate to his little front deck, and Mark is standing just inside the open doorway. He seems really happy to see me, and says, "Hey, Fin!"

Sitting behind him at the little bar is Rhonda, his fiancé, all aglow with her big brown eyes. And another girl I've never seen before. She has blonde wavy hair, sparkly blue eyes and a bright smile.

"Hey Fin," Mark says again, "This is Nancy. She sings in a band!"

That stops me in my tracks. We say hi, and then I say, "You sing in a band? What kind of music do you guys play?"

She laughs, and then says, "Oh, we do some Pat Benatar, Linda Ronstadt, Fleetwood Mac…" In the same breath she says, "but I'm quitting that band. The lead guy is a little too… pushy."

I can't believe what I'm hearing. And I'm also laughing to myself. We just learned a Pat Benatar song, 'Hit me with your best shot', with no one singing.

I cut to the chase. "So you can really sing Pat Benatar?"

She laughs again. "Oh yeah, I love Pat Benatar!"

Mark hands me a glass of wine, and Rhonda says, "Nancy is really good Ben. She's singing at our wedding."

"Oh yeah?" I say, and my wheels are spinning. I can't believe that we were just talking about getting a vocalist, and now here's this girl sitting in front of me who can sing Pat Benatar, and is quitting her band.

She pulls out a micro-cassette recorder from her purse and says, "This is a song that my friend Rene and I wrote, and we're singing it at the wedding. Do you wanna hear it?"

Before I have a chance to answer she pushes the button and I hear a piano starting an intro. Then she starts singing. And wow, what volume, what passion! And I can tell that she probably doesn't even need the recorder to accompany her. She seems to have no inhibitions about singing in front of me, which is impressive.

When she's done I say, "Wow, you sound great! You really wrote that?"

"I told you Ben!" Rhonda says, gushing.

Nancy blushes just a little bit. Then she looks at me and says, "You're a Pisces, aren't you?"

I laugh. "As a matter of fact I am."

"When's your birthday?" she asks.

"February twenty second."

"You lie! That's my birthday! Let me see your driver's

license!"

I start pulling out my wallet, laughing that this girl is 'carding' me.

She looks at my license and then says, "Oh my God, that's unbelievable!" She looks at me again and says, "Has anyone ever told you that you look kind of like Shaun Cassidy?"

Rhonda giggles.

"No," I say. "I've never heard that one. Is it a compliment?" She just laughs again. "Maybe."

I try to work the conversation back to the band. "So, I'm sure Mark and Rhonda have told you that I play drums in a band. We just happen to be looking for a vocalist. Would you consider giving our band a try?"

She bites her lip, then says, "Sure, I guess... But I still have to quit my other band. He doesn't know that I'm quitting yet."

"Oh well, yeah, definitely take care of that first." I say, but my wheels are still spinning. "So, I'm wondering when would be a good day to have you, um, audition."

"Well..." she says, "maybe we could do it on the Saturday of the wedding, like after the reception? You're coming to the wedding, right?"

"Oh yeah, absolutely." I think about it some more. "Okay, lets plan on that."

And I can't believe this is happening, that I just happened to come over here tonight. It's like it was all meant to be, and I'm getting excited. She just might be perfect for our band.

The four of us spend the rest of the night laughing and talking, and drinking wine and listening to music. I find out that Rhonda is Nancy's boss at 'The Flytrap' clothing store that they work at in the Westminster Mall. And Nancy is positively cracking me up, the way she's teasing Rhonda, calling her 'wifey'.

A couple of weeks later I'm at Mark and Rhonda's reception, and I'm really happy for them, but now I've got something else on my mind. And then I see Mark and Nancy dancing, spinning each other around and falling down on the dancefloor. So now I'm thinking, maybe this isn't such a good idea to do this today...

It does happen a few weeks later though, with Nancy showing up with a support team, about six of her girlfriends. Mark C. peeks through the front window as they walk up to the door and says, "Yes!"

We'd been working on an original song that Mark and Eric wrote, and Nancy surprised us by saying, "Play that." She pulled some lyrics out of her purse that she had written down, a song she called 'Everlasting Love Affair'. She sang her words to the song, and she managed to make them fit perfectly. Mark and Eric and Matt were really impressed, and after playing the song a couple of more times it was a done deal. She was hired.

Not long after Nancy was in the band the other guys warned me not to get intimate with her. "You know Ben, that's how bands break up," they told me. I told them not to worry, that the band was first and foremost on my priority list. But after a while I couldn't deny what my heart was telling me anymore. I was falling for her.

To this day October 9th is Nancy's and my unofficial anniversary. On that date in 1981 the band played at Laguna Hill's High School Prom, and we got paid eleven hundred dollars for it, the most we'd ever earned for one gig. When it was over we brought the band equipment back to Matt's house in Costa Mesa, where we had been rehearsing. It turned into an after party there, splitting up the money, and Matt telling me, "Ben, you're paid up. The drums are officially yours." That was great news to me. We drank beers and talked about our next gig.

At some point Nancy went to the bathroom. I waited a few minutes, and then went back there myself. When she came out of the bathroom door into the dark hallway, I cornered her and went to kiss her, not sure how she would react. But she kissed me back. And I mean really kissed me back. When we finally broke it off she smiled and put a finger to her lips, and then walked back to the living room. I went in the bathroom, shut the door and looked in the mirror. It was official. I was in love.

From then on we spent every spare minute being together as much as we could. We were so totally in love that the rest of the world could just go to hell for all we cared. She would come over to the Cabin, or I would go to her parent's house, and we would make love morning, noon and night.

To try to keep our 'affair' a secret we would go to rehearsals in separate cars. We were practicing at Eric's condo in Huntington Beach at that point, and one night Nancy and I showed up at the same time. I told her to go ahead on up, and I waited five or ten minutes. When I got up there everyone was smiling, and not saying a word. "What?" I said. Nancy laughed and said, "They know."

They all laughed, and it was like a great weight had been lifted off our shoulders. It felt so good not to have to hide it anymore.

Entry
Bullet Hill Diary
January 3rd, 1979

This is the first time I've written in this journal since I've been back. Ever since that day that Gina dropped me off things just feel weird... I had a life over there on Maui, and now here I am back again. Oh well, I wanted to go skiing, and that's what I'm going to do.

I'm in the room above my parents garage now, the studio apartment that my dad had built for my grandfather. After he passed a few years ago my brother moved up here. But now he has moved out, so it's mine. It's mainly one big room with a bathroom, and it's almost like having my own place. Mom is of course extremely happy that I'm back, and I've been making her omelets in the morning sometimes. She says I should go to Chef School and become a Chef, and I laugh at that.

Entry

Bullet Hill Diary
January 5th, 1979

Von's been calling me... He wants to come by and talk to me about something. I get the feeling that he wants to go somewhere, maybe a backpacking trip to Catalina Island, or maybe something more... he sounds serious. He's coming by tonight, so I guess I'm gonna find out.

In 1987 I turned thirty, and for our birthday (Nancy is six years younger) we went to Mexico, to Rosarito Beach. We ate a most historic lobster lunch in Puerto Nuevo, complete with tortillas and refried beans, and cervesa's. Then we drove a little farther south and stayed in the wonderfully old and oh-so-cool Rosarito Beach Hotel. We drank margarita's and Pina Colada's out of coconut shells outside by the pool, while the exceptional old piano player played 'As Time Goes By' every time we requested it. We were Bogey and Bergman living the Casablanca life, with a Mexican twist.

We were still living in our apartment on Ocean avenue in Seal Beach, just across the alley from the beach and right next to Dolphin Market. It had a small living room, a big bathroom and a tiny kitchen, but we loved it anyway.

Later that year I quit my purchasing job at CDI, an electronics company where I started out as a delivery driver. After not finding new employment in a reasonable amount of time things got a little strained with Nancy and I, and we temporarily split up. I spent most days at the beach or walking out on the pier, listening to a lot of The Cure and The Smith's on my Walkman.

I helped Nancy move into an apartment in Huntington Beach with a friend of hers, and since I couldn't afford our apartment alone, the easiest place for me to go was back to the Cabin. By coincidence my friend John R., whose dad owned the Abbey in Westminster, had recently moved back into his parent's house also. His dad had sold the Westminster property, where the house was torn down and condos were built.

John's parents lived just around the corner from my parents, and when he found out that I was back up in the Cabin he started coming by at night. Sometimes he would bring a bottle of wine that he would abscond from his father's extensive collection, and we would drink wine and play backgammon. It was during one of these nights that the topic of climbing the oil towers came up, and when John heard that we had climbed them, he was intrigued. In fact he was a little more than intrigued. He wanted to experience it firsthand.

He showed up a few nights later wearing a dark hoodie and a daypack, with a couple of bottles of wine and a corkscrew. So, no backgammon that night. We were off on a Tower climb, and John wasn't messing around.

When we got to the bottom of the trees and started making our way to the towers he asked me, "Which one do you think is the highest?"

I pointed towards one with a pyramid shaped top.

John smiled. "Let's climb that one."

Since it was in the approximate center of the oil field there was no need to hop the fence. Without seeing the Man anywhere around we just walked right through the open front gate, something that we would have never done before, and quickly made our way to the Pyramid Tower. Once at the top we could clearly see that this tower was indeed the highest, and we even took turns climbing the little ladder that went to the peak of the pyramid, swinging our legs around and sitting on the square metal plate.

After that John caught the tower climbing fever, and was on a mission to climb every one of them. And we almost did, climbing almost twenty towers in one night, spending maybe five minutes at the top of each one. It was exciting, but exhausting.

One night, as John and I are sitting around the Cabin drinking beer and playing backgammon, my friend Kim pops by. John soon tells her about our tower climbs. Kim looks at me, starting to smile, but also maybe looking a little perturbed, probably because I hadn't told her about this before.

She comes over one night in a dark jumpsuit, a dark hoodie and wearing a fanny pack. It isn't big enough to hold a bottle of wine, but a small bottle of Jack Daniels fits in there just fine.

Kim doesn't look it but she's somewhat of a tomboy, and turns out to be a good climber. She's a little nervous at the top, but that's to be expected. We figure out that we can see the restaurant that she works at in the nearby Marina Center, and she can't wait to tell her Swedish co-worker friend Janne about this.

So, not too long later I end up taking Kim and Janne up the tallest pyramid tower, and Janne is absolutely thrilled. We pass the bottle of Jack, and then those two sit on the platform and watch me as I climb up the little ladder that leads to the very top, and then stand on the top plate, showing off like an idiot.

Later that year we got a powerful tropical storm that came up from Baja, with thunder and lightning, and high winds. With the wind and the thunder the storm was loud, but also during the night I could've sworn that I heard crashing steel. The next morning, with the storm gone, my suspicions were confirmed. After walking down through the trees to take a look, I saw half a dozen oil towers on their sides. Sometime later the fallen ones were dismantled, along with all of the standing ones. Just like that, and maybe just in time, our tower climbing days were over.

Entry
Bullet Hill Diary
January 6th, 1979

My hunch was right. Matt wants to go to Lake Tahoe and spend the winter there, and he wants me to go with him. Maybe we could get jobs at one of the ski resorts... I'm excited to be going somewhere again. I wanted to go skiing and this could be the cheapest and best way to do it. It's good having a plan again...

Entry
Bullet Hill Diary
April 30ᵗʰ, 1979

Been back for a few weeks and I'm finally writing. The trip was great... working at Heavenly and meeting new friends, skiing a lot and going to Emerald Bay was fun as hell. I just really wish that Von or I would've won that damn 4 x 4 Truck. We could've drove it back down here, sold it and split the money, and then I could pay Von's mom what she wants for the damage to that girl's bug. That goddamn accident is really biting me in the ass now... Matt's mom sent me a letter asking for the money, and I just don't have it. Fifteen minutes of stupidity is costing me fifteen hundred dollars and/or my relationship with the entire Janssen family. Agghh!!

September, 1989

In 1985 one of our last gigs by the band known as Flurry was at the Lion's Club in Belmont Shore, where we had probably played two dozen times. We always played to a full house, courtesy of Josh. All we had to do was set a date, then Mark would tell Josh, who would put the word out and then it was a guaranteed two hundred people or more. I should say kids, because most of them were under twenty one, but they would get served anyway, which definitely helped with the turnout.

After a while we found out that the Lion's Club was raking in around five thousand dollars each night in alcohol sales alone, not counting what they got at the door. And for playing three solid hours we got a whopping four hundred bucks. At the end of one of our gigs I hit up Tom, the fifty something in charge, and asked him for another hundred. But he instantly got defensive and threatened to not let us play again. That kind of got to me, so I let him know that we knew he was serving underage kids alcohol, and without us he wouldn't be making so much. He told one of his security guys to throw me out, but the guy felt awkward, and ended up helping me carry my drums out to my truck.

The next time we played there Tom actually paid us five hundred, but it ended up being our last gig anyway, and for completely different reasons. Eric was having some marital problems, and needed a break.

So that was it. Flurry was done. For a while.

We had four good years with Nancy singing for us though, and she took our band to a whole new level.

So, four years after that I finally pulled my head out of the sand and decided to look for another band to play in. I'd seen the Musicians Wanted section in the 'Recycler', a free want ad paper, and called a number for a drummer wanted. I ended up meeting the guitarist, Shawn, a petite brunette who looked to be part Hispanic, and when I met her she told me that the ad was supposed to say 'Christian band'. If I knew that I probably wouldn't have called, but she laughed and said that she didn't write Christian music, she just wanted people that weren't hard drug users. The problem was that she kicked the other two members of the band out because they started doing hard drugs. She asked me if I did drugs, and when I told her I smoked a little pot she kind of laughed. She made me a copy of her demo tape with three songs on it, and I talked with her a few more times on the phone but nothing ever came of it. And it was too bad, because I liked the songs on the tape, and the drumming was good and challenging. Her band was 'Condition Red', and she was the songwriter, and she sounded kind of like Chrissie Hynde. What a shame. Oh well.

Every Sunday I would grab the 'Calendar' section out of my parents LA Times and check out all of the clubs that catered to the hopeful up-and-coming bands. For some reason I kept looking at the Redondo Beach clubs, and one Thursday night I decided to drive up there alone and check one or two of them out.

I walked into the first one, much tinier than I expected,

and it was packed, not a single empty seat at any of the tables or at the bar. I walked by the band, the stage taking up the entire wall on the right. I looked up at the singer, a fairly tall blonde dude about my age singing the Stones, but not necessarily trying to emulate Mick Jagger. Since I had to pee, and there was no place to sit anyway, I just kept walking to the bathroom. As I stepped up to the urinal I heard the band stop, and pretty soon someone came in and started peeing in the urinal next to me.

Looking straight ahead the guy suddenly says, "You lookin' for a band?"

I couldn't believe my ears, and looked over at him. It was the lead singer. "Um yeah... I am."

Still looking straight ahead he says, "MCS."

"MCS?"

"Musicians Contact Service. They're on Sunset boulevard in Hollywood. You pay a hundred bucks and they give you access to all kinds of bands and musicians seeking other musicians. You'll find something for sure."

"Wow, really?" I was incredulous. "Okay, thanks man!"

"No problem." We both finished peeing and then he looked at me. "Good luck."

"Thanks." He left, and I walked up to the sink and looked into the grimy mirror. Did that really just happen? How in the hell did he know I was looking for a band? Was it written on my forehead? Oh well, no matter. I knew what I had to do now. I walked straight out of the club, straight to my truck and started driving back home. No reason to go anywhere else. Mission accomplished.

Entry
Bullet Hill Diary
May 4th, 1979

Dean called me today and he wants me to meet him and Sara at the pancake breakfast tomorrow. They'll be on their bikes, and so will I. The weather's turning nice and tomorrow should be a perfect day. I'm ready for it... I'm ready for Summer and days at the beach.

I ended up meeting about a dozen bands through Musicians Contact Service, with almost as many auditions, most of them in the Hollywood area. And most go really well, but they all have the same question: Since I live in Seal Beach am I really going to drive to Hollywood to rehearse all the time? I tell them yes, I will, but they're being a little more realistic, and are having a hard time believing me.

I met some really interesting people, along with some downright weird ones, and got a lot of cool demo tapes. That was my routine; I would meet with them first, bring a blank cassette with me and hopefully get a copy of their songs so I could practice to them. This meant a lot of practicing at my parent's house, down in my old bedroom, where I could keep my drums set up, the windows looking out on Bullet Hill. My dad was surprisingly supportive, sometimes even helping me carry my drums out to my truck on audition nights.

Out of all of these auditions two really stood out. The very first one, and the very last.

I found MCS on Sunset, went up the narrow creaky staircase to the second floor, and after paying the hundred dollars I started looking through hundreds of bands seeking drummers. I decided to shoot the moon and picked one called 'The Six O'clock News'. The first thing that caught my eye was that they were produced by Ronnie Wood, of Stones and Faces fame. They had a professional portfolio, complete with eight by ten glossy color pictures. This band definitely had the look, the lead singer a gorgeous leggy blonde wearing mini-skirts or tight black leather pants, and the guys all looking like 80's rock bordering on alternative.

The number that I called ended up being the lead guitarist's, and he gave me directions to his apartment in Hollywood. When I got there I slowly realized that his was the penthouse suite on the top floor. This place was right out of the movies, with big plate glass windows looking out onto Holly-wood, the Capitol Building front and center.

The girl was there too, and yeah, she was beautiful. She had a British accent and looked amazing in jeans and a T shirt. I took a seat on their large couch and quickly realized that they lived here together. They both asked me a few questions while he took my blank cassette and started making me a copy. He did it with the volume off though, so I couldn't hear what the songs sounded like.

She was being very polite and friendly, and her accent seemed to intensify her sexiness. I tried not to look only at her while I was talking to them. I wanted to keep things light, so I laughed about something and tried to keep my attention on both of them equally. They asked me a little bit about my musical history, and I briefly told them about Flurry. Pretty soon I heard the tape deck click, and he got up and retrieved the tape he made and handed it to me. I stood up to take it from him, and then shook both of their hands, thanking them for their time. He said he'd call me in a week or two when they lined up a studio for auditions.

When I got to my truck I could hardly wait to hear the tape, and popped it into my stereo. On the ride back to Seal I started getting a smile on my face. This stuff sounded pretty easy to drum to. Pretty much straight forward rock n' roll. And she sounded okay, but she definitely didn't have Nancy's range or passion.

There were four songs on the tape, and I learned them pretty quickly in the next few days.

Almost two weeks later the guitarist called me and told me the time and place of the audition, and it was at SIR Studios on Sunset Boulevard. I find out that SIR is like the work horse rehearsal studio of Hollywood, with many rooms, some big and some small, and it's always a bustle of activity.

When I get there I find out that they've reserved the 'Big Room', and that they might audition a hundred drummers in one day. Wow. That seems daunting.

I sit outside the door on a small couch and can hear them playing in there, the songs already sounding familiar. I didn't have to wait long before the door opened and the previous drummer left. The guitarist ushered me in and told me to go ahead and rearrange the drums if I needed to. I looked around the room and it was indeed big, probably twenty by thirty, with a ratty old couch and a few lounge chairs facing the stage. The stage was big also, with all of the lights and bells and whistles. The drums were on a drum riser, and the whole thing almost made me laugh. I'd never played on a drum riser before.

We ended up playing the same songs on the tape plus one more, and I felt good because I knew I was nailing these songs. At the end they all seemed happy, especially the girl, and I started thinking damn, maybe I have this!

The guitarist guy shook my hand and thanked me for showing up on time, then said he'd call me in a week or so, reminding me that they still had a lot of auditions to go through that day. I drove back home in pretty high spirits, but tried not to get my hopes up.

After a few weeks I realized that he was probably not going to call, that they probably found someone else who lived close by and had 'the look'. I needed to know though, so I called him, but just kept getting his answer machine. So I accepted defeat and kissed it off. Oh well, I couldn't expect to get lucky my first time out.

My last audition was another one that stood out to me, and even though I wouldn't get this job either, it had a special moment.

After going to MCS so many times now a few of the employees got to know me by name, and knew that I was a drummer. I came in one morning and the girl that was working saw me and said, "Hey Ben, did you see this one?"

She handed me an ad for the band 'Agent Orange' looking for a drummer. Agent Orange was a well-known band in the LA area, mainly punkish but they did some surf tunes too. KROQ would play their songs sometimes, and to me they were the

Big Time.

The girl looked at me and said, "You should go for it!"

They were having auditions in a couple of weeks at SIR, and I decided I would.

Agent Orange had rented out the same Big Room as The Six O'clock News, and they were doing the hundred drummers a day thing also. When it was my turn I went in and shook hands with Mike Palm, the guitarist and songwriter. He was very cool but looked tired. It was understandable though. He had probably been through close to fifty drummers, and had fifty more to go.

After meeting me he asked, "Are you left handed?"

I kind of laughed and said no. Then he nodded towards the drums and said, "The last guy was, so go ahead and do what you gotta do. We're gonna go take a smoke break."

This was kind of a blessing in disguise, because it gave me something to occupy my mind and helped to ease my nervousness.

They came back right as I was finishing up, and took their places to the left of me, Mike being the closest. When they were ready Mike looked at me and said, "Okay, here's the deal... we're gonna play three songs, all new songs that you've never heard before, and just try to play to them the best you can."

I swallowed hard and nodded.

The first song they played I caught onto fairly quickly, and despite a few parts I thought I did pretty well. The second song, not so good. It had a lot of stops and starts, and at one point a change in tempo. And having not ever heard it before I was at a loss most of the time.

When it ended Mike nodded at me and said, "Everyone has a little trouble with that one."

The third song was more like the first, and I thought I did okay.

The three of them talked a little bit, and then Mike turned to me and said, "We've got a little extra time. Is there anything you wanna do?"

This definitely took me by surprise. I thought of one of my friends, John H., who had one of their albums and played it a lot. My favorite song on it was a cover of Dick Dale's 'Miserlou'. It was all I could think of, so I said, "Miserlou?"

Mike turned to the bass player and said, "He wants to do Miserlou."

The bass player laughed, and they just went into it. I loved this song, always had, and I liked their punkish version of it. I just bashed away, really having fun.

When it was over they all laughed, and Mike actually high fived me! "Okay man, that's it!"

I shook hands with all of them and walked out of there on cloud nine.

I knew I didn't get the job, but I didn't care. I got to play Miserlou with Agent Orange, and I would never forget it.

Entry
Bullet Hill Diary
October 3rd, 1979

So now, everything looks good again! Andy called last night, telling me that he's working at the Hyatt Regency Maui for the drywall company, and that he can get me a job there. He really wants me to come back to Maui, says I can stay with him and Ken at their condo until I find a place. And now I've decided… I'm gonna do this. I don't know how mom and dad are going to take it, but my mind is made up. I'm already getting excited and I don't even have my ticket yet.

Entry
Bullet Hill Diary
October 30th, 1979

Tomorrow is the day that I go back to the island that I love, back to Lahaina that I have been dreaming about for the past year.

And I'm really glad that Mark is going with me. We are the Maui duo! I'm taking my backpack again, because I'm planning on hiking through Haleakala Crater again. I'm so excited I probably won't be able to sleep tonight... Aloha!

After all of the auditions I went through with bands that I found at MCS, the one that I finally hooked up with happened the other way around. They actually went there, looked at my bio-sheet, and called me. And wouldn't you know it, they lived in nearby Belmont Shore, and they had a rehearsal studio in Signal Hill. No more worrying about driving to Hollywood.

I talked to Jeff the guitarist on the phone and he gave me directions to his place, which was an upstairs apartment off of second street, just behind Panama Joe's. We instantly hit it off, Jeff being about my size with black hair, long on top but short on the sides, and looking like a rocker.

He had already made me a demo tape with six songs on it, and he told me that their plan, him and the bass player John, was to go back into the studio and re-record those songs, plus a few new ones. They called themselves The Sundials, and they even had a music video with one of their songs, 'Century Sky', that John wrote.

We had a great talk and I was already getting a good feeling. When I was about to leave I turned to Jeff and said, "What made you guys pick me?"

He kind of laughed and said, "If you wanna know the truth, it's what you said about Keith Moon."

I laughed. On my bio-sheet, where I explained what kind of music I was into and what bands I liked, at the very bottom I wrote 'Keith Moon Rules Forever!'

Lucky for me Jeff was a Who fan. As I walked back to my truck I silently thanked Keith Moon, once again.

Listening to the tape on the short drive back to Seal I started getting really excited. These guys were alternative rock, and they had their own sound, and they had it down. I got back home and instantly started practicing to the tape.

A few weeks later I met them at their rehearsal studio in Signal Hill. It wasn't their studio, but a good friend of theirs who only charged them twenty five dollars a week, and they practiced three to four nights a week. I met John the bass player and immediately liked him too. He was tall, probably six four, slender with short brown hair, and looking like a hipster with an easy going personality.

And it's a good thing I did my homework, practicing to those songs. These guys put me through the ringer, playing all of the songs on the tape, some of them twice. After almost two hours we finally took a break and went out front into the cool night air.

They both looked around, looked at each other, and then looked at me. "Well man," Jeff said, "the job's yours, if you want it."

After playing for almost two hours I kind of expected it, but then again I still couldn't really believe it. " Yeah, I want it."

They laughed, and then they both high fived me and shook my hand, and they seemed to be just as excited as I was. And I felt a lot of things, but I mostly felt like I had finally come home, and had found my long lost brothers.

For the next six months we practiced three nights a week until we finally went into the studio to record. The studio was Earl Mankey's house in Ventura, and I soon learned on the ride up there with John in his Wagoneer, that Earl recorded the Beach Boys and Concrete Blonde, among many others. The house was a sprawling Ranch style place, and everything was recorded in different rooms. The drums were in the living room, while Jeff and John were in separate rooms on either side of me. The vocals were recorded in the bathroom, and that made me laugh. It reminded me of Eric back at Tim and Troy's house, and the 'Bathroom Sessions'.

After being with the Sundials for a year we had still never played live anywhere, and now some of my friends, my friend Heidi in particular, was openly wondering if I was really in a band at all. I couldn't blame her, and I was itching to play live myself. I hit up Jeff and John about it, and John was for it, but I soon found out that Jeff had had a string of bad luck playing live gigs. His main complaint was that there was never enough people. I told him about Flurry, and how we always had a guaranteed turnout. As I was telling him this I started realizing just how lucky we were, having someone like Josh to get the word out.

The next time I talked to Heidi she was planning a thirtieth birthday party for her sister's husband Larry, and asked me if we would play at it, at her house on fifth street in Seal Beach. I told Jeff and John about it, and they ultimately agreed to do it.

The party was great, went off without a hitch, and I was noticing how much fun Jeff and John were having, rocking out and really having a good time. And I guess this really put a fire under them, because they were both ready to start playing more live gigs now.

John took control of this, and started booking us at different clubs. But most of these gigs were kind of a let-down, playing on a Monday or Tuesday night with hardly any people, and causing Jeff to start having flashbacks.

One night in particular was actually kind of funny. We played at Senor Frog's on Santa Monica boulevard on a Tuesday night, and even though this place was packed on the weekends, we literally played to the bar tender and two go-go girls hanging from the ceiling in cages on either side of the stage.

Another one was in a very small club in downtown LA, high above and right next to the Harbor Freeway. We were opening for Chuck E. Weiss, a fixture on the LA music scene, and the subject of the song 'Chuck E's in Love' by Rickie Lee Jones. It was a very cool place and we had fun, but we only played to maybe a dozen people.

And then there was the one in Fountain Valley somewhere, playing in front of a mostly girl band who looked like they idolized the Bangles. It was their CD release party, so there were a lot of people there, but as we were playing we got nothing but a bunch of dirty looks. They just wanted us to finish our set and get the fuck off the stage.

Another bad one was a club in Hollywood called the Ice House. It was on a Thursday or Friday night, but we were the first of four bands, and even though there was a fair amount of people, when we finished not one person clapped. I guess we weren't 'Hollywood cool' enough. And oh yeah, we had to pay to play there. 'Pay to play in LA'. It was by far the 'coldest' reception we ever got.

At this point Jeff had about had enough, but I got us one more gig in Seal Beach at our local hang out, Dave's Other Place. Big Dave the owner was Heidi's uncle, but it was actually Lisa the bartender who asked me if we would play there. Dave's is a small place, and they had to turn the pool table sideways to make room for us. It was a good turnout though, and we got a good reception and had fun.

After almost two years with the Sundials John reluctantly announced to Jeff and I that he was going to another band, a band that was already signed to a record company. I was really bummed to hear this, because I liked John a lot. But Jeff was downright devastated.

And at about this same time their friend who owned the rehearsal space in Signal Hill was selling it. Jeff, worried that the band would just fizzle out and die, insisted that he and I keep practicing once a week. The closest place was a Trojan Studios in Garden Grove, and after meeting there a few times he started asking me about my old bass player from Flurry, Mark C. I called Mark one night and he agreed to meet us there.

Mark showed up at the studio, and after meeting Jeff and talking for a while we jammed a little bit. I realized that Mark probably hadn't played in a while, maybe since Flurry broke up, but it didn't take him long to get right back into the swing of things. He eventually got us a gig at Josh's restaurant, Tsunami's Sushi in Sunset Beach. Jeff of course was worried that this was going to be another humiliating gig with no people, and probably no girls. Mark and I laughed, because Jeff was definitely surprised to find the place packed, and with a lot of girls.

Not long after the Tsunami gig my work started taking a downhill turn. I was still working with Steve, building houses in Seal Beach mostly, but the housing boom was slowing down. At this same time my friend John M. was talking about building a house on his property that he had on the island of Kauai.

I would go by his house some days after work and find him in his living room with pieces of paper scattered everywhere, makeshift drawings of what he wanted his house to look like. He would ask me a few construction questions, and then tell me that I should consider going over there and help his cousin Leon and his friend Tram build his house when construction started. I had to think about it though, because Nancy and I now lived in an apartment in Fountain Valley, and we had our son Dustin, who was just shy of two years old. But as the weeks went by, and my work situation got worse, I started seriously thinking about John's offer. He now told me that he would pay me my current wage, but cash under the table, and buy me my round trip ticket. After thinking about it a little more, I decided to go for it.

Nancy of course wasn't too happy about this, but I told her it would probably only be three or four months, and that I would make good money and send her some each month.

The other person who wasn't happy to hear about me leaving was Jeff. He knew that if I left, the band would most likely dissolve, and he practically begged me not to go. My mind was made up though, and I told him to just keep playing, that there were other drummers out there. But it didn't help. I didn't want to leave on bad terms, but try as I might I couldn't say anything to cheer him up.

So, in early November of '93, after John sent some of my tools and some other stuff in boxes ahead of us, he and I boarded a plane at LAX bound for Kauai.

I was going back to the Islands of Aloha once again for a while, but I had no idea of what the future really held... or that Andy and I would live together in Hawaii one more time.

'A RIVER RUNS THROUGH IT'

'Comin' down the mountain
One of many children
Everybody has their own opinion
Everybody has their own opinion
Holding it back
Hurts so bad
Jumpin' out of my flesh'

'Mountain Song'
Jane's Addiction

Early March, 1994
Wailua Homesteads, Kauai, Hawaii

I'm racing up Kuamo'o Road on my dirt bike, the wind in
my face feeling really good after a full day of working on John's
house. The bike is a 250 two stroke, and as the roar of the
engine splits the air I find myself wishing that I had a quieter
motorcycle. I'm heading up to the State Park, which is actually called the Keahua State Park and Forestry Arboretum, but
we just call it 'Jurassic Park' because a lot of the movie was
filmed there. I've been making a habit of coming up here sometimes after work lately, knowing that my time here on the island is precious, and limited.

My ultimate destination is a very special little pool that
Leon and Tram showed me, and it is actually part man-made.
On the right side of the pool is what appears to be a cave, but
it's really a tunnel that has been dug straight through the hill.
The water flows out of that tunnel to feed the pool, and on the
left side is a small waterfall, ten to twelve feet high, which also
feeds the pool. The water is then channeled into an open air
concrete canal about two feet wide, and then continues down
the mountain and out of sight, eventually reaching the sugarcane fields far below. And that's what this is. It's part of an
elaborate irrigation system built by the Sugarcane Plantation,
channeling rainwater from Mt. Waialeale down the mountain
to feed the thirsty sugarcane. Leon and Tram tell me that
there's many of these canals and tunnels all over the island,
some of them very old.

After three or four miles of dirt road, some of it fairly
steep, I reach the pool and park the bike. I strip off my shirt
and shoes and jump in, and it's bracingly cool. I turn to my
right and look into the tunnel. It's just high enough to walk
into, with green foliage framing the entrance. The water is
about waist high, and I wade through it against the current towards the opening. I slowly venture in, doing the same thing

that I always do when I come up here, and that is to go as far as I dare up the dark tunnel until it gets too spooky, and then turn around and float back down and out into the pool again.

I do this a couple of times until the shadows start getting long, and then put my shirt and shoes back on. I hop on the motorcycle and start heading back down the mountain.

When I first got to the Island with John in November of '93, I didn't know that he would be shipping this bike over here, but now I'm really glad that he did. I bought it off of John a year or so ago and had no place to keep it, so he let me store it at his house in Seal Beach. He then loaded a container with all kinds of things for the new Hawaii house, like doors and windows, and light fixtures and plumbing fixtures, and he still had some room for some toys, like his two dirt bikes, his Avon rubber boat and motor, and my dirt bike and my mountain bike.

Just by chance, at this same time Andy had quit his job with S.E. Rykoff up in the Bay area, and had temporarily moved back in with his parents in Seal Beach. He just couldn't take the life of a traveling salesman anymore, working for a big corporation, driving a company car, and feeling like a number. Of course he would want to get out of the house sometimes, so he would go over to John's to hang out, and that's when he soon learned that I was over here on Kauai, helping build John's dreamhouse.

Sometimes Leon would call John on the telephone from the guesthouse that he and Tram lived in, which is just a few doors up from John's property, and I happened to be there one evening when he called. After a while I heard Leon say, "Yeah, he's here." Then he handed me the phone and said, "Someone wants to talk to you."

And I was indeed surprised when I heard Andy on the other end of the line say, "Aloha Benoit, son of Droit!"

After some laughter and some 'howzit's' he told me his situation, and how he had been helping John load this container with all kinds of things, including the three dirt bikes.

Then he surprises me. "I'm coming back over there Ben. I'm coming back to the islands. And for good this time."

I turn off of Kuamo'o and onto Kaholalele street, John's property being the last one down on the left. I go down the long dirt driveway to the house and park the bike in the open garage. I then walk down behind the house to the Shed that I stay in, and this is possibly the coolest place that I've ever lived. Tucked into the valley behind John's house, you really get the feel of the Kauaian countryside. Tram and Leon built this Shed out of wood that literally blew onto the property from hurricane Iniki, which hit the island as a category five storm a little over a year ago. They used it to store things and take refuge from the rain while they were landscaping the property. And it's pretty good size, about ten by fourteen, and actually has a covered lanai. It has a front and back door, a bunk to sleep in, a table and bench seats, which John and I converted into another collapsible bunk bed, a screened window with a storm shutter, a sink and an outdoor shower (cold water only) and power from an extension cord that we ran from the house above.

I pay a hundred dollars a month for the use of the kitchen and bathroom at Leon and Tram's guest house, but I sleep and spend most of my off time in the Shed. It looks out onto the valley which is basically John's backyard, where Leon and Tram have planted a lot of grass and fruit trees, including Papaya, Banana, and Avocado. I also helped them plant a large garden. When it rains a creek will form running through the little valley, and when it rains for an extended period of time the creek will start looking more like a river, taking things with it.

"A river runs through it," Leon said one time, quoting the movie. Tram and John and I nervously laughed. We had been trying to get things done, but It had been raining all day, and now that sunset was coming on it started raining even harder. We were standing in the cover of the Shed, watching and listening as the river got louder and really started flowing through it.

John shipped over an Isuzu Trooper from the mainland, and some nights, usually when the moon is big, I'll take the Trooper up into Jurassic Park, sometimes stopping on a straight stretch of road bordered by tall trees. This happens to be the road in the movie where T-Rex came crashing out of the woods and started chasing them in the Jurassic Park jeep. At night it's easy to imagine T-Rex busting out of the trees and giving chase...

On the way back down I might stop at the beginning of the park, where the tall and magnificent Rainbow Eucalyptus trees grow on grassy hills. Sometimes we'll come here in the morning or afternoon and walk the hundred yards or so to the Rope Swing Pool, swinging out and taking the plunge.

Hurricane Iniki definitely took its toll on the island, making landfall in Poipu on the west side and wreaking havoc with high winds. A year later there was still a lot of rebuilding going on, and this backed up the building permit process. So when I got here expecting to immediately start working on the foundation, things got put on hold. This briefly threw me into panic mode, until Leon and Tram talked to the neighbor, Walter, whose property was adjacent to Johns, but in a different sub-division.

When Walter learned of our situation he came to our rescue, saying that he needed a Gazebo built and some landscaping work done in his backyard. The timing was perfect, and as soon as we were finished with Walter's projects, John's building permit came through.

Tram and Leon and I spent the better part of a week building the forms for the concrete slab, but as soon as we were ready to pour, it started raining. And it continued raining, and raining, and kept raining for the better part of two weeks. In one day it rained thirteen inches, and on that day huge Koa trees got washed out of their roots and floated down the

Wailua River, taking out the bridge at the main highway on the coast.

Kuamo'o road skirts the Wailua River for the first two miles or so, and with nothing better to do Leon and I drove down it to check out the damage to the bridge. There we saw some of the Koa trees piled haphazardly on the beach. After a while we ran into a friend of Leon's. He was cutting four inch slabs off of one of the Koa trees with a chainsaw to make into tables. I guess when there's trouble in paradise some of the more creative take advantage.

At the end of almost two weeks the rain finally started to subside. Leon was in touch with the concrete contractor, and a few days later they decided to go for it. All went well at first. They got the entire slab poured and were putting the finishing touches on it, getting it nice and smooth, when it started sprinkling. And then it started raining. We took cover under a makeshift lean-to made out of plywood and watched as their hard work of making it smooth all went to crap.

That evening when the rain finally quit for good, under a dramatic Hawaiian sunset, Leon and Tram and I proceeded to try to smooth out the slab with some trowels that the concrete guys left with us, but we only half succeeded in our attempt. We didn't know what John was going to think about this, and he was due to come back out again in three or four weeks. But when he did arrive he was so happy to see the house mostly framed that he didn't even care about the roughness of the slab.

During this time while building John's house and spending nights in the Shed I started keeping a journal, which I called the 'Shed Diary'. I didn't have any notebook paper on hand, but what I did have was a large stack of white paper plates.

Entry
Shed Diary
Friday, February 11ᵗʰ, 1994

We had to cancel the pour for tomorrow. I'm sitting at the table in the Shed at 12:43 am and I'm looking at lightning flashes over the mountain. I'm hearing thunder... I hear the river, starting to really run through it. I guess it was a good idea to cancel...

A few days later.
Entry
Shed Diary
Tuesday, February 15th, 1994

Rain, rain, rain... It's coming down, and it continues to come down. How long? Who knows? It could last for an hour, a day, a week, a month... We did get half a day in though. Leon and John Hankinson showed up with the two beams and a full load of chicken shit. Now those beams have that unique chicken shit smell!
Trees the size of Seal Beach are coming down the Wailua River and making it all the way to the beach. I guess this really is the wettest spot on Earth.

The next entry was obviously a couple of days later... I didn't write down the date.
Thursday, February...
We poured. It rained. We drank.

We will usually work Monday thru Saturday and take Sunday off, but occasionally we will take the whole weekend. The Trooper is really for Leon to use, and Tram has a small pick-up, and if they go somewhere for the weekend, like maybe up to Haena on the North Shore to a friend of Trams, or maybe to Poipu where their friend Bruce the ambulance driver lives, they will usually take Tram's truck. When this happens this will mean that I am free to use the Trooper to go anywhere I want. And it's finally going to happen for the first time.

My very first entry into the Shed Diary:
Wednesday, December 1st, 1993

Dropped John off at the airport at 1:00 o'clock, came back and worked 'til 5:00. Around 7:00 Leon and I went to get propane and ice and make an Oar House run. (A very old and very cool bar.) *Got back around 11:00 and made drunk video.* (John left me a video camera to record progress, but I usually filmed other things.)

Entry
Shed Diary
Thursday, December 2ⁿᵈ, 1993

Leon showed up around 9:30, we made compost pit. Lumber didn't come. While making ice-beer run I call Earl. He says Lumber tomorrow around 9:00 or 9:30. Cool. Leon isn't coming tomorrow. After the lumber comes I'm free… Kalihiwai here I come.

Entry
Shed Diary
Friday, December 3ʳᵈ, 1993

The lumber came at 9:20 but they couldn't unload it. I went to the North Shore at about 10:00. I found sun at the end of the road. While I was sitting in Chuck's Steak House I see Bruce drive by in the ambulance. I pick up Leon and Tram at exactly 7:00…

It had been raining all night and into the morning, and the truck driver didn't want to try to unload the huge load of lumber and risk getting stuck. He just unhooked the trailer and left it there until the next day.

About a month later I get use of the Trooper again.

Entry
Shed Diary
January 9ᵗʰ, 1994
Today was finally the full snorkel mission. Went in at the end of the road for a while, then back halfway to Hanalei. Waves at this spot were six to eight feet. Immediately went in and almost got sucked out to sea. Then went and checked out the Hotel (at

Princeville) *and found a way down to 'Hideaway's'*, (A little cove that most tourist's don't know about). *Ultimate sunset on forbidden beach!*

Andy will be here soon, and I can't wait to show him all of the places that I've found, especially the sugarcane tunnel pool up in Jurassic Park. There's also a two mile hiking trail at the beginning of the park that I want to show him. It comes to a plateau with a great view of other valleys and has a covered picnic table. I've ridden my dirt bike up it a few times (totally illegal) but I did it at dusk so I hopefully wouldn't scare any hikers.

When the day comes Leon picks Andy up at the airport, and we give him a grand welcome, drinking many Steinlager's. (Tram's favorite beer. It's from New Zealand, and so is Tram). Leon tells Andy that he can stay at the guesthouse with him and Tram, but after seeing the Shed and noticing the other bunkbed he asks me if he can stay in the Shed instead. I tell him that's fine, there's plenty of room, and we'll be able to do a lot of catching up.

Andy has a pretty good idea that he could probably get his job back at Duke's, but he doesn't want to. He tells me that he wants to get out of the restaurant business, and the main reason being the long hours. He worked ten to twelve hours a day, six days a week, and just didn't have any time to do anything else. So, he has got on with the electrician at the house, learning to pull wire and set receptacle and light switch boxes. He likes learning this new trade, excited about doing something different.

After Andy's been there for about a week or so Tram, Leon, and Andy and I take the Trooper up to the sugarcane tunnel pool. We hang out in the pool for a while, and Andy is pretty impressed. Then Leon tells us that it's a short hike over the hill to the other side, where you can see the entrance to the tunnel. Andy and I really want to see this, so we follow Leon up and over to the other side, and lo and behold, there it is.

Now we're thinking, wouldn't it be cool to float all of the way through and come out on the other side? But we're also thinking, what if the tunnel gets really low in the middle somewhere and we hit our heads. Or what if we get stuck? Leon, always the practical one, suggests that maybe we should send an innertube through with a dummy on it (not one of us, but a real dummy) and see if it comes out the other side unscathed. Andy and I laugh, but we like this idea. With that in mind we hike back over the hill, and Andy and I go back in the pool again. We wade farther up the tunnel than we ever have before, to see if we can see light at the other end. But we never do.

When we get back to the house Andy and I go down to the Shed and have a beer at the little table. Pretty soon Andy notices my little stack of paper plates with writing on them. "What's this?" he laughs. "The Shed Diary?"

I laugh and say, "Yeah, I've been keeping kind of a log. Go ahead and read it if you want."

He does, and after he's done he starts chuckling. "Paper plates Ben?"

I shrug, and nod at the large stack on the counter. "It's all I had available."

Almost exactly a year from now Andy will take this journal, diary thing to a whole new level. Literally.

He will embark on his 'Himalaya Trek', starting out from Kathmandu, Nepal and eventually hiking to the Gokyo Peak, a base camp of Mount Everest. Elevation, 17,990 feet. Andy will keep a handwritten journal, and it won't be on paper plates.

Andy's father Blaine will copy Andy's journal word for word onto the typewritten page so that he can make duplicates, and he will be kind enough to give me one. In his introduction he will explain that Andy wrote this on a 'Lotka paper booklet', better known as rice paper. According to the maker it is 'moth proof, and can be used as an antiseptic to stop bleeding from cuts.'

Andy titles it 'The Himalaya Trek', and his first entry is on 'March 20th, 1995, Monday, Kathmandu.' He talks about waking up early and running errands, buying some personal items and getting passport photos for permits. He talks about Kathmandu being a remarkable place, and how it smells much better than Bangkok. (He must've had a stopover there.) He says that the local people are very kind and helpful, even though they appear to live in poverty. He ends this first entry with this:

'Other than motors, I'm sure this place hasn't changed much in the last hundred years. It's hard for me to describe the feeling here, so I won't elaborate on my excitement of what feels like stepping back in time. I'm staying at a lodge called 'Karki' in the Thamul area, which seems to be a very nice place. It's clean and has a hot water shower.'

Stepping back in time...

This actually isn't the first time that Andy and I have been together on Kauai. In 1986 when I was working at CDI and got my first ever paid vacation, Nancy and I took the same week off and went to Maui for four days and Kauai for three. Andy was living with Leon at the time in Poipu and working at Keoki's, another restaurant that he helped open. Andy picked Nancy and I up at the airport in Leon's small pick-up and took us to Keoki's for dinner. The next day he took us up to the Northwest shore to 'Barking Sands' beach. When we came back we went to Keoki's again and had their oh-so-good nacho's with beers.

The next day Leon needed his truck so we rented a jeep and went to the other North shore, to Haena and the end of the road. We went for a swim at the beach there, which is the beginning of the Na Pali Coast trail. Andy told us that he had hiked this trail all the way to Kalalau Beach, a grueling eleven miles.

On the way back we stopped at Chuck's Steak House for cocktails, and Andy couldn't stop laughing when Nancy went to the restroom, and soon came back asking, "Which one am I, Kane or Wahine?"

The bartender said, "You're a Wahine honey."

Stepping back in time...

About a month before Andy got to Kauai my friend Dave came over for a short visit. Dave grew up in Seal Beach with John and I, and in fact lives right down the street from John. Dave's a commercial sword fisherman, along with his two brothers Steve and Jeff, and their father before them. And they're not Longliners or Gillnetters, they're Harpooners. Among the last of a dying breed, they take only what they spear.

In 1987 I had the privilege of going out on Dave's boat, the 'World Famous'. The boat is about forty feet long, with a thirty five foot plank mounted to the bow that can be winched up and down. It was the beginning of the season and there were reports of swordfish being spotted fairly close to Catalina Island.

Most of the sword fishermen have spotter pilots, usually flying Piper Cubs or Citabria's, planes that can fly low and slow, making it easier to spot fish. Dave didn't have a plane yet, so he paid for a pilot he knew who happened to have the day free. His name is Ernie, and we would be meeting up with him later in Avalon.

As we were heading out to the fishing grounds that morning, Dave and his harpooner Mike, were telling me about another sword fishing boat a few miles to the west of us. They called him the 'millionaire guy'. Apparently this guy had a huge boat and *three* planes, a lot to compete with.

I was there with our good friend Jon, and Jeff, Dave's older brother. On our way out Jeff spotted a school of Albacore, and asked Dave to slow down so that he could throw a line out. Dave, driving the boat from the Crow's nest, grudgingly agreed. Very soon Jeff hooked into one of the small tuna, and the second he landed that fish on the deck Dave punched the throttle back up.

Jon and I, just along for the ride, were in for a treat. About fifteen minutes later Jeff emerged from the galley with freshly sliced sashimi and cold beers on a large tray, and we enjoyed an extremely good and unexpected brunch.

Not long afterwards we hear the radio crackle to life. Ernie has found a swordfish. As we're racing to the spot I start getting excited. I've heard these guys talk about harpooning swordfish for years, but now I'm finally going to get to witness it for myself.

Jon, who has seen this before says, "You're in for another treat Ben," Then he whispers, "Unless he misses."

But Mike is reportedly one of the best, and that's why Dave hired him away from another captain who Mike was having problems with.

Pretty soon Dave slows the boat down and Mike starts heading out onto the plank, harpoon in hand. Jeff sees the fish and points it out to me, a tall dorsal fin and a tail sticking out of the glassy water. Dave inches up on it ever so slowly so that Mike is right on top of it. Mike slowly raises the harpoon, and then throws, pretty much straight down.

It's a hit!

Line starts going out, and eventually it's followed by a bright orange buoy with a black flag attached to it on a stick. Dave turns the boat and punches up the throttle again.

"Now what?" I ask.

"Now we go look for more!" Mike says, laughing.

We all high five Mike, the hero of the moment, but he just shrugs it off. Just another day at the office for him.

I look back at the black flag receding in the distance. Mike just put a brass harpoon into that fish and now it's down deep, wounded and dying. The reality of it all is hitting me, and I suddenly feel bad for this fish. I can't believe that they're leaving it here, but they don't seem worried. What if someone comes along and steals it, I wonder. But Jon tells me that they'd be strung up from a yardarm for that.

Later on that day Ernie will spot two more, and Mike will successfully stick both of those also. They're good sized fish, but not as big as the first one. Three or four hours later they call it a day and we go to retrieve the fish. We get to the first one last, and I try to help Mike and stay out of the way at the same time. As Mike is hauling it up he tells me that he might have got it through the heart, which is actually what he tries to do, because he can tell that the fish is dead.

He gets it to the surface, and from the tip of the sword to the tail it looks at least twelve feet long. He slips a rope around its tail and winches it onto the back deck. It looks positively huge, and Mike says, "Nice one!" Him and Dave are clearly happy.

It ends up weighing just under four hundred pounds, and with the other two fish they've had a really good day.

Just then Ernie flies low over us and throws something out of his window. It lands right next to the boat, and I see that it's a big zip lock bag with yellow liquid in it. Everyone else starts laughing. It's Ernie's piss bag.

I climb up and sit next to Dave in the Crow's nest as we head on into Avalon. Dave gets on the radio to someone, and after a while I hear him say, "Tell him I'll take it." He puts the mic back down and looks at me smiling. "I just bought an airplane."

Once we're in Avalon they sell the big fish to the restaurant 'El Galleon'. They keep the other two on ice in the boat to sell back on the mainland. We go there for dinner, and the chalkboard out front is boasting fresh swordfish. The big round table to the right of the door on the patio has a reserved placard on it. Dave pulls up a chair and sits down, and I say, "Dave, this table is reserved for someone."

He laughs and says, "That's right. It's reserved for us!"

Ernie meets us there, having landed at Catalina Airport and getting a ride into town. We all order swordfish, of course, with beers and bottles of wine. And it's all complimentary, courtesy of the owner, who is running around and happily buzzing the customers about the fresh swordfish.

We're being treated like kings, the owner and a waitress

making sure that we have everything we want at all times. I slowly realize that this will probably never happen again, not to me anyway, and I'd better enjoy it while I can. Jon looks at me smiling, like he's thinking the same thing, and we clink glasses.

Dave would go on to having the best season of his career that year, catching more swordfish than all of the other Harpoon boats. And that's including the 'Millionaire Guy'.

Back on Kauai, my entry into the Shed Diary on Tuesday, March 8th, 1994:

Dave finally got to take the car and go surfing today. We got the first wall of the second floor up. After work I took the 250 up the road and up the Kuilau Trail. Scared the hell out of some tourists at the beginning of the trail. All in all a day of firsts.

I assumed that by late afternoon, early evening there wouldn't be any hikers on the trail, and I was wrong. About a quarter of the way up, and moving along at a good clip, I was surprised by a couple coming down the trail. I could see the alarm on their faces, and I'm sure that they weren't too happy about my breaking the rules. In about a month from now I will be showing Andy this trail, and we will bring a six pack of beer along to have at the picnic bench.

Dave and I got to spend a few days together, snorkeling near Poipu and eating at Keoki's. We also went up north and I eventually showed Dave 'Hideaway's, where I went snorkeling alone and was startled by a large sea turtle. Dave, up on the rocks, saw it too, and said that it was pretty big indeed.

I keep a picture of my son Dustin, who is two and a half, tucked in a corner of the screen window in the Shed. When Andy arrived I was eager to show it to him, because he hadn't seen him yet. But when we got down to the Shed that first day it was gone. I often leave the front and back doors open, and I figure that the wind must have blown it down. I look everywhere, but it's nowhere to be found. I'm really bummed because I couldn't wait to show him this picture, but Andy says not to worry, it'll show up.

Stepping forward in time...

After Andy was done with his errands in Kathmandu he had to take a bus from there to a place called Jiri, about a hundred and eighty eight kilometers away, to begin his hiking trek. He bought two seats on the bus so he could put his pack next to him, but they would cram three people into two seats, so they had to put his pack on top of the bus. He talks about how they kept picking up more and more people, until they started putting them up on the top of the bus also. After five hours of this they stopped for lunch. He met some people from England and said he had 'good conversation' with them.

About a third of the way down on his entry into his journal on March 23rd, 1995 Thursday, he wrote:

After lunch, the English group and myself decided to sit on the rooftop and get some fresh air and a better view. I spotted my pack and went to get my camera for some rooftop pictures, only to find it was stolen as well as two hundred of hundred note rupees, which is ten thousand rupees. About two years wages for the average person. Needless to say I was crushed, not so much about the money as I was the camera. It had my roll of film in it of Thailand and Kathmandu, plus the whole rest of my trip wouldn't be recorded. I certainly hit my lowest point. The valleys of Rhododendron and the terrace mountainsides were just stunning, although it was hard for me to enjoy it. Throughout the ride we kept picking up more people to the point where it was comical. Probably eighty people on top and a hundred inside. Driving on unpaved mountain roads with steep drop offs all along the way. Occasionally far below I'd see other (busses) that have gone over the side to their unquestionable death. All in all it was the bus ride from hell.

I can't help but wonder when Andy was experiencing this 'bus ride from hell' that it didn't remind him of a certain 'train ride from hell', albeit not nearly as scary, that he and I took almost twenty years earlier.

The day of Andy's graduation from Huntington Beach

High School, in June of 1976, he talked to someone who had taken a train from Mexicali to Mazatlan, Mexico. The trip took twenty four hours and only cost twenty five dollars. Andy thought that this would be a fun way to celebrate graduating High School, and asked me if I wanted to go. I'd been to Mexico many times but never that far south, and it didn't take that much persuading for me to say yes.

We didn't know how we were going to get to Mexicali, but we definitely didn't want to leave one of our cars there for two weeks. I told my dad what we were planning to do and his eyes lit up. He said no problem, he'd fly us to Mexicali. Not what I was expecting, but I told Andy and he was thrilled. He'd never been up in a light plane before, and was really looking forward to it.

My dad brought along our neighbor Russ, who was a co-partner with the plane. Dad loved any excuse to fly somewhere, and they seemed as excited as we were. I also suspected that once they dropped us off at the Mexicali train station my dad would take Russ to 'Alley Nineteen', a favorite restaurant of his that we would always stop at when we went on one of our many Mexico hunting trips.

Andy and I are standing at the train station, and the whole scene is something right out of a Sergio Leone spaghetti western. Our train is sitting there, hissing and steaming, seemingly as impatient as we are. We buy our tickets and the conductor shows us to our car, and our seats. The seats are big and comfy, and they even recline a little.

Directly behind our car is the bar/dining car, with little tables and bench seats that face each other. As we're sitting in our seats and the train finally starts moving we look at each other, and then get up and head straight for the bar car. We sit at a table and order up a couple of beers, something that we've never legally done before. Feeling like Clint Eastwood and Lee Van Cleef, we clink bottles. Let the celebration begin!

After two or three beers, and looking out the window and watching the Mexican countryside going by, we head back to our seats. Every half hour or so the train stops in little towns and lets on more people. A few more stops and it's starting to get crowded, with women and children starting to sit on our armrests. After a few more hours of this we're getting hungry, and head back to the bar car again. We enjoy some good authentic tacos and another beer. When we go back to our seats there's people sitting in them, but when they see us coming they get up and give them back.

It starts settling into a routine, the train stopping about every forty five minutes and more and more people getting on. And it seems like no one is getting off.

At one point the train stops, and then we feel it backing up. Then it stops again, and after a few minutes it resumes going forward. We both take naps for a little while, and when we wake it's dark out. Even more people have got on, and now our car is jam packed. At this point it's actually more comfortable in the bar car because there's always an open table. We get up and go through the connecting doors, and the bar car... is gone! It's just another car jam packed with people! Now we feel like we've stepped into the Twilight Zone. We go through that car to the next one, and it's the same thing. We keep going back and it just gets worse. Now the cars aren't air conditioned and some of the windows are busted out, the hot night air streaming in. Even further back and there's no seats, and no lights, and amidst the people there's goats and chickens scurrying around.

Suddenly two Americano guys about our age pass us going back the other way, and they have three or four bottled beers in their hands. Andy stops them and asks them where they got their beers. They tell him that a porter is selling them a few more cars back. We thank them, and continue to delve deeper into the ghetto, until we find him.

He's in between cars with the hot air swirling around him. He's selling warm beers out of a milk crate for three bucks apiece, about quadruple the normal price. We get two apiece anyway and start the long trek back to our car. When we reach

it, even though it's packed with people, at least it's air conditioned, and feels like heaven compared to the rest of the train.

We are given our seats back again, and after we get settled
Andy looks at his watch. I have no idea what time it is. He
looks up at me and says, "We're about halfway Ben." He gives
me one of his comical sardonic looks, and cracks a beer.

Many hours later, after a fitful night of sleeping on and off,
Andy wakes me and I notice that it's light out, and the train
is slowing down. In just a few minutes the nightmare will be
over. We're finally in Mazatlan.

As we're stepping off the 'train ride from hell' Andy says,
"That was more like twenty nine hours. If I ever see that guy
from school again, I'm gonna kill him."

We hop in a taxi and Andy says, "Airport, por favor."

I look at him.

He says, "We're buying airline tickets right now for the
trip back. Even if we have to cut our trip short a week, I'm not
taking that damn train home."

I laugh, and I agree. And that's exactly what we do.

When we finally get to our hotel on the beach, it's like it
was all worth it. It's a beautiful place, with a huge pool and
a large outdoor bar, and coconut palms everywhere. We commence to having a celebration.

We rent trail bikes and ride from one end of the city to
the other. We go parasailing, something that neither one of us
has ever done before. We rent surfboards and try to surf, but
mostly just wipeout all the time. I get my arm wrapped in the
hair like tentacles of a jellyfish, a Portuguese Man of War, and
it burns for about twenty minutes. The locals tell me to rub
wet sand on it, and that kind of works. But then Andy brings
me a shot of tequila and a margarita, right there on the beach,
and that seems to work even better. God love him!

We go downtown and try some of the restaurants there,
and find a couple of good ones. One of them is seafood only,
'mariscos', with many varieties of fresh fish. We stuff our-

selves with shrimp cocktails and as many different kinds of fish that we can. And margaritas. And more margaritas.

It turns out that one week of this was plenty, two weeks might've killed us. The day comes to fly home and Andy wants to go to the airport early, like five am, just to make sure that nothing stupid happens. Something that would make us have to take that train again.

We finally board our flight and it takes us to Calexico, on the U.S. side of the border. When we get off the plane Andy kisses the ground. Mexico was fun, but he's glad to be back in the good ol' U.S.A.

I call my dad, and in a few hours he shows up, this time with my mom, and Russ and his wife. As we're boarding the plane my dad says, "We're glad you guys are okay. To celebrate we're going to Alley Nineteen!"

Andy and I look at each other. We're exhausted, and a little hungover, and the last thing we want to do is go back into Mexico. My dad mistakes our look and says, "Don't worry you two. It's on me!"

Andy's journal, March 24th, 1995, Friday:

Woke up at five am and out the door by five fifteen. Still dark and I knew I had a tough day ahead of me. Here I go! Ten minutes into my walk I came to a crossroad and not quite sure which way to go. Along came a young man who not only directed me, but also took it upon himself to be my guide. He was the most gracious person I ever met. I'm two hundred pounds and out of shape and needed time to rest on a regular basis. Like every five minutes. It got to the point that he could listen to my breathing and knows to rest. His eyes were the most understanding eyes. I could see there were no judgement only respect and understanding and being with him made me feel totally at ease with very little embarrassment of being less than adequate.

And then, a little further down;

Well anyway (we) made it over the first pass and down to Shivayla, and let me add that's no minor feat. After a fifteen minute rest we started up the second pass, which is twice as high as the first. Every step I took I (felt) was a blessing from God. I've now walked up seven hundred meters (2300 feet) towards the top of the pass where I came upon two small wooden huts where they serve food. Sitting at the only table were two couples that rode with me on the bus ride from hell. They had left a day before me and on my first day I had caught them already. They were very impressed. I can't put into words how good that made me feel. They informed me that to do Jiri to Bhandar is the hardest day of the whole trek, which I have to agree. I decided to spend an hour or two here at the hut (then) ascend to the ridge and stay at Deurali for the night. Deurali in height is only 200 meters higher but two hours away. I've been here twenty minutes and my muscles are tightening already.

Well I arrived at the top of the pass called Deurali and I'm thoroughly exhausted. From Jiri to here was over 3460 feet in altitude at which at times I would have to head down in order to get up. Anyway I survived and feel good for doing so.

Back on Kauai things are a little easier. Andy is still helping the electrician, and Tram has hired on a couple of more carpenters, two guys named John and Jeff. They are both very cool, and with their help we have almost got the roof completely framed in.

While we're up there setting rafters I look down at Leon, who is running pipes in the freshly dug leach field. It's about four feet deep and looks almost the size of an Olympic swimming pool. I feel kind of bad for him down there alone, but he seems to be enjoying himself.

My entry into the Shed Diary, 10:38 pm, Tuesday March 29th, 1994:

Got all of the jack rafters in today, just the ten commons in the center of the house are left. It looks like a twin door missile silo right now. The wind and rain have finally stopped. Today was the first 'normal Hawaii' day that we've had in about three weeks.

John comes out again for one of his ten day visits, and he works with us almost the entire time. At the end of his visit we all take a few days off, and John and Andy and I take the trooper and drive all over the island. We go up the mountain for a view of Waiamea Canyon, and then through Kokee to the end of the road where we spend some time at Kalalau Lookout. Up at four thousand feet it's a spectacular view all the way down to the ocean.

There's a few tourists there, and we see one guy pointing at some clouds off in the distance and telling his girlfriend, "See that way out there honey? That's the mainland."

We try not to laugh, but we're not doing a very good job of it. I want to tell him that there's no possible way that you could see the mainland from here, but I just let it go. As they turn to leave he gives us a dirty look. Andy looks at John and me and shrugs.

From there we go all the way back around to the north shore at Haena, and go swimming in a big cave that's right off the side of the road. If you know about it, at one end of the cave if you dive down you'll see a bluish light, and if you follow it you'll come up into a hidden pool in the sunlight that the locals call 'Blue Hole'. John really likes to go to as many places as he can while he's here, so from there we go all the way back to Poipu and have Nachos and beers at Keoki's.

The next day is John's last day, and Andy and I take him to the airport. After we drop him off we decide to have a couple of beers at a bar I've been to a few times with Leon. I never knew what the real name of the bar was, but Leon calls it 'The Birdcage'.

As we're sipping our beers Andy tells me that the people at Duke's have found out that he's back on the island, and they want him to come back to work there. But Andy is adamant about not going back into the restaurant biz. But at the same time his work with the electrician has run out, and he needs a job.

Duke's has been closed this whole time since Iniki, but it's about to re-open. "It wouldn't be so bad," Andy says, "In fact it would be great, if it wasn't for those long hours."

THE BULLET HILL DIARIES

I think about that for a minute, and take a drink of my beer. Pretty soon I say, "What if you told them that you only want to work five days a week, eight hours a day. Do you think they'd go for that?"

Andy thinks about it. "Hmm," he says. "Maybe..."

"It sounds like they want you pretty bad, man."

"Yeah it does, doesn't it?" He takes a drink of his beer. "I'll have to think about that Ben."

We drain our beers and start heading back up the mountain. During the drive I tell him that I've been here for almost seven months, and I told Nancy that it would only be three or four. "I need to get back to California. And I miss Dustin terribly."

Andy looks at me with a frown.

"But," I say, "I want to go to Maui first before I leave. You know, go to Hana, and maybe up to the top of Haleakala, and Lahaina of course. Would you want to go with me?"

Andy's eyes light up. "That's an excellent idea Ben! Hell yeah, I'll go with you!"

We high five each other, happy with our new plan.

A few days later we're in the guest house making phone calls. It's a Sunday, and Tram and Leon are gone. Andy's been calling his mom once a week. "She worries about me," he says. When he's done I call Nancy, which I do about twice a month. When I'm done I hang up and stare out the window.

"What's up?" Andy asks.

"Well," I say, "I guess when I leave here I'm moving to Arizona."

Andy's eyes go wide. "Wow Ben. That's quite a change."

"Yeah, right? From paradise to the desert." I tell him how Nancy's parents moved out there a few months ago, to Scottsdale, and that Nancy is going through a job change. "And I guess there's all kinds of work out there."

As we mull this over we decide to take the dirt bikes up into Jurassic Park. While I'm riding behind Andy I realize that I'm already going into 'leaving' mode, making every last minute count.

Back in January, before Andy arrived, I noticed that someone had moved into the tiny room in the back of the house in between Tram and Leon's guest house and John's property. One night after having dinner at the guest house I'm walking back to the Shed, and I see our new neighbor standing in his doorway. He says hello, and introduces himself. His name is Wayne, and looks to be in his late twenties, and is built like a linebacker. He invites me into his small room for a beer.

Wayne turns out to be an extremely likeable guy, open and funny. He tells me that he likes to go hiking up in the park sometimes, and asks me if I'd like to go. I say sure, thinking that it might be a good change from riding the dirt bike up there all the time. We plan it for the upcoming Sunday, and Leon decides to go with us.

We take the trooper to the beginning of the park and then start walking from there. Instead of taking the road that I usually take on my motorcycle, we take a different road, and Leon tells us that this is the road where The Jurassic Park entrance gate was set up for the movie.

This road leads to a large waterfall, but we decide to cut the trip short and turn around about half way up. Pretty soon we see three men walking towards us heading up to the falls. The one in the middle is tall and slender, wearing a wide brimmed leather hat and large sunglasses. We say hello as we pass each other, and then Wayne tugs on my arm and whispers, "That's Peter Fonda!"

Leon overhears him and starts laughing. Wayne says, "Really man, I've seen him up here before. He likes it up here."

I look at Wayne. "You mean that's Bridget Fonda's dad?"

"Yeah man, I swear."

He senses that we're looking for some kind of proof, so he suddenly turns around and cups his hands to his mouth and yells, "Where's Bridget?"

Without missing a beat the tall one half turns his head and yells back, "With her boyfriend!"

My entry into the Shed Diary on Sunday January 23rd, 1994:

Wayne, the new neighbor, has been initiated into the Shed Hall of Fame. He became one with the spirit of the Shed. He felt it. He liked it here. We drank and toked in his honor, with 'Jane' and 'Ned' playing in the background.

Andy's entry into his journal on April 6th, 1995, Thursday:

Woke up at Machherma about 5:30 am and out the door at 6:45 am. There was fresh snow that covered the ground and the trail. As it so happens someone left just before me and I followed his footsteps. It was quite an exciting day. Had to walk over and through this waterfall. All that was covered with ice. Upon arriving at the falls, I had to walk along a trail carved into the mountainside with water from the snow dripping down onto the trail. Just before arriving at the falls something hit me on my shoulder and I damn near lost my balance. By the time I looked up there was a small avalanche of small rocks showering down on me. I was lucky enough to regain my balance thanks to my walking stick and hid behind the nearest big rock. It was over in seconds but seemed like a lifetime. Within the next hour I was above the falls and feeling a lot better about things.

And further down in the same entry:

I arrived at Gokyo at 11:00 am, altitude of 15,585 feet. I was relieved to get a private room at the Gokyo Resort Lodge for two hundred rupees a night, about four bucks. They have a sunroom just outside the lodge with all glass windows that reflects the heat inside the room, which raised the temperature to a warm 75 to 80 degrees. It's just heaven. A nice place to read and write and have some lemon tea. I'm darn near the top of the world!

I can just see Andy in this sunroom, with his books and his journal laid out on a table, sipping lemon tea and looking out at what must've been a breathtaking view of the surrounding mountains. Andy, the world traveler.

The next day he would make his final hike to the Peak.

His entry on April 7th, 1995 Friday:

Left Gokyo for a day hike to Gokyo Peak of which turned out to be the hardest day of hiking yet. The reason being that from Gokyo at 15,585 feet to Gokyo Peak is 17,990 feet and two and a half hour walk. The lack of oxygen was strangling at times. Once at the top though it was my finest moment I've ever experienced, it was an accomplishment that I did alone without any assistance etc. It got to be quite an emotional moment for me. I'm proud of myself for the first time in a long time. The views from up there are incredible of Mount Everest. ABA Dablum etc. I hope my photos come out, for this morning I found my batteries were dead. Even if they don't come out, that moment was truly mine alone.

And then the next day, April 8th, 1995:

Woke up early and decided to stay another day at Gokyo and just hang out. My friends from Holland left and everyone else except Hans who didn't feel well. He asked me if he could walk with me down to Namache Bazaar, which was just fine. I hung out all day in the sunroom reading and talking with all the people from around the world. Germany, Belgium, Canada, Norway, South Africa, England, Israel and Denmark. It was quite a collection of people, all of which speak good English and know more about America than I do.

Our plane touches down in Kahului, and in that instant I realize that I haven't set foot on Maui in eight years, since Nancy and I came for our visit in '86. Eight years, and it feels like twenty.

Both Andy and I are excited. Our plan is to get a rental car and go straight to Hana. Get some dried cuttlefish and some bottled Budweiser's like we used to do, and take our time on that road of roads.

But when we go to get our rental car there's a problem. Neither Andy nor I have a credit card, and they need one for the deposit. We both have plenty of cash though, and offer the guy two thousand dollars, but he won't take it. So Andy gets an idea.

Drew ended up being the only one of us from the old days that came back to live on Maui. I remember him saying 'Maui me' all those years ago, and he was true to his word. Andy calls Drew and he agrees to meet us at the airport and let us use his credit card for the deposit. But when he gets there he first wants to show us his house, so we hop in his small pick-up and take a ride up country to Kula where he lives with his wife Nikki. It's a really nice place with a grand view, and Andy and I are duly impressed. We don't stay long though, Drew has to get back to work and Andy and I are eager to get on the road, so Drew takes us back to the airport and we say our goodbye's.

In our rental car, a convertible of course, we put the top down and finally get on our way to our favorite place in the world. And talk about stepping back in time. Tram and Leon had warned us that Maui was different now, with more people, more traffic, and more tourists, and we do notice that. But now, on the road to Hana, it might as well be 1978. Everything looks the same, and we're both incredibly happy about that.

A little before the halfway point to Hana is the Wailua Lookout, and we stop there. This was tradition. We always stopped here on every one of our Hana trips, and looking around I noticed that it hasn't changed a bit. In front of us is a sweeping view of the ocean, endlessly blue and serene, and far below us is the little village with its colorful taro patches. Behind us is the Wailua Valley, stretching lush and green off into the distance, a true and seemingly endless paradise wilderness.

We continue on, the road weaving in and out of the most beautiful valleys anywhere, until we finally reach Wai'anapanapa State Park. I stop at the entrance to the park and look at Andy. "You wanna jump in the cave pool?"

He thinks about it. "I will if you want to."

It's raining, which is the norm for this place, and we have the top up. After thinking about it for a minute I say, "That's okay. Let's just keep going."

As I get us back on the road Andy says, "You know Ben, I still get the shivers when I think about that cave to the Gollum Pool." Then he says, "But to make up for it we could stop at Red

Sand Beach. You ever been there?"

Red Sand Beach. I've heard of it and seen pictures, but I've never stopped there. At that point on the road I was always eager to get to the Seven Pools. "No, I haven't," I say. "Let's do it."

By the time we get to Hana it has quit raining, and we stop at the Hasegawa General Store and pick up sandwich makings and more beer. We get back on the road with the top down again, and Andy takes us the short distance to Red Sand Beach. It's an easy trail, but slippery in spots. We go out and around a point towards the ocean and then wind back to the secluded cove that is really called Kaihalulu Bay.

The contrast in colors is the most striking that I've ever seen. Red volcanic rock, along with the red sand of the beach itself, is framed by bright green vegetation and the turquoise blue water of the bay. Dark volcanic rock, looking like broken teeth, form a barrier to the ocean and create somewhat of a lagoon. Andy tells me that this is one of the few red sand beaches in the entire world, and now that I'm finally seeing it for myself I realize what I've been missing.

We get down to the beach and take off our shirts and run and jump in the water of the lagoon. It's shimmering and clear, and we swim out close to the rocks that protect us from the crashing sea. Now I wish I'd brought my snorkeling gear, and say as much to Andy. Pretty soon we swim back and plop down on the soft red sand.

The sun shines down on us and it feels fantastic, giving us that 'true paradise' feeling. After a while Andy gets a far off look in his eyes and says, "You know Ben, I brought Mary Beth here once."

Mary Beth, the love of Andy's life. And by the look in his eyes I can tell that he's still in love. "I did not know that."

"It was in the early eighties, a while after you left."

That had to have been when Mary Beth was first working in Hollywood, on her way to becoming a soap opera star. Thinking about Mary Beth, and looking out at the ocean, I suddenly remember something and start to laugh. Andy looks over at me questioningly.

"Remember that time a bunch of us ditched school and went to the Wedge, and you brought Mary Beth?"

Andy slowly recalls the day, and kind of laughs and looks down. "Yeah, I remember. Definitely not one of the smartest things I've ever done."

The Wedge in Newport Beach, one of the most famous body surfing beaches in the world, was breaking close to sixteen feet that day. It was 1975, my senior year, and some of us were hanging out at the edge of the 'Quad' at Huntington next to the parking lot in the late morning. While we're standing there, up drives our friends Rich and Paul in Rich's convertible MG. They stop in front of us with inspired smiles on their faces. In black spray paint down the entire length of the car are the words 'The Wedgemobile'. Rich is a bona fide Wedge maniac, and he and Paul inform us about the size of the surf that day.

A bunch of us decide to car pool and follow them down there and check it out. Dean rides with me in my Ghia, and Mary Beth rides with Andy. When we walk out onto the beach there's a pretty good sized crowd standing and watching. The towering faces of the waves are the biggest I've ever seen. Dean and I look at each other and shake our heads. There's no way we're going out in this craziness.

Andy gets wind of this and says, "Come on, you pussies!" But we're not budging. He grabs Mary Beth by the hand and says, "Mary Beth will go. C'mon Mary Beth."

He leads her down the beach towards the water, and she looks back at us and rolls her eyes and shrugs. They reach the water and start swimming out. She's right next to Andy, one hand holding tight to his swim trunks. A set comes in and they barely make it up and over the first wave. As they reach the top I see her turn her head and look back down the face of the wave, and her eyes are as big as silver dollars. They make it through the next few waves, and then we can see Mary Beth punching Andy in the back, and shouting at him.

Now Andy's job is to get Mary Beth safely back to shore, and it takes him about twenty minutes to do it.

Back on Red Sand Beach I ask Andy, "I forget. Did you ever go back out after that?"

"Hell no," he says. "I was wiped out after that ordeal, and I felt kind of stupid for dragging her out there just to prove a point."

"Those were some big waves, man," I say.

"Yeah they were. You and Dean were probably right not to go out." Then he looks over at me. "But I still say that you're both pussies!"

No argument here, and we both laugh and he claps me on the back. Then he says, "Hey Ben, I have an idea. Let's go to the Seven Pools."

Now that's a great idea.

We walk slowly towards the middle of the bridge, looking for any sign of the red cross that is painted on the top of the stone guardrail. The cross that marks the spot from which you jump, if you're crazy enough. We've been crazy enough many times, and now it's been many years.

"I think this is it," Andy says. We barely make out a little bit of red mixed in with the white. We look over the side at the stream roughly fifty feet below us, and we seem to be in the center of it. We know that it's deep enough. One time after we both jumped Andy dove down trying to find the bottom. After two attempts, coming up for air and then going back down again, he surfaced shaking his head. "It just keeps going."

We arrived here in the early afternoon, our favorite place in the world, the Seven Sacred Pools. It's really called Oheo Gulch, and there's obviously more than seven pools, but the name seems to stick. We were surprised to find a parking lot, or a parking area really, no asphalt or concrete thank God. And a brand new payphone, out here on the far side of the world.

After parking the car we made our way to the cow pasture

to the right of the pools, knowing that we had a pretty good chance of finding mushrooms over here. As we were searching I remembered one time when I was here with Dean. He had got ahead of me, going higher and higher up the grassy hill, until I heard him calling to me. When I reached him I suddenly stopped and stared in amazement. Dean, with a capital smile on his face, was sitting in the middle of a large 'Fairy Ring', an almost complete ring of mushrooms about ten feet in diameter, probably enough for fifty people.

Andy and I didn't find a Fairy Ring, but we found enough for the two of us. Me eating them as I found them, and Andy saving them up in his hand and then stuffing them in his mouth all at once, almost gagging, and making me laugh.

When we feel ourselves start to come on we know what we have to do. Make our way to the stream, and the Pool of Life, which seems to be pulling us like a magnet. We come out of the tree lined barrier just above the Pool of Life, something that for some reason I don't believe we could've done so easily if we weren't shrooming.

The pool was pulling us to it. We could feel it...

We positioned ourselves over the pool and jumped, feeling like we just did this yesterday. We could feel the vortex just pulling us in, the memory of doing this so many times before making it second nature. And we just flowed with it, down and out of Dean's Pool of Life, through the long narrow 'guava pool', and eventually standing at the top of the Pool of Death. It was long ago, but seems like yesterday, when I was standing here the last time with Mark and Drew and Rick, looking through a rainbow at a full moon rising.

Andy and I backtracked from there to the trail, and took it down to the road, following it left to the bridge. So here we are, about to jump this bridge again. I'm hesitant for some reason, maybe because I haven't jumped it in almost fourteen years, but probably more so because it's the scariest fucking thing I've ever done.

Having found what's left of the red cross, Andy steps over

the stone rail and positions himself on the little ledge. He looks back at me for a second, giving me a look that seems to say 'maybe we really are fucken crazy', and then he steps off. I hear a woman scream, one of the few tourists that are milling about the far end of the bridge, and I look over to make sure that Andy landed okay. I see him swimming to the side of the creek, and he seems fine.

As I swing my legs over the rail and get into position I notice a Japanese couple approaching with cameras around their necks. I want to jump before they get close, but then I hear the woman say, "Wait, wait. We want to take picture." I wait maybe thirty seconds, look over at them, and then step off. And something didn't feel good right from the start. I feel off balance and start waving my arms, and sit back a little. My ass slaps the water, and I feel it all the way up my back.

When I come up and swim over towards Andy he says, "That didn't sound so good Ben."

Grimacing I say, "It didn't feel so good either." We climb out of the water and Andy looks concerned. "I'll be okay," I say, as we walk to the top of the next waterfall. The only way to go is down, so we both jump to the next pool, and this time I do my usual 'Pin', landing like I should. If only I was this focused when I jumped the bridge. I let it get the better of me this time, and I'm definitely going to feel it for a few days.

Later that night around ten, after we've eaten our dinner of sandwiches and we're drinking a few beers, Andy says, "Hey Ben, remember that pay phone that we saw up by the road?"

"Sure."

He gets that twinkle in his eye and says, "Let's go call Dean."

I laugh. "You know it's like one in the morning there, right?"

"I know. But he'll answer."

Andy has to call collect, and Dean does answer, accepting the charges. "Hey Deano," Andy says. "Guess where Ben and I are?"

We trade off talking to him, and he's just as surprised as we are to hear that there's a pay phone at the Seven Pools now. We say as much as we can in the three minutes that we have, ending it with a chorus of Aloha's. Dean responds by saying, "You fucken guys!"

The next morning we wake early, and after a quick dip in one of the lower pools we get on our way. It's kind of emotional for me. I don't when I'll ever come back here again.

We decide to keep going around the island, taking the 'bad road'. But the bad road is in much better shape these days. We both notice a few new bridges, and other improvements where the road would sometimes be washed out. Taking our time we eventually reach Kaupo, and stop at the Kaupo Store for some munchies and fruit juices. We reminisce a little bit about our Crater hikes, and Ken picking us up in the van with the cooler of Heinekens, right here at this very spot.

We continue on through the desert side of the island, through the lava flows, until it starts getting green again and we're coming into Ulupalakua. Andy's driving, and pretty soon he says, "So Ben, we're still planning on going up to the top of Haleakala right?"

"Yeah, I'd like to."

"Whaddya say we stop at the winery and get a couple of bottles of wine to take up there with us?"

I look at him, and his smile turns into my smile. We get two bottles of the Tedeschi Winery pineapple wine and continue on up to the top of the world, to the House of the Sun. It's very late afternoon when we find ourselves walking down Sliding Sands Trail, two bottles of wine and a newly bought corkscrew in our daypack. We don't hike down very far, picking out a rock ledge that's pretty far off of the trail. We settle into what feel like naturally carved seats in the rock, the daypack between us.

Our view... well, our view is just.. unbelievable.

Smaller craters within a large Crater, immense walls of

perpendicular rock. But it's really the things that we can't see, the things that we know are down there... Bubble Cave, and Pele's Pig Pen, the Mars landscape in general, and... Paliku.

As we sit in silence, Andy opens one of the bottles. Pretty soon he says, "Look where we fucken are, Ben."

Look where we fucken are, indeed. The late afternoon sun is casting long shadows across the Crater, a sharp contrast to the terrain still shining in the sun. A little below us and off to our left we see maybe a dozen Silverswords clumped together, glowing with a light of their own.

Andy takes a good long pull off of the bottle and hands it to me saying, "Hiking through this Crater is still the most amazing hike I've ever done."

I nod my head in agreement and take the bottle from him and take a drink. Damn, this stuff is good! Grown and bottled right here on the slopes of Haleakala, I feel like I'm tasting the essence of the Island itself. I look over at Andy. "You hiked the Kalalau Trail on Kauai too right? How did that compare?"

"Oh it's amazing also," Andy says. "But it's grueling. You go in and out of so many long, sometimes steep valleys, and a lot of it is muddy, and it's slow going." He looks out over the Crater below us. "There's just nothing like Haleakala. You see so many different landscapes. And even though it's a long way, it's not as hard of a hike as Kalalau."

I take another drink and hand the bottle back. "John and I hiked the Kalalau trail one time, but only as far as two mile beach. We spent the night in that cave on the left side of the beach."

"I stopped at that beach one time, I know the cave you're talking about."

I tell Andy about the sign in the middle of the beach on top of a sixteen foot pole that said, 'Water level can reach this point'. "The surf was huge and loud, and during the night it rained hard, and I kept waking up thinking that either the ocean or the rain were going to wash us away."

Andy laughs and hands the bottle back to me. "Yeah, I've

seen some big surf at Kalalau too."

I drain what's left in the bottle, and Andy is already opening the second one. Sunset is coming on, and the Crater seems to get brighter instead of darker, reds and yellows and greens starting to come alive. I shift my gaze to the far end of the Crater, where I know Paliku lies. I mention the Paniolo that rode up to our campfire on his horse with the bottle of Tequila.

Andy laughs again. "I remember you guys telling me about that. It must've been a wild night."

"That it was." Still gazing down there I say, "So many memories on this island."

Andy hands the fresh bottle to me. "We have a lot of great memories on Maui Ben. I love this island." After a second he says, "I just might move back here."

I look at him. "That would not surprise me." I take a drink and hand the bottle back to him. "By the way, do you have as good a buzz as I do right now?"

He looks at me with a big smile. "I have a fantastic buzz!"

We both laugh, and then we continue laughing for an indeterminate amount of time, which is, of course, the best time. Andy says, "Look where we're sitting right now. Look at this view!" Looking over at me he says, "I wish we could get everyone we know, all of our friends, and bring them to this spot that you and I are sitting at right now."

"That would be something else."

It's twilight now, and as the colors in the Crater fade, the colors in the sky seem to get more intense. We sit in silence again, and finish what's left of the second bottle.

Pretty soon Andy starts getting up. "I hate to leave this place Ben, but I'm getting hungry. Whaddya think about dinner at Kimo's?"

I laugh and say, "I hate to leave too, but that sounds really good."

Andy takes one step and bows low, paying his respects to Haleakala, and to 'Princess Pele, Goddess of Volcanoes and

Fire'. Impressed and amused by his action, I follow suit, and bow myself.

We stuff the empty wine bottles in the daypack and slowly make our way back to the trail, feeling a high that is unparalleled to any we've felt before. I'm sure that the altitude has something to do with it, but I think it has more to do with the magic that is Haleakala.

Back in the car, winding down the switchback road that takes us down the slopes of the mountain, we're finally on our way to Lahaina, where it all started so many years ago. When we're almost there Andy suggests trying to get a room at the Pioneer Inn. We actually luck out and get one, on the second floor facing Front Street.

As Andy is taking a shower I walk out onto the lanai and look across the street at what used to be the Whale's Tail. It's called something else now, but looks exactly the same as when I worked there. I look over at Blackbeard's, which has also changed names, and then at the Banyan Inn, which hasn't changed at all, and then the Banyan Tree. So many memories...

After my shower we start walking down Front Street towards Kimo's, literally walking down memory lane. We're on the seawall side of the street, and look over at what used to be the Blue Max, where Chris worked. I bring up the night when Linda Ronstadt played, and Andy laughs. A little farther on and we're in front of the Lahaina Market Place, and I mention Roadie. Andy tells me that he's pretty sure that Roadie still cooks at Kimo's, and we'll say hi to him if he's there.

As we're nearing Kimo's I look over at what used to be Nimble's, and is now a Moose McGillycuddy's. Remembering that New Year's Eve, I wonder what ever became of Peter Nimble.

We go into Kimo's and head straight for the bar, and Andy tells me not to say anything. He wants to see if anyone recognizes him, and vice versa.

We order up a couple of beers from the bartender, who Andy does not recognize. After a while he asks him if Jack the Manager is working tonight. The bartender says yes, and Pretty soon Jack appears, and Andy and him hug and shake hands.

After Andy introduces me, he asks Jack about Roadie. Jack says, "Yeah, he's working tonight. You guys want to say hi to him?" He leads us upstairs to the kitchen, and on the way he adds, "Your timing is unbelievable. It's Roadie's birthday."

We sneak up on Roadie, who is very busy, but takes a minute to hug us and say hey. Still with his signature pony tail, he looks at me and says, "Tom! Howzit?"

After wishing him a happy birthday we say Aloha and go back down to the bar, but they tell us that our table is ready. Andy and I look at each other. We didn't even request a table yet. The hostess leads us to a two-top right next to the water, and we take our seats. We order up the fresh catch of the day, and they bring us a bottle of Champagne, and it's all comped, courtesy of Jack. We feel kind of guilty, so we leave a very generous tip.

We're at Kimo's for probably two hours, enjoying the food and drink and talking with Jack. We go back up to the kitchen to talk to Roadie again, and he's more at ease since it has died down. "You really helped us out back in the day man," I say. "Thanks for that." He just laughs, but tells us to make sure to say hi to Chris and Dean for him.

We finally say our goodbye's and head back out onto Front Street. Andy says, "Let's go to Longhi's and see if Peter's there."

I want to see Longhi's also, it being the last place that I worked when I lived here. When we get there we walk straight into the kitchen, but we don't see anyone we know, which isn't surprising. I look at my prep station, and it feels like yesterday that I was here prepping food, making salads, squeezing orange juice, and eating fresh Ono.

Pretty soon the manager approaches us, and Andy asks him if Peter is around, but he tells us that Peter has the night off. We start to leave, and then I notice a local Lahaina newspaper on a table with a picture of Peter on the front page. I show it to Andy, and the caption says, 'Lahaina's Most Eligible Bachelor'.

Andy laughs in disbelief. "You've got to be shitting me."

I laugh at his response, and then say, "Remember his birthday, and all that champagne?"

Andy nods his head. "That was quite the party." Then he starts laughing. "I think we drank close to four hundred bucks worth of champagne that day."

We leave Longhi's and start heading back to the Pioneer Inn. It's been a long day, and we're ready to call it one. On the walk back down Front Street Andy says, "We had a lot of good times here Ben. A lot of good memories."

I look all around me, at Front Street in all of its nighttime glory, and then the twinkling lights of the boats out in the harbor.

"Yes, we did at that..."

Andy's entry into his journal on April 9th, 1995 Sunday:

Woke up at 5:30 am, had breakfast, paid the Lodge bill, took some pictures of some friends I had made, packed and said good-bye to everyone. Paid my last respects to Gokyo of which is absolutely beautiful and stunning place to stay for three days. Gokyo is as close to the top of the world as I'll ever get to. I worked hard to achieve a goal and I really didn't think I could do. Bravo!!

And now, back on Kauai, it's time for me to say goodbye. I still have one more day though, and tell Andy that I want to take the dirt bikes up to the Tunnel Pool one last time. We wade up the tunnel farther than we've ever gone before, still seeing no light from the other end. We float back out into the pool and just hang out for a while, not saying much.

That night the four of us, Leon, Tram, Andy and I go to the 'Bull Shed' for dinner. It's a nice steak house with an extensive salad bar. Tram is a vegetarian, but he loves coming here for their salad bar, which among other things has fresh California avocados. It's a great place, and we have a great time.

The next morning, right before Andy is about to take me to the airport in the Trooper, I say goodbye to the Shed. Just a stupid little wooden shed, but it's my most tearful goodbye. It has been my sanctuary in this period in my life, and I know it will be a long time before I see it again, if ever.

We climb in the Trooper and Andy says, "Oh crap, I left my wallet in the Shed. I'll be right back." When he returns he's got something else in his hand besides his wallet. "Look at this Ben. It was laying right in the middle of the floor!"

It's the picture of Dustin that I lost. The mystery picture that disappeared on the day that Andy got here, and now re-appears on the day that I leave.

He hands it to me. I look at it, and hand it back. "You keep it," I say. "I'm going to see him, and be with him, and watch him grow up. I'll be taking more pictures."

"Thanks Ben," he says. "I'm gonna tack it up in the Shed so it can't get away again."

We start heading down the mountain, and off to our left is the low mountain ridge known as 'Sleeping Giant'. While Andy is looking at it out his open window he says, "The Islands are my home now Ben. I'm here for good." He looks over at me. "I'm gonna live the rest of my life here."

I look back at him, and I can tell that he means it.

Looking back out the window he says, "You'll be back, Ben. I know you. Someday, you'll be back."

I have a feeling that he's probably right. But when that will be, and why, I have no idea...

IN MEMORY OF...

Andrew Joseph Kramer
March 10th, 1958 – August 26th, 1995?

John Dean Gerber
August 10th, 1958 – July 29th, 2002

Gary Gerard Kramer
July 10th, 1955 – April 25th, 2016

Andrew Main Janssen
December 2nd, 1955 – December 24th, 2019

AFTERWORD

Sometime in late 1992, my friend Kim told me that she wanted to buy a mountain bike, and asked me if I would give her a ride to the bike shop in my Toyota pick-up. After getting there and looking around for a little while, she ended up falling for a beautiful black and purple Pachanga twenty one speed mountain bike, which also had fuchsia colored speckles sprinkled here and there. Somewhere around a year later Kim got married, and she and her new husband Ulf were moving to Nevada. She didn't have room for the bike, and wanted to give it to me. I didn't feel comfortable about taking it, and I couldn't afford to buy it off her. But she insisted. "Please take it Ben. I want you to have it."

I lived on top of the Dolphin Market in Seal Beach at the time, and I would ride the bike to John's after work almost every day, right up until the time came to go to Kauai to start building his house there. And I left the bike at John's. When John and Andy loaded the container with the dirt bikes and all of the other stuff, they put the mountain bike in there as well. And this is the bike that Andy would start doing his workouts on, riding it up into Jurassic Park. Or sometimes he would go down the mountain, where he would occasionally go to a bar. When he did this he would more often than not call Leon and offer to buy him a drink if he would come and pick him up, which I'm pretty sure Leon was more than happy to do. And of course this ends up being the bike that Andy disappears on...

There has been no shortage of scenarios on what happened to Andy. Tram and Leon (Heroes, in my opinion) rented a helicopter for a few days, and then organized a search party from the house. Fifteen to twenty people, many of them from Duke's, would show up and then fan out in all directions looking for any sign of Andy or the bike. And they did this for weeks with no success. Andy's younger brother Tom flew in from the Philippines to aid in the search, and Ken came also. It was initially thought that maybe Andy was struck by a vehicle, and that perhaps the driver panicked and dumped the bike and Andy somewhere. Another theory was that Andy might've inadvertently wandered onto someone's marijuana patch and was assaulted. Whatever happened, it definitely started feeling more and more like foul play was involved.

In a five to six year period during the time that Andy disappeared, there was believed to be a possible serial killer on the island, preying on Haole men. Other guys, one of them much bigger than Andy, had also disappeared without a trace. I started thinking about this, and remembered that Andy would sometimes ride the bike down the mountain to that bar. And then I thought, what if that guy was there, and after talking with Andy for a while offered to give him a ride back up the mountain. It's a chilling thought, what might've happened, and I don't even like to think about it. But then, during the writing of this book, Andy's brother Ken sent me all kinds of Andy memorabilia, including a lot of pictures, and a Kauai newspaper called 'The Garden Island'. It was dated Wednesday, September 13th, 1995. The headline on the front page reads: 'Still No Clue About Fate of Missing Man'. Among other things the article states that Andy's 'passport, bank cards, wallet, etc.' were left at the house. That got me to thinking, and set my mind somewhat at ease. If Andy had planned to go down the mountain to that bar, he would've taken his wallet.

So, this all points to Andy going up the mountain, to really get a workout. Did he get too close to the edge of the road somewhere, and then fall down a steep cliff, the jungle just swallowing up both him and the bike? I just have a hard time believing this. He wasn't the only one mountain biking on that road, and he wasn't a klutz. But then again, could something like that really have happened? It just seems like a million to one.

It was just after noon on a Saturday when Andy went for his bike ride. On the weekends we would sometimes see local pig hunters in their four wheel drive trucks at Keahua Park. We might pass them on our way to the tunnel pool, and sometimes we'd see them hanging out there in the afternoon, drinking beers, with their rifles on their tailgates and their truck beds full of empty beer cans. Did one of these guys accidentally run into Andy up where the road is narrow, maybe on a curve? Did they panic, and hide the body and the bike? It's just another theory, and I guess we'll never know.

But I think somebody knows...

In 1976, the Friday after Thanksgiving, Andy and Scott got the idea of getting all of the boys together and having a poker game. But since we all still lived at our parents houses, and they might've frowned upon the amount of beer we planned on drinking, Andy and Scott decided to rent a hotel room at the Edgewater Hyatt, just across the river in Long Beach. We dressed up in suits and ties, put a keg of beer in the bathtub full of ice, and proceeded to have a good ol' time. We had so much fun in fact, that we did it again the following year. And then the year after that. And now, 43 years later, we're still doing it. Even though it's always held in the summertime now, we still call it the PTPG, for Post-Thanksgiving Poker Game.

Those first games were held in hotel rooms, in Long Beach, or Huntington Beach, or Seal Beach, or even Palm Springs. But later, as we got older and a lot of us got married, we started having them at someone's house, trading off with someone different hosting it each time. In April of 2002 I hosted it at our house in Scottsdale, Arizona. Our friend Josh flew out, and having just won an unexpected amount of money on a basketball bet, he showed up at my house in a fifty foot stretch Limo, taking all of us out on the town.

Dean hadn't made it to one of these party's in many years, living with his friend Ian in the Bay Area and then Colorado. At some point during the night Scott called Dean, and we passed the phone around, trading off talking to him. I talked to Dean last, and he soon told me that he was really bummed that he didn't make it. "I'm coming to the next one Ben, no matter where it is. This is too cool that you guys have kept this going, and I'm not gonna miss another one."

I was glad to hear that, happy to hear the conviction in his voice. But sadly, it wasn't to be.

Later that summer Dean and Ian would rent a large passenger van, and along with Dean's kids Angela and Max, and Ian's wife and their kids, they would take a cross country trip to New York, where Dean wanted to visit relatives, some of whom he had never seen. For the trip Dean and Ian had taken out all of the rear seats and put in mattresses and pillows to sit and lay on.

And then, after they had made it all of the way across the country, somewhere in New York, something went terribly wrong. Dean was driving, and apparently had a coughing spasm, and veered off the road. The van flew through the air, finally smashing into a large concrete abutment on the driver's side. The mattresses in the back actually cushioned those who were in the back, but Max broke his arm, and Ian's wife had other pretty severe injuries. But Dean bore the brunt of it, and was very critically wounded with blunt force trauma to his head. He was later airlifted out, and shortly after reaching the hospital... he died.

When Dean's sister Nancy called me with the tragic news, I refused to believe it, sliding down the wall of our bedroom to the floor, slowly going into shock. I silently cried while tears streamed down my face. Not Dean, not my good friend, my co-conspirator, my brother! No... This just can't be...

Someone once asked me if I believed in ghosts. I can tell you this... I definitely believe that the spirits of the dead can haunt you in your dreams. Both Andy and Dean haunt me regularly in mine, but it always seems to be on the humorous side. They delight in fucking with me...

The PTPG's have morphed into a full blown event, renting out large houses in California somewhere for three days and nights, usually with a pool, and a tennis and basketball court. Tim will bring his Rock Blocker so that we can all play our different music selections. Eric will bring a turntable and all kinds of vintage vinyl. Scott will bring his state of the art ping pong table, and there will be many other games, like washer toss and corn hole, and a multitude of frisbees to play frisbee golf. And oh yeah, Eric and Matt will bring all of their guitars, and Matt will bring a PA system and microphones, and a really nice drum set for me. We'll play music and play games and tell stories, and drink and eat to our hearts content.

At some point during the night, like if you're holding the cards and you have the deal, you can set the cards down and say, "Andy story!" or, "Dean story!" (And now, unfortunately, Gary and Drew are added to that list.) But the stories are always pretty comical. Humor that can only come from the intimate knowledge of special memories with special friends.

ACKNOWLEDGE-MENTS

I would like to thank first and foremost my loving and super patient and devoted wife Nancy, who helped me to navigate through the electronic side of the story, and did all of the computer work necessary to finally publish my book. Without her I would have been lost. I also want to thank Lorraine Gerber, Dean's mom, who was also very patient with me, sending her rough drafts usually later than I promised them. I definitely want to thank Mark Hjelm, Scott Weir, and Paul Finchamp, who I also sent some rough drafts, and their encouragement after reading them. A huge thanks to Ken Kramer. Getting in touch with Ken again has been really uplifting, and that's thanks to his younger brother Tom, who emailed me Ken's address. I emailed Ken many times with questions, to which he was more than happy to answer to the best of his recollection, which I was hoping to be better than mine. Thanks also to Chris Collier (Maui brothers forever), Mary Ann Kramer, Matt Janssen, Eric Janssen, Andrew Janssen, Todd Stegen, John Rossi, Jon Wright, Dave Earle, David Lynn, Jacki Rigney, Mary Beth Evans, Steve Jones, Ron Juler, Bruce Powers, Mark Cunningham, Josh Peasley, Tim Young, Troy Wickline, John Tosdale, and Jeff Donahue. And I know I've forgotten someone, and I'm sorry, but please consider yourself included. And I also have to thank Carl Safina for his quote of Mary Shelley in his book 'Eye of the Albatross', which I shamelessly stole for my epigraph. After reading it a few times it just seemed to fit so perfectly to my story, and I couldn't help myself. Thank you Carl. And finally thanks also to the staff at the Seal Beach Public Library, they were very helpful.

Made in the USA
Columbia, SC
08 March 2020

88877081R00238